ROUTLEDGE LIBRARY EDITIONS: AGRIBUSINESS AND LAND USE

Volume 1

AGRICULTURAL MARKETING AND THE EEC

AGRICULTURAL MARKETING AND THE EEC

MICHAEL BUTTERWICK
AND
EDMUND NEVILLE-ROLFE

LONDON AND NEW YORK

First published in 1971 by Hutchinson & Co. Ltd

This edition first published in 2024
by Routledge
4 Park Square, Milton Park, Abingdon, Oxon OX14 4RN

and by Routledge
605 Third Avenue, New York, NY 10158

Routledge is an imprint of the Taylor & Francis Group, an informa business

© 1971 Home-Grown Cereals Authority and the Meat and Livestock Commission

All rights reserved. No part of this book may be reprinted or reproduced or utilised in any form or by any electronic, mechanical, or other means, now known or hereafter invented, including photocopying and recording, or in any information storage or retrieval system, without permission in writing from the publishers.

Trademark notice: Product or corporate names may be trademarks or registered trademarks, and are used only for identification and explanation without intent to infringe.

British Library Cataloguing in Publication Data
A catalogue record for this book is available from the British Library

ISBN: 978-1-032-48321-4 (Set)
ISBN: 978-1-032-49845-4 (Volume 1) (hbk)
ISBN: 978-1-032-49863-8 (Volume 1) (pbk)
ISBN: 978-1-003-39581-2 (Volume 1) (ebk)

DOI: 10.4324/9781003395812

Publisher's Note
The publisher has gone to great lengths to ensure the quality of this reprint but points out that some imperfections in the original copies may be apparent.

Disclaimer
The publisher has made every effort to trace copyright holders and would welcome correspondence from those they have been unable to trace.

AGRICULTURAL MARKETING AND THE EEC

by

MICHAEL BUTTERWICK AND
EDMUND NEVILLE-ROLFE

HUTCHINSON OF LONDON

HUTCHINSON & CO (*Publishers*) LTD
178–202 Great Portland Street, London W1

London Melbourne Sydney Auckland
Wellington Johannesburg Cape Town
and agencies throughout the world

First published 1971

© Home-Grown Cereals Authority and
The Meat and Livestock Commission

This book has been set in Times type, printed in Great Britain on antique wove paper by Anchor Press, and bound by Wm. Brendon, both of Tiptree, Essex

ISBN 0 09 108100 9

Contents

ACKNOWLEDGEMENTS	ix
INTRODUCTION	xi

Part One The Background to Intervention in Agricultural Markets

Ch. 1	An Incomplete Policy	3
Ch. 2	The Marketing Gap	10
Ch. 3	The Work of Intervention Agencies	37

Part Two The Principal Farm Products

Ch. 4	Cereals	57
Ch. 5	Milk and Dairy Products	79
Ch. 6	Livestock and Meat	123
Ch. 7	Eggs and Poultry-meat	152
Ch. 8	Sugar	171
Ch. 9	Horticulture 1) Fruit and Vegetables	186
	2) Non-Edible Products	205
Ch. 10	Vegetable Oils and Oilseeds	208
Ch. 11	Other Farm Products	218

Part Three The Future for Regulated Agricultural Markets

Ch. 12	EEC Farmers' Marketing Organisations and their Future	231
Ch. 13	The Future for Intervention	243
Ch. 14	Implications for the British Market	249

Part Four Appendices:

A.	Agricultural Marketing in other Countries applying for ECC Membership	259
B.	Intervention Purchases EEC 1967/8—1969/70	268
C.	Expenditure from Guidance Section of FEOGA 1964/68	271
D.	UK/EEC Conversion Factors	273

INDEX	275

Foreword

This study was commissioned jointly by the Home-Grown Cereals Authority and the Meat and Livestock Commission. A substantial grant towards its cost was given by the Agricultural Market Development Executive Committee whose generous help in this connection is acknowledged by the sponsors and the authors.

Acknowledgements

A large number of people have given us encouragement and assistance in writing this book. Our sponsors, the Home-Grown Cereals Authority and the Meat and Livestock Commission, have been most helpful to us. We are grateful to officials in the Ministries of Agriculture in all the countries that we have visited and to those in the various Boards, Commissions, Farmers Unions, etc., concerned with our enquiries.

In particular we must mention the directors and staff of the various intervention agencies in the present member countries of the Community, who have been very generous with their time for discussing the work and problems of these agencies. We extend special thanks to Herr Ernst Freisberg of the Agricultural Section of the Community's Information Services, Mr Derek Prag and his staff at the European Communities Office in London, Mr John Morley of the Central Council for Agricultural and Horticultural Co-operation, and Mrs J. Morrice who coped most efficiently with the preparation of the typescripts.

Introduction

At a fairly early stage in the negotiations begun in 1970 for British entry into the EEC the British Government made clear its full acceptance of the Community's common agricultural policy. Adoption of the CAP would involve major changes in economic circumstances and outlook for producers, processors, distributors, and consumers of foodstuffs in Britain. Though these changes may to some extent be anticipated by government action during the negotiating period, most of them would, in the event of Britain signing the Treaty of Rome, be spread over the subsequent transition period, now agreed at five years. A majority of the hundreds of Community regulations on agriculture issued since 1962 and still in force, and many of those that will come into force before the end of the transition period, concern one stage or another of the marketing of farm produce. Besides dealing with imports and subsidised exports, with official market intervention, and with the storage and disposal of intervention stocks, the regulations also touch at a number of points the processing and distribution of foodstuffs, and are becoming increasingly concerned with the organisation by producers themselves of the disposal of their produce.

Entry into the EEC would therefore profoundly affect every aspect of agricultural marketing in Britain. This study has two main objectives: to compare the marketing systems on both sides of the Channel, and to suggest what changes would be likely to occur on this side in the event of Britain joining the Common Market. In Chapters 1 and 2 the two systems are placed in their historical and political perspectives. Some knowledge of their origins is clearly necessary to an understanding of their differences. So is a knowledge of the background of official support policies to agriculture against which they have evolved. We also discuss the important developments in food processing and distribution which are tending to face farmers in all liberal Western economies with similar problems of how to concentrate their output on the market to their best advantage. The methods adopted by producers in Britain and in the EEC to meet this situation, and the additional measures of official support, sometimes inspired as much by political and social motives as by strictly economic ones, are described. Chapter 3 is devoted to the scope and constitution of the so-called intervention agencies in each EEC member country which are responsible for implementing most of these official support measures.

Readers to whom the historical background, including the development of the British system of marketing boards, is already familiar may prefer to turn to Part Two. There, for each group of products in turn, the EEC marketing system and the main features of the market structure in member countries are briefly described. The implications for Britain are then examined. What changes, if any, in current British arrangements would, in the strictly legal sense, be mandatory to make them conform to Community rules? What is likely to be the effect of those rules, in a broader context, on the structure of marketing? What institutional changes or innovations might be necessary in the official machinery for agricultural support? Appendix A considers in summary form the main issues for Britain's three fellow applicants, Ireland, Denmark and Norway.

Finally, Part Three takes a general look at the future. First, it examines the way in which EEC member countries have been encouraging more effective participation by producers in the disposal of their produce, and how it is proposed by the Commission that these sometimes disparate measures should be harmonised to form a distinct Community policy for producer organisations. Second, we discuss whether the present system of market intervention is, despite its high cost, likely to continue for the foreseeable future. Since we conclude that it will we end by summarising the institutional arrangements which we consider would be necessary in Britain for implementing it and the other forms of support for agricultural production and marketing authorised by the CAP.

Oxford,
January 1971

PART ONE

The Background to Intervention in Agricultural Markets

CHAPTER 1

An Incomplete Policy

A major aim of government support of agriculture in most Western European countries since World War II has been to maintain the incomes of farmers and farmworkers at a level reasonably close to those of comparable groups of entrepreneurs and wage earners outside agriculture. A basic objective of enabling legislation has been to ensure 'a fair standard of living for the agricultural population' (Treaty of Rome, Article 39) and 'proper remuneration and living conditions for farmers and workers in agriculture' (Agriculture Act 1947). There are of course other important policy objectives, notably the provision of adequate low-cost supplies of food to consumers. The Agriculture Act refers to 'minimum prices consistent with proper remuneration . . . for farmers', and Article 39(e) lists 'to ensure reasonable prices and supplies to consumers' as one of the five objectives of the CAP. Even allowing for the difficulty of defining precisely the meaning of 'comparable', 'fair' or 'proper', there is a widespread feeling, not confined exclusively to farmers, that these aims have not up to now been achieved. However much farm people may have shared in the material benefits of economic growth during the past twenty years the majority of them, both in the EEC and in Britain, still work longer hours for a smaller return, whether in cash or in kind, than most people in other forms of employment. Real incomes in agriculture have stagnated or at any rate not increased at a similar rate to those outside.

Official policy on both sides of the Channel for increasing farm incomes has so far mainly consisted of manipulating producer prices, though using different methods. The development of the British system could be ascribed as much to past historical circumstances and to geographical accident as to any intrinsic merits which it may have. Long before the 1947 Act enclosures, primogeniture and landlords had over several centuries already made their mark on the structure of farming; 150 years of industrialisation on the proportion of the working population engaged in agriculture; and a century of free trade on the price of food. A system whereby freely formed market prices for the main farm products, competing with imports, were topped up to a guaranteed level by means of deficiency payments made directly by the government to producers was tailored to this situation. In the EEC, where, except for some 'minority' products like durum wheat and olive oil, the producer receives prices that are no higher than those of the market, the market itself is manipulated through official intervention buying and the systematic exclusion of lower-priced imports. With the exception of Belgium and the Netherlands a century of high protection for domestic agriculture in the EEC countries has left an indelible mark. The designers of neither system reckoned sufficiently with the effects of the technological revolution which hit British agriculture during the fifties and that of the Community a decade later. In Britain surpluses of 'review products' have been kept at arm's length by means of complicated devices which limit the quantity, and sometimes also quality, of products qualifying for the full guaranteed price, and the Treasury commitment to meet guarantees has not in recent years been open-ended. In the EEC, on the other hand, surpluses of produce in excess of current demand within the Community have not been avoided. This is largely because the common Fund has been obliged to honour at unlimited cost its obligation to purchase, at prices well above their value on international markets, unwanted supplies of wheat, dairy products and sugar.

These large outlays from the guarantee section of FEOGA[1] have contributed little to raising the general level of farm incomes relative to incomes outside agriculture. Intervention buying has of course helped to prevent them falling to a wholly unacceptable level. However, to the extent that it enables large numbers of producers to operate at a profit (often a small profit, but on larger holdings sometimes quite a comfortable one) regardless of what the true market demand may be for a given product, surpluses are likely to persist. It is arguable that if intervention prices were substantially lowered, or intervention discontinued altogether, many farmers would be obliged to switch to other products for which there existed a ready demand. If for financial or technical reasons they could not do so, then they would have to cease production altogether, dispose of their land to other farmers with better resources of land, capital and managerial ability, or, if the land were of poor quality, to forestry and recreation. Retraining grants or accelerated pensions are already available in all member countries to farmers wishing to move to another industry or retire prematurely. Community policy is to strengthen and extend such arrangements in the future. In this way the primarily social nature of the present price support payments would in the long run become clearer. Farmers' incomes would either be supplemented in a way which would not encourage them to add to unsaleable stocks of produce, or farmers would have to produce commodities for which there existed a clear market outlet even at prices below the former intervention level. Ideally the return received by farmers from their markets would no longer depend on official support buying, though it would still be protected from the effect of low-priced imports by the levy system.

[1] Fonds Européen de Garantie et d'Orientation Agricole (the European Agricultural Guarantee and Guidance Fund).

Levies, by artificially raising the price of competitive imports on the domestic market, lead, by strict economic reasoning, to a distortion of the market similar to that caused by intervention buying, and to a misallocation of resources on an even grander scale. On the principle of comparative advantage North American farmers should, for example, even without the extensive subsidies they receive, be able to provide consumers in Western Europe with products processed from their wheat and feed-grains, and New Zealand farmers provide them with dairy products, at not much more than 60 per cent of what they are paying for them at present in the EEC. Given an equivalent level of producer prices (whether supported by intervention or not) in Europe the present surpluses of wheat and butter would begin rapidly to disappear—along with a very large number of the farms and farmers contributing to them. This being, except in the long run, politically unacceptable, the apparatus of threshold prices and levies is likely to persist.

Support measures for agriculture are, of course, seldom justifiable on exclusively economic grounds, but have political and social aims which isolate and protect farmers from the strict operation of market forces. These may include devices which either artificially raise producer prices to a guaranteed level above those of the market (deficiency payments and production grants), relieve producers of unmarketable surpluses at a guaranteed minimum price (intervention purchases), maintain market prices at above those prevailing on export markets (levies and restitutions), restrict imports (quotas), lower the cost of farm inputs (cheap credit, fertiliser and fuel subsidies, etc.), or discourage certain types of production (grants for slaughtering dairy cows, grubbing up orchards, etc.). Social measures of a positive kind may consist of grants towards improving rural infrastructure, subsidies to rural industries, retraining grants to persons moving out of farming, or accelerated pensions for farmers. These are designed to raise the incomes of a disadvantaged minority, to avoid rural depopulation, and contribute to the preservation of the countryside for general enjoyment. Only a small number of persons living there can be profitably engaged in producing food. Any assessment of the cost of agricultural support must therefore make allowance for the need to maintain the environment, ecosystems, and the 'quality of life', aims to which attention is increasingly given, but whose cost is not always appreciated. The recent report of the Strutt Committee[1] has also underlined the risks of applying short-term economic criteria to agriculture.

Assistance to the minority is likely more and more to consist of measures to strengthen their position in the market so that the food which they do produce comes to correspond more and more closely to what consumers want to buy. These measures consist largely of incentives to the formation of producer marketing groups. Closely linked to them are the so-called 'structural' aids, aimed at creating more economically

[1] *Modern Farming and the Soil*. The Agricultural Advisory Council. London, HMSO, 1971.

efficient production units. The EEC Commission has been giving increasing attention to these since the single-market regulations for the main products were completed in 1967/68—an attention forced upon it by the evident inadequacy of those regulations in face of mounting surpluses of unmarketable produce. The Commission's Memorandum on the Reform of Agriculture submitted in December 1968 to the Council of Ministers—the so-called Mansholt Plan[1]—had a predictably cool reception in both farming and official circles in the member countries. At the time of writing the Council has never even discussed it formally, nor did it accept the short-term recommendations to lower intervention price levels which the Commission had tacked on to its main structural proposals. These proposals are now of mainly historical interest. The Commission has already had second thoughts about some of them. Two major ones have been dropped; others have been either modified or elaborated in subsequent draft proposals, sometimes known as 'mini-Mansholt'.[2] The importance of the original Plan remains its unvarnished statement, for the first time in an official Community document, of the great unresolved problems of EEC agriculture. It stated frankly:

> 'The Community's agricultural policy has so far given priority to action on markets and prices.
>
> The introduction of single prices has certainly opened up national markets and made room for a very appreciable increase in intra-Community trade; but in the case of most agricultural products, these prices do not seem to have been fixed primarily with reference to economic criteria and the requirements of the specialisation that should exist in the common market. More often than not the price fixed was the result of political compromises acceptable to all Member States.
>
> The Community was thus led to fix the prices for most agricultural products at a level generally well in excess of the prices currently ruling in international transactions or even on the domestic markets of countries with which the Community is in competition.
>
> While this price policy has helped to raise farm incomes, it has not enabled farmers to catch up with the incomes of other comparable social and occupational groups. On the contrary, the income of certain farmers is declining in real terms. The present system of market intervention, with its quantitatively unlimited market support at high prices,

[1] *Memorandum sur la réforme de l'agriculture dans la Communautée Economique Européenne* Com (68) 1000, Brussels, Commission of the European Communities, December 18th, 1968.

[2] These were first included in a document entitled *L'équilibre des marchés agricoles (communication de la Commission au Conseil)*, Com (69) 1200, drawn up by the Commission just before The Hague Conference in November, 1969. Its main purpose was to demonstrate how savings on the Guarantee Section of FEOGA between 1970 and 1975, brought about by a lowering of certain intervention prices, could be applied to finance structural reforms out of the Guidance Section. The price proposals were in the event rejected by the Council, but the proposed structural measures have been elaborated into a series of draft directives (see page 9, footnote 1).

encourages marginal farms to stay in business and thus constitutes an obstacle to a Community-wide division of labour in agriculture and to the modernisation of farming. It holds up the diminution in the number of farmers, which is one of the essential factors for an increase in farm incomes, and at the same time enables certain more competitive farmers to batten on the support given.

The system is also extremely costly for the public at large. The policy of high prices, coupled with progress in chemistry, animal health, plant protection and genetics, has greatly raised unit yields. Since demand expansion is limited by the rate of population growth, the Community now finds itself saddled, in the case of many products, with surpluses of which some cannot even be disposed of on the saturated world market. Even when there are outlets, the surpluses bear on the market so heavily that they can be disposed of only at a price which is very costly for the Community. The cost of intervention and refunds in an agriculture producing structural surpluses is a burden which is becoming intolerable for our Member States, and their economies are in consequence being deprived of resources which could be used to better advantage in improving the competitive strength of other economic sectors.'[1]

In developing this theme the Report did not pull its punches:

'It is . . . illusory to believe that market policy and price policy alone can make a major contribution to the improvement of the farmer's standard of life.'[2]

'It is impossible to introduce adequate guarantees for a certain number of products important for the income of the small farmer, except at the risk of finding production expanding beyond all limits.'[3]

'The only way to provide farmers with an equitable income and better living conditions, and at the same time ensure the indispensable balance between output and sales outlets, is to reshape the structure of production.'[4]

'The problem of the structure of European agriculture is not that there are so many small farms but that . . . more and more farm enterprises are becoming marginal.'[5]

Appearing at a moment when most people were still enjoying a certain euphoria about the completion, after herculean efforts of political compromise, of the unified market system (a euphoria to which the Commission itself had done much to contribute), the Memorandum seemed to many disagreeable and ill-timed. It was as if they had climbed arduously up a mountain side only to be told that what they took to be the top was only a ridge on the way to a still distant summit.

A rapid switch from a system of indiscriminate price support to all farmers by means of price manipulation to one of direct and selective income support to non-viable farmers on social grounds, however desirable

[1] *Mémorandum sur la réforme, op cit, ibid*, para 55.
[2] *ibid*, para 38.   [3] *ibid*, para 38.   [4] *ibid*, para 38.   [5] *ibid*, para 37.

theoretically, must be out of the question. The traditional structure of agriculture, in which unwanted surpluses and low farm incomes have for some time been uneasily accommodated, will never undergo a single thorough overhaul; it will only be modified by successive bits of political carpentry. But at least the Mansholt Plan has provided the nucleus for a coherent policy for the future at Community level, which may be subsequently refined and adapted in the light of technical and political debate. The only comparable exercise in any member country was carried out by a committee appointed by the Minister of Agriculture to consider the long-term development of agriculture in France up to 1985, the so-called Vedel report.[1] Neither Mansholt nor Vedel have minimised the extent of the revolution involved. Mansholt estimated that 5 mn persons and 5 mn hectares in the Community would have to cease agricultural production during the current decade. According to Vedel these numbers should reach about 2·3 mn and 12 mn respectively in France alone, though the exodus would be spread over half as much time again, to 1985. Taken out of context and headlined these forecasts, suggesting social engineering on an almost stalinist scale, aroused alarm and fury. Dr Mansholt pointed out that the movement of farmers envisaged in the Commission's memorandum was no greater than that which had occurred in the six member countries during the previous years. On the other hand M. Jacques Duhamel, the French Minister of Agriculture, who had votes to count, explained after an early unguarded remark that he would make the Vedel report his bedside book, that it was not an official policy document and that anyway he was treating it as general reading and not as the Bible. All this bad publicity had unfortunate results. First, more measured and constructive comment, notably official Dutch and German criticisms of the Mansholt proposals, was less widely reported.[2] Second, although both reports closely argued the need for farm supply to be adjusted to demand and for complementary regional and social programmes, neither of these fundamental aspects of future changes in agriculture and rural life received a fair share of public attention. Inevitably this tended to be focussed on that part of the Commission's package which recommended immediate cuts in the butter target price and changes in quota arrangements for sugar-beet. The Vedel report also recommended price reductions, especially for cereals and sugar, stressing that the present level of prices disadvantaged the poorer consumer without bringing any notable benefit to any but the largest producer. It pointed to the absurdity of a system whereby the market was underwritten for products such as cereals and dairy products for which the prospect of expanding demand was relatively

[1] *Rapport général de la commission sur l'avenir à long terme de l'agriculture française présidée par M. le doyen Georges Vedel*, Paris, Ministère de l'Agriculture, 1969.
[2] It is significant that the German government's annual 'Green Report' in 1969 recognised that agricultural problems can no longer be solved by traditional policies only, but require a co-ordinated problem of economic, educational and socio-political measures.

limited, whereas producers of beef, pigmeat and poultry-meat, of which per capita consumption was tending to rise, were burdened with the high price of grains.

From its politically detached position the Vedel Committee was able to be more uncompromising than the Commission in its analysis of the shortcomings of existing price support and structural policies. But, predictably, no action has been taken in France on the report. The Commission's memorandum, on the other hand, was a good deal more precise than Vedel in its practical recommendations. Its thinking has since developed, *via* 'mini-Mansholt', into a series of draft directives[1] submitted to the Council of Ministers for its consideration. In these a common framework for reform is laid down, as well as the extent of the contribution available from the Guidance Section of FEOGA (generally 50 per cent of total cost towards what are deemed to be 'common actions' in the sense of the regulation for financing the CAP whose principles were agreed at the 1969 Hague Conference). It would be illusory to imagine that the proposals will be accepted by the Council without prolonged delay and substantial amendment. They concern measures to be taken over the next five years for farm modernisation; improved technical and managerial training for persons remaining in agriculture; encouragement of producer groups; redistribution of the land of farmers who have retired, where it is of suitable quality, so as to enlarge other holdings; and transfer of less suitable land to forestry and recreational purposes.[2] These are all tentative steps along the Community's arduous road towards a common agricultural policy that is both complete and coherent, or at any rate as complete and coherent as any agricultural policy is ever likely to be. There is, however, a strong risk that even larger unsaleable surpluses might result from combining improved production structures with continuing technical progress. This was a point made forcibly in the Vedel report. To mitigate it two things are necessary. First, the social and marketing measures now proposed would have to be complemented by changes of policy on prices. This is, however, a course which the Council of Ministers is, for political reasons, unlikely to adopt. Second, farmers themselves will have to recognise clearly, as a minority of them have already done, the dominating power of the consumer in the developed economies of Western Europe. To this aspect we shall now turn our attention.

---

[1] *Réforme de l'agriculture (propositions de la Commission au Conseil)*, COM (70) 500, Brussels, Commission of the European Communities, April 29th, 1970. Legally, directives oblige member countries to introduce or adapt national legislation in order to give effect to them.

[2] As a corollary all national aids to reclamation of land for agricultural purposes would be forbidden. The question whether such a directive, if eventually adopted, would apply in new member countries during a transition period, could be of some relevance to UK farmers.

CHAPTER 2

The Marketing Gap

The relative failure of price policy by itself to maintain average levels of real farm income underlies the need for other policies designed to promote more efficient marketing of farm produce. Although the importance of adapting their supply to the demands of the market is becoming better understood by farmers there is still a big gap between understanding and achievement. In this chapter we compare the attempts made up to now in Britain and in the EEC countries, taken with official support and by producers acting independently, to bridge that gap. We examine the extent to which these attempts have been successful in the past and analyse the future challenge of an ever-increasing concentration of demand on the part of food processors and wholesalers.

Schooled by the year-to-year vagaries of the weather farmers often tend to become resigned to the pressure of outside forces over which they seem to have little control. Each is well aware of the very limited impact which his own output can have on the total market situation, and is often ill-informed about the state of markets other than that in which he is selling. His produce being either highly perishable, like fruit, vegetables, milk or eggs, or preservable with difficulty or for relatively brief periods of time, like grain, potatoes or fatstock, the possibility of withholding it from the market at times of low prices is limited. The individual farmer has traditionally produced goods without much forethought about who will buy them and has usually in the end had to accept the market price offered to him. As long as his production was confined, as it has been for generations, on hundreds of thousands of peasant smallholdings of continental Europe, to the needs of his family and his neighbours, and to a modest saleable surplus disposed of in the local country market or to a local miller or dealer, there was little risk of a serious long-run imbalance between supply and demand. Gluts, of eggs or fruit or vegetables for instance, would be mainly seasonal, and generally short-lived. Hunger was in any case a more likely risk than over-abundance. There might also be occasional surpluses of a more cyclical nature, such as those of pigs or potatoes. More or less passive acceptance, though an attitude which still prevailed even fifteen years ago in some regions of what is now the EEC, has largely disappeared during the past decade. For farm people in general, the consequences of rapid economic growth, not least in the form of television and the spread of car ownership, have opened windows on to a wider world, encouraging a desire for more consumer goods and the higher-income expectations that go with it. At the same time they have become aware that their real incomes have been rising relatively slowly compared with those of persons outside agriculture. To farmers themselves, trying perhaps by increasing their output to overcome this disparity, its causes, though simple in origin and familiar enough to many, sometimes unsympathetic observers, may seem remote and incomprehensible. These are, briefly, the limited capacity of human beings to absorb a greater volume of food once they have reached a certain level of day-to-day satisfaction, even if food suddenly becomes cheaper; their inclination once they have acquired a certain standard of comfort to devote a steadily diminishing proportion of any additional earnings to buying food; a parallel tendency to purchase more elaborately processed forms of food so that the value of the raw material falls relatively to the value of the processed product;[1] and, last, the rapidly rising yields of land and livestock, whose large additional output often exceeds such limited additional demand as may arise from an increase in the population and from its higher consumption per head.

Of course not all farmers are unaware of these adverse factors, and a minority, varying in importance from country to country, has responded to the challenge which they present. The intensity of this response is also uneven and reflects one of the remarkable characteristics of agriculture in highly developed countries: in no other industry have traditional practices survived on such a large scale alongside modern production techniques and management methods. This is equally true as far as marketing practices are concerned. In small local markets farmers and their wives can still sometimes be found devoting most of a day to selling a single duck or lamb or calf, a few vegetables, and a small pile of eggs. This presents a striking contrast to anyone who has visited the office of any large grain trader, with its worldwide telex links, or talked to the manager of a production co-operative accustomed to purchase batches of several hundred young stores for its beef-lots, often from government agencies in Eastern Europe, and contracting with supermarket chains for its output. Indeed the gap between the old and the new, between the peasant wedded to a way of life and the career farmer confident in his business ability and fully conscious of consumer demand beyond the confines of his local market square, is continually widening. This awareness has been much stimulated, as has the adoption of new technology in all its other aspects, by the better education of young entrants into farming, by the wide range of official and private advisory services available to older farmers who are willing to try new methods, and by improved communications and the mass media.

[1] It has been estimated that in Britain between 1958 and 1967 spending on marketing services per head of the population grew at a rate three times greater than that on food valued before processing and distribution. See G. H. Woollen and G. Turner, *The Cost of Food Marketing*, Journal of Agricultural Economics, Reading, Vol. XXI, No. 1, 1970.

For historical reasons already touched upon, the contrast between the modern and traditional in agriculture is more marked in the EEC countries than it has been in most of Britain for a decade or more. Thanks largely to a free trade tradition established by the middle of the 19th century, British farmers have until recently suffered much severer exposure than their continental neighbours to the external economic pressures of an expanding industrial society. French cereal growers in the 1880s, for instance, were rapidly accorded tariff protection against the imports of North American grain which had brought to such a sudden close the so-called golden age of farming in England.[1] Even in the thirties of this century when government help eventually arrived for British agriculture, almost the first occasion in time of peace, it was only partly in the form of the tariffs and quotas then being stepped up all over the rest of Europe. It consisted also of deficiency payments[2] and of the Agricultural Marketing Acts of 1931 and 1933 which gave to farmers a potential influence over the disposal of their produce greater than that enjoyed by producers anywhere else in Western Europe. Even so, as will be seen, their privileged position was in some ways more apparent than real and even where it existed may perhaps in the long run even prove to have been disadvantageous.

The most widely publicised and most durable results of this inter-war legislation were the Milk Marketing Boards. In setting up a producer marketing monopoly for milk, the product with the greatest effect on most farmers' incomes, the motives of the government of the day were, as usual, mixed. First, it gave the impression to the public of making quite generous amends for the fact that British agriculture had been 'let down' after World War I, notably by the repeal in 1922 of the war-time Corn Production Act. Farmers had been led to believe by an Act of 1921 that this would be maintained and ensure the continuance of guaranteed prices for wheat and barley more or less indefinitely in peace-time. Second, it reorganised milk distribution in a way that no longer gave large distributing and processing firms an undue influence over the wholesale market, often at the producers' expense. It promised an assured outlet, at prices that would neither fluctuate violently nor fall disastrously low, for a commodity on whose sale the majority of farmers, especially small farmers, relied for their livelihood. Third, and perhaps most important in a period of economic depression, it allowed producers, through their Boards, to fix their own price for liquid milk. The balance used for manufacturing could be disposed of at a lower price competitive with that of imported dairy products. Demand for liquid milk being relatively strong in Britain and rather inelastic as to price, as well as being stimulated by new government subsidies

[1] The far from beneficial long-term effects on French farming of increasing doses of protectionism has been stressed by critics like Augé-Laribé, who ascribes to it the lack of incentive to any but a pioneering minority of farmers over a period of forty years to introduce technical improvements that would lower their costs of production per unit of output. See A. Augé-Laribé, *La politique agricole de la France de 1880 à 1940* (PUF, Paris, 1950), pp. 63 *et seq*.

[2] For wheat in 1932 and for barley and oats in 1937.

to schools and welfare schemes, dairy farmers could be assured of a major part of their income from the liquid sector of the market. At the same time the low-priced imports of butter and cheese which had formerly disrupted the market still continued to enter at relatively low rates of duty or on fairly generous quotas, and help keep down the general level of food costs to the hard-pressed urban working population. Such is the fame (some might say notoriety) of the milk marketing scheme, and of the unprecedented market power originally given by it to producers, that there is still a widely held belief on the Continent that its principles have been extended to most farm produce in Britain. In fact up to 1939 hops, potatoes and bacon pigs were the only other products for which schemes were established. After World War II the pigs scheme was not renewed except in Northern Ireland. Since 1945 one for tomatoes and cucumbers has come and gone. One for eggs is already on the way out. The only post-war scheme which seems permanently established is that for wool. More detailed consideration will be given to some of the Marketing Boards' activities in the separate product chapters of Part Two.

The hops marketing scheme, the first and only one instituted under the 1931 Act, brought to an end a period of extreme fluctuations in which price had varied inversely with yield for a number of years. Throughout the thirties and since World War II real producer prices have remained stabilised at a level considerably above the average of the years of fluctuation. Before 1932 efforts to achieve producer solidarity had been spoilt by an unco-operative minority. Under the scheme, however, farm quotas by weight are administered by the Hops Marketing Board. These are transferable and have been known to change hands in recent years at up to £50 a cental (100 lbs) against a general selling price of around £34. There is no provision for new entrants. Brewers' own hops are exempt from the scheme, but have never been grown on a sufficiently large scale to provide an alternative source. Imports, mainly from Central Europe for lager and from the USA for stout, are limited by agreement, and constitute under 10 per cent of total demand. The Board has thus a virtual monopoly, but the cost of hops to the consumer being less than 2 per cent of the cost of a pint of beer it cannot be considered as a very harmful one.

The Potato Marketing Board, set up in 1932, has been notably less successful than the Hops Board in ironing out year to year price fluctuations for main-crop potatoes despite possessing rather similar restrictive powers over output (through acreage quotas) and over imports and, in addition, of market intervention. This is partly attributable to the susceptibility of the crop to year-to-year climatic variations. At any rate in promoting market intelligence, technical research into disease, fertiliser use, mechanisation, etc.; encouraging, in its early days especially, through licensing, an improvement in the business morality of merchants; and, more recently, promoting higher standards of product to meet modern retailing requirements, the Board has been of general assistance to producers.

The Pigs and Bacon Marketing Boards (1933–9) during a brief and troubled life enjoyed considerable powers to regulate imports of bacon and also gave producers a certain protection against the tendency of the domestic bacon industry to come under the control of a few large firms. They may also have helped to strengthen those tendencies by eliminating numbers of small firms on hygienic grounds through its control of licensing. The scheme covered only bacon pigs. The Pigs Board's price policy was never very attractive to producers, many of whom seem to have been content to torpedo its operation by evading contracts made with the Board for bacon pigs and selling their produce on the uncontrolled pork market if prices there proved temporarily more favourable.

These pre-war producer marketing schemes should perhaps be viewed not exclusively in the light of the immediate economic crisis which provoked them, but also against the background of earlier unsuccessful attempts to persuade producers to organise their output for the market. As early as 1922 the Linlithgow Committee[1] was drawing attention to distributors' unduly wide margins, to the necessity for a comprehensive approach to marketing involving producer, distributor and consumer, and to the producer co-operation which was essential to satisfy consumer demand for home-grown food of a standardised and reliable quality. Nearly half a century later such exhortations have a familiar sound, on both sides of the Channel. In an attempt to give producers a marketing sense and make them understand the importance of reflecting consumer preference back to the earliest stages of primary production an Act of 1928 introduced the National Mark scheme, which, it was hoped, would counteract the effect of foreign competition in grading and packaging, especially of dairy products, eggs, bacon and fruit. Two years of world crisis and imports at dumped prices almost immediately engulfed a scheme whose chances of success were anyway fairly slender in view of what the Lucas Committee was later to deplore as the 'ingrained individualism' of the British farmer.[2]

It was the intention of the 1931 Marketing Act to clip this individualism by means of monopoly Boards to whose direction all producers were obliged to submit once they had been voted into existence by a two-thirds majority of them. The Boards could be empowered to fix grades and prices, and also if necessary quantities to be sold, in order to improve the machinery of marketing and distribution. To protect consumer interests special committees would watch over any tendency to collusion between monopolistic Boards and oligopolistic distributors. The Act of 1933 added to the Boards' already considerable restrictive powers a right to impose production quotas based on producers' past output. Whilst also imposing tariffs and quotas on imports it was the Act's intention not to give too exclusive an advantage to home producers, but in the long term to regulate

---

[1] *Final Report of the Departmental Committee on Distribution and Prices of Agricultural Produce.* Chairman, the Marquis of Linlithgow. London, HMSO, 1924, Cmd 2008.

[2] *Report of the Committee appointed to review the working of the Agricultural Marketing Acts.* Chairman, Lord Lucas. Ministry of Agriculture and Fisheries, Economic series No. 48, 1947, p. 5.

The Marketing Gap

supply in an equitable manner between each sector. In considering in 1946 the National Farmers' Union's case in favour of a return to pre-war marketing arrangements the Lucas Committee had pungent comments to make on the extent to which the general interest had been served by the two Acts. The Report did not accept the view that the interest of producers in a market right up to the point at which a commodity reached the consumer was in any way exclusive; nor should it be allowed to become so. That producer controlled Boards would expand the market for commodities whose price was guaranteed by the government could also only be considered true up to a point. One of the principal means of expanding consumption is by reducing prices through minimising marketing and distribution costs 'throughout the whole process of production and marketing'. Boards, on the other hand, are likely to give primary consideration to reducing costs up to the stage at which the price guarantee is applicable, i.e. the point of first sale. Thereafter they might consider the advantage to producers of cost reduction rather uncertain.[1] Since the operating costs of Boards are met from a levy on producers any effort to expand demand which failed would involve them in an unrequited loss; and successful efforts to cut distribution costs would be principally of benefit to consumers. Last, the Lucas Committee did not consider that producer control over Boards was necessary in order to persuade producers to co-operate in improved packaging, grading and presentation of their products.[2] In its view pre-war experience offered little evidence of producers being persuaded by their Boards to play such a part. Indeed in the case of sugar-beet where producers did respond keenly to the contract system, with differential prices ensuring prompt and level deliveries, the NFU had said that no Board was necessary. The Hops Board was almost exclusively concerned with quantitative restrictions. The Pigs Board was merely 'a piece of negotiating machinery'. The Potato Board did pioneer a certain amount of advertising, as did the Milk Boards, which also, under the stress of war, had taken an interest in promoting producer efficiency. But by and large, the Report concluded, producers should no longer, now that the economic conditions of the thirties no longer prevailed, retain exclusive control of the continuous process of marketing.

The then Labour government, feeling perhaps that it already had the public reorganisation of enough industries on its hands, set aside the Committee's main recommendations to set up independent Commodity Commissions, state Boards under whose direction the producer Boards would confine their activities to production alone. The Marketing Act of 1949, with the important exception that it gave the Minister of Agriculture

[1] The absence of economic incentive to producers' organisations to promote expansion in the consumption of liquid milk was to be remedied with the introduction of the 'standard quantity' when the Boards resumed their pre-war role in 1953 (see page 21 below). It is interesting to compare a similar lack of incentive resulting from the EEC system of intervention buying of butter and dried skim (see pages 87, 95 and 97).

[2] *op cit*, pp. 53 *et seq.*

and Food a veto over the regulatory and price-fixing powers of the Boards —in the case of retail prices and margins for milk it took them away altogether—virtually restored the *status quo ante bellum*. There was, however, one other respect in which the situation differed from pre-war. The 1947 Agriculture Act had introduced guaranteed producer prices for all main products. In the case of potatoes and milk these reached producers through the intermediary of the established Boards, and one of the arguments advanced for the setting up of the Egg Marketing Board in 1958 was that it would provide a means for channelling the government subsidy to producers who marketed their eggs through the packing stations to be licensed by the Board. The argument was a doubtful one since the subsidy had until then been paid through packing stations by the Ministry without undue complaint from producers. Nor did the Wright Commission[1] consider it necessary to maintain the Board in existence in order to administer the subsidy during the final three years of its operation between 1971 and 1974.

The only other product to which producer price guarantees apply and for which a marketing scheme operates is wool. The Wool Marketing Board, the first to be set up or revived under the 1949 Act, provides a clearcut example of countervailing power exercised by producers in an oligopolistic market. As sole purchaser of the British clip since 1950 it fairly rapidly secured a reduction in trade margins, and consequently higher producer prices, while managing also to keep its own operating costs per pound of wool sold at a low level. There is no restriction on producers' output or tariff protection, and the Board sells in the open market.

The Tomato and Cucumber Board, also set up in 1950, enjoyed some fifteen years of chequered, and sometimes tempestuous, life. Its regulatory powers were limited to setting quality standards. Plans for raising a levy to finance its activities and for fining offenders, were bitterly contested by a powerful minority of growers and never obtained the two-thirds majority necessary to achieve such a degree of control over producers. For the same reason the Board never acquired any trading powers. In the absence of direct control over imports it is, however, doubtful whether these would have been very effective.

It is ironical that British marketing boards should be regarded as an enviable model by many continental farmers. If anything the system has tended to shelter producers in Britain from the realities of the markets for products for which schemes operate. The legislation of the thirties probably overcompensated for the official neglect from which agriculture, except for the brief interval of World War I, had suffered for half a century or more. Were the statutory and other props which keep Boards in existence with quasi-monopoly powers now to be removed farmers would in many cases find themselves ill-equipped to compete commercially on even terms in a free market. On the Continent, on the other hand, where tariff protection

[1] *Report of the Reorganisation Commission for Eggs*. Chairman, Rowland Wright, Esq. London, HMSO, 1968. Cmnd 3669.

has been the traditional method of supporting agriculture, farmers were left to organise themselves as best they could without direct government intervention (though in some countries co-operatives have enjoyed certain tax advantages). Producer co-operatives in the EEC have, of course, not been uniformly successful in steering a majority of farmers in all member countries unscathed through the technical and marketing revolutions of the past decade. The failure of producers to equip themselves collectively to meet a demand for food, increasingly exacting in terms of quality and regularity, is manifest from the Mansholt, Vedel and other reports. In the co-operatives themselves there is much deadwood, but without the co-operatives that failure would have been substantially greater. It could be argued that in some ways continental farmers through their co-operatives are better prepared at the opening of the seventies than are British farmers to meet the commercial challenges of the coming decade.

Agricultural co-operation took root in the EEC member countries during the last quarter of the 19th century, largely under the impulse of the depression of the 1880s, though the pioneering work of F. W. Raiffeisen in the Rhineland dates from thirty years before. Many co-operatives are mutualist in origin, associations of like-minded neighbours pooling their savings to meet each other's needs of harvest credit or other short-term working, and even investment, capital. Some insured their members against the consequences of fire, hail or illness. Others were formed for the common purchase of farm supplies, especially of chemical fertilisers when these first became available, and others for collective marketing of produce, usually confining themselves to a single crop or product, such as cereals, milk or wine. The dairy co-operatives of Charentes in Western France were started after phylloxera had wiped out the traditional wine-growing in the mid-seventies. The cheesemakers' *fruitières* of the Alps and Jura have an even longer pedigree. Over a period of ninety years co-operatives have, through the formation of regional and then national unions, acquired a position of considerable economic influence both in the supply of farmers' inputs and the marketing of their output. Although this position has been consolidated mainly since the end of World War II (and not without internal stresses), it could not have been achieved without the earlier formative period. Nor, outside the Low Countries, has the movement always been marked by that absolute loyalty of producers to their co-operative which has been a notable feature in Scandinavia. Nevertheless in terms of percentage of produce now marketed in some countries the achievement has been impressive: for cereals, about 15 per cent only in Italy and Belgium, but 45 per cent in Germany, 70 per cent in France, 80 per cent in Luxemburg, and 40 per cent in the Netherlands; for milk 90 per cent in Luxemburg, 84 per cent in the Netherlands, 83 per cent in Germany, 62 per cent in Belgium, 52 per cent in France, and 50 per cent in Italy. For livestock products, which until quite recently at any rate lent themselves much less readily to marketing on any scale, co-operative effort has been on a good deal more modest scale. But in the case of those produced industrially progress is being achieved, around a quarter of egg and broiler production being in the hands of the co-operatives in some countries. Finally, no summary of co-operation in the EEC would be complete without reference to the formidable position built up in the fruit and vegetable sector since before the last war by the co-operative clock auctions in the Netherlands, where they control 100 per cent of the market, and in Belgium, where their share is about 60 per cent of fruit and 40 per cent of vegetables.

Although agricultural co-operative associations first came into existence in Britain at a fairly early date[1] it is remarkable that the Rochdale pioneers, who directly or indirectly inspired many rural co-operatives on the Continent, should have had such relatively little influence on farmers in their own country. Co-operation remained largely an urban consumer movement in England. A major reason was the generally better structure of English farming, the origins of which have already been briefly described. On the Continent holdings were almost always too small to generate the financial reserves needed as a hedge against poor harvests, the savings with which to buy new implements, or the necessary countervailing power in bargaining with millers, dairymen and other country merchants and dealers. For the same historical reasons a substantial number of English farmers, whether tenants or owner-occupiers, held a social position equal, or at least not markedly inferior, to that of the merchants, brewers, professional men, and (an important factor) bankers of the small market towns which they frequented, and with whose families, indeed, they often intermarried. In this world of *Middlemarch* many farmers enjoyed a standing and creditworthiness which made unnecessary the type of mutual assistance developed by the European peasantry. It was also a state of affairs which caused the farming community to be divided socially. On the Continent it was more homogeneous. In England not only were the poorer farmers and smallholders cut off from their more prosperous and well-educated neighbours, but also from the minor professional men of the villages and small towns who often provided the inspiration and drive for agricultural co-operatives abroad. The cement to this rural social structure was provided by the predominant system of land tenure, that of landlord and tenant,[2] which gave tenants of holdings that were already in any case larger on average than those on the Continent a number of advantages not enjoyed by the owner-occupiers of tiny peasant farms. Whilst in good times their incomes benefited from the capital improvements that were provided by the landlord, often at a low rate of interest, in bad times they might be remitted rent or allowed to be in arrears without eviction.[3] Though improving and benevolent landlords

[1] The first, a requirement society, was started at Aspatria in Cumberland in 1869 to safeguard its members against fraudulent sales of chemical fertilisers.

[2] The system accounted for 90 per cent of land in England in 1890. In 1969 the proportion was 46 per cent.

[3] The situation of the average tenant should not of course be idealised. The series of Agricultural Holdings Acts passed between 1875 and 1908 indicate how few rights he

were by no means universal (and many of them suffered severe financial difficulties as a result of the crisis of the 1870s) the system was in some sense both a substitute for and an obstacle to the development of co-operation on the continental model. It is significant that the growth of co-operation was particularly feeble in England. Elsewhere in the British Isles social and economic conditions were in general less inimical to it. In Ireland the prevalence of absentee landlords and the scarcity of improving ones, combined with the gradual transfer of small tenanted farms to owner occupation by successive Land Settlement Acts, produced a situation out of which arose the co-operative movement pioneered at the turn of the century by Horace Plunkett, himself an improving landlord. The producer co-operatives which enjoy a monopoly of butter manufacture in the Irish Republic and which predominate in the western part of the Six Counties, are thus more typical of the continental than of the English situation today. In the northern part of Scotland the two Milk Marketing Boards still preserve much of the old spirit of the co-operatives from which they took over. The aid given to crofters in the Highlands and Islands remains one of the few examples of government promotion of agricultural co-operation in Britain.

A central organisation, the British Agricultural Organisation Society, was founded in 1900, on lines established six years earlier by Plunkett's Irish AOS, to provide overall guidance to agricultural co-operatives.[1] Those in England numbered only 19 at the time, of which 12 were requirement societies. During the following two years, however, a further 14 marketing societies came into existence, making a total of 11 milk-collecting and 8 egg-collecting co-operatives. A fairly rapid expansion in the number of societies before and during World War I encouraged the AOS, which for a ten-year period from 1909 received some modest financial help from the government, to sponsor in 1918, in an atmosphere of post-war enthusiasm for agricultural co-operation in general, the Agricultural Wholesale Society. Within six years this co-operative trading venture had foundered, a victim of the collapse of corn prices in 1922 and of the lack of any established tradition of loyalty on the part of its producer customers. But the Linlithgow Report attributed its failure mainly to indifferent management. The event had a traumatic effect on would-be promoters of centralised co-operative trading for a generation. Locally and regionally requirement societies continued slowly to expand their business, but distinguished from other agricultural and corn merchants by

originally enjoyed, how slowly they were extended, and how tenaciously the landed interest in Parliament resisted their extension. The 1923 Act further consolidated the tenant's position. Virtually total security of tenure to the farmer who maintains proper standards of husbandry was assured by the Act of 1947, thought at the time to be 'the *nunc dimittis* of the country squires'. Some alleviations were granted to the landlord by the 1958 Act.

[1] For a detailed description of developments in agricultural co-operation in England since the beginning of the century see J. G. Knapp, *An Analysis of agricultural co-operation in England* (London, ACAA, 1965).

the fact of their shareholders being farmers, rather than by any particular, let alone exclusive, loyalty on the part of their farmer customers. The marketing societies, especially those for eggs, received some boost from the National Mark scheme of 1928, but the dairy co-operatives ceased to have much *raison d'être* after the introduction of the milk marketing scheme in 1933, becoming little more than transport agencies for the Milk Marketing Board.

The AOS disappeared in the wreck of the AWS. Organisation Societies were maintained in Scotland, Wales and Northern Ireland throughout the inter-war years, and still exist there today, but from 1924 onwards England was left without any effective voice for agricultural co-operation until the constitution of the Agricultural Co-operative Association in 1945. The collapse of the AWS appeared to justify the scepticism of farmers' union leadership, which may have reflected correctly the opinion of a majority of their members, about co-operative ventures generally. The National Farmers' Union felt no obligation to help keep the AOS in existence, preferring to take upon itself the mantle of representing co-operatives in England, to the extent of the essentially limited view which the Union took of its role, especially in marketing. Little effort was made, for instance, to promote any central schemes for training co-operative managers. As early as 1927 the official NFU Year Book stated flatly that 'the farmer's business is to produce foodstuffs. ... The business of the wholesale or retail dealer in foodstuffs is something which lies completely outside the farmer's province.' If this point of view was to be modified somewhat over the following five years it was not in the direction of giving co-operatives a more powerful role in farmers' control over the disposal of their produce. In the desperate situation prevailing by 1932 it is hardly surprising that official farmer leadership succumbed to the immediately attractive idea of producer monopoly over the much disturbed market for liquid milk. No doubt the MMBs managed to acquire a certain share of the market for dairy products by means of investments in manufacturing plant of its own, financed by a levy on producers. It is nevertheless arguable that a vigorous expansion of co-operative effort in the thirties might, given the sort of official encouragement and fiscal privileges enjoyed by co-operatives in some continental countries, have afforded producers in the long run a more effective countervailing power against oligopoly among private dairy firms than has actually been provided by the Marketing Boards.

Profound differences of outlook, policy, and personality between farmers' co-operatives and their professional unions have by no means been confined to Britain. Where, as on the Continent, the two sectors are fairly evenly balanced, no great harm, and even some good, may eventually emerge from such tensions. In England the conflict has been more one-sided. The origins and course of the long and at times bitter controversy between the NFU and organised co-operation, which can only now be said to be drawing to a peaceful close after nearly fifty years, have been described with great fairness in the Knapp report.[1] It need only be noted here that, however the blame may be allocated, the only real losers have been the majority of farmers. It must however be admitted that their silence and apparent indifference makes them no less culpable than any who may have claimed to be representing their interests.

However complex and deep-rooted its causes the failure of co-operatives to establish themselves as a force to be reckoned with in agricultural marketing in Britain undoubtedly reinforced the tendency, encouraged by official policies, of farmers to become insulated from the full effects of their markets both during the late thirties and for the first ten years or so after the passing of the 1947 Agriculture Act. To the extent that government policy succeeded in the pre-war period in rescuing agriculture from the consequences of a catastrophic fall in world prices the generous privileges accorded to certain producers can be considered to have been both socially and morally acceptable. The more comprehensive post-war price guarantees also sprang from a laudable determination that there should be no repetition of the farming slump of the twenties. They were thus designed to deal with a situation which to a great extent no longer existed and devised without regard to changes in the nature of demand and in the volume of supply which could not be foreseen in 1946. There being only partial restriction of imports, domestic production, raised to unimagined levels by the combined efforts of plant breeders, research chemists, mechanical engineers, and the government's own advisory services, began so far to outrun the inelastic and increasingly discriminating demand for food as often to depress market prices below guaranteed levels, and thus create a steadily rising trend of Treasury liability. At the time of the restoration of the milk marketing scheme to peace-time conditions in 1953 a new support system had been introduced which for each Board area restricted the volume of milk for which producers could obtain the guaranteed price in any one year to a standard quantity. This is based on the previous year's consumption of liquid milk plus a reserve of 20 per cent. Producers thus benefit from any increase in liquid consumption and are penalised for any decrease. Since then it has been found necessary from time to time to incorporate similar devices in the guarantees for other products so as to provide an incentive to producers to adapt their output, both as regards quantity and quality, to the demand of the market. The originally more or less flat rate deficiency payment on fatstock has, for instance, been refined so as to reflect the impact of seasonal supplies on the market, as well as to encourage production of carcases of suitable weight and conformation. The guaranteed price for fat pigs is related to a forecast level of production. If marketings fall below this level the price is automatically raised, but if pig numbers increase unduly it is lowered. In 1964 standard quantity limitations were also introduced for wheat and barley, though they were later abolished in the context of both the government's expansion programme for domestic agriculture and of its commitments under

[1] *op cit*, pp. 54 *et seq.*

the Kennedy Round. In these and other ways the original open-ended nature of Treasury liability for deficiency payments has been gradually modified.

A generalised system of support to agriculture through deficiency payments on the British model was, for a variety of reasons both technical and political, not adopted by those responsible for framing the basic principles of the EEC's Common Agricultural Policy. Although at the time the first market regulations had not yet appeared, this position remained impregnable to all argument by the British delegation during the early months of the 1961/63 negotiation for British entry into the Common Market. One of the most strongly held objections was the potentially enormous cost to Community funds of deficiency payments which were open-ended, as experience had already shown in Britain. On the other hand if the system were to be hedged about with the sort of limitations that had gradually been introduced across the Channel it would start to involve quantitative restrictions on production and internal trade which it was the Commission's main object to avoid. Any allocation, for instance, of standard quantities as between farmers would in addition be politically delicate. They would be almost bound to involve discrimination between member countries and end up on the lines of the sort of national quota system which the Commission had later to propose, with great reluctance, for sugar.[1] The free play of market forces being fundamental to Community philosophy, in order to ensure the uninterrupted movement of agricultural produce both across and within the common frontier quantitative restrictions of all kinds were to be as far as possible abolished. Within this 'liberalised' system Customs duties and levies, set at a level that allowed domestic producers and processors judged efficient to compete on fair terms with imported goods, would be wholly non-discriminatory. However, the decision to set intervention prices as well which would officially underwrite the level of the internal market for certain key products seems to have introduced a flaw in the pure logic of this system. It has certainly added greatly to its cost. Total net expenditure on intervention went up steadily from UA 22·0 mn in 1964 to UA 410 mn in 1969 and is expected to have amounted to about UA 2,500 mn in 1970.

The framers of Regulation 19/62 which first introduced the principle of intervention buying (for cereals) have been proved as little prescient about the consequences for their market system of the technological revolution in agriculture as were those of the Agriculture Act of 1947. Likewise, the stimulus to production provided by the Community's agricultural price policy was seriously underestimated. As in Britain in the fifties so in the EEC during the sixties, farmers were encouraged by prices raised artificially in one way or another, above a level at which supply would balance demand in the open market, to produce goods of a quantity too great, and often of a quality insufficient, to clear the market. The situation in the Community was, however, different in two important respects. First, the

[1] See pp. 124–5.
[2] Unit of Account, equivalent to the value of the gold dollar.

prices for cereals, beef, veal and dairy products were (and are) guaranteed not directly to the producer but at wholesale level. Second, they are set right at the bottom of the market. Those in Britain were (and are) set above, sometimes well above, market level. In the early post-war years the British farmer had, for some products, little incentive to fit in with the quality, quantity, or timing of his finished product demanded by the market. He was almost entirely out of touch with the needs of the consumer. In the EEC the wholesale purchaser of the farmer's produce, whether merchant or processor, has, in respect of a considerable proportion of his merchandise at any rate, also been absolved from any need for hard selling. This is especially notable in the dairy industry, where relatively inefficient enterprises have managed to coast along by selling their butter and skim powder to intervention and avoid the investment and sales effort that would be required to diversify into other products for which demand is more elastic. Farmers' co-operatives have, in order to raise their members' returns above the very modest level ensured by selling at intervention, tended to pursue a more aggressive marketing policy. To this extent the unamended intervention system may be said to have been less inhibiting to farmers' enterprise in marketing than was the unimproved system of deficiency payments.

There is a third respect in which the agricultural marketing situation in the EEC during the formative years of the CAP has differed from that which evolved in Britain after 1947. The pace of change in the pattern of demand for food has been greater during the sixties than the fifties, though transatlantic influences in retailing were already making themselves felt in Britain in the earlier decade. The initiative at that time seems to have come more from those food processing companies in which North American capital had acquired a controlling interest than from the retail sector itself. Retailing was adapting relatively slowly to the opportunities for increased turnover at more competitive price margins offered to it by new techniques of preserving, packaging and presentation being developed by the food industries. By 1960 Britain had more self-service stores and supermarkets than any country of the Community except Germany. Elsewhere in Western Europe only Sweden and Switzerland had made comparable progress. The correlation between these trends in retailing and general economic growth has been illustrated still more forcibly by developments during the sixties. France, the Low Countries, and Italy (northern Italy at any rate) have made up for their slow start, the number of modern retailing units there rising proportionately more than in Britain, whilst in Germany 70 per cent of all food shops have now been converted to self-service. The changing pattern is beginning to have an appreciable influence on the attitude of farmers and their organisations to their markets.

In view of the ultimate importance for farm incomes of this evolution in retailing, a brief consideration of its causes and effects seems indispensable to this study of farmers and their markets. Although periods of economic growth are marked by a transfer of resources, especially of labour, from the primary sector into industry and services, a point is quite soon reached where the cost of even unskilled labour, inflated by high earnings conceded to scarce skills and by general wage drift, becomes a decisive factor in any retailer's profit-and-loss account. Only in small family enterprises, where the opportunity cost of his own labour and that of his dependants is reckoned by the proprietor to be very low or zero, do under-employment and low labour productivity continue to be acceptable. This is still the situation in many tens of thousands of food retailing (and of course of farm) businesses. But even in quite modest enterprises the pressures in favour of higher labour productivity soon begin to operate.

Understandably self-service, as the main means of reducing labour costs, was first introduced by enterprises where the scope for such economies was greatest such as department and variety stores and the major chains. The practice of transferring to the customer the share of the distributive labour load involved in collecting goods from shop shelves and bringing them together at a central point for payment has also spread to non-food shops, notably those of the drink, pharmacy, stationery and ironmongery chains. But self-service in the form of customers being channelled with their purchases through a limited number of check-out points is still almost exclusively confined to shops selling mainly food, or to the food sections of department and variety stores. It was logical for the larger enterprises to become the pioneers of self-service, since its introduction, like farm mechanisation, involves a certain substitution of capital for labour: reorganisation of shop fittings, purchase of gondolas, checkouts, wire trolleys, etc. The increased turnover per person employed was not, however, a sufficient end in itself. There arose an immediate need to reduce the cost of overheads, including depreciation of the new equipment, per unit of merchandise sold. To achieve this a more rapid turnover of a wider assortment of goods became necessary. Except for a few perishable commodities rapidity of turnover in the grocery trade had previously been of secondary importance. Although the introduction of refrigerated and deep-freeze cabinets to some extent preceded that of self-service, their use received a great boost from it, enabling grocers to start to invade retail territory formerly held by specialist dairymen, fishmongers, and butchers, and, thanks to deep-freezing, that of greengrocers and fruiterers as well. This was, however, a development requiring still greater investment, not only in shop equipment but in refrigerated storage and distribution plant and transport. Cost reduction could at the same time be further promoted by increased bulk purchase, and optimum use made of scarce skilled labour, such as butchering, by centralised pre-packing. The possibility, arising from new methods of procurement, distribution and selling by the larger food chains, of satisfying an ever-increasing volume of customers was inevitably accompanied by a change of approach to the economics of food retailing: an increasingly high turnover could now be linked with a much lower average level of profit margin than had ever been possible in the old days of mostly slow-moving dry goods.

The Marketing Gap

These developments coincided with changes in shoppers' tastes and habits. Each acted strongly upon the other and it is difficult to disentangle cause and effect. A glance at an income-per-head map of the Common Market will confirm that the spread of supermarkets is closely associated with economic growth. Of the 355 supermarkets and 1,037 multiple self-service stores in Italy in 1969 only 62 were located in the south.[1] In Bavaria the density of self-service stores is almost half the average for West Germany as a whole; that in North Rhine-Westphalia just over twice the average.[2] Supermarkets in western France are, except in the largest towns, still relatively rare.[3] If they have tended to be established initially in urban areas this is a reflection not only of the higher level of earnings there but also of the higher proportion of wives going out to work. The supermarket provides opportunities for the once-a-week shopper to satisfy her main food requirements with the minimum expenditure of time, energy and, as often as not, money. It has increasingly provided her with the labour-saving convenience foods in ready-to-cook form which form an increasing proportion of supermarkets' stock. In some countries, too, late opening hours are an additional attraction to the working wife, whose custom has also been a major incentive to the widening of the assortment of goods offered not only of food but of an extensive range of non-food day-to-day household items as well. The largest supermarkets may offer a total assortment of anything up to 8,000 items, compared with the few hundred usually stocked by a small retail food shop. The logical extension of this is of course the discount store (in France *hypermarché*) which caters not only for householders' food needs, but also for their longer term demand of furnishings and electrical goods, toys and leisure equipment of all kinds. This generally demands a suburban site, with relatively low ground rents and room for free parking. For, along with higher incomes and greater opportunities for female employment, economic growth has brought wider ownership of the automobile. After the refrigerator (and generally before the deep-freeze) it has probably contributed most to the revolutionary change in consumer demand. The shopper can empty his trolley straight into his waiting car, and when traffic congestion begins to present parking problems in city centres then the supermarkets move, as they started to a generation ago in the United States, to suburban areas where land is cheaper and customers increasingly numerous. At the same time the spread of car ownership among farmers and farmworkers has also brought the country shopper into the towns. A recent IFOP poll of supermarket customers in France established that a third of them travelled more than 5 km to do their shopping.[4]

[1] ISTAT study, quoted in 'Retail Newsletter' of the International Association of Department Stores.
[2] 'Selbstbedienung und Supermarkt', October 1970, p. 40.
[3] 'Libre Service Actualités' No. 326, 1970, p. 43.
[4] Institut Français de l'Opinion Publique, quoted in 'Les Echos', September 22nd, 1970.

26 The Background to Intervention in Agricultural Markets

The introduction of the supermarket, with its wide assortment, its loss leaders, and the overall lower level of profit margins and prices which its large and rapid turnover has made possible, presented a threat to traditional food retailing (whether the multiple with a limited sales area or the small independent shopkeeper) which it could not afford to ignore. Of itself self-service offered relatively little scope for the chain store to reduce costs, and even less to the independent with a single shop. Indeed, wage economies might in both cases prove to be not much greater than the cost of amortising investment in new equipment, and for the independents the financial outlay involved in competing with supermarkets in assortment and price may prove prohibitive as well. For the chains of what were originally small multiple stores conversion to self-service and the establishment of additional superettes or supermarkets with larger sales areas has inevitably involved considerable streamlining of their procurement policies. At least these were already geared to certain economies of scale. The only possibility open to the independent single shop trader has been to group his purchases not only of a wider assortment of goods but also of the equipment required to convert his enterprise and maintain his competitiveness. This has been achieved partly by means of retailing co-operatives, initiated by the most enterprising retailers themselves, and partly by so-called voluntary chains. Here the initiative has come from wholesalers who, appreciating the threat to their own interests of the larger supermarket chains, offer special discounts, as well as free marketing and technical services and financial assistance with re-equipment, to retailers who are willing to trade exclusively with them.

The number of supermarkets[1] in EEC member countries increased from about 350 in 1960 to nearly 4,500 at the end of 1969, and will probably go on growing at a rate of well over 10 per cent per annum for some years to come. The main impetus has been in Germany, where they were expected to pass the 2,000 mark in 1970, and in France, with over 1,500 at the beginning of the year.[2] The other member countries, except Luxemburg, each have between 300 and 400. In Luxemburg their development has until recently been prevented by legislation favouring the small shopkeeper. These figures include a growing number of very large out of town stores of 2,500 m^2 (about 27,000 ft^2) and over. Forty-six of these *hypermarchés* and 380 other supermarkets were opened in 1969 in France alone,[3] and there are more than 100 in Germany. Rapid though this development has been on the Continent, the number of supermarkets having risen by more than 50 per cent between 1956 and 1969, multiple food retailing has not yet achieved the formidable concentration of economic power with which it is associated in Britain. Taking together *The Times* list of leading British and

[1] Supermarkets, as defined by the International Self-Service Organisation, have a minimum of 400 m^2 (4,300 ft^2) of sales area. Superettes (between 120 m^2–1,300 ft^2 and 399 m^2) are considerably more numerous, over 4,000 of them in France.

[2] There are no homogeneous statistics of distribution in the EEC, and the figures in this and the following paragraphs have had to be collated from a wide variety of sources.

[3] 'Libre Service Actualités', *ibid*, p. 38.

continental enterprises and a list of forty-eight European distributive firms with a turnover of more than $200 mn published by the International Association of Department Stores, five British companies, all with a turnover of $440 mn and over, were in 1969 first in order of those engaged mainly in food distribution: Associated British Foods (Fine Fare and Melias), Unigate (United Dairies), Tesco, Sainsbury, and Allied Suppliers (Unilever). These were followed by Casino and Docks Rémois of France, J. Lyons, the Dutch Albert Heijn, and another British multiple group, International Stores. Multiples with a turnover of around $200 mn were the three German companies, Albrecht, Kaiser Kaffeegeschäft, and Tengelmann. Groups of department stores like Kaufhof, La Rinascente, or John Lewis, and chains of variety or discount-type stores like Marks and Spencer, Standa and UPIM (Italy), GB Enterprises (Belgium) and Carrefour (France), all of which have substantial food retailing interests, are fairly evenly spread, as far as size is concerned, between the EEC and Britain. Though representing only 18 per cent of the total number of shops, multiples and co-operatives accounted for 56 per cent of total grocery turnover in Britain in 1969.[1] A major part of this business was handled by the fifteen to twenty chains and co-ops with an annual turnover of more than £20 mn ($48 mn). The proportion of larger supermarkets has been increasing, the average sales area of all self-service stores of 200 m² and over having risen from 392 m² to 652 m² between 1967 and 1969. According to the British Institute of Distribution there were 3,800 superettes and supermarkets of this size in 1969, of which nearly 70 per cent were multiples, 15 per cent co-operatives, 10 per cent belonged to voluntary and co-operative retail chains, and about 1 per cent constituted the food sections of department and variety stores.

Although the changing structure of food retailing has, as would be expected, left its mark on wholesaling, a surprisingly large number of small wholesale firms still survive. In 1965, the most recent date for which information is available, the 280-odd firms in grocery and provision wholesaling in Great Britain which recorded receipts of under £50,000 ($120,000), averaged less than half that sum, and accounted between them for less than 1 per cent of total receipts.[2] The total number of firms engaged in all types of food wholesaling was just over 8,000. However, in France in 1969 there were still over 25,000.[3] Some wholesalers have retained the custom of the unaffiliated shops by opening cash-and-carry centres. Appealing mainly to the small man, who probably puts no value on his time spent collecting goods from a centre, cash-and-carry has

[1] 'Nielsen Researcher', March–April, 1970.
[2] *Wholesale Trades 1965*, 'Board of Trade Journal', July 26th, 1968.
[3] *Variations de structure de l'appareil commercial français. Année 1969*. AFRESCO, Paris, 1970. Although some of these would be supplying the catering trade, etc., the proportion to the total number of food retail shops (about 180,000) is still remarkable. This fragmentation of resources contributes directly to the high cost of food at retail, and goes a long way to explaining why 60 per cent of those replying to the IFOP poll already quoted gave lower prices as their principal reason for shopping at supermarkets.

developed strongly in France, which now has about 400 stores, and in Britain, where there are over 600. In Germany, however, where the number of independents has been falling more rapidly than in other EEC countries, cash-and-carry seems to be losing its impetus. Not all stores belong to independent wholesalers. Some have been started by the voluntary chains, and in Britain the largest chain of them, Alliance, is part of the Associated British Foods (Weston) group. Indeed, as with the other links in the distributive chain, modern wholesaling demands ever larger investments, not only in stocks and storage space but in modern, often computerised, techniques of stock control, thus further jacking up the minimum level of throughput at which operation is economic. Resources on this scale would be available to the major multiples who do their own wholesaling; to the joint buying organisations serving a number of corporate chains which provide a means of securing economies of scale in countries where the corporates tend to be less individually powerful than in Britain[1]; to some of the larger consumer co-operatives, which are particularly strong in Germany; to the principal co-operative groups of independent retailers, such as Unico in France, which covers 6,500 sales points, and Edeka and Rewe, which account between them for about 18 per cent of the German food market; and to the larger voluntary chains. These 'symbol' organisations, which account for nearly half the turnover of the independent sector of the British grocery trade[2] also exercise considerable purchasing power in France, Germany, Belgium, and the Netherlands, where the original Vege (Verkoop Gemeenschaft) shops first became associated in the thirties. Some of them, like Vege, Spar and Vivo, cover most of the EEC, as well as Britain and the other applicant countries.

The consequences for the food manufacturing industry of the restructuring of distribution can become dramatic. In Britain a recent estimate puts the number of buying points in the non-independent grocery trade (but including the symbol independents), accounting for 77 per cent of total turnover, at 746.[3] Taking into account the cash-and-carry stores serving a growing number of the remaining independent retailers, the concentration of demand at wholesale level is formidable. In the EEC that part of the food processing industry which is owned by firms of member-country nationality has only recently begun to take account of the changes in demand now facing it. Part of the original responsibility for those changes lies with their international rivals, mainly North American but including some European transnationals, such as Nestlé-Oursina and Unilever. Experienced in the effects of the retailing revolution outside the EEC, they have fomented it from within by means of their greatly superior knowhow and resources for technical and market research and for develop-

[1] For instance, Paridoc, with which 15 French chains are associated, embracing over 200 supermarkets, Socadip (6 companies, 36 stores), Difra (9 companies, 72 stores), etc. ('Techniques Marchandes Modernes', No. 232, January, 1970).

[2] 'Nielsen Researcher', March–April, 1970.

[3] 430 co-ops, 100 head offices of multiples and 103 of their subsidiaries, and 113 wholesalers serving 23 symbol groups. 'Nielsen Researcher', *ibid*.

The Marketing Gap

ing new processes and products. A recent French study[1] provides estimates of the 'levels of effectiveness', in terms of turnover, at which firms should be capable of acting on their own account in the various aspects of launching a new food product. For research, for instance, the minimum turnover would be not less than Fr 500 mn ($91.0 mn). Only five firms in France answered to this criterion. For advertising it would have to be anything from Fr 130 mn ($24 mn) up to Fr 200 mn ($36 mn). About a dozen French food firms would qualify for the upper limit and another half dozen would fit in above the lower one. But these include five flour mills and three sugar refineries, enterprises not always notable for developing new products. A survey carried out in 1966 showed that 66 firms were in fact carrying out research and development in some form. This suggests that many of them were doing so with inadequate resources, and in any case the number only represents about one-half per cent of all firms in the food industry, and less than 2 per cent of the 5,000 firms that account for 95 per cent of total turnover. Of these there were only 1,000 with a turnover of over Fr 10 mn ($1·8 mn) competing effectively on EEC markets; only 100 had a turnover of more than Fr 100 mn ($18 mn).[2] Quite apart from whether it has the resources available for investment in new food technology an industry on this scale is in no position to compete with the international giants on the product innovation that is a main dynamic element in the development of modern retailing. As self-service stores employ no salesmen, the manufacturer is involved not only in high costs of technical research but also in those of marketing and promotion through mass advertising, and through packaging that will itself help to sell his products. Despite this whole apparatus of pre-selling the failure rate of new products in test markets is said to be very high. In the USA food manufacturers may have between 4,000 and 5,000 such products on offer every year,[3] of which supermarket chains may perhaps be prepared to accept 1,000 to replace items that they are discontinuing. Whilst customers' tastes on the Continent may still show a conservativism that would hardly warrant such a high level of innovation, demand for pre-packaged, ready-to-cook, easy-to-handle foods is, even in France, increasing rapidly.

In these circumstances, and using the yardstick suggested in the study referred to above, it would appear from a list of leading firms in the food and drink industry in the EEC, published in a working document of the French Planning Commission,[4] that the industry in some other member

---

[1] By CACEPA (Centre d'Action Concertée des Entreprises de Produits Alimentaires), quoted in *Rapport sur la situation et les perspectives d'avenir des industries agricoles et alimentaires* (ANIAA, Paris, 1968), p. 16.

[2] P. Lescanne, *Analyse de la situation économique des industries alimentaires françaises dans le cadre européen*. Proceedings of the Annual General Meeting of CACEPA, Paris, 1969.

[3] *Food marketing and economic growth* (OECD, Paris, 1970), p. 102, footnote 1.

[4] *Stratégies d'expansion en Europe et dans le monde des firmes de l'industrie alimentaire*, Commissariat Général du Plan, Commission des industries Alimentaires, VIème Plan, Paris, October, 1970, Annexe IV.

countries is little better equipped than it is in France with the necessary resources for product innovation and promotion. In Italy 5, in Belgium 2, and in the Netherlands 4 (including Unilever and subsidiaries of two US corporations) food firms have a turnover exceeding Fr 500 mn. Italy also includes 10 with a turnover of between Fr 130 and Fr 500 mn. Germany, on the other hand, has 16 firms in the upper group, including subsidiaries of Unilever, Nestlé-Oursina, Corn Products and National Dairy Products, and 29 in the lower group, including three US subsidiaries, two Swiss and one French (of Gervais-Danone). In Britain there are 27 food firms with turnover exceeding Fr 500 mn (£38 mn), including conglomerates and the leading flour millers and sugar refiners, in all but three of which British interests at present hold control.[1] The much greater degree of concentration of resources in the British industry, mirroring that in food distribution, is illustrated by the fact that whereas some 25 food firms are included in the first 200 of *The Times* list of British companies, of which 14 have a turnover exceeding £100 mn ($240 mn), only five EEC based firms find a place in the top 200 Continental companies; three with a turnover above the £100 mn mark: Unilever, the German Oetker group, and Lesieur-Cotelle in France. The next list will, however, include the recently formed French dairy product and soft-drink combine, Perrier-Sapiem-Genvrain, whose turnover, probably slightly exceeding that of Oetker, should bring it into third place on the Continent—rather a long way behind Unilever and Nestlé-Oursina. In France, too, the expansion of Générale Alimentaire's activity through the acquisition of holdings in the company, by, amongst others, Gervais-Danone and Général Sucrière; in Germany the merging of Unilever and Nestlé's subsidiaries to form a new group marketing frozen-food, frozen poultry, and ice-cream; and in Italy the take-over of Motta and Pavesi, the confectionery firms, by the state-financed IRI-Montedison, which already have interests in fruit and vegetable canning and freezing, including Cirio, are all signs of the quickening pace of concentration in food manufacturing in the EEC. Market research confirms that, predictably, a greater degree of concentration has been already achieved, generally speaking, in the production of modern convenience foods than in the traditional sector.[2] The process of concentration is likely to become intensified, especially in France, which, accounting for a third of the Community's agricultural output, but for only a fifth of its output of processed food, is in a particularly weak position relative to its potential. A long tradition of protection by governments, which obliged them at the same time to purchase raw materials from domestic and colonial agriculture at preferential prices, has left French processors ill-equipped to face the cold winds of Community competition.

[1] For a recent analysis of trends in the British industry, see K. Van Musschenbroek, *Developments in the food manufacturing and distributive industry*. 'Journal of Agriculture Economics', Vol. XXI, No. 3, September 1970, pp. 435–43.

[2] Proceedings of AGM of CACEPA summarise recent findings of Nielsen, Attwood and other surveys in Western Europe, *op cit*. Annexe 62.

The significance for farmers of the revolution which we have been describing is clear. In both the EEC and Britain ever greater concentration in food processing and distribution are mutually reinforcing, both for technical reasons and because countervailing power is called forth on both sides. Mass production demands mass distribution in order to be fully profitable. The converse is also true because of distributors' needs for assured volume, uniformity of product, and heavy advertising to keep goods moving. There is a constant tension between the two, with the balance of advantage always tending to shift marginally to one side or the other, as is shown by the extent to which large retailers can exact favourable terms for the manufacture of 'own-brand' products, often enabling them to undersell the same manufacturers' brands on their own shelves. Into this conflict the primary producers must insinuate their own interests as powerfully as they can. Apart from putting pressure on governments to maintain prices on agricultural markets at an acceptable level by one or more of the several methods available producers may respond in three different ways: by arranging to sell their product for a year or some other fixed period ahead, by integrating forward into processing, or by integrating into retailing. They may act individually or attempt to influence supplies and markets through collective action by offering their produce on a substantial scale, whether to processors, wholesalers, or the buying organisations of the multiples. In southern Germany, for instance, a company, Berland GmbH, formed by local farmers started five years ago to contract with Latscha of Frankfurt to deliver date-stamped eggs to the firm's 125 branches.[1] Similar arrangements for direct delivery by own transport have been developed by, amongst others, UDCA, a co-operative whose sales cover 22 departments in eastern and south-eastern France, and by Thames Valley Eggs and Yorkshire Egg Producers, which between them supply branches of multiples over the whole of England. Marks and Spencer's Provision Department contracts direct with growers for high-grade supplies of apples, vegetables, and table chickens.[2]

Forward selling of agricultural produce by contract—commitments entered into by farmers to deliver certain quantities at certain prices in the future—has been commonly used in the United States for many years. This method of marketing is a comparative innovation in Western Europe, where, until recently, it has been virtually confined to sugar-beet and processed peas. A farmer is unlikely to want a forward sales contract unless he has a fairly accurate idea of what his costs of production are and therefore what his level of profit would be at various price levels. There has been a major trend in agriculture over the past generation towards costing of the production process. Peasant farmers often do not know what it costs

[1] W. Fleck et al, *Wettbewerbs- und Absatzprobleme bei Landwirtschaftlichen Erzeugnissen in der BDR* (Forschungsgesellschaft für Agrarpolitik und Agrarsoziologie, Bonn, 1966), Annexe, p. 13.

[2] M. J. Sieff, *The expanding market for quality produce*. Proceedings of the 20th Oxford Farming Conference, January, 1966, pp. 53–61.

them to produce even the simpler products such as grain. Costing is less important to them as they use fewer purchased inputs. The more sophisticated farmer is now able to forecast accurately what his production will cost and is therefore in a position to be interested in forward selling at prices to cover his costs and leave him with a profit. Further, the new technologies in agriculture have made it possible for farmers to control to a much greater extent both the quality and quantity of their production. Developments in livestock breeding and techniques of livestock feeding, plant protection, fertiliser application and harvesting, grading and storing of crops, have made it possible for the farmer to deliver an increasing number of products to a specification. This is an important cause of the spread of contract selling. For some farmers marketing on contract has more appeal than spot selling on markets. Others, undoubtedly the majority, prefer traditional methods and the freedom associated with them, and are only drawn into contracts because of the economic pressures and other inducements associated with contract selling. If profit margins become very tight, farmers are more likely to be receptive to any arrangement which secures them a known profit and avoids the danger of a loss. Other benefits to the farmer, which can accompany contracts and are often used to sugar the pill of loss of freedom, include the supply of credit facilities and the provision of technical assistance. As farming becomes increasingly intensive throughout Western Europe and the average size of enterprise increases, the former is of particular importance.

Vertical integration is a stage beyond contract marketing which effectively removes altogether the need for a marketing process. The recent progress of integration in Britain and some EEC member countries has been described at length elsewhere.[1] For many years dairy farmers in Western Europe have, individually or collectively, been integrating their milk production with either its direct sale to consumers or its processing. Egg producers have also traditionally sold direct to consumers and fruit and vegetable growers have been involved in retailing, usually in local markets, as well as in the grading and packing of their own produce. In this sense there is nothing new in forward integration. The streamlining of retailing and the interaction of this with developments in the processing field has, however, offered considerable new opportunities for extending integration as well as for the spread of contract selling. As noted above, farmers or their co-operatives may sell direct to supermarkets and chains, by-passing traditional dealers and wholesalers, and themselves engage in large-scale processing. In a few cases they have already integrated as far forward as the retail stage. UDCA of Bourg-en-Bresse, for instance, owns a small chain of shops, Agrilait. The MacMahon group of co-operatives has through its subsidiary, Comptoir Agricole Français, acquired holdings of up to 51 per cent in a dozen or more supermarkets in the Paris region and is

[1] M. W. Butterwick, *Vertical integration and the role of the Co-operatives* (Central Council for Agricultural and Horticultural Co-operation, 1969).

planning to extend its control.[1] Until fairly recently co-operative activity on the Continent has been confined to basic and bulky products such as cereals, milk, and ordinary wine. Indeed, in France and the Netherlands the co-operatives have established a formidable position in the grain market. In Germany they dominate the dairy sector. These are fields in which farmers themselves are each producing a relatively small quantity of a product that they could not easily process themselves, like wheat, or that which is highly perishable, like milk. Thus no very severe strain has been placed upon their loyalty to a co-operative. In any case the co-operative was usually in no position to enforce that loyalty should members decide for any reason to sell elsewhere. With livestock products and plant products like potatoes, fruit and vegetables, however, seasonal and cyclical price variations have tended in the past to discourage co-operative marketing, farmers being more inclined to sell privately when prices are good and use their co-operative as a last resort when prices are bad. In the Netherlands and Belgium producers have been tied by a mixture of loyalty and self-interest to using the co-operative clock auctions, standing to obtain at least a withdrawal price paid out of a fund to which they have themselves automatically contributed by a levy on all sales. In some areas co-operatives may even be said to suffer from an excess of loyalty and to be so firmly attached to the social means of co-operation as to have lost sight of its economic ends. This is often the case, for instance, with butter manufacturing co-operatives formed, sometimes seventy or more years ago, to conform with a local pattern of milk delivery which disappeared with the horse and cart. In Charentes (western France) we visited one co-operative which after installing up-to-date equipment has established for its butter a brand name and reputation for quality that enables it to be sold at a premium in Paris. Although it had capacity for twice its present output loyalty demanded that there should be no poaching of members from neighbouring co-operatives although they farm within a radius which is quite economic for milk collection by motor transport. Misplaced loyalty to their organisation and its paid staff equally prevents these co-operatives from contemplating any merger with their more go-ahead neighbour. Since any surplus butter which they produce can be sold at a profit of sorts to the intervention agency, the economic spur to amalgamation is also lacking.

The obligation which the law lays upon co-operatives in some countries to purchase all its members' output has to some extent made the co-operative form of association unsuitable, or at any rate adaptable only with difficulty, to recent developments in the pattern of demand. If produce of a previously defined quality and quantity is required by a wholesaling/retail-

[1] Integration backwards by processors or wholesalers into farm production is still also a fairly rare phenomenon. Compound feed manufacturers have largely confined their farm activities to experimental work. In Britain Sainsbury's production of eggs and chickens, in conjunction with Spillers, who provide the feed, and of a limited quantity of beef, provides an exceptional example of this type of integration by large groups, Associated British Foods having disposed of their interest in the Ross Group (which includes major egg and broiler production enterprises) to Imperial Tobacco.

ing organisation for supplying its chain of supermarkets, stores or independent shops, it is clear that any consortium of producers entering into a contract with it will require an equivalent discipline from its members. Since producer groups of this kind must clearly be selective in membership, other formulae than the traditional co-operative ones may often seem more appropriate. Concentration of demand has in fact resulted in a wide variety of legal arrangements for the production and supply of farm produce both in the EEC and in Britain. A common feature of all of them is a requirement that the goods be of level quality, delivered punctually, and, where appropriate, all the year round. The broiler chicken and the hen's egg are the farm products which, thanks to technological developments, answer most easily to these criteria. It is now fairly rare anywhere for broilers to be produced without their sale having been assured beforehand, at least at a basic price to cover the cost of their production. Output of other forms of table poultry, especially turkeys, is increasingly being tailored to demand. The less predictable performance of the laying hen, even in controlled environment, and her longer time-scale, may still, however, present even the most efficient co-operative or marketing group with problems of shortages and surpluses of supply.

In the case of poultry-meat and eggs it is now accepted that the producer may be financially involved in the processing of his output. Both are packed ready for display in the purchasers' shops.[1] Increasingly in the EEC the same is applying to fruit, vegetables, and potatoes, which may be graded and packed to their customers' specification by co-operatives and producer groups. Processing by producers has developed much more slowly in the case of pigmeat (and its by-products), beef, veal, and lamb, partly because of the larger capital investment required in processing equipment, partly because these items have only gradually entered into the assortment of supermarkets and chains, and partly because of a certain difficulty in laying down and achieving product standards.

Producer processing of relatively new types of food has thus been making variable progress. Development of marketing outlets by established co-operative groupings for more traditional products has, for all the reluctance of some constituent co-operatives to abandon ingrained attitudes, not stood still. Cereal co-operatives have extended their processing activities at regional and national level, but into the production of compound animal feeds rather than into milling, *pasta* manufacture or biscuit making, where private interests are already strongly established.

---

[1] Establishment of brand names by producer organisations has met with varying success. UDCA (Union Départementale des coopérative Agricoles de l'Ain) have successfully established the punning label 'Coqu' Ain' for their poultry and eggs, under which their produce appears on the shelves of a number of the largest chains of supermarkets, including Carrefour. Another important multiple customer, on the other hand, insists on its own brand name. British egg co-operatives and broiler groups have also encountered uneven response to their labels. In Italy, on the other hand, where mass retailing is still relatively weak, there is strong competition on brand between the two major broiler groups, Cipzoo and Pollo Arena.

The Marketing Gap

In the case of dairy produce co-operative action has been much stimulated by the expansion of exports both to third countries (with or without restitution according to product) and within the Community, especially since the boost given by the establishment of a unified market in 1968. Although some co-operatives, like some private firms, have preferred to rely on the easy way out offered by intervention buying of butter and dried skim, others have diversified vigorously into products with higher income elasticities such as yoghurt, cream cheeses, ice-cream, and flavoured milk drinks. Sodima-Yoplait, which claim to have captured 20 per cent of the French domestic market for yoghurt in little over five years, have been increasing their sales in Germany and Britain. The Comptoir Agricole Français (belonging to Groupe MacMahon, one of the two main co-operative groupings) have in conjunction with their affiliated company, Union Laitière Normande (Elle & Vire), established selling agencies in several Western European countries. Their subsidiary Fromançais distributes on the domestic market. The Milch- Fett- und Eier-Kontor, which groups all German dairy co-operatives, is energetically establishing an international brand name, 'Delicado', for a wide range of products. Dutch dairy co-operatives, while adapting their supply to the Netherlands' highly developed modern retailing system, do not yet seem to have made any major dent in Dutch consumers' very clearly established preference for cheese over all other forms of processed milk. Demand for yoghurt is lower than that in any other EEC country. Export promotion of dairy produce is in the hands of the dairy *Produktschap*, which, while also representing both private and co-operative trade and industrial interests in this field, is financed by a levy on producers.

These are a few examples of the way in which producers are adapting themselves to changing markets. Other aspects will be described during the course of the separate product chapters in Part Two. In Chapter 12 we shall discuss likely future developments. Although producer organisations already have much solid achievement to their credit, and many groups present a very encouraging picture of producer activity, it would be wrong to give the impression that farmers as a whole in the EEC, or in Britain for that matter, were organised to meet the challenge of an increasingly concentrated and selective demand for what they produce. The marketing gap is still a very wide one. A few individuals producing on a relatively small scale will undoubtedly continue in agriculture, as in retailing, to cater efficiently for minority needs. It may be expected, for instance, that the demand for both health and luxury foods will expand in a richer society. 'Farm-fresh' products of this type may be supplied direct by the enterprising small producer. There will also be room for the small general food shop 'round the corner' catering for the housewife's *ad hoc* needs between her weekly visits to the supermarket or discount store.[1] Some of these

---

[1] In the United States 'convenience stores', remaining open for eighteen hours and sometimes twenty-four hours a day, have developed to satisfy this need. Most of them are now, however, themselves organised in chains.

may even manage to survive without joining a voluntary chain, or making use of cash-and-carry. But, generally speaking, for the unaffiliated independent retailer, still in a majority in some EEC countries and in a large minority even in Britain, the writing is on the wall.[1] Political pressures in favour of limited shopping hours, retail price maintenance or planning restrictions on very large-scale self-service units, especially out-of-town ones, may, however, continue to protect him for some time to come. In Italy the authorities seem, largely from political motives, to look indulgently upon a retail sector continually swollen by refugees from agriculture. The protests of M. Gérard Nicoud and his fellow activists have served a warning on the French government that surplus shopkeepers can present almost as intractable a problem as surplus peasants. On the whole, however, food producers seem more likely than food retailers to continue to obtain the lion's share of official consideration and financial support during the coming decade. Despite the irreversible trends eliminating the majority of those who fail to 'organise' themselves and their markets, the intervention by government (or Community) agencies in those markets will continue, in one way or another, for the foreseeable future. Their role will be examined in the next chapter.

---

[1] One estimate, perhaps exaggerated, is that with an efficient food retailing structure less than 40,000 retail outlets would be necessary in England. The 1961 Census listed 235,000. Quoted in OECD, *op cit*, p. 70 (footnote).

CHAPTER 3

The Work of Intervention Agencies

With certain exceptions, always limited in duration, the numerous and intricate regulations which comprise the CAP are binding on all member countries equally. The principle is fundamental to the Community. Virtually unlimited discretion is, however, given to individual governments in their choice of administrative arrangements for putting the regulations into effect. These arrangements do in fact differ substantially from country to country. To a great extent they reflect the type of agricultural policy and mechanism of government support to farming operating at the time the Rome Treaty was signed and during the following four years before the CAP came into force in 1962. This absence of uniformity has sometimes led to a slowing down in the development of a common policy inasmuch as some member countries have tended to press for arrangements best suited to their own institutions and administrative traditions. French advocacy of certain intervention procedures for cereals and Dutch predilection for withdrawal from the market by producer organisations of surplus fruit and vegetables are only two examples. The variety of systems has also unfortunately led to a certain amount of mutual suspicion. During the course of our enquiries we were told how country A's intervention agency distributed illegal subsidies, country B's gave special privileges to the co-operatives, or country C's connived at dubious import practices. We found only limited evidence to justify such suspicions, which seemed to arise mainly from differences of national temperament. No doubt they will continue to be held by some people for many years to come, and be suitably embroidered by and about new member countries. Largely they are due to ignorance of how each country's agencies do in fact operate. We hope that the following pages may at least help to dispel this. They describe the origins and organisation of each country's arrangements. A description of how they operate for particular products will be found in each of the commodity chapters.

Belgium

Oddly, half the activity of the Belgian intervention agency, OBEA (Office Belge de l'Economie et de l'Agriculture) has not the remotest connection with food or farming, but concerns government aid to the coal and textile industries, trade with East Germany, and space research. The divisions dealing with these matters are still administratively independent, but under a proposed reorganisation plan they would share a common secretariat and accounts division with the two agricultural divisions (one for livestock and one for plant products). The Inspector-General for each of the two main sectors, Produits et Industries Agricoles et Alimentaires (the intervention agency) and Economie Industrielle, would also be responsible to a single Director-General. At present each division has its own Director-General. This somewhat anomalous juxtaposition is inherited from OBEA's two predecessors, the Office Commercial du Ravitaillement (OCRA) and the Office de Récuperation Economique (ORE), both set up immediately after the end of World War II to administer food rationing and industrial reconstruction respectively. After the end of rationing, OCRA operated intervention buying of butter and of meat (mainly on behalf of the armed forces) during the fifties, and became responsible for administering the EEC agricultural regulations from 1962 onwards. OCRA and ORE were merged in OBEA at the beginning of 1968.

The agricultural sector has a staff of 70, of which 24 work on livestock products and 14 on plant products. There is a directing staff of four, and the remainder consist of those members of the the general services and accounts divisions occupied full time on the non-industrial side of OBEA's activity. Although a request has been made to increase total staff to 130, which would involve bringing the strength of the livestock and plant divisions to 36 and 31 respectively, an addition to the establishment of 19 has only so far been authorised. OBEA's main work, as far as the EEC regulations are concerned, is the administration of intervention arrangements for all products to which these apply. It is not responsible for the issue of import or export licences, the collection of levies, or payment of restitutions. These are all dealt with by the Office Centrale des Contingents et Licences (OCCL), the Central Quota and Licence Office, a branch of the Ministry of Finance.[1] OBEA does, however, handle and pass on to the Commission all tenders for restitutions (e.g. on sugar), as well as dealing, of course, with tenders submitted for the purchase of intervention stocks.

OBEA's Board of Directors (*conseil d'administration*), consisting of a Chairman and anything between 14 and 19 members, appointed by the Ministers of Economic Affairs and Agriculture for a term of six years, meets two or three times a year for largely formal purposes such as approving OBEA's budget, passing the annual accounts, and confirming staff appointments. In addition, each of the two sectors has its own Standing Committee (*comité permanent*) composed of the Inspector-General and six members of the Board of Directors, again jointly nominated by the two Ministers concerned. The agricultural Standing Committee

[1] Any net annual cash balance between levies and restitutions is at present paid into the Fonds Agricole, and passed on to OBEA for financing its intervention operations.

meets every three weeks, mainly to consider the current market situation. It has no executive role. The members of the Board who sit on the Committee are all nominated *qua* representatives of producers, the food industry and the trade. The Standing Committee thus provides a forum for general discussion by all interested parties of Community (and government) policy. Recommendations and representations may be made to the Ministers of Economic Affairs or Agriculture through their representatives attending committee meetings. The sort of issue on which the Committee might have some influence would be the choice of storage points. Nor has the full Board much more power than its Standing Committees. Effectively the Minister (and, in most matters, ultimately the EEC Commission) is in control.

The members of the Board are paid expenses but no salaries. The administrative costs of OBEA are shared equally by the two Ministries concerned. They are not large, $540,000 in 1970. For its intervention and other activities the office works on a float of $4 mn from the Ministry of Finance as well as any balance due to it from the Fonds Agricole. Since it may have anything up to $40 mn worth of produce in store at any one time, additional financing is available from the Institut National du Crédit Agricole (INCA) on the security of warehouse warrants issued by the Société Anonyme des Warrants in respect of the commodities stored. These are then rediscounted by INCA with the Belgian National Bank. As INCA has only been authorised to finance storage of up to 4,000 tons of butter on public premises and up to 8,000 tons in private stores, OBEA may be obliged to draw on its float, or hope that funds will filter through from FEOGA, for financing larger amounts. These difficulties, which have been largely connected with the National Bank's tight money policies, should cease after the end of 1971, when FEOGA will be making substantial payments on account against anticipated costs for each current year. Hitherto settlement of national treasuries' claims has been retrospective after scrutiny, resulting in delays extending to months, even years.

Luxemburg

The Ministry of Agriculture and Viticulture is responsible for administering all aspects of the CAP, including levies and restitutions. These are dealt with by the Office des Licences which works under the Ministry. Subsidies for storage of butter and for end-of-season carry-over stocks of cereals and on liquid skim, are also paid direct by the Ministry's accounts department. Representation on management committees in Brussels and intervention arrangements are the responsibility of its Service d'Economie Rurale, Section Office du Blé for cereals, and Section Cheptel et Viandes for all livestock products. The two sections employ under ten persons between them. They have not, however, until now had any occasion to intervene on any market owing to the provisions of the Protocol to the Treaty of Rome, which remained in force until May 1st, 1970. This permitted a continuance for twelve years of Luxemburg's special status under the 1921 Belgium Luxemburg Economic Union whereby agricultural imports were subject to variable quotas. Internal consumer prices were also held at below European levels by means of deficiency payments (*subventions structurelles*) made to farmers by the Ministry of National Economy after vetting by the Section Cheptel. Under the Protocol, wheat, pigmeat, beef, butter, raw milk and unsweetened concentrated milk were therefore exempted from the provisions of the CAP until 1970. The Ministry owns no grain storage and would be obliged to rent silo space from any merchant or co-operative submitting grain for intervention purchase. Intervention stocks of butter would be stored in Belgium. As far as sugar is concerned, Luxemburg has a joint quota with Belgium. Production is in any case confined to a small area in the north farmed by Dutch growers who contract with a Belgian factory.

Netherlands

Responsibility for administering the EEC regulations is divided between the Voedselvoorzienings In en Verkoopbureau (VIB) (Food Purchase and Sales Office) of the Ministry of Agriculture and the *Produktschap*[1] (Commodity Board) for each product or group of products subject to the CAP. VIB, which is financed out of the Ministry of Agriculture vote and uses the Ministry's letterhead, was formed out of the war-time and post-war Netherlands Office for Relief and Rehabilitation (NOR). It later became responsible for administering the variable import levies, deficiency payments, and drawbacks on exports of pig and poultry products, and other measures which characterised Dutch agricultural support policy up to the introduction of the CAP. Its staff was therefore already well experienced in many of the aspects of the Community regulations, though not in market intervention. One hundred and forty of the Bureau's 220 employees are engaged on field work, 70 mainly on livestock products, and 40 on sugar and cereals, with 30 part-timers, but all are trained to deal with any product. Their work includes control of denaturing of wheat and sugar, inspection

[1] The Dutch Commodity Boards, which have no commercial function, are public bodies with statutory, advisory and regulative powers, most of them dating from before the war. Each has a Board of Management consisting of 9 employers' and 9 employees' representatives (3 Protestant, 3 Roman Catholic and 3 non-sectarian in each case) from agriculture, processing, wholesaling and retailing. Advisory Committees (with similar representation), whose number varies from Board to Board according to circumstances, deal with individual products and with matters such as retail prices, consumer relations, and regulations (national and international). Each has a standing sub-committee to consider urgent business arising out of developments in the EEC regulations. Statutorily the Boards enjoy direct access to the Minister of Agriculture and his officials. On questions relating to Community regulations, therefore, they may be dealing direct with branches of the Ministry other than VIB. To the outsider this may give the appearance of a triangular relationship, *Produktschap*—'the Ministry'—VIB, but effectively the Boards and VIB remain in close touch on all matters of mutual interest.

and control of quality of all products subject to intervention, and supervision of storage arrangements. At, or based on, the modest-looking head office are an administrative and accounting division and a technical division comprising three sections for dairy produce, cereals and all other products respectively. These are mainly engaged on processing licence applications for exports and denaturing, and dealing with offers of, or tenders for, intervention stocks.

The various *Produktschappen* play a complementary role in administering the EEC regulations. They have no power of autonomous action in this field, operating always on Ministry instructions and in association with VIB. It is, however, they and not VIB which supply the intervention agency representative on the Dutch delegation to each Management Committee[1] in Brussels, the other four being Ministry officials, including one from the legal department. In order to conform with a Community rule that only public servants may attend Management Committee meetings, the *Produktschap* official concerned has been transferred to the Ministry's pay-roll. Nevertheless, he is usefully placed to represent and watch 'interprofessional' interests over the relatively wide range of aspects of the EEC regulations on which the Commission is bound to consult a Management Committee.

Apart from this, each *Produktschap* is involved in the day-to-day administration of the regulations inside the Netherlands in a number of ways. On behalf of the Ministry of Agriculture its permanent staff (foreign trade division) receives and passes on to the Commission all applications for export restitutions, and, if and when these are granted, eventually issues the appropriate certificates. Applications for import certificates are, however, dealt with by Customs (Ministry of Finance), copies of documents being merely sent to the *Produktschap* for record purposes. Although offers of produce for intervention are made to, and purchases made by, VIB, sales of intervention stocks, including forwarding of tenders to Brussels, come under the *Produktschap*. The *Produktschap* for Grains is also responsible for calculating local freight and storage costs in connection with grain intervention.

The importance of the EEC regulations in relation to their other activities obviously varies from one *Produktschap* to another. In the case of dairy products about 80 of the 275 people at headquarters staff are engaged on EEC work, though it has not been necessary to take on any new staff to deal with it. For cereals and for meat, of which there has been relatively little intervention buying, the numbers involved are very much smaller.

Germany

Like the VIB and the Commodity Boards in the Netherlands the Einfuhr- und Vorratstellen (EVSt) (Import and Storage Agencies), set up about 1950,[2]

---

[1] See p. 52 for note on the Management Committee procedure.
[2] Effectively they took over from the earlier Reichsnährstand.

already had considerable experience in administering regulations of the type introduced into the EEC after 1962. Indeed, the previous national support arrangements for cereals, livestock and meat resembled more closely the Community system than those of any other member country, particularly in their use of intervention buying and storage and eventual resale of seasonal surpluses. The four EVSt (for cereals; livestock; dairy products, oils and fats; and sugar) are statutory public boards directed and controlled by the Federal Ministry of Agriculture. Each has a Board of Administration consisting of 24 representatives of the Federal Ministries of Agriculture, Finance and Economic Affairs, the Länder governments, farmers' and producer co-operative organisations, wholesalers' and retailers' trade associations, the processing industries, and consumer organisations. The Board meets only two or three times a year, mainly to conduct formal business. The participation of non-government interests appears to be nominal. The agencies, all four of them in Frankfurt, are essentially bureaucratic. They employ between them an administrative staff of about 710, including those in branch offices (cereals 450; livestock 100; dairy products, etc., 120 and sugar 40), at a total annual administrative cost of about $4·8 mn. Some of the staff of each Board are concerned with storage for defence purposes and other matters unconnected with the CAP. Although located under the same roof and maintaining a certain liaison on questions of general policy, and with central computerised accounting in the hands of the cereals board, the EVSt operate independently of each other under the close control of the Ministry of Agriculture in Bonn. They have little autonomy in the purchase and resale of intervention stocks. This is of course partly in the nature of the EEC system, especially where tendering is concerned, but they appear to be a good deal less independent than, say, ONIC in France,[2] whose 'interprofessional' role, even if not particularly effective, is much stressed.

Italy

Before the introduction of the EEC regulations market intervention had formed no part of official support policy for agriculture in Italy. This had consisted mainly of protection at the frontier by means of quotas and minimum import prices. In the case of wheat, foreign trade was entirely in the hands of the government. Domestic production of wheat was subject to compulsory collection of part of the crop at fixed prices. This collection was carried out on behalf of the government by the Federconsorzi,[1] which continued to operate the new EEC intervention system after 1962 on behalf of the government pending the establishment, in time for the 1966/67 harvest, of AIMA (Azienda di Stato per gli Interventi nel Mercato Agricolo—State Agency for Intervention on the Agricultural Market). This is the agency concerned with applying the EEC regulations for all products in Italy. It does not, however, deal with levies and restitutions,

[1] For an account of the role of the Federconsorzi in Italian agriculture see p. 234.
[2] See pp. 44–5.

application for, and payment of, which are handled by the Customs authorities.

Although nominally autonomous, AIMA is inextricably geared into the government machine. Of the 10 members of its Board of Directors, five are senior civil servants from the Ministry of Agriculture, and one each from the Ministries of Finance, Labour, and Industry and Commerce. There are two outside 'expert' members, professors of economics and law. The Minister of Agriculture is *ex officio* chairman, but the Deputy Minister normally presides. The Director-General and two auditors (one from the Treasury, one from the Court of Accounts) attend but may not vote. Although AIMA's statute allows other persons outside government to be co-opted on a non-voting basis, none have so far been called in. There seems to be little room for 'inter-professionalism' in the Italian concept.

The Azienda has a staff of 150, including some five travelling inspectors. It has an administrative budget of $960,000, which also covers the salaries of senior staff who are seconded from the Ministry of Agriculture. Besides the administrative and accounting divisions and one dealing with studies, the organisation includes five separate divisions, for cereals (with 15 inspectors), livestock products, fruit and vegetables (including sugar), vegetable oils and fats, and wine.

AIMA has received a great deal of criticism from farmers as being a very slow payer, especially of the deficiency payments for hard wheat and olive oil. The elaborate procedure involved with these is discussed elsewhere.[1] The agency seems to have more than its fair share of financial difficulties. First, it is subject to a particularly cumbrous form of auditing, being submitted not only to the type of control usually reserved for state agencies, but also to that required for government departments, plus some additional supervision of its day-to-day transactions applying especially to itself. Second, like OBEA in Belgium, it has been the victim of the government's day-to-day monetary policies, and third, the Italian treasury's chronic financing difficulties have made AIMA especially vulnerable to delays in settlement by FEOGA. To an initial float of $233 mn made in 1966, $160 mn was added subsequently. Otherwise AIMA has had to rely on its funds being topped up from time to time by FEOGA payments, or when particularly large sums are involved (sometimes as much as $260 mn in a season has been required to settle claims for deficiency payments), the agency has been obliged to borrow from the banks. This situation should become regularised by 1972.

France

The French system has been left to the last since it is by far the most elaborate and, although it embodies many features of the other member countries' systems, it also has a number peculiar to itself—notably the sharing out of intervention functions among several autonomous agencies.

[1] See pp. 211–12.

ONIC (Office National Interprofessionnelle des Céréales), the intervention agency for cereals whose ancestry dates back to 1936, is the *fons et origo* of the French system of managed marketing, rather as the MMB is the British prototype. Its long-established constitution has influenced that of the other more recently created French agencies, FIRS for sugar, SIDO for oilseeds, and FORMA for all other products.[1]

ONIC is a public body (*établissement public*) under the joint aegis (*tutelle*) of the Ministries of Agriculture and Finance. Effectively this means that it comes under the first for technical purposes (using its letter-head for the issue of regulations, lists of charges, etc.) and under the second for accounting purposes. Its Central Council (*conseil central*) which meets twice (exceptionally three times) a year, consists of 43 members appointed by the Minister of Agriculture (or the Minister of Social Affairs in the case of the consumers' representatives) on the nomination of the organisations which they represent: 22 producers, of which 9 are elected by producer members of departmental Cereal Committees (see below); 15 from the grain trade and grain utilising industry; and 6 consumers, representing trade unions, consumer co-operatives and farming organisations. Members are nominated for three years, but are re-eligible. The Chairman is always a producer. Five officials attend Council meetings: representatives of the Ministries of Agriculture and Finance and the Caisse Nationale du Crédit Agricole (CNCA), and two government auditors, a *contrôleur d'etat and a commissaire du gouvernement*. A Standing Committee (*comité permanent*) of the Central Council, consisting of 7 producers, 5 from trade and industry, 2 consumers, and 5 officials, meet once a month under the chairmanship of the Chairman of the Central Council to consider current problems connected with the administration of the regulations, including any proposals for their modification. Commissions of experts may be set up *ad hoc* by the Central Council, and chaired by its Chairman, to advise on specific questions. Finally, in each *département* there is a Cereal Committee, consisting of 7 producers, 2 merchants, 2 millers, 1 baker, and the departmental Director of Taxes and of Agriculture. Representatives of ONIC and the CNCA attend in an advisory capacity. These Committees supervise the application of the market regulations, and draw attention to any special local difficulties or anomalies.

At the head office in Paris the Director-General has assistant directors for administration and finance, technical affairs, commercial affairs, and international relations. There is an inspectorate-general and an accounts branch. The general secretariat and statistical services are directly under the Director-General. The total headquarters staff numbers about 360. Sixteen regional offices, each covering one or more administrative regions (*régions du plan*), consist of three sections, technical, inspectional and

[1] Except potatoes. For a description of the activities of SNIPOT in this sector which is not at present covered by any EEC regulation, see page 223.

accounts, under a Chief. Each *département* has its office, which also provides administrative services for the Cereals Committees. The largest ONIC region covers 13 *départements*, the smallest 2. There is an average of about 12 sedentary office staff per region (including the departmental offices), the remainder being itinerant, supervising the technical standards and financial probity of accredited merchants, policing denaturating, and so forth. About 780 persons in all are employed outside Paris.

A unique feature of ONIC is that its administrative budget, some $9.1 mn a year, is entirely covered by a levy on producers (*taxe statistique*). This is collected for ONIC by the Ministry of Finance (department of indirect taxation), at an appropriate charge, from authorised merchants (*collecteurs agréés*), who in turn deduct it from their payments to producers. Currently (1971) the levies average Fr 2·50 ($0.45) per ton on all cereals.

The concept of 'interprofessionalism' embodied in ONIC has provided a pattern for similar organisations and agencies set up in France since the war, though in no case has their day-to-day administration been financed by a producer levy. The Groupement National des Produits Laitiers (GNPL), founded in 1939, associated all sides of the dairy industry with war-time and post-war rationing and import licensing measures. For its peace-time successor, Société Interprofessionnelle du Lait et de ses Dérivés (or Interlait for short), which was responsible for intervention buying of dairy products from 1954 onwards, a new variation on the interprofessional theme was devised. This involved the formation of a limited liability company (*société anonyme*) whose shares were divided equally between producers, co-operatives, industrial processors and the trade (mainly corporate but also including a few individuals in the case of the non-co-operative group). This balance must be maintained if the share capital is increased. The quadripartite structure is also reflected in the composition of the Board of Directors. Interlait was set up in 1964 within a framework of a series of decrees on agricultural marketing passed a year earlier which allowed private intervention agencies to 'carry out trading operations designed to bring equilibrium to agricultural markets'. The company's articles of association included among its aims the conclusion of export and import contracts, and the subsidised storage, denaturing, etc., of surplus dairy products. Since none of these operations could be carried out without the approval, and in most cases financial participation, of the government, the influence to be enjoyed by private interests over the markets was largely notional. A Government Commissioner (*commissaire du gouvernement*) has a power of veto on virtually all important decisions taken by either the Board of Directors or by a shareholders' meeting, subject only to confirmation by the company's two tutelary Ministries, those of Agriculture and Finance. Although this in practice left a good deal of discretion to Interlait in day-to-day market operations, the company was effectively only an agent for carrying out whatever the government's agricultural support policies happened at any given moment to be—during the fifties mainly guaranteed producer prices ensured by payment of subsidies to processors.

An almost identical company, Société Interprofessionnelle du Bétail et de la Viande (SIBEV), was formed for regulating the market for beef, veal and pigmeat. The autonomy of both organisations became still further restricted after 1962 by the setting up of the Fonds d'Orientation et de Régularisation des Marchés Agricoles (FORMA). This assumed responsibility for administering the policy of target prices and intervention buying which had been introduced in 1960 after the breakdown of an earlier system of guaranteed prices. Henceforward Interlait and SIBEV merely carried out FORMA's instructions, an arrangement which has remained virtually unchanged since FORMA assumed the role of intervention agency in connection with the EEC market regulations for livestock, horticultural products and wine.

Although FORMA's own constitution pays some lip-service to 'professional' participation, in its management it is essentially a government-controlled organisation, more so than ONIC. Half of the 24-man Board of Directors consists of government representatives (6 each from the Ministries of Agriculture and Finance), and the Chairman, currently a *conseiller d'état*, is appointed by the two tutelary Ministers. The 12 'professional' representatives[1] receive expenses and the Chairman an official allowance (*indemnité de fonction*). Meetings are also attended *ex officio* by the Director of FORMA (a senior civil servant, also appointed by the Ministers) and the *contrôleur d'etat*, an auditor with the power of veto over expenditure against which appeal is only possible to the Minister of Finance, who appoints him.

On the financial side it is perhaps worth noting that in FORMA it has been possible to avoid maintaining an absolute distinction between *ordonnateur* (the official who has to authorise all payments in advance) and *comptable public* (the official who makes the payments, but must first check the legal validity of the *ordonnance*, since he is personally accountable for all disbursements). The Director of FORMA, by delegating his responsibilities as *ordonnateur* to the head of his accounts department, who is the officially designated *comptable public*, has combined the two functions in the same person. Since each aspect is dealt with by two branches of the same department working in close association, reasonably prompt payment is ensured. This is important in purchasing stocks offered to intervention, paying restitutions, etc. Delays in settlement are, it seems, normally a bane of the French system of public finance, since a disputed account may spend many weeks passing to and fro between *comptable public* and *ordonnateur*.

FORMA's administrative budget, amounting to some $1·6 mn a year,[2] provides for the employment, under the Director, of a Secretary-General

[1] 2 from trade and industry, 3 from the FNSEA (farmers' unions), 3 from the co-operatives, 3 from the Chambres d'Agriculture, and 1 from the CNJA (young farmers).

[2] The equivalent of less than 1 per cent of the agency's total turnover in recent years.

and permanent staff of 180 divided into six commodity divisions (for meat, dairy products, poultry products, fruit and vegetables, wine, and miscellaneous). Each division draws up measures (strictly within the framework of national and Community legislation) for action in the market appropriate to the commodity with which it deals. Such measures are executed by the division after prior consultation with its equivalent interprofessional Advisory Committee (*comité consultatif restreint*—CCR), and after formal approval by the Board of Directors and the relevant Ministry. The technical execution of the measures (e.g. intervention purchases and storage) is delegated in the case of meat, dairy products and potatoes (not an EEC regulated commodity) to the relevant interprofessional companies, SIBEV, Interlait, and SNIPOT (Société Nationale Interprofessionnelle pour les Pommes de Terre). Their full-time administrative staffs total about 320 persons, including field men, and their administrative budgets amount to about $1·3 mn. In the case of fruit and vegetables, intervention at a state of crisis would be delegated by FORMA to regional economic committees (the umbrella organisations of the producer groups). First-stage withdrawal of fruit and vegetables from the market is now the responsibility of the growers themselves,[1] but the necessary funds for compensating producers are obtained through FORMA.

Besides direct market support, FORMA is also responsible for the distribution of indirect subsidies, both those reimbursable from FEOGA and those still permitted under EEC regulations to be charged to national budgets. Such structural measures mainly involve grants towards the initial expenses and working capital of new producer groups, but also include the cow-slaughtering subsidies and those now available to farmers converting their enterprises from milk to meat production. Applications for investment grants are vetted by a separate division (*division des études*), which is also responsible for providing the commodity divisions and the CCRs with rapid up-to-date market intelligence. Besides investing in new food-manufacturing processes, FORMA also assists the development of export markets for French farm produce and sales promotion at home. SOPEXA (Société pour l'Expansion des Ventes de Produits Agricoles et Alimentaires) and CENECA (Centre National des Expositions et Concours) are both financed by FORMA for this purpose. Much of the aid to producer groups is channelled through a third dependent agency, COFREDA (Compagnie pour Favoriser la Recherche et le Développement des Débouchés Agricoles), whose field men are active in a number of regions promoting their formation and development.[2]

FIRS (Fonds d'Intervention et de Régularisation du marché du Sucre)

[1] See pp. 191-2.

[2] It is no doubt this wide range of activities not directly connected with its intervention role which has aroused the suspicions sometimes expressed to us in other member countries that FORMA provides a cloak for improper subsidies. So far only one instance is recorded of the Commission having objected to a grant disbused by FORMA on grounds of its incompatibility with Community rules on distorting competition. This case is likely to be settled before it reaches the European Court of Justice.

resembles ONIC in being concerned with one type of product only, sugar, but the concept of its organisation is much closer to that of FORMA. Set up as an *établissement public* in 1968 to administer the new EEC common policy for sugar,[1] it has a Board of Directors of 16 persons under a chairman, appointed as usual by FIRS's tutelary ministers. The present Chairman, formerly *préfêt* for the Seine, combines his appointment with the chairmanship of the Coal Board. Of the 8 civil servants on the Board, 3 are from the Ministry of Agriculture, 3 from the Ministry of Economy and Finance, and 2 from the Ministry of Overseas Departments and Territories. The other half of the Board, nominated by the Ministers on the recommendation of their professional associations, consists of 3 *fabricants*[2] from metropolitan France, and one from the DOM,[3] 3 beet growers and 1 cane grower. As in the case of FORMA, these all receive expenses (including travel) and the Chairman an official allowance. The Director (chief executive) of FIRS and the official auditors attend all meetings *ex officio*. The Board, whose role is mainly consultative, meets once a month. It advises the Ministers of Agriculture and Finance on the French brief at the Council. It is represented, usually by the Director, on the Management Committee for sugar at its weekly Thursday meetings. The Board also maintains a general supervision of the finances of FIRS, discusses its budget (to which it may propose amendments), examines and adopts the annual report and accounts, and reviews FIRS's borrowing policy. In all financial matters its decisions are subject to confirmation by all three ministers; in other matters to that of the Minister of Agriculture.

The permanent staff of FIRS (whose administrative budget is about $0·7 mn a year) numbers about 60, including drivers, doormen, etc. Its relatively large size is due in part to the complicated paper-work connected with the application for and authorisation of restitutions, not only on bulk sugar but on all processed products containing sugar. The regulations for these are particularly intricate, since their other ingredients are often also subject to regulations, those for cereals and dairy products for instance. The manufacturing industries concerned being not much concentrated, and consisting of numerous small specialised firms, they require, at this early stage at any rate, considerable guidance on the regulations. The section dealing with restitutions and tenders for restitutions, issuing export (and import) certificates and checking all supporting documents, numbers about 16 persons. In the long run its work is likely to decline as the regulations become better understood, and the possibility of a reduction in the staff is envisaged. A second section, employing a staff of 18, carries out purchases and (if necessary in conjunction with the section dealing with restitutions) resales of stocks offered for intervention; arranges their

---

[1] This came into force on July 1st. FIRS opened its offices a week later in a state of unpreparedness caused by the events of May and June.
[2] The term does not distinguish between crushers and refiners.
[3] Départements d'Outre-Mer, i.e. Guadeloupe, Martinique and Réunion.

storage; and carries out inspection (*contrôle*) as necessary at all stages of purchase, storage, denaturing, and export. An accounts section consisting of 15 persons handles all payments, and there is a fourth section, for economics and statistics, with a staff of 6, whose activities are still rather embryonic. They help compile the annual report. FIRS's price-reporting role seems to be confined to keeping Brussels posted with offers on the Paris market, about which the Commission already has other sources of information.

The fourth French intervention agency, SIDO (Société Interprofessionnelle des Oléagineux), is modelled more closely on SIBEV and Interlait. Indeed, SIOFA (Société Interprofessionnelle des Oléagineux Fluides Alimentaires), from which it is directly descended,[1] also dates from the early fifties. It served as an import monopoly for oilseeds from third countries outside the franc zone and to administer support arrangements for domestic oilseed production. The three tutelary Ministries to which SIDO is responsible, those of Agriculture, Finance, and Industrial Investment, as well as producers, crushers and the trade, are represented on its Board, whose Chairman is currently a former high Customs official. The Board meets monthly. There is an administrative staff of 90, including 14 regional inspectors and 5 or 6 accountants and auditors. The chief accountant is nominated directly by the Ministry of Finance. Its administrative budget is about $0·9 mn. Apart from administering the EEC deficiency payment system for colza, sunflower seed and grape-seed, and handling applications for restitutions on re-exports of olive oil, the staff also carries out the national support arrangements for linseed. This commodity is, however, marketed by a separate company, SILIN (Société Interprofessionnelle des graines et huiles de Lin), with a different Board of Directors but the same Chairman as SIDO.

NATIONAL ARRANGEMENTS COMPARED

Both the differences and points of resemblance between national arrangements for implementing the EEC regulations may be summarised under four main headings: whether they are operated by a single 'umbrella'-type agency or by several different bodies; the limits of these agencies' financial competence; their staffing; and the extent to which they are 'interprofessional'. All four aspects are strongly influenced by national tradition and convenience. The first three will continue to be for the foreseeable future. Only in the case of the last might some effort be made in the long run to harmonise national arrangements at Community level within the framework of greater professional participation in administering the CAP.[2]

The choice between single and multiple agencies has been largely a matter of historical accident. In Benelux and Italy all products come under

---
[1] SIDO's take-over from SIOFA in 1970 effectively involved little more than a change of name.
[2] See p. 240 *et. seq.*

a single agency. In the former this is largely due to the small size of the countries. In Italy, where no semi-autonomous agency already existed, and AIMA is ruled entirely by civil servants, with no professional participation, it seemed logical to create a compact organisation. In Germany, on the other hand, a bureaucratic tradition has favoured multiple agencies, though they are of identical constitution and all in the same building. France presents the greatest variety. This is partly because at the time of the setting up of FORMA in 1962, ONIC was already long-established and operating an entirely different type of support system for cereals from the intervention arrangements being applied to meat and dairy products. The same was true of SIOFA's support for oilseed production. The decision to create a special agency for sugar, and not add it to the list of products for which FORMA is responsible, was partly so as to prevent FORMA from becoming too unwieldy an organisation. Otherwise it would have risked turning its interprofessional Board of Directors into, as someone expressed it to us, 'a sort of agricultural parliament'. Partly no doubt the government were influenced by the economically and politically entrenched position of the *betteraviers* and *fabricants* to hive them off into an organisation of their own where they would not have a disturbing effect on their fellow professionals from other sectors.

The scope of the agencies' financial competence in fact differs very little from country to country. None are concerned with the collection of levies, which are usually administered by Customs authorities. All *ipso facto* purchase and resell intervention stocks, and finance their storage. All deal with applications for export licences and restitutions, including tenders for restitutions where applicable, and with their eventual payment. Promptness of payment, on the other hand, varies a good deal, depending on local financial and monetary policies.[1]

Permanent staffs of agencies in all member countries are public servants, including that of ONIC, whose salaries are paid out of the levy on grain producers. Those of the so-called 'companies' like Interlait have, however, preferred to subscribe to forms of contract of employment used in private enterprises. The proportion of seconded career civil servants on agency staffs varies from country to country. The intervention agencies of the five member countries employ between them some 2,700 personnel of all kinds and have a total annual administrative budget of roughly VA20 mn.[2] France accounts for about 60 per cent of both staff and cost. This is largely a reflection of the wide geographical extent there of the intervention process, especially for cereals. $20 mn, although in itself a not inconsider-

[1] In the Netherlands, where official policy has, on principle, been inimical to intervention, settlement by VIB of intervention purchases was until recently subject to a two-month delay. As a result of complaints from the trade over a long period this has now been reduced to one month.

[2] Estimates of cost have been made in the case of the Netherlands and Luxemburg, where the agencies form an integral part of the Ministry of Agriculture. To allow for their activities in sectors not covered by EEC regulations one-third only of FORMA's staff and budget is included, and an appropriate reduction made in that of the EVSts.

able sum, should be seen against the background of a total estimated gross Community expenditure on all forms of agricultural price support in 1970 of VA2·4 bn.[1]

As will already be apparent, there is considerable diversity in the extent to which producers, processors and the trade participate in the running of the intervention agencies—i.e. to which they are 'interprofessional':[2] not at all in Italy or Luxemburg, only nominally in Germany, a little more in Belgium, in France to a varying degree according to the agency. Only in the Netherlands do professionals have any part in the day-to-day running of the EEC marketing system, thanks to the special role allotted to the Commodity Boards. But even there influence is, as it were, at one remove, with executive responsibility effectively in the hands of the *Produktschappen* permanent officials, who tend to act more as civil servants than one would normally expect in employees of a trade association. In France and Belgium professionals' participation being confined to membership of the Boards of the various agencies, their influence is more limited. Where Boards hold plenary meetings only infrequently, mainly for the conduct of formal business, provision is made for a standing committee to meet monthly, or more often, to keep track of developments in Community policy and discuss current problems arising out of the application of the EEC regulations. It should be noted that in the case of OBEA in Belgium and ONIC in France, the Boards consist entirely of professionals. So do those of the French 'companies'. On the Boards of FORMA and FIRS, however, officials and professionals are evenly balanced. This is also the case with the Boards of Management of the EVSt in Germany. Since there are no equivalent standing committees, professional participation there is insignificant.

We have a general impression that, whatever provision may be made in their constitutions to correct it, all intervention agencies have a very strong official bias. Governments in all cases possess powers of veto. Professional influence is at best diluted even at national level, and in Brussels, with not more than one representative from each national agency on a Management Committee, it is virtually non-existent. This is still a far cry from the idea floated in the 1968 Mansholt Plan[3] of interprofessionally constituted 'product councils' at Community level. These would be responsible, amongst other things, for establishing and maintaining a 'permanent information system', involving comparable price quotations for agricultural markets throughout the Community; for organising quality checks; for sales promotion; and for encouraging the growth of contractual and similar relationships between producer organisations and processors and wholesalers. The paragraph concludes:

[1] *Avant-project de budget supplémentaire des Communautés Européennes pour l'exercise 1970, No. 4*, COM (70), 810 final, EEC, Brussels, July 1970, III/10.
[2] Fruit and vegetables, support arrangements for which are essentially in the hands of producers, are here left out of account.
[3] *op cit*, para 111 (English translation as published by the Commission).

'The Commission intends to propose rules to govern such product councils and groupings of product councils, so as to make it possible to hand over to them wider responsibilities in the above-mentioned fields as and when further progress is made with the common agricultural policy.'

One of the 'above-mentioned fields' in which product councils are expected to be active is the examination 'at the beginning of each marketing year, and in the light of market prospects (of) the conditions that will prevail and the arrangements to be enforced'. 'Wider responsibilities' in this field could give professionals a far more effective *entrée* into the Berlaymont building than they have at present.[1] It would be more effective for instance than that enjoyed by the National Farmers' Union in Whitehall, since the intention seems to be to institutionalise the presence of farmers (and in this case of processors and the trade as well) within the framework of the Commission. The proposals are, of course, in an embryonic stage and need a good deal of clarifying. Their basic concept will inevitably be challenged by the usual centrifugal forces in the Community, political, bureaucratic, and probably professional as well in this case. At any rate it will be a long time before they reach the Council table in the form of a proposed regulation—if they ever do.

Note on Management Committees

The only direct link between national intervention agencies and the Commission in Brussels is provided by their representation on the Management Committees (*comités de gestion*) for each of the groups of products subject to regulation under the CAP. The agencies are represented by one of their senior officials, usually the Director-General, within the team of officials attending from each member country. Not more than five of these may be present at a Committee meeting at any one time. Although contacts at all levels between agency staffs and Community civil servants can, and do, take place at other times, the Management Committee provides a unique forum for formal discussion of national viewpoints both on the application of existing regulations and, perhaps even more important, on the drawing up of proposals by the Commission for amendments or new regulations. Apart from discussion of technical criteria the Committee's routine work also includes fixing, sometimes weekly, of levies and restitutions—though, as will be apparent in the commodity chapters in Part Two, for certain products these may be fixed directly by the Commission without prior reference to Management Committee.

The reasons for this are evident. The day-to-day working of the CAP involves large numbers of regulations of a technical nature, often the result of decisions having to be taken at short notice. The Commission is in any case empowered to issue these so-called 'regulations of the

---

[1] The concept of greater responsibility for producers is further discussed in Chapter 12.

Commission' without prior reference to the Council, which only meets, on average, once a month. The Commission may, in theory at least, be required to justify such actions to the Council *a posteriori*. In fact this necessity is virtually excluded by the Management Committee system. These have the same weight of national representation and voting powers as the Council except that their chairmen, who have no vote, are members of the Commission, which also provides the secretariat. They may turn down any Commission regulation other than those to which, for reasons of urgency, prior Management Committee procedure is inapplicable. They are, however, prevented by the voting arrangements from completely hamstringing the Commission's administration. A majority of at least 12 out of the 17 votes is required to enable a Committee to stop any action by the Commission and have it referred back, within a month, to the Council, which may then, by a similar qualified majority, oblige the Commission to withdraw the measure. Therefore as long as the Commission can carry with it at least one of the major member countries (with four votes) and either Belgium or the Netherlands (with two votes each), on any Committee, giving at least six votes in favour of its action and only eleven against, its wishes cannot be frustrated. In fact this is all rather theoretical as questions tend to be thoroughly thrashed out and compromises reached long before they are put to a formal vote. In the case of amendments to Council regulations or new regulations such preliminary discussions and negotiations in Committee may continue for weeks or even months.[1] The Committees thus play a key role in policy making.

---

[1] They are also discussed, of course, in the relevant special Committee (e.g. for Agriculture) by officials on the staffs of the member countries' Permanent Representatives, and in the Working Parties (*groupes de travail*).

PART TWO

The Principal Farm Products

CHAPTER 4

Cereals

Throughout Western Europe the climate is suitable for growing cereals. The limitations to the use of land for this purpose are mostly topographical and economic: steep slopes, thin or stony soil, poor drainage, remoteness from centres of demand. In the minds of many people cereal growing represents the typical farming activity, with its strong seasonal character and identification with harvest. Cereals are also generally still associated with bread, despite the fact that they are to an ever-increasing extent used in Western Europe as feedingstuffs for livestock rather than for the production of flour. Of total supplies of cereals in Britain, for instance, less than a third is used for direct human consumption by the milling, breakfast cereals, malting and distilling industries. In recent years an average of about half of the British wheat crop has been used as animal food.

The British marketing system for cereals has recently been examined, by a team of economists working under the direction of Professor D. K. Britton, in an invaluable report, the first comprehensive treatment of the subject for about forty years, published in 1969.[1] In view of the existence of so much up-to-date information, the discussion that follows on the British cereals market will be limited to a brief outline of those points which seem most relevant to the objectives of this study.

So far as complexity of marketing is concerned, cereals seem to lie somewhere between the more or less homogeneous agricultural products such as milk, poultry and eggs, ready subjects for grading, and livestock, for which the varieties of breed and qualities still inhibit a movement towards greater market transparency. In North America, where the major cereal growing areas enjoy very similar soil and climatic conditions, cereals are bought and sold on the basis of accepted grades. If the same conditions existed in Britain it would be possible for a much larger proportion of the cereal crop to be sold direct by farmers to end-users, and for the structure of the marketing system through merchants to take a form different from that which exists at present. Grading of cereals has made some progress in Britain but, as the Britton report points out, the day is far off when all domestically produced cereals will be sold without visual examination.

[1] D. K. Britton, *Cereals in the United Kingdom: Production, Marketing and Distribution.* Pergamon Press, 1969.

It is this lack of accepted grades for home-grown cereals that provides the main *raison d'être* for merchants as intermediaries for most transactions between producers and end-users.

Corn merchants in Britain number about 1,500. Many of them are very small. Of the 260 firms in the Britton report's sample survey, 86 had a turnover of under £150,000 a year. An outsider visiting some corn merchants' offices might gain an impression that little had changed in fifty or even a hundred years. Clerks still sit on high-backed chairs and the smell of samples is evocative of the chandler of the last century. It is true that many firms are old established and based on family connections. About half the firms in the Britton report's sample had been established before the First World War. But it would be a mistake to conclude that the structure of the trade has become ossified. Since the last war, as the report shows, not only has a large number of firms gone out of business, but there has also been quite a flood of new entrants, to the extent that nearly one-third of the firms trading today were established after 1947.

While the need for visual inspection of grain may be the principal *raison d'être* for the corn merchant, as well as the main explanation for the structure of the trade, there are several other important functions which he performs. At least as important as the prices which the merchant agrees with the farmer and the end-user are the arrangements for transport of the cereals. For all but very short journeys it is most important to arrange a return haul for the truck transporting cereals from the producing farm. The intense competition for farmers' business forces the merchant to make the most economic use of transport. Much of the art of running a corn merchant's business consists in ensuring that the merchant's, or his contract haulier's, transport is kept employed to the maximum. Typically the return haul is composed of compound feeds from the mill receiving the grain, or from another mill nearby. These compounds may or may not return to the farm from which the grain originated. Occasionally, the return haul might consist of another product, such as fertilisers, in which the merchant is also trading, but such possibilities are becoming fewer as grain and feed transport becomes more specialised.

Second, there is the important credit function. In the past, merchants have come in for some criticism for the high cost of the credit they extend to farmers. These criticisms are less justifiable now that farmers must surely be aware of what it costs to take credit from a merchant and the manner in which the credit charge arises, usually through a discount being disallowed. The extension of credit to farmers undoubtedly suits merchants very well under conditions of normal farming prosperity. Indeed, some firms claim they make as much out of their profit on extending credit to their customers as they do on trading margin. But it can be argued that if this profit on credit did not exist, merchants would be forced to push up their margins on transactions which, at around 50p per ton on grain (about 2 per cent), appear to be modest.

Third, merchants play some part in keeping farmers informed about market developments. Fewer farmers now attend grain markets. Instead they obtain market intelligence from corn merchants who are constantly in touch with cereal growers in their area advising them about prices. This function is becoming rather less important as other sources of information, including the Home-Grown Cereals Authority's bulletins, become available. When it comes to making transactions with farmers, merchants are sometimes criticised for making different offers to different farmers. In a sense this is inevitable, as all transactions are individual. While there may be going prices for the various cereals at market centres (particularly at the ports), there are no equivalent going prices at the farm-gate, as these prices will be greatly influenced by the transport arrangements that can be made, including the return haul. Variations in the quality of the grain, difference in farm access and loading facilities, and credit arrangements all have to be taken into account in setting a price. The results of the Britton report's sample probably underestimate the degree of price variation that occurs. Such variation seems to be inevitable because of the complexity of each transaction in grain, apart from considerations of getting other business from the farmer in question.

Over the past decade, two important developments have occurred in British agricultural marketing. First, all the national compound feed manufacturers who were not already selling direct to farmers have bought up firms of corn merchants. The number acquired, several being large and well-known, exceeds a hundred. The principal motives for this move had no direct connection with grain marketing. In the first place the feed manufacturers concerned wanted to secure sales outlets for their feed more closely tied to them than independent merchants. Also the move, which was initiated by a feed manufacturer less committed to the ports than some others, was seen as a means of acquiring country compounding facilities belonging to these merchants which would be cheaper than erecting new mills from scratch. As a consequence of this development, the compounders in question find themselves heavily involved in grain trading. The Britton report reveals that these firms account for 22 per cent of all domestic grain transactions. This foray into merchanting on the part of the feed manufacturers has now largely come to a halt. The short-term effects on profitability of the feed companies have probably not been very satisfactory, and it seems unlikely that the development will be carried much further in the near future. In other words the compounders seem to have found that margins in merchanting are not very attractive. Other things being equal, these companies may give their merchanting subsidiaries some preference over grain purchases. But it seems unlikely that they would go further than this and attempt to channel grain through them which could be more economically bought elsewhere. It would hardly be in their own interests to do.

The other potentially important development has been the growth of farmers' trading groups. Some of these sell their members' grain as an activity secondary in importance to the main purpose of the group, which may be requirements purchasing or the marketing of some other agricultural product or products. A few, perhaps a dozen of any importance, specialise in grain marketing. The former often sell their members' grain to merchants, but the policy of the latter is usually to market direct to end-users and thus retain for themselves the merchant's margin. If this activity, particularly of the specialised groups, developed on a large scale throughout the country, it could alter the present structure of cereal marketing.

Clearly both these developments, the integration of feed manufacturers and of farmers into agricultural merchanting, are not in the interests of the independent corn merchants. No doubt they will put up resistance against a continuation of them, and particularly against farmers' groups, which most directly threaten them. To resist effectively, merchants may have further to improve their services and perhaps work on tighter margins. The economics of the operation of many of the cereal groups seems to be questionable. Many of them are not achieving the turnover that is required to justify the employment of the manager and small staff necessary if marketing is to be performed efficiently. The transport problems for groups may often be more severe than for merchants. On the other hand, it must be recognised that in integrating into merchanting, British farmers are doing little more than has already occurred in the EEC countries through farmers' co-operatives. The Britton report attributes only 8 per cent of British grain as being sold to co-operatives. After allowing for the grain requirements of co-operative feed mills, the significance of the co-operative sector in marketing alone is even less than this figure.

It might be appropriate at this stage to summarise what will be the principal influences on the future British cereals market regardless of possible EEC membership. First, if government policy continues to favour expansion in cereals production and assuming continued (and perhaps even dramatic) improvements in plant-breeding and hence in yields, there will be a considerably larger quantity of cereals to be marketed. Aside from exports, the only major user of this increase is the compound-feed industry, involving some displacement of imported maize. Second, it is to be expected that farmers' groups will expand their activities (possibly in the direction of groupings of groups in order to save on overheads), particularly if they receive favoured treatment by way of government grants for the erection of grain drying and storage installations. Third, as a result of competition from this source and from merchanting firms controlled by the feed companies, there will be some acceleration in concentration among the independent merchants. One could readily envisage that the number of firms could be halved down to about 700 by the end of the decade, and the reduction might well be even greater than this. Groupings of farmers' groups might be countered by groupings of merchants. During this period there will certainly be some rationalisation of the traditional co-operative sector as well. Finally, it must be expected that the continuing trend towards country mills expanding at the expense of the port mills will have some effect on cereal marketing. Medium-sized country compounders operating over a small area can do their own grain gathering with less difficulty than the large port mills which tend to be remote from the main cereal-producing regions. Whether they consider it worth while will depend on the efficiency of the service performed by the merchants in their area and the costs of the operation. Merchants dealing in a number of commodities, including fertilisers and feeds, should be able to compete on overhead costs with this part of the country compounders' business. Much will depend on whether the compounders decide to sell their own feed direct to farmers, in which case it would be logical also to handle the grain side themselves.

Government policy will affect the British cereal marketing system through prices for agricultural commodities and through decisions over aid for grain storage. The trade would also be affected by changes in import policy. Market prices could be pushed up closer to the desired level of farm-gate prices than is already being achieved by minimum import prices, by means of variable levies on imported cereals. If Britain in this way moved closer to the EEC system, outlined in the following pages, merchants would have to familiarise themselves with a new range of techniques. But the main change would be to insulate the British market from fluctuating world prices. The possible effects of this on cereal marketing are indicated at the end of this chapter.

Market structure in the EEC

The response of Britain to the agricultural crisis of the thirties differed markedly from that of most other Western European countries. Through the 1932 Wheat Act and the 1937 Agriculture Act Britain began to lay the foundations of an agricultural policy which although based on free entry of food and feedingstuffs was accompanied by guaranteed prices to farmers implemented by transfer payments to make up the deficiency between the guarantee and the market. With modifications this still remains a principle of British agricultural policy. Elsewhere in Europe governments were also attempting to protect their farmers from ruin through guaranteed minimum prices. In France, for instance, a succession of laws was enacted early in the thirties designed to stabilise market prices, culminating in the Law of 1933 which laid down a minimum price below which wheat could not be sold. These prices were, however, sustained by import controls, exercised through the CICIB (Comité Interprofessionnel du Contrôle des Importations de Blé) which had been set up a few years earlier. In fact import controls proved insufficient in the face of the bumper French harvests of 1932–4 even though they were accompanied by other measures, including rules about incorporation of domestic grain by millers, and special credits. Stronger and more co-ordinated regulations were required and for this purpose the Office du Blé, the predecessor of ONIC (Office National Interprofessionnel des Céréales), was established. Elsewhere, in the countries which are now members of the EEC, generally similar measures were taken designed to insulate domestic markets from outside pressures, state or interprofessional organisations being given powers to regulate markets, including intervention buying if this proved necessary to sustain farmers' prices at the required level. Only the Netherlands with its major interest in exports of livestock and livestock products pursued a more liberal policy towards cereal imports.

This divergence of policy over cereals between Britain and the Continent, which had existed for a generation prior to the first negotiations over British entry into the EEC, was due to complex causes. But perhaps the overriding reason has been fiscal. In Britain the cost of implementing the guarantees for cereals has often seemed to be a very severe burden on the Exchequer. For instance, in the early sixties when the domestic harvest was usually about 11 mn tons, the guarantees were costing about £70 mn a year and the production grants relevant to cereals probably a further £30 mn, to give a total cost to the Exchequer of about £100 mn a year, or about £9 per ton. Allowing for the higher cereal prices prevailing at the time in the Common Market countries the cost per ton of this type of support would have been very much greater. In France, for example, where cereal production in the early sixties was running at between 20 and 25 mn tons a year (and the *collecte* at about 15 mn tons), the total cost of a British-type system for cereals would have exceeded £300 mn a year, a gigantic burden to a country for which the raising of tax revenue has always posed particular problems.

In the EEC countries, as in Britain, most cereals are marketed through merchants (the word here being used to include co-operatives) rather than direct from producer to end-user. As the present structure of the merchanting sector existed in much the same form before the EEC was created, it seems logical to include at this stage a brief description of the trade in the Common Market countries before turning to discuss the cereals regulations, the role played by the intervention agencies and the effect of these regulations on marketing.

There are many points of similarity between the work of corn merchants in Britain and in the EEC countries. In both there is a co-operative and a private sector. In both merchants (of each kind) deal in a wide range of agricultural commodities other than cereals, including feeds and fertilisers. As in Britain, merchants in the EEC develop close links with farmers; this helps them to decide what amount of credit they can afford to extend to each customer. Other similarities include a tendency towards concentration in the trade and a continuing decline in the importance of grain markets as places where transactions are made. So far as the latter is concerned the process has gone further in Britain than in the EEC countries where local markets, for example at Groningen in northern Holland, still provide quite important meeting places for farmers, wholesalers, manufacturers, traders and importers, in fact anyone who has any business to do which is concerned with agriculture and the agricultural industries.

Another similarity is presented by the new links that are being made between domestic merchants and feed manufacturers and some of the international grain shippers and importers. In Germany, for instance, some of the largest importers are also engaged in the domestic grain market, as well as owning compound feed mills and/or flour mills, but unlike the position in Britain, these companies which now have diverse interests in the cereals/compounds/flour-milling complex generally started life as grain importers. The degree of penetration of domestic markets by the international shippers has been greater than in Britain. Three or four of the large shippers have extensive interests in internal markets, mostly through subsidiary companies. The lines of demarcation between shippers, importers, wholesale merchants and local merchants are disappearing rapidly. For example, shippers are selling direct to local country compounders, by-passing the intermediaries. Clearly the objective is to make up in domestic business what may be lost in international trade through greater self-sufficiency in cereals in the EEC member countries.

The two major differences between cereal marketing in Britain and in the EEC countries are related to the comparative importance of co-operative activity and to the location and control of storage.[1] The two differences, which are partly connected, have both been influenced in some member countries by government action. The most striking example comes from France, where in the period from 1936, when the Office du Blé was started, until 1952 the cereal co-operatives were given substantial advantages over private merchants, largely through credit terms, and were thus able to gain a big proportion of the grain trade, currently about 80 per cent of wheat sold off farms and 65 per cent of coarse grains, and also to construct a large number of grain silos. Co-operatives and private merchants now compete on more equal terms and both are eligible to take their part as *collecteurs agrées* (formerly known as *organismes stockeurs*) in the intervention arrangements of ONIC described later.

Recent statistics prepared by ONIC show that there has been a considerable increase in storage capacity in the hands of both co-operatives and private merchants. Over the three years to July 1969 capacity increased by slightly over 3 mn tons, about 2 mn tons by the co-operatives and rather over 1 mn by the private sector. This increase took place without any appreciable change in the number of silos, the average capacity of which has risen greatly. At this date the former held a total of 8·3 mn tons of capacity and the latter 3·4 mn tons. The increase in new capacity has been particularly strong since the middle of 1968. To this total of 11·7 mn tons under the control of the *collecteurs agrées* can be added the facilities of transit silos and the storage of the processing industry, which together total about 2·5 mn tons. Despite this increase in available storage for French cereals, capacity is still insufficient in relation to the *collecte* which in 1968/69 totalled 21·7 mn tons, a higher figure than had been

[1] Cf. D. K. Britton, *op cit*, Part VI, Chapter I, 'Grain Marketing in some Western European Countries', contributed by M. W. Butterwick.

envisaged by the Planning Commission even for the 1970 harvest. In fact, increases in storage capacity have hardly kept pace with increases in the *collecte*. In 1960 capacity of 5·2 mn tons was available for a *collecte* of 11·1 mn tons, compared with 11·7 mn tons in 1969 available for the 1968/69 *collecte* of 21·7 mn tons. This lack of adequate cereal storage puts a considerable strain on the French marketing system, especially at harvest time.

Estimates of on-farm cereal storage capacity are inevitably much less reliable than those for commercial silos. ONIC's calculations show on-farm storage at about 3·5 mn tons. This is so far below the difference between total production of cereals and the *collecte* that it must be an underestimate. Here the difficulty is to define what can be classed as storage capacity. Elsewhere in the Community the amount of cereals stored on farms and then sold is very small. Effectively it can be said that the quantity deliberately held back and stored on farms with a view to subsequent sale is nearly negligible. Thus commercial storage arrangements for cereals in the EEC member countries are entirely different from those in Britain. Figures for total storage under the control of British merchants, including co-operatives, are at present lacking. Some evidence is provided by the Britton report's survey of 260 merchants which shows that only 30 merchants without feed manufacture had storage capacity exceeding 500 tons. In view of this, it seems unlikely that total capacity in the hands of merchants in Britain could exceed half a million tons. The implications of this on intervention activity are discussed at the end of this chapter.

Control of the storage of cereals profoundly influences the system of marketing them. In the Common Market countries cereals are normally moved into central grain stores either straight from the harvest field or from the farm after a short stay in temporary store, often consisting merely of a heap on the ground. In dealings with private merchants the sale is usually made at the time of the movement of the grain, but occasionally the farmer may retain ownership while it is in the merchant's silo until it suits him to make a sale, at which time storage costs (and any other costs, including drying) are deducted from the proceeds. A farmer dealing with a co-operative can usually sell in either of these two ways, but a third alternative is also available. This involves the farmer delivering his grain to the co-operative and receiving immediately a payment on account against a nominal price. The selling of the grain becomes the responsibility of the co-operative. At the end of the season each farmer is paid on a pooled basis after the deduction of the co-operative's costs and after allowing for any quality differences between the deliveries of the various members. Clearly this method puts the co-operative in a strong position to negotiate the best possible prices. It is becoming increasingly common and many co-operatives, notably in the Netherlands, more or less insist on their members adopting it.

Once a local co-operative has gained control of marketing of cereals on behalf of its members, the next stage is for co-operatives to join together in order to strengthen still further their selling position. This can occur at either regional or national level. In France and Germany where the co-operatives are organised regionally (in the latter based on the Länder), the local co-operatives are encouraged to sell all or part of their grain to the regional co-operatives and thus, in effect, to delegate to them part of their marketing function. Co-operation among co-operatives is particularly relevant to export business. In France the two central cereal co-operatives, to which practically all the co-operatives are affiliated, handle a large amount of cereal exports. Grouping together of co-operative cereal marketing is making most progress in the Netherlands. The central organisation, CEBECO, is taking a positive line in encouraging the Dutch grain co-operatives to hand over responsibility for marketing all their grain both to domestic users and for export. CEBECO already handles all imports of cereals on behalf of its members. The Dutch are taking a leading role in promoting closer links between national co-operative organisations. Trade across national frontiers is already occurring between co-operatives, notably from the French regional co-operatives to Dutch and German buyers. Eurograin, the co-operative cereals brokerage organisation, which established a British subsidiary in 1970, handled nearly 2 mn tons in 1969/70, its third trading year. A much closer commercial collaboration on cereal marketing among the Western European co-operatives can very well be envisaged as a viable possibility, despite the obvious differences of interest between buyers and sellers.

The EEC system

The basis for a common policy for cereals for the Community was established in April 1962 through Regulation No. 19. The main features of this and subsequent regulations affecting cereals have been described elsewhere.[1] For the purposes of this study, it seems most relevant to describe the mechanics used by the Commission in setting the levies, which are designed to enforce the threshold prices for cereals, and for deciding the level of restitution payment on exports, since the national agencies are closely concerned with both imports and exports. In practice, the daily routine for levy fixations begins about 12.45 when quotations begin to come in by telex from the reporting agencies. These are ONIC in Paris, the EVSt for grains and feedingstuffs in Frankfurt, the *Produktschap* for Grains in The Hague, the Grain Union in Antwerp and the Italian Ministry of Agriculture in Rome. By about 14.15 the quotations, numbering roughly 500–600, have been received. These are then converted into units of account per metric ton and quality coefficients are applied. The quotations are transferred to punched cards for the Directorate-General for Agriculture's computer and arranged in ascending order of price. Quotations

---

[1] Butterwick and Neville-Rolfe, *op cit*, p. 91 *et seq*.

which are considered to be unrepresentative, either because the offers involved are small (under 500 tons) or for any other reason, are disregarded. The Commission frequently checks on any quotations which it considers out of line, either with the reporting agency or direct with the market in question. By about 15.45 the lowest c.i.f. offers for the various cereals have been established and the information passed from the telex room to the Commission's Secretariat. A checking copy is returned to the telex room by the Secretariat. At about 16.00 a message is received back from the Secretariat confirming that the rates of levy have been agreed and signed by one of the Commissioners. These rates are then communicated to the Official Journal published in Luxemburg and notified to the various national agencies and the Customs authorities of the member countries. The levies come into force from 0001 hours on the following day and remain in force until they are altered. The regulations provide that changes are not made to take account of very small changes in the lowest c.i.f. price, for instance UA 0·75 per ton in the case of maize.

Levies are fixed at the moment when an importer applies to his national agency for permission to import a certain quantity of grain in a certain month. Applications are made by telex or telegram, usually the former, which have to be despatched before 16.00 in order to obtain the levy applicable to the day in question. The national agency then confirms back the licence on which is stamped the appropriate levy. Levies can be fixed for shipment during the current month and the three following months. The rate of levy is always the same for the current month and the next month. For the next two months levies may be different if the futures market and the threshold price (after allowing for the monthly increments) do not keep in step. If an importer wishes to fix the levy for these next two months he has to pay a so-called fixation charge representing this difference. The fixation charge is announced daily at the same time as are the levies for the current (and the following) month, and is likewise published in the Official Journal.

Levies are payable by the importer after the grain has been cleared through Customs, when the exact quantities are established. A deposit amounting to UA 5·00 per ton has to be made at the time when the levy is fixed, but this is normally done by bank guarantee, the cost of which is under 1 per cent per annum. If a licence is not used there is anyway a penalty of UA 0·50 per ton. In addition, if at the end of the third month following the month of application the licence has not been used and the levy is then higher than that applicable to the licence, this difference has to be paid as well. The levy set on the last day of each month (being the day on which licences lapse) is therefore particularly important for the trade. Naturally it is also the day on which the Commission and the national agencies have to take particular care to make sure that the market is not being rigged. A similar penalty is payable when a vessel arrives after the end of the month in question and the levy applicable to the actual arrival date is higher, except when the delay is due to acts of God and strikes.

Cereals

For vessels discharging at Rotterdam, passing the Hook of Holland constitutes arrival, the date and time being certified by Dirkzwagers.

Restitutions are normally fixed weekly on Thursdays and become effective from 0001 hours on Fridays.[1] In order to establish the most favourable export prices for cereals the Commission obtains reports from the national agencies, ministries of agriculture and other market sources in much the same way as for the levy fixations. Restitutions are common to all ports in the Community but vary according to country of destination. An exporter may either take the restitution of the day when he applies for the export licence, fix an advance restitution (as for levies), or simply leave the rate unfixed, in which case he must take the restitution applicable to the day on which the export of the cereals takes place. In the case of large export opportunities, notably to state trading countries, special restitutions are awarded as a result of tenders by the trader.

Before turning to the work of the cereal intervention agencies, some comments must be made about the other method that is used to shift surplus cereals, denaturing. Two types of operation are involved. Where wheat exports are required to be denatured (i.e. distinguished from wheat for milling) by the country that is buying the wheat, the treatment, usually by a dye, is carried out, in conformity with the importing country's regulations, either on board ship or in bond. The wheat is known as *blé traité*. The other, and more important, type of denaturing is confined to the internal market. Basically it consists of offering a premium (or subsidy) per ton to induce those holding high-priced wheat for which there is a surplus in the Community to sell at or near the lower price level of coarse grains in which the Community still has a deficit. To avoid the possibility of wheat that has received this premium re-entering the market (and either being offered to the intervention agency or even attracting a second premium) the wheat has to be treated so that it can be permanently distinguished from milling wheat. There are harmonised regulations concerned with this process. The normal method is to taint the wheat with fish oil or cod-liver oil. In some cases lucerne meal is mixed in with the wheat. Where a dye is used the regulations lay down that it should be Hoechst *bleu patenté* 5. Direct incorporation (or *Beimischung*) of wheat in compound feeds without denaturing is also eligible for the premium payments. The mixing is closely supervised as is also the denaturing process, the responsibility for supervision lying with the national agencies.

There is little or no economic sense behind the policy of paying subsidies for denaturing. Clearly it is a method of 'turning wheat into coarse grains' without adjusting the basic price differentials for the various cereals, and in particular without touching the sanctity of the wheat price. The original intention was that the premium should vary from region to region according to local fluctuations between wheat and barley prices. The

---

[1] The difference in timing between levy and restitution fixations might indicate that the Community is more anxious to prevent disruptions of its own domestic market than to stop excessive exports of cereals due to over-generous restitutions.

premium was therefore first fixed (July 1967) at the difference between the basic intervention prices for wheat and barley at Duisburg, but some variations were permitted through the Community. Later it was found necessary to increase the premium to take account of the cost of the process and differences in feed values between the cereals. The premium now stands at the difference between the intervention prices at Duisburg plus UA 2·50 per ton, and at this level wheat is competitive with maize in certain areas.

The origins and forms of organisation of the intervention agencies have already been described (Chapter 3). A more detailed account of their work in cereal markets is now required.

In France the prices at which ONIC will buy cereals at intervention and the months when the buying will take place (an important point which is discussed later) are announced before the season begins.[1] Grain may be offered for intervention buying by any accredited merchant to the departmental section of ONIC in whose area the parcel is stored. Offers must be made in writing (on a form issued by ONIC), giving particulars of quantity and quality, location in store, choice of intervention point, distance from store to intervention point, and particulars of available rail or water communication between the two. At present minimum lots that will be accepted for intervention buying are 500 tons of soft wheat, barley and maize, 100 tons of durum, and 50 tons of rye. These minima may be varied by ONIC in special circumstances provided they are no lower than those specified in EEC Regulation 1414/69.

The departmental office must acknowledge an offer within 4 working days of its receipt stating whether the quantity and designated delivery point are acceptable. Within 15 working days of receipt firm refusal or provisional acceptance of the offer on grounds of quality (after analysis of the sample) must be communicated to the offerer. Non-reply implies provisional acceptance. At or soon after acceptance ONIC must supply the offerer with the name of the storer-purchaser (*stockeur-acheteur*) (see below), location of his store, and the date on which delivery is to begin. Not less than 10 per cent of the parcel is to be delivered on each successive day, and in any case not less than 40 tons a day by road or rail and not less than 125 tons a day by water. Failure to observe delivery dates, other than that due to transport breakdowns, involves the offerer in a fine. He is, on the other hand, reimbursed (at fixed storage rates per day) in the event of the storer-purchaser being unable to accept all or part of a parcel on the due date. In fixing his intervention point (*centre de commercialisation*) the offerer has the choice between the three official points nearest (in

[1] Except, of course, so-called 'Type B' intervention. This involves the agency entering a weak local market *before* prices fall to intervention level. Originally introduced into the EEC system experimentally for one season at the request of France, where it had formed part of previous national arrangements, this preventive type of support buying seems likely to remain a permanent feature. It may only be rarely authorised by the Commission. It can have the effect of forestalling a general collapse of prices and thus of avoiding a greater volume of intervention purchases.

the sense of accessible at lowest cost) to the parcel in store. He is paid the intervention price for grain delivered by him alongside the centre of his choice. In addition he receives payment (at rates laid down according to the mode of transport) from the storer-purchaser towards the cost of moving the grain from store to centre.

Cereals which have been the subject of intervention buying from accredited merchants are not in fact purchased by ONIC but by the accredited storer-purchasers themselves. Normally these are designated by ONIC for a single harvest period on the basis of tenders submitted by owners of storage capacity (minimum 500 tons) to store a given quantity of grain at an offered daily rate. The technical suitability of the storage must previously have been vetted by ONIC's regional services and the store accredited by the departmental cereals committee. Stores and silos used for supplying industrial users are ineligible. The storer-purchaser is obliged to accept all cereals of suitable quality offered him up to the contracted quantity, and not less than one-thirtieth of the quantity per day over any period of one month. The contracted quantity may, by mutual agreement, be increased by up to 5 per cent. Normally storage is not in use for more than $4\frac{1}{2}$ to 5 months. Contracts oblige the storer-purchaser to store grain no longer than up to March 31st of the harvest year following that in which the grain was produced. In order to ensure it greater flexibility, however, ONIC was authorised in 1970 for the first time to enter into long-term contracts. The long-term contracts are of two types, 'A', exclusively for cereals on which payment for storage is guaranteed for 205 days in any harvest year, and 'B', in which other types of goods may be stored, ONIC guaranteeing only 155 days' use and 3 months' notice of need. Purchases of cereals by the storer-purchasers (of whom there are usually about 200, including the two central co-operative unions—but not their regional member co-operatives as such) are financed by means of bank loans guaranteed by ONIC, which also bears the interest charges.

There have been a number of different schemes for intervention since 1962. Up to 1967 (i.e. in the transition period leading up to a full common policy for cereals) intervention was differentiated on the basis of a few main production zones with prices tapering off round the edges of each zone to a roughly similar level, the object being to reduce the incentive to move grain for short distances from one zone to another. For 1967/68 principal intervention points were established with a large number of secondary centres with intervention prices derived from the main centres, the difference being the transportation cost. From 1968/69 one further principal intervention point was added and the number of secondary points reduced to about 250. In this apparently complicated structure there are four main elements. First, the Duisburg price (the highest) is also used at Marseilles. Second, the main Channel and Atlantic ports all have the same price as Rouen, which is derived from Rotterdam (derived in turn from Duisburg), except that allowances are made at the smaller ports for higher handling costs. Third, the principal inland grain centres have prices derived from the points already mentioned, e.g. Compiègne from Duisburg, Chartres from Rouen, Châteauroux from La Rochelle and so on. Fourth, the secondary points derive their prices either direct from Duisburg, Rotterdam and the ports, or from the main centres. For calculating transport costs and therefore the difference between these various intervention prices the regulations specify that a 10-month average of freight rates should be taken. In France most medium and long hauls (over 50 miles) are made by canal or rail, both of which are fixed for inland transportation. For road rates, which are not fixed, a return load is always assumed, which gives the cereal producer an advantage by lowering the cost and thus raising the intervention price. There are no fixed rates for international barge traffic and this presents some problems for settling intervention prices in France which are derived from Rotterdam or from Duisburg or Mannheim.

The method of disposal of grain bought at intervention which is basically the same for all the agencies, is described later in this chapter. In France losses and profits on sales in relation to original purchase prices paid by the storer-purchaser are reimbursed by and paid over to ONIC respectively.

In view of the fairly exhaustive account that has been given of the intervention arrangements in France, the description which follows of the work of the national intervention agencies in the other member countries will be limited to the main differences between their practices and the French. The differences are related to organisation, including price reporting and licensing, the storage facilities available to the agency, some details of the purchasing arrangements, and the general policy towards market intervention activities for cereals in the member country in question.

In Germany the organisation responsible for intervention in the cereals market is the Einfuhr- und Vorratstelle (EVSt) für Getreide und Futtermittel whose head office is in Frankfurt. Like the other EVSt it is established under Public Law (*Anstalt der öffentlichen Rechts*) and is closely associated with the Ministry of Agriculture, which provides funds for its administrative budget. The Board of Directors (*Verwaltungsrat*) consists of 25 members representing producers, the grain trade, grain users, etc., the Chairman being an official of the Ministry of Agriculture. The Board, which only meets twice a year, has a rather nominal influence on the running of the EVSt, which effectively takes its orders from the Ministry of Agriculture. The EVSt lacks the general responsibility for cereals (statistics, quality control, some research, etc.) which ONIC still possesses and does not have the interprofessional character of the French organisation. There are six sub-offices, in Berlin, Hamburg, Duisburg, Mannheim and Bremen, each of which has a staff of about 10. Total employees of the EVSt, including head office, number about 450. Many are engaged in checking quality of cereals in store, including the German strategic stockpile which amounts to several million tons. Another activity is price reporting in which it collaborates with Zentrale Markt- und Preisberichtung (ZMP) in Bonn. The EVSt receives price reports from its sub-offices, from the large cereal importers and from a number of grain markets. These quotations are then forwarded by telex to the Commission in Brussels. Comments are included concerning any oddities in the quotations. All applications for import and export licences are handled by the EVSt, as are the receipt of the downpayments, or guarantees, which have to accompany these applications. Levies are collected by the Customs office of the port of entry. Restitutions are paid by the Hamburg Customs office known as Zollamt Jonas.

Intervention arrangements correspond to the French, except that the EVSt demands a minimum of 100 tons of any one quality in any one place. The EVSt prides itself on paying promptly for grain bought at intervention, settlement being usually made within a week of receipt. At present there are 24 main intervention points, all of which are derived direct from Duisburg with the exception of the two large grain ports, Hamburg and Bremen, and Regensburg and Passau in Bavaria, to which special intervention prices have been allotted. There are about 200 secondary points which correspond with the location of silos where the EVSt will accept delivery of grain for storage. Estimates of total grain storage capacity in Germany are inevitably inexact as the trade can if necessary make use of non-specialised facilities, old warehouses, barges, etc. Unlike ONIC the EVSt itself owns about 4 mn tons of capacity, but some 1·7 mn tons of this is at present let out to the trade on contract and about 0·3 mn tons are used for the food aid programmes. The possibility of large intervention buying has forced the EVSt to replace by other facilities the capacity that it has let out. In addition, the EVSt has extended some income guarantees to companies erecting new silos in order to secure further capacity. Clearly the creation of a balance between available storage capacity and anticipated intervention buying is very difficult for the EVSt.

German policy towards intervention in the cereals market has an ambivalent character. On the one hand the tradition of state intervention in the market is well established. There is less of the reluctance to get involved in state trading in agricultural commodities which is prevalent in the Netherlands. On the other hand the experiences of 1969 when, owing to speculation over the revaluation of the Deutschemark, storage became overburdened and markets confused, are too recent to be ignored. Besides, Germany as the largest net contributor to FEOGA must be very conscious of the costs of dealing with surpluses by intervention or other means. Government policy is now directed towards obtaining still higher prices for barley and maize so as to encourage their production in preference to wheat.

In the Netherlands intervention for cereals is handled by VIB in The Hague (see Chapter 3). Rotterdam is the sole official intervention point. Merchants are, however, free to enquire about whether VIB will accept grain at other locations and in practice unofficial intervention points were established in 1968/69, the first year when any intervention buying occurred in the Netherlands, about 100,000 tons of wheat and 50,000 tons of barley being acquired. The minimum quantity per offer has been established at 250 tons for wheat and 100 tons for rye and barley, and the minimum which can be offered at any store is 50 tons. The intervention prices derived from Rotterdam are readily calculated because most of the movement takes place by barge, the rates for which are settled at auction and are therefore publicly known.

The last enquiry into Dutch storage facilities, carried out in 1964, showed that the private merchants owned about three-quarters of the total of 2 mn tons capacity in the trade. Since then the position has changed, the co-operatives having built a number of new silos, and it is now the private sector that appears to be particularly short of storage. The position is aggravated by VIB's policy of paying for grain bought at intervention about two months after delivery. The consequence is that private merchants who are short of either storage or capital have had to sell grain on the open market in August/September at prices below the intervention level. The discount in this period of 1969 was around 5 guilders (about 55p to 90p) per ton. By contrast the co-operatives have avoided any sales of grain to VIB until the end of the season and have therefore been able to take the maximum premium on monthly increments.

As one would expect, the Dutch policy is anti-intervention, with a preference for leaving grain in the hands of the trade. The government has also aimed to keep the professional interests involved. VIB is largely an executive department of the Ministry and is not concerned with policy to any great extent. Far more influence is exerted by the interprofessional *Produktschap*, which is a closer equivalent to ONIC so far as giving advice to the government and taking part in discussions in Brussels are concerned. The *Produktschap* has a direct responsibility for deciding how and when to sell grain owned by VIB (see below).

The responsibility for market intervention for cereals in Belgium lies with the Food and Agriculture Section of the Office Belge de l'Economie et de l'Agriculture (OBEA). The present relatively small staff can mostly be explained by the arrangement whereby the Ministry of Agriculture performs all the field work on behalf of OBEA, and by the fact that OBEA does no price reporting to Brussels. There are only two official intervention points, Antwerp and Liège. OBEA pays promptly—within a month—for grain that it buys. This is quicker than the payment terms usually given by Belgian merchants, and farmers sometimes prefer to take the intervention price rather than a slightly higher price from the trade with delayed settlement.

Belgium is very short of storage capacity. The co-operatives claim that they lack the capital to make these investments, and the private merchants are similarly placed. In 1968-9 when OBEA bought some 220,000 tons at intervention, storage space could only be found for less than 180,000, and no more than 100,000 tons of this was efficient storage. Consequently,

OBEA had to take immediate steps to export the grain. The Belgian authorities would prefer a much reduced number of intervention points in other member countries, and they are critical of some of the calculations of transport costs which are used to arrive at prices at these intervention points.

Despite large increases in domestic production, Italy still draws much of its total supplies of cereals from abroad. Hence the importance in grain trading of the importers. This trade is rather highly concentrated, the two largest firms (Ferruzzi and Pagna) doing more than half the business. The major firms also trade on the internal markets in domestic grain and sell both direct to mills, and even to farmers. For this purpose they have a large number of selling agents all over the country and own some terminal elevators. There are a handful of medium-sized grain merchants, such as Mantovani, and many small firms which are tending to shrink in number as the trade becomes more concentrated.

Of the two principal buyers of cereals, the *pasta* industry has become highly concentrated and now often buys direct from farmers. Most of the important companies producing *pasta* have interests in other food processing. The compound feed industry, centred on the Po Valley, has expanded very rapidly over the past ten years and production now exceeds 3 mn tons a year. The industry is based on the by-products from *pasta* manufacture or oil-crushing and there are relatively few port mills. There is some tendency towards concentration, but there are still over 1,000 factories making compounds, most of which are small firms trading only in their immediate locality. About 15 per cent of production is in the hands of the provincial co-operatives.

The *consorzi agrari*[1] occupy a strong position in the grain trade. At the centre the Federconsorzi is a major importer of oats and maize, the latter to the extent of about half a million tons. Much of its position on the domestic market must be due to its responsibility between 1962 and 1964 for intervention buying. The *consorzi agrari* have built up a network of grain stores throughout Italy numbering over 2,000. Many of these are multi-purpose on-floor stores, which accounts for the total grain storage capacity of the Federconsorzi being higher than its annual trade. It also operates a type of contract storage system. Under this so-called *ammasso volontario* any producer wishing to participate in the scheme may receive spot price for grain delivered into store after harvest, and a subsidiary payment at the end of the season based on the Federconsorzi's average realisation price from its market operations during the course of the year.

At the beginning, from 1962 to 1964, the Federconsorzi carried out all intervention procedures on behalf of the government. During the subsequent two seasons it shared this task with other co-operatives and with private millers. Since it was set up in 1966 AIMA, the official intervention agency, has issued licences to *assuntori* (equivalent to the *stockeurs-acheteurs* in France) who purchase, store and resell intervention grain on

[1] See p. 234 for an account of these co-operative-type bodies.

its behalf, the agency subsequently reimbursing them for costs and any trading loss incurred. Although the Federconsorzi and its member *consorzi* constitute the majority of the *assuntori* a certain number of co-operatives are usually licensed as well. Nevertheless the privileged position enjoyed by the Federconsorzi during the early days of the common cereals policy, involving special access to market information, continues to be resented, and the Federconsorzi regarded with suspicion, by the private trade even though the *consorzi* are today subject to the same regulations as their fellow *assuntori*. In ensuring that these are correctly observed AIMA is handicapped by a shortage of staff, with only about 15 persons in the cereals division including inspectors. The agency would prefer a larger field staff, its local responsibilities in the administration and supervision of the deficiency payment (*integrazione di prezzo*) system for durum wheat having to be carried out on its behalf by offices of the provincial food inspectorate. For a detailed account of the working of this system the reader is referred to a description of the identical procedures used for the deficiency payments on olive oil in Chapter 10.[1]

Luxemburg's small production of cereals (about 40,000 tons each of wheat, barley and oats) is mostly marketed by private merchants, some of whom have storage facilities. The co-operative system is less well developed. The Fédération d'Achat et de Vente in the capital and Caisse Rurale in the town of West both have small silos. The largest silo is a co-operatively owned facility at Mersch in the centre of the country, where there is also a compound-feed mill. Despite Luxemburg's surplus of cereals, mostly wheat, there has been no intervention buying. A small amount of denaturing has occurred under the supervision of the Office du Blé, the organisation which would have the responsibility for any market intervention activity.

Very little has been said so far about how the agencies dispose of cereals that they have bought (or in the case of ONIC have been bought on their behalf). The reason for this is that whereas there are, as has been shown, a number of other differences between the agencies, the same procedures are followed with few exceptions when it comes to selling intervention stocks, an operation which is very closely supervised by the Commission. Three ways are used for disposing of grain bought at intervention. It can be sold back on to the domestic market, but here there is a risk that the sale will further disrupt the market. The EEC has therefore decided that the intervention agencies can only sell provided the market price is at least UA 1·50 per ton above the intervention price, and, secondly, that the sales will not disturb the market. At times when market prices are at or about intervention prices (or even below them) there is clearly very little scope for this method. The other two ways are export and denaturing, methods which are, of course, already available on a permanent basis.

[1] See pp. 211–12.

IMPLICATIONS FOR THE BRITISH MARKET

At first sight, consideration of intervention activities in the British cereals market might seem of more theoretical than practical interest. Britain is a major deficit country for cereals. Despite large increases in home production, notably of barley, imports still total around 8 mn tons a year. The question of whether intervention buying of cereals might occur in Britain following adoption of the CAP is, however, a perfectly relevant one. The reason for this will only be briefly noted since this study is concerned more with the means of intervention and similar methods used to influence the cereals market than with the situation which may create the need for using them. The very large differences between prices currently obtained by producers in the EEC countries and the guaranteed prices for cereals in Britain do provide a warning that production might rise rather steeply following adoption (over a transitional period) of the EEC price level. At the time of writing, however, it is not clear whether or not Britain will have a price structure for cereals in which intervention price levels will be derived from Duisburg.[1] This would make them somewhat lower than if they were fixed for, say, Manchester/Liverpool at the same level as for Mannheim (UA 98·75)[2] or Rotterdam (UA 98·51), taking no account of real transport costs from Duisburg to the British ports. The justification for this latter alternative would be that, like the Rhineland ports, Manchester/Liverpool would be the centre of a 'zone of major deficit' in an enlarged Community. In some respects London, considered in isolation, is another such zone, but given the large volume of cereal production in East Anglia, central southern, and southern England, the South-East as a whole could not be described as deficitary—rather the opposite. Despite the importance of London as a centre of consumption, therefore, it would hardly be logical for it to be one with a high intervention price, and certainly not as high as Manchester/Liverpool, which is not only a large consumption centre but also relatively remote from the main English production areas. If the intervention price there were set at Mannheim level, it would be perfectly logical for intervention prices at appropriate marketing centres in the production areas, Bury St Edmunds or Gainsborough say, to be derived by means of true transport costs (effectively road transport costs of, at current rates, around UA 7·00 a ton) from Manchester/Liverpool. The intervention price at London would then lie somewhere in between the two. At present EEC price levels, market prices for homegrown wheat in eastern England might therefore become established around UA 92·00–93·00, especially if the pull of continental demand in this area is taken into account. Corresponding market prices in the west and south of England, although somewhat higher, would, on the other hand, be barely high enough to attract supplies from France. Merchants in

[1] For an explanation of the system of derived intervention prices see Butterwick and Neville-Rolfe, *op cit*, p. 98.

[2] Prices in each case for soft wheat, July/August 1970. They rise by monthly increments thereafter.

the Chartres area, for instance, would find it more profitable to offer grain at intervention at Rouen, where the intervention price is UA 95·48, than to deliver to Liverpool, Avonmouth, or to southern ports such as Poole. This would clearly be an anomaly. But consideration of intervention price levels may in fact be somewhat academic. In a basically deficit region such as Britain they probably do not provide the main key to the problem of the level at which market prices are likely to become established. A peculiarity of Britain's position as an island within the EEC—though perhaps not one that ever occurred to General de Gaulle—is that no inland area is much more than a hundred miles from a port at which grain prices would come under the influence of the Community's common threshold price. This is currently UA 104·38 for wheat. The high price of imports which threshold prices imply cannot fail to affect the level of internal cereal prices even in the surplus areas of eastern England, and will certainly do so in Scotland and Northern Ireland.

There are three other relevant factors in assessing the possibility of intervention buying and its associated tools having to be made use of in Britain. First, in comparing imports with home production it is important not to lose sight of the fact that it is impossible at present to find a substitute from home production for imported hard wheat and part of the imports of maize (including maize consumed for industrial purposes and breakfast cereals). Second, the very large reduction that EEC compound feed manufacturers have achieved in the grain content of their compounds —in the Netherlands by about half—indicates that other feed ingredients would be imported in much larger quantities by Britain if the existing EEC price relationships were maintained. Third, it seems highly unlikely that there will be any significant increase in the uptake of grain in Britain by the two principal outlets, that is to say flour-milling and animal feedingstuffs, if EEC cereal prices are applied to Britain, even if they are set at the lowest possible level consistent with the CAP. The total effect of all these factors is extremely hard to quantify with any precision at all. But for our purposes it is sufficient to state that there is every reason to think that if the UK subscribes to the CAP there will be excesses of at least some cereals at some times in the season and in some places. These excesses might have to be dealt with by intervention buying. The remainder of this chapter will be concerned with examination of the problems of market intervention in cereals peculiar to Britain and with discussion of how intervention might be undertaken.

Fortunately, the question of what organisation might become responsible for cereals intervention in Britain requires very little comment. Unless the British Government opts for an umbrella organisation charged with intervention for all the relevant products (this issue is discussed in Chapter 14), it seems obvious that the Home-Grown Cereals Authority should take on this responsibility. The Authority, whose constitution provides for the possibility of market support buying, would be well suited for this purpose. The Council consists of 23 members, all appointed by the Minister, of which 9 are drawn from users of cereals and merchants, 9 are farmers, and 5 are independents, the last including the Chairman and Deputy Chairman. To date the Authority's main task has been the administration of the Forward Contract Bonus Scheme for which funds have been made available to the Authority by means of deductions from deficiency payments on wheat and barley. Administrative costs amounting to about £200,000 a year have been paid half by the Ministry and half by deduction from deficiency payments. This system proved a neat and inexpensive way of raising money until the 1970/71 season when market prices rose above the guaranteed prices, deficiency payments were no longer necessary, and these deductions could therefore not be made. While the Forward Contract Bonus Scheme has occupied most of the staff (about 50 in number), the Authority has fulfilled other functions including the operation of a price-reporting service and sponsorship of research.

At the time of writing, the future financing of the Authority is being considered by the Treasury, the Ministry of Agriculture and the Authority itself. As Government policy is now directed towards the gradual elimination of deficiency payments, the problem will have to be dealt with even if world market prices fall back from the high levels of the 1970/71 season and regardless of British membership of the EEC. The alternatives are clear-cut: the Authority's administrative costs can either be met by an increase in the contribution from the state or by the raising of income through a levy. If the latter is preferred, the levy could be collected either from growers or from merchants or from processors of cereals. To collect a levy from farmers is likely to be more cumbersome and more expensive than the other two methods.

If the HGCA became the cereals intervention agency for Britain the costs of its administration would depend on the way in which intervention was conducted (see below). Intervention activity would take the place of the administration of the Forward Contract Bonus Scheme, which may well be phased out regardless of British membership of the EEC. Initially it will be difficult to know how many staff would be required. Judging from the experiences of the intervention agencies of the existing member countries (none of which are directly comparable), it seems likely that the Authority might need to have about the same number of staff as at present and incur approximately the same total administrative costs when it operates as an EEC intervention agency. The method of meeting these costs would be at the discretion of the British Government. In ONIC's parafiscal arrangements there is a precedent for a levy. The EVSt provides a precedent for a direct grant from the government. The Authority would no doubt prefer to have its own source of income via a levy, as this tends to give any organisation of this kind a greater feeling of independence. The sum of money required is anyway not (by government standards) very large, and no doubt it would be sensible to continue with the same method of providing income as is decided upon for the Authority prior to its assumption of the EEC intervention responsibilities.

A far more important question is how intervention would be done. In Britain most grain is stored on the farm of origin and moved direct from the farm to the user. There are very few centralised grain stores operated either by co-operatives or private merchants. On-farm storage has been encouraged by government policy, notably through grants under the Farm Improvement Scheme. Failing a reversal of this policy and the construction of a number of new centralised grain stores, it would be necessary for the intervention agency to acquire cereals at the farm store. This raises at least three problems: more and smaller parcels would have to be bought; it would be difficult to ascertain reliably and accurately how much had been acquired as exact measurement of farm-stored cereals is usually impossible; and quality control would be harder.

These problems could most easily be solved if the intervention agency worked in close collaboration with recognised agents throughout the country. These agents could correspond closely with the authorised wheat merchants, who already have the important role of certifying the quality of wheat for subsidy payments, operating in conjunction with the local Wheat Committees. The merchants would buy on the authorisation of the intervention agency and subsequently be responsible for selling when so instructed. They would be compensated for costs incurred in this work, including interest costs involved in financing the purchases. Responsibility for ascertaining the quantity offered and purchased could therefore become the responsibility of these merchants acting on behalf of the intervention agency, as would also the job of checking quality at the time of purchase and ensuring that storage is adequate to prevent deterioration. Some inspectors under the direct control of the intervention agency would also be required. Without experience of the scale of intervention activity it is difficult to estimate how many staff would be needed for this purpose, but it could hardly be more than a dozen. It should be possible for some inspectors to be made available from staff at regional offices of the Ministry of Agriculture.

For cereals, as for other intervention products, it is a mistake to be too dogmatic at the initial stages as to how intervention would be conducted, how much staff would be needed, etc. The important thing is to set up a system which is inexpensive and flexible, which makes use as much as possible of existing people and facilities, and keeps the commodity, where possible, within the normal pattern of trading. With its system of on-farm storage Britain will not need to set up an elaborate network of intervention points as in France, Italy and Germany. British policy is likely to resemble the Dutch and to aim to discourage intervention buying of cereals as much as possible, and to favour disposal of local surpluses through trade channels without direct market intervention.

CHAPTER 5

Milk and Dairy Products

Adoption of the CAP for milk and dairy products has given the Six some of their worst headaches. For many reasons its adoption in the UK would also present considerable problems. In the Community as a whole milk accounts for a higher proportion of the value of gross farm output than any other single product, 19·3 per cent in 1967, the most recent year for which figures are available, ranging from 36 per cent in Luxemburg to 10·5 per cent in Italy (where horticulture accounted for a record share for any form of husbandry in any member country of 31·5 per cent). If production of beef and veal, which except in France and Italy are joint products with milk, is taken into consideration, the contribution of the dairy cow to the Community gross farm income comes close to 30 per cent. In the UK the situation is similar: sales of milk and milk products have over recent years accounted for between 21 and 23 per cent of the total value of farm sales. Beef and veal account for around 15 per cent, so that allowing for the higher proportion of these originating in single suckled herds, the overall economic importance of dairying is closely comparable to that in the EEC. The producer price of milk is thus a lively and constant political issue on both sides of the Channel, aggravated in the case of the Community by the problem of trying to ensure a decent living from milk production to several million farmers, the average size of whose herds is still only seven cows.

The cash cost of the EEC dairy policy falls mainly on the consumer and only partly on the taxpayer. The cost in wasted resources of disposing of unwanted surpluses of dairy products has also been considerable. The surpluses, mainly butter, are the combined result of, over the past five years, high intervention prices, a steady rise in average yields per cow and a very large increase in the proportion of milk delivered to dairies. Thanks to fortuitous demand from a number of Socialist countries' butter stocks had by spring 1970 declined to a level well below the gloomiest official forecasts and a dry summer has helped to keep them there. With relief the Council of Ministers seems to have considered itself exonerated from taking any immediate action to lower prices or adopt in any haste the Commission's proposals for structural reform designed to eliminate many thousands of uneconomic dairy herds. Nevertheless it may well prove that the check to the expansion of milk production which occurred in 1969 was only a temporary one. Rising yields seem likely, in the short term at any rate, to more than compensate for declining numbers of dairy cows. Indeed it is believed (and even evident to the casual observer) that in France, the member country still with the greatest potential for increased yields as well as by far the largest cow population, a fresh expansion of production is in the making thanks to a widespread raising in the past two years of Friesian replacements for cows of local dairy breeds.

Milk therefore has major political and economic implications for the future of the Community. We propose in this chapter to describe the EEC support system; to give an account of the structure of milk marketing and of the dairy industry in each of the Six; and finally to discuss what modifications of the British system might be necessary to accommodate it within the CAP.

First it is important to appreciate substantial differences between the EEC countries and Britain in the production, processing, and consumption of milk and dairy products.[1] Conditions in the three other applicant countries resemble more closely those in the Community. In Britain in 1970 there were 106,000 registered milk producers supplying a population of 55 mn. In the EEC, with a population of 186 mn, there are probably still almost 3 million holdings producing milk. Nearly 80 per cent of herds have fewer than 10 cows. Under 5 per cent have over 20. Under 1 per cent have more than 50. In England and Wales nearly 40 per cent of all cows are in herds of over 50, and although 45 per cent of herds still have under 20 cows they only comprise 16 per cent of the national total. Only in the Netherlands, where average yields per cow are also highest, 4,250 kg (905 gallons), is herd size significantly above the average for the Community. In Belgium and Germany average yields are not far below those of the UK (3,815 kg (815 gallons) in 1968/69). In France they are still relatively low (3,120 kg (665 gallons) in 1968), but rising rapidly. Thanks to the generally primitive state of dairy farming in the Centre and South, yields for Italy as a whole are the lowest in the Community (2,740 kg (585 gallons) in 1968), but in the main dairying area of the North are rather above the French level. Most of the additional output of milk between now and 1975 will be due to increased yields, mainly in France. Cow numbers are unlikely to expand very much.

Seasonality of milk supplies, being largely influenced by the demand for liquid milk, is dissimilar in the EEC and Britain, where the price incentive to produce winter milk is made much stronger. Both the depth and length of the production trough is affected. In the UK in 1968/69 the lowest monthly level of daily supplies delivered to dairies was 12 per cent below the annual mean; in the Benelux countries it was well over 30 per cent; in

[1] The statistical information used in the following paragraphs to highlight the main differences is drawn largely from the 3rd edition of *EEC Dairy Facts and Figures*, prepared by the Milk Marketing Board's Economics Division (Thames Ditton, February 1970). For fuller details of all aspects of milk production in the EEC the reader is referred to this invaluable publication.

France and Germany between 15 and 20 per cent. In the UK the trough (say, 10 per cent or more below annual mean) lasted for three months, in France and Germany for four, and in the other countries for five. In northern Italy despite a relatively high demand for liquid milk the less extreme winter climate tends to reduce the difference in production costs between winter and summer, resulting in more level all-year-round deliveries than elsewhere in the Community. Although the producer price structure is largely responsible for this differing pattern of seasonal supplies, close comparison between prices is made difficult by the generally much greater regional and local variations which go towards making up the national average in most EEC countries compared with Britain.

Price policy in Britain has a rather opposite influence over the levels of national self-sufficiency from that in the EEC. British producers are penalised for any output over 25 per cent in excess of the requirements of the domestic liquid market,[1] whereas under the Community system support from FEOGA for the very large excess of supply over liquid demand is virtually open-ended, even if at a level below that of the target price. Besides price, traditional trade patterns strongly affect self-sufficiency. Whereas in 1968 Britain only produced about half its requirements of milk, in terms of milk fats, the Community had a 10 per cent surplus.[2] France and the Netherlands are the main exporting member countries, supply and demand being approximately in balance in Germany and the US Forces in Italy alone being a net importer. Like Britain, all six countries are self-sufficient in liquid milk, apart from Luxemburg, which exports to Belgium and Germany. Even in frontier areas intra-Community exchanges are fairly exceptional. Italy has imported supplies from France in drought years.

The way in which milk is disposed of differs very considerably in Britain and the EEC, mainly as between the liquid and manufacturing markets, but also as regards the proportion delivered to dairies. Although this has been rising steadily during the past seven years, contributing to the Community's surpluses of dairy products, it still represented only 73 per cent of total production in 1968, compared with 86 per cent in the UK. In both cases, however, about half of that retained on farms is fed to livestock, the main difference between the two being the higher proportion still made into butter in the EEC (18 per cent compared with 4 per cent), and the fact that 40 per cent of what is retained on farm in the UK is consumed or sold in liquid form compared with under 30 per cent in the Community. Producer-retailers with a milk round, although rapidly disappearing, still play a proportionately more important part on this side of the Channel.

[1] See p. 105, footnote 2.
[2] This figure, which does not of course reflect the large surpluses of solids-not-fat, is likely to have been considerably exceeded in 1969 and 1970, and the situation is expected to persist until 1975 and beyond.

As far as utilisation by dairies is concerned, liquid sales, which accounted for 72 per cent in the UK in 1967, only represent 21 per cent of total intake in the EEC, ranging from 41 per cent in Italy to as little as 13 per cent in France. Just over half was made into butter and a fifth into cheese. Butter production predominates in all member countries except Italy, where cheese, representing 40 per cent of manufacturing output, is traditionally the milk product for which demand is strongest. In the Netherlands cheese absorbs almost as much milk as butter, and production of condensed milk is higher than in any other member country. Only in the Netherlands and Belgium is any substantial proportion of throughput transformed into milk powder. In Britain cheese is the principal manufactured product, followed by butter and condensed milk, but even cheese only accounts for about 10 per cent of total dairy throughput.

The EEC system

The policy for a unified market for dairy products is laid down in Regulation 804/68. No basic regulation for liquid milk and cream (section 04.01 of the CET) has yet been issued. The Commission's most recent draft[1] is still the subject of certain reservations on the part of the Special Committee on Agriculture. It would be surprising if a regulation were finally agreed and issued by the Council in time for the beginning of the 1971/72 EEC milk market year on April 1st 1971.

Under Regulation 804/68 a target price (in 1970/71 UA 10.30) per 100 kg of milk of 3·7 per cent fat content delivered at dairy is fixed, from which threshold prices are derived for butter and for pilot products of each of twelve groups of other dairy products. The derivation takes into account the quality of the milk required for the manufacture of the product in question, production costs, and the value of the fat and skim incorporated in the product. E.g. for butter the threshold price works out at UA 191·25 per 100 kg, on the basis of 1 kg of butter equalling 28·2 kg of milk at 3·7 per cent butterfat.

Import levies, consisting of the threshold price minus the lowest reported offer c.i.f., are fixed on 1st and 16th of each month. The fixing is done by the Commission on the basis of various sources of information, mainly special price bureaux which have been operating for the purpose since 1964.[2] Their information is checked against other reports from Comtel-Reuter, trade journals, and interested parties, such as, for instance, the association of Emmenthal cheese producers, who may volunteer evidence of imports at lower prices than those on which the Commission

[1] R/1874/70 (AGRI 603) Council of the European Communities, Brussels, September 24th 1970.
[2] Belgium and Luxemburg: Commission des Cotations; France: Commission Officielle de Constation des Prix; Germany: EVSt für Fette; Netherlands: Commissie Officiele Nederlandse Zuivelnoteringen; Italy: Giunta Camerale della Camera di Comercio di Milano (a trade organisation).

has been basing its recent levies. There is no facility for forward fixing of levies by importers.

Restitutions on exports are based on the difference between prices on Community and on world markets. The regulation is not precise in its definition. During the transition period leading up to the unified market in 1968 restitutions were inclined to be high, up to maximum level of the levy, since they were fixed by member countries, whose governments tended to compete on behalf of their own exporters, thus contributing considerably to the general fall in world market prices. Since 1968 there has been a single level of restitution for the whole Community regardless of differing manufacturing costs in member countries. For certain groups of products (e.g. soft cheese and whey) for which world markets operate fairly normally, no restitutions are granted on exports. For skim milk powder, butter and other bulky products a special (*exceptionnelle*) restitution may be granted if the exporter can supply clear proof that the normal restitution is insufficient to enable him to meet an offer from a third country and cover his costs and margin. This usually arises where a foreign government is inviting tenders for bulk purchase. It is very seldom that the Commission grants the full amount of the restitution requested, and the exporter's aim must be to sell the largest quantity at the least disadvantageous price. Normal restitutions have to be fixed by the Commission at least every four weeks, by Management Committee procedure (which is not required in the case of fixing levies). For certain products exporters to certain countries may pre-fix their restitution, for the current month and the following two months in the case of exports to European countries, and the following five for those with other destinations.

Intervention prices are set for butter and skim milk powder (and, in Italy only, for Grana-Padano and Parmigiano-Reggiano cheese), at which agencies will purchase at designated storage points those commodities offered to them, subject to fixed quality and other criteria, and to minimum size of lots which may be varied from country to country. There are no derived intervention prices, which are uniform throughout the Community, and no seasonal variations. As an alternative to intervention buying, subsidies are also available at a fixed rate per 100 kg plus a daily rate up to six months towards the cost of storing butter in private cold-stores (*prime de stockage*), as well as compensation for the stored butter's loss of value (*prime de dépréciation*).[1] The large stocks of unwanted butter which the intervention scheme has caused to accumulate is perhaps the most widely known single fact about the Community's agricultural policy. In the first three years of the unified market a total of 1·2 mn tons was bought at intervention in the five countries other than Italy. Disposal of these huge stocks, of which 131,000 tons still remained in store at the end of 1970, has been achieved by a variety of expedients. Apart from restitution with export to third countries the basic regulation

[1] *Stockage privé* of skim powder is allowed only 'if market conditions permit'.

only envisaged sales of ex-cold-store butter, after a minimum period, at a reduced price on internal markets. During the course of 1969 it was found necessary to introduce other means of disposal, all subsidised out of the Guarantee Section of FEOGA. These fall into three main categories: export (commercially as cocoa butter, or free as food aid through FAO); internal (to the biscuit and confectionery industry, to welfare institutions and to the armed forces, or as blending fats); and denaturing for incorporation in animal feed (see below).

In the case of dried skim, of which 418,000 tons were purchased during 1968/69 and 1969/70, and of which 92,000 tons remained in store at the end of 1970, the intervention price for roller powder (Hatmaker process accounting for about 50 per cent of German production) is set UA 3·50 below that for spray powder. Disposal of powder is by export with restitution, resale within the Community at UA 2·00 above intervention price level, sale for incorporation in pig and poultry feeds, subsidised sale for calf feed (this also applies to liquid skim), or export as animal feed after incorporation with grass and lucerne meal. In the case of sales for pig and poultry feed, stocks are open to open tender (*adjudication permanente*) on the basis of a minimum price fixed weekly by Management Committee procedure, tenders being submitted to and awarded by the Commission each week. The same system applies to denatured butter sold to compounders.

Certain basic features of the draft regulation are likely to remain incorporated in any ultimately agreed Common Market organisation for liquid milk. Sales will only be permitted in one of four forms. Raw untreated milk may be sold only by a producer on his farm. Heat-treated milk sold from dairies must be of three types only: wholemilk of not less than 3·5 per cent fat content; semi-skim milk of between 1·5 and 1·8 per cent fat content; skim milk of a minimum fat content of 0·3 per cent. All will be subject to hygienic and compositional criteria. Payment to producers must be according to quality.[1] No alteration to composition may be made by dairies except by the addition of skim or butterfat. Member states are free to fix prices, differentiated by region if they wish, for all types of liquid

---

[1] This means, effectively, payment according to fat content. The first-hand purchaser of milk will therefore pay a higher price for all milk with a fat content exceeding the minimum of 3·5 per cent. In Britain this is only done in the case of Channel Islands milk, which is then sold to the consumer at a correspondingly higher price. There will be nothing to prevent this differential from being maintained in the EEC. Since at present all other milk receives the pool price regardless of any percentage of fat above the legal minimum which it may contain, it can be resold by the Board at a uniform price without loss. Once differential payments to producers for all milk (and not only Channel Island) are introduced, however, the Board, or other first-hand buyer, would be bound to incur a loss unless the extra fat which it had paid for were removed before the milk were resold at a uniform price, and the fat content reduced to a uniform 3·5 per cent. The value of the surplus fat can then be realised in the form of butter. At likely levels of national milk consumption in the late seventies this standardisation could in the view of the Board's Economics Division result in an additional output of some 20,000–25,000 tons of butter a year.

milk 'provided (their) free circulation within the Community is not impeded'.

The regulation is, by Community standards, a simple one. However, a number of substantial differences of national opinion on the draft regulation remain unresolved. The Commission's wish to define by means of subsequent regulations the conditions governing the clause about price fixing and free circulation is opposed by most member countries. The Working Party had already had removed from an earlier draft of the regulation a clause defining the three components of which maximum prices were to consist: (a) the average price of manufacturing milk in the region concerned, (b) the cost of any special treatment by producers, dairies and retailers, necessary to the marketing of liquid milk, and (c) an additional sum sufficient to encourage them to undertake such treatment. Second, application of the regulation should, in the French view, await agreement of a common regulation on the health aspects of liquid-milk marketing. These, it is considered, should be clearly distinguished from the aspects concerning compositional quality. Without simultaneous harmonisation of health regulations conditions for a truly free circulation of milk would not be met. Third, the Italian government is not satisfied with certain details of the special provision that wholemilk produced in southern Italy should have a permitted fat content of only 3·2 per cent. The French delegation has taken the view that any such exception should in any case be limited in time.

Pending an eventual consensus on the draft regulation, agreement on two other aspects of milk marketing has been reached. First, zoning has been ended in all member countries except Italy, where it will be allowed to continue until the end of 1972. All producers are free to deliver milk to any dairy. Dairies are no longer obliged to collect from a restricted area. Second, it has been established that, subject to national health regulations, bulk milk in road tankers of not less than 5,000 litres (1,100 gallons) capacity, shall be permitted to transport milk across intra-Community frontiers. Although it is possible for health regulations effectively to nullify such liberty of movement it must be reckoned a step of sorts towards the establishment of a unified market, and away from a concept, which has been aired in France at any rate, of setting up a series of more or less autonomous supply zones (*bassins d'approvisionement*). Such a system would, of course, have isolated a large liquid market like that of Paris from distant sources of supply, and given protection to the dairies which are already finding the supply of the city unremunerative. It should be stressed, however, that sterilised milk, being a product subject to Regulation 804/1968, may circulate quite freely in the EEC. As elsewhere, the development of a long-keeping ultra-heat-treated milk with a taste acceptable to a majority of consumers could have a revolutionary effect on the marketing of liquid milk in the Community.

THE MARKET STRUCTURE IN THE EEC[1]

Belgium

The 25 per cent increase in producer prices between 1962 and 1965 involved in adopting the Community target price for milk had only a very gradual effect. Indeed, total output in 1968 had after two or three years' recession barely recovered to its 1963 level. The proportion delivered to dairies had, however, risen from 55 per cent to 74 per cent during the five years. The effect of prices, assuming they remained at their present level, and of improved techniques (Belgium already has the second highest average yields in the Community) during the early seventies is expected to be to a considerable extent compensated by the disappearance of small, and especially of part-time, herds. Projections of national output for 1975 range between 104 per cent and 110 per cent of the 1968 level.[2] By EEC standards Belgians are average milk drinkers, just over a quarter of national production being consumed in liquid form. The liquid milk market is characterised by the relatively large number of producer retailers, who still account for nearly a quarter of liquid sales. House-to-house delivery in the larger cities is widespread, but a recent enquiry indicated a low level of profitability and scope for a substantial degree of rationalisation.[3] The trend in consumption has, however, been downward during the sixties, while that of cream and condensed milk has been increasing. The relatively high level of butter consumption is likely to decline or remain stagnant, but demand for cheese will rise substantially.

There has been considerable concentration in the dairy industry since the war. There are now about 140 dairies, whose ownership is divided about half and half between the private and co-operative sector, but with the volume of deliveries in favour of the latter (about 60 per cent), which in the North are closely linked with the Boerenbond, the Flemish-speaking farmers' union. The linguistic boundary also to some extent follows that between the two distinct forms of dairy production in Belgium. In French-

[1] J. Gay, *Structure et évolution de l'industrie de transformation du lait dans la EEC* (Informations Internes sur l'Agriculture No. 34, EEC Commission, Brussels, 1968) provides an exhaustive and, to the extent that the various national statistics permit, comparative analysis of the dairy industries in the EEC countries. Unfortunately most of the data is no more recent than 1965, since when the industry's structure has continued its rapid process of change. Where possible this has been illustrated by more recent information, much of it obtained in the course of private conversations in the member countries.

[2] H. Schmidt et al, *Aggregation of future demand and supply for agricultural products in the ECC 1970–1975*, Ifo-Institut für Wirtschaftsforschung, Munich, 1969.

Vernon L. Sorenson and Dale E. Hathaway, *The grain-livestock economy and trade patterns of the EEC, with projections to 1970 and 1975* (Michigan State University, Institute of Agricultural Research, Report No. 5, East Lansing, 1968).

Agricultural projections for 1975 and 1985. Production and consumption of major foodstuffs (OECD, Paris, 1968).

[3] A. Verkinderen and H. de Baere, *La distribution des produits laitiers en Belgique* (Cahiers de l'IEA, No. 39/R13, Ministry of Agriculture, Brussels, 1965).

speaking Wallony, where average herd size (9 to 10 cows) is larger than in Flanders, there is a much higher level of on-farm use, deliveries to dairies being mainly in the form of cream. In 1964 two-thirds of deliveries were in this form. Sixty per cent of cheese production (mainly Gouda, but some Cheddar and a growing proportion of cream cheese) takes place in Flanders. Concentration in both regions is greater than the number of dairies would suggest, many of them (including the co-operatives) having little autonomous existence and virtually serving as collecting centres for the 25 or so second-tier co-operatives and 15 private firms which are likely to emerge from a further series of mergers now in progress. Although producers have been nominally free to change dairies since the end of the war the *status quo* tended until 1968 to be frozen by a system of near-guaranteed area prices (*prix de direction*). Competition for new customers was thus only along the margin, the co-operatives paying a bit over the odds in the form of rebates, and private firms retaliating to some extent with quality premia, collection bonuses and suchlike. The advent of the CAP has had two contradictory effects. The possibility of offering all surpluses to intervention has on the one hand retarded the development of vigorous marketing attitudes. On the other hand it has opened up opportunities for export to other EEC countries, as well as stimulated rationalisation in face of increasing imports from them. We learned from the chief provision buyer of the largest Belgian food multiple that there was a rising demand for French butter in preference to Belgian. There seem, however, to be good prospects for delivery of Belgian sterilised milk on the Paris market. Since there is little scope for reducing producer prices, economies in distribution and manufacture are being forced upon the dairies. In Wallony, for instance, the co-operative Société Beurrière d'Ardennes has recently concentrated production of its ILA brand butter into two factories, one of which, at Recogne, will be a modern plant, said to be one of the largest in the Community, with an annual output of 6,000 tons of butter and 25,000 tons of milk powder. It is also diversifying into yoghurt and other fresh products.

Intervention is administered by OBEA.[1] Butter is either purchased by the agency, in minimum lots of one ton, for deposit in stores hired by OBEA, or may be stored privately, OBEA paying storage and depreciation costs as laid down in the EEC regulations. Judging from the volume of butter involved in 1968 and 1969, the second method appears to be preferred by the trade. Of the 39,000 tons of dried skim purchased by the agency during 1969 about three quarters was resold, mainly to the animal feed industry (at BFr 5·50 per kg, against a purchase price of BFr 22·0 per kg). Relatively little was exported, and OBEA have not been much involved in the open tender system of disposal.

In Belgium the Office Nationale du Lait (ONL), financed about half from levies paid by producers and the trade and half by the Ministry of Agriculture, is a parastatal organisation, with an interprofessional

[1] See pp. 38-9.

majority on its Board of Management, charged with inspection of dairies, licensing of wholesalers, quality control of milk and dairy products, etc. It also supervises the commodity market in dairy products.

The Netherlands

The Netherlands differ from other EEC countries in a number of important respects. Their cows have the highest yields, their average herd size is much the largest (15 cows), and a smaller proportion of milk (7 per cent) is retained on farms than in any other country. Cow numbers have risen steadily since 1964, and with yields, despite their already high level, also marginally higher than six years ago, total output has been moving steadily towards the 8 mn ton mark. Projections for 1975 have ranged between 7·7 mn and 8·4 mn tons.[1] Except for condensed milk, of which consumption per head (10·7 kg in 1969) could well reach the level of 12·0 kg projected by OECD, no marked increase in demand for any form of dairy product is anticipated except as a function of population growth. Consumption per head of liquid milk has been falling and that of butter was already down to 2·8 kg by 1969, the level projected by OECD for 1975. By then there is a general consensus that the Netherlands will have a surplus equivalent to around 3·5 mn tons of milk.

The spur of the export market has led to much rationalisation of processing, especially in the North. The structure of the country's dairy industry is largely determined by its geography. In the northern and eastern provinces the bulk of raw milk goes to manufacturing (as much as 95 per cent in Friesland), whereas dairies in the West and South are mainly engaged in supplying liquid milk to the conurbations of the seaboard. The liquid market absorbs about 20 per cent of supplies, including the rather high proportion of sterilised milk. The Netherlands is the only member country in which retail sales are still predominantly by house-to-house delivery, by means of a highly rationalised system from which consumer choice of dairyman has been largely eliminated. Seasonality of liquid supplies is mainly assured by summer and winter price differentials wider than anywhere else in the Community. But recourse is also necessary during the trough to an open market for accommodation milk purchased, sometimes at a relatively high premium, from the North, where price incentives to winter production are negligible. These purchases consist partly of skim imported in order to standardise fat content, which tends to be higher than the 3·5 per cent standard in winter. Three-quarters of liquid consumption in the Netherlands is covered by fewer than 60 dairies, most of which specialise in liquid sales and fresh products and a majority have an annual throughput of 30 mn litres (6 mn gallons) or more. They are predominantly private firms. However, one of the largest co-operatives, CMC, has contributed to the concentration of the industry not only by absorbing or federating with small co-operatives but

[1] See footnote 2, p. 86 for sources.

also by taking shares in a large number of private firms and forcing their amalgamation.[1]

In 1968 there were 347 dairy establishments receiving milk, of which about a quarter had an annual intake of over 30 mn litres (6 mn gallons) and accounted for well over half of total national throughput. Nearly 80 per cent of milk produced passes through co-operatives, which predominate in butter and cheese manufacture. They account for over two-thirds of milk powder and whey powder production, about 50 per cent of condensed milk, including the big condensery at Leeuwarden, and just over 40 per cent of liquid supplies. The incentive to producers close to the liquid markets of the seaboard to join co-operatives is less than in the North. Many have been able to enjoy the benefits of CMC's countervailing power without having to submit to its discipline. Private interests are chiefly active in the production of spray powder, ice-cream and cream cheeses. But even in the private sector about a third of the 100-odd dairies are operated with an element of producer participation. The very large enterprise is dominant in the private and mixed sector, CMC being one example, in which two-thirds of the dairies have a throughput of over 30 mn litres.

Intervention in the Netherlands is carried out by VIB[2] in close collaboration with the *Produktschap* for dairy products, which also handles demands for restitutions and issues certificates when they are granted.

Luxemburg

Increases in both cow numbers and yields have resulted in an unequivocally upward trend in milk production during the past decade. The proportion delivered to dairies has also risen sharply, from 84 per cent in 1963 to 92 per cent in 1968, almost as high as in the Netherlands. There are no projections of future output and consumption separate from those made for the BLEU.

As a result of official pressures and incentives to rationalisation nearly 200 dairies disappeared during the fifties, so that by 1961 90 per cent of raw milk was already passing through three co-operative dairies, Laduno in the North, Luxlait in the Centre, and Celula in the South. Since 1968 the co-operatives have been paying a pool price negotiated centrally by Central-marketing under the auspices of the Centrale Paysanne Luxembourgeoise (CPL). Just under a quarter of national output is consumed either as milk (14 per cent) or cream (8 per cent). Pasteurisation is compulsory except for raw milk sold at farm-gate. House-to-house delivery is strictly zoned. Cream, butter and cheese production is concentrated in the northern part of the country. Half of the market for cream and between 40 per cent and 55 per cent of yoghurt and cheese, depending

[1] *The Coöperative Melkcentrale, The Hague* (MMB, Economics Division, Thames Ditton, September, 1967), p. 7.
[2] See pp. 40–1.

on the variety, is claimed by the only private dairy, Ekabe. Having entered into exclusive contracts with about 500 producers in the North this hustling enterprise provides a useful spur to the economic efficiency of the dominant co-operatives.

The equivalent of about half of Luxemburg's milk production is exported, mainly to Belgium. Butter, being of high quality, seems to find a ready market, especially for blending. Summer surpluses have sometimes been transferred at government expense to Belgian co-operative stores for resale during the winter. Ekabe deliver surpluses of manufacturing milk by bulk tanker to ILA's factory at Recogne. The Luxemburg co-operatives do not view a free market for liquid milk with any apprehension. Indeed, they are confident that its known high quality, which has earned them a contract to supply the US forces in Germany, gives them good prospects for exporting it, especially to the neighbouring Saar.

Before the Protocol arrangements[1] ceased to operate on May 1st 1970 the government subsidies to butter storage were paid direct by the Service des Laiteries of the Ministry of Agriculture. Future intervention buying, if any, would be carried out by two officials of the Ministry's Service d'Economie Rurale.

Italy

Three features clearly distinguish dairying in Italy from that in the other member countries. The first is its very uneven geographical dispersion. Well over 90 per cent of cows' milk is produced north of the Apennines, and mainly in the four regions comprising the North's central and eastern plain. In the Centre and South of the country and the Islands production of cows' milk is confined almost entirely to the coastal areas, with sheep and goats' milk predominating in the hills and mountains. Second, cheese, of which Italy is the world's third largest producer, is the key product in the manufacturing industry. It accounts for a third of total milk production and for 40 per cent of dairy output. Less than 20 per cent of the milk passing through dairies is made into butter, much of it the lower quality whey butter (*burro di affioramento*) that is a by-product of the Grana cheese-making process. Third, a far higher proportion of dairy supplies than in any other member country, over 40 per cent, goes to the liquid market.

The sharp division between North and South distorts the significance of the statistics for the country as a whole. The national yield, for instance, is, at around 2,800 kg (600 gallons) per cow, far the lowest in the Community, and in no way reflects the generally high level of technical efficiency already reached in Lombardy and some of the other northern regions. The average will therefore rise only slowly as yields in the Centre

[1] See pp. 39–40.

and South gradually improve. Nor will cattle numbers tend greatly to increase. Unlike other EEC countries Italy does not have a preponderance of those herds of between 5 and 20 cows upon whose owners there tends to be the greatest economic pressure to expand. The numbers of very small, small, and larger herds are about equally balanced. A likely consequence of this better structure is that in Italy the disappearance of very small herds of under 5 cows will only be slightly more than compensated, over the next five years, by additions to herds in the 5 to 20 and over 20 size groups. The level of total production will probably therefore not exceed 11 mn tons by 1975. It averaged 9·8 mn tons in 1966–8. Prospects for increased per head consumption, especially of liquid milk, are, on the other hand, more favourable than in other parts of the Community, particularly in the South and Islands, where improved communications, rising living standards, the spread of the milk-drinking habit among the families of former emigrants to other parts of Europe, and the elimination of climatic obstacles to, and improved facilities for the distribution of, sterilised milk should all contribute to a rising demand for cows' milk.

The level of liquid consumption is at present closely related to both the density of population and to the pattern of production. 60 per cent of liquid sales are concentrated in four northern regions which comprise nearly 40 per cent of the total population, three of these coinciding with three of the four major producing ones. The supply of liquid milk is subject to a system of zoning which dates back to 1929 and was introduced in order to promote the sale of safe and hygienic milk. Although, under the EEC regulations, this system is due to come to an end by the beginning of 1972, its past effects have been sufficiently marked on milk marketing in Italy for its future disappearance to have perceptible consequences, and a brief account of it seems therefore appropriate. Each of the so-called white zones (*zone bianche*) at present established in and around 44 cities on the mainland and in Sicily has a single *centrale di latte* (central milk processing organisation) with a monopoly of sales of the liquid wholemilk (including sterilised) within the zone. The *centrale* is obliged to accept all milk offered to it by producers in the zone, who may, however, deliver to manufacturers (both inside and outside the zone) if they prefer. The abolition of zoning will lay open the *centrali* to competition from liquid dairies outside the zones. On the other hand it will free them of the obligation, and inconvenience, of accepting all milk, and becoming embarrassed with residual supplies at times of surplus production. It will enable them to plan and rationalise their throughput by means of contracts with producers. Unfortunately most of the *centrali* are ill-prepared to meet the conditions of a free market. About half of them are under the control of the local authorities, many of which have for some time past been subsidising their inefficient operation out of the rates. The Rome *centrale* notoriously contributes to the city council's already substantial deficit, its overstaffed offices allegedly constituting a useful source of minor political patronage.

Of the remaining 22 *centrali* 10 are run by private companies and 12 are co-operatives.

Generally speaking it is considered that the removal of zoning could have nothing but a beneficial effect, in the case of the municipal monopolies at any rate. Some of the co-operatives appeared apprehensive, complaining of unfair price-cutting inroads already made by outsiders in the sales of low-fat and skim milk, over which the monopoly of the *centrali* does not extend. On the other hand we were assured that a number of the more thrusting producer co-operatives were eagerly awaiting the opportunity of establishing processing dairies within the erstwhile white zones in competition with *centrali,* or of taking over and running more efficiently the installations of the *centrali* themselves. Some of the stronger co-operatives are already able to exert considerable bargaining power over their local *centrale* over price, playing it off against other *centrali,* or even, at times of cyclical milk shortage, against manufacturers. Indeed at such times *centrali* are often obliged to buy in depot supplies of liquid milk from outside their zone, even from abroad. The *comitato prezzi* which under the guidance of an interministerial price control committee is responsible in each province for fixing maximum retail prices and distributive margins, is motivated mainly by considerations of the cost of living, though not to the extent of threatening producer interests by lowering prices at times of glut. In 1968 the Parma *centrali* was having to bring milk from France at Lit. 80/litre (including freight costs of Lit. 17 from Normandy), the target price at farm-gate being Lit. 61, because local producers were being offered Lit. 100 by cheese factories.

The milk price cycle, a phenomenon seldom encountered outside Italy, is linked to cyclical movements in the price of Grana-Padano cheese, as well as to the pig cycle. This is now (1970/71) in a price trough, but at its previous peak in 1969/70 coinciding with a reduction in imports into Italy from Eastern Europe (itself part cyclical but also structurally connected to rising living standards in the Socialist countries), the cycle exercised a strong upward pressure on the price which Italian cheese manufacturers were bidding for raw milk supplies. This reflected the higher marginal return obtainable from the whey-fattened pigs which are a joint product of cheesemaking in most Italian factories. Some were paying up to Lit. 120/litre during the early part of 1970. Of the expected average return to producers of Lit. 80/litre for the 1969/70 year some Lit. 10 to 15 would be attributable to the pig price element. In 1968, with a glut of cheese dating from an earlier trough period of pig prices, factories were paying as little as Lit. 50/litre. As milk prices fall in sympathy with pig prices, cheese factories are again encouraged to increase the volume of their purchases of raw milk and thus of production of the local long-maturing Grana (known generically as Parmesan in Britain) and Provolone cheeses. Since the maturing process takes from one to two years the effect of any consequent excess supply, and falling prices, of cheese is correspondingly lagged.

In some areas co-operatives store and market as much as 50 per cent of their output. In others, notably Emilia, the majority of cheeses are traditionally sold for maturing to specialist storage firms (*staggionatori*) with access to the necessary finance. Indeed, many of them have close ties with banks. The mature cheeses are marketed through the storers' own selling organisations. Recent high interest rates have tended to circumscribe the activities of these wholesalers, and co-operatives (often second-tier ones formed for the purpose) have been undertaking a greater share of storage, not always with conspicuous financial success.

The dairy industry is still highly fragmented, and concentration, as in most other fields of food processing, wholesaling and retailing in Italy, has been relatively slow. At present there are only five enterprises marketing dairy products (including sterilised milk) on a national scale, three private companies, Galbani, Invernizzi and Locatelli (a Nestlé subsidiary), and, next in order of importance, with a daily throughput of its two plants of 300,000 litres (66,000 gallons), Polenghi-Lombardo, in which the Federconsorzi purchased a 99 per cent interest in 1951. The largest co-operative, Soresina, comes a close fifth. The total number of collecting dairies, 3,365 in 1967 according on one source,[1] has apparently not been greatly reduced since the 1961 census of businesses recorded 3,647 dairy enterprises, of which only 11 per cent were employing more than 10 persons and 77 per cent were employing fewer than 5. The manufacturing sector is equally fragmented, with over 1,800 factories (including 1,300 independent co-operatives) making Grana cheese alone. Only 3 per cent of them had an annual throughput of more than 1·5 mn litres (330,000 gallons). Possibly no major rationalisation will occur in cheesemaking until imports of cheese from elsewhere in the EEC, particularly of Emmenthal, begin seriously to compete in price and taste. Not only is the structure of production excessively fragmented, but there is a plethora of varieties, shapes, and qualities. There are said to be 40 different types of Gorgonzola alone. Only in Emilia do the co-operatives appear to have succeeded in imposing quality standards, mainly for export purposes, for Parmigiano-Reggiano, the regional type of Grana.

Since the coming into force of the unified market for dairy products AIMA has been obliged to make intervention purchases of cheese. The bulk of the 13,000 tons bought in 1968 had been resold in five lots, by tender, on the Community market by the middle of 1969. It is noteworthy that on three other occasions tenders were made for purchase of stocks for export to third countries, but none were considered by the Commission to be sufficiently high.

France

France is the world's third largest producer of milk after the USSR and the USA, and has the fourth highest output of dairy products after those

[1] IRVAM (Istituto per le Ricerche e le Informazioni di Mercato e la Valorizzazione della Produzione Agricola).

countries and the Federal German Republic. After stagnating between 1964 and 1966 the number of dairy cows increased during the following two years, but fell back again slightly in 1969, to 8·7 mn, probably as the result of culling of lower-yielding animals. Indeed, yields per cow have risen steadily throughout the decade, though at just over 3,000 kg (640 gallons) they are the lowest in the Community outside Italy. In 1967, 70 per cent of farms in France had dairy enterprises and the average size of herd was 8 cows, only 5 per cent of cows being in herds of over 30 cows. Over 40 per cent of dairy cows are, however, located on farms of between 50 and 125 acres. About 36 per cent of total output of milk was still retained on farms in 1968, but ten years earlier the proportion was 53 per cent.

The main areas of milk production lie in the West and North-West of the country, deliveries to dairies being concentrated in Lower Normandy, Poitou-Charentes, Brittany, and Pays de la Loire. Well over half the establishments processing over 50,000 gallons of milk a day are located in these regions, and the first three regions account for over 60 per cent of French butter output. Cheese production is also concentrated geographically, in eastern France, though Normandy and Cantal are also important centres for soft paste and mountain cheeses.

OECD forecast that by 1975 cow numbers would not have greatly increased beyond the 1965 level of 7·2 mn. They had in fact risen by over 7·3 mn by 1968. It is, however, possible that the disappearance of small herds in the early seventies will more than compensate for the increasing size of large ones. Average yields, on the other hand, are certain to rise steadily towards the 4,000 litre (880 gallon) mark, giving a total output of not less than 29 mn tons of milk by 1975.[1] Although some further increase in the already high level of per head consumption of butter is considered possible, and even a slight rise in that of cheese, liquid-milk consumption is expected to continue downwards. These trends present a challenge to the French dairy industry to intensify its marketing efforts outside France.

As in most other EEC countries there has been a marked concentration over the past five years at all levels of the industry other than that of production. There was certainly scope for it. In 1965 out of 3,900 dairies, including some 600 serving as depots only, just under 80 per cent were collecting an average of under 3 mn litres (0·66 mn gallons) a year. A quarter of them were collecting under 180 gallons a day. Only 40 per cent had an annual throughput of over 25 mn litres (5·5 mn gallons). Seventy per cent which employed under 5 persons each accounted for under 5 per cent of total turnover.

If precise statistics were available for 1970 it is possible that numerically the reduction since 1965 would not appear very startling. This would, however, belie the organisational changes which have been taking place, especially in the co-operative sector. There are still about 2,600 co-operatives, but half of these are small traditional *fruitières* manufacturing Gruyère cheese in mountain areas. The remainder are divided

[1] See footnote 2, p. 86 for sources.

about half and half between milk processing and manufacturing. Co-operatives account for just over 40 per cent of liquid-milk distribution, a slightly higher proportion of butter manufacture, and about 30 per cent of cheesemaking. The main change of direction has been a move away, for marketing purposes, from the traditional pyramidal concept of local co-operatives grouped in regional and national federations. In the past, local independence has been so strong that regional unions were often little more than the residual recipients of their constituent co-operatives' surpluses. Recently, however, a few central co-operative marketing agencies of national, and, increasingly, international, significance have emerged, cutting across the formalised legal and political structures of unions and federations, and demanding of the first-tier co-operatives absolute discipline in the supply of specific products or groups of products. The aims and methods of enterprises such as Sodima-Yoplait (marketing fresh products), Fromançais (butter and cheese) and Gama (fresh products marketed under the brand name Nova), are avowedly commercial.

A major aim of the co-operative groups has been to overcome the built-in disadvantage from a purely commercial point of view, compared with private industry, of their close association with the producers of the basic raw materials of their industry. It is significant that whereas they have had access to 40 per cent of raw milk supplies, their sales have represented only 30 per cent of the total turnover of the French dairy industry. Apart from the sheer market inertia of local co-operatives, there are two important causes of this state of affairs. First, government policy, and since 1964 Community policy, has tended to discourage diversification by providing an assured, if only modest, return from manufacture of basic products like butter and skim powder. With the intervention agency ready to purchase in bulk there has been a minimum of incentive even to undertake the additional effort of packaging and branding. Second, co-operatives have generally been operating on a scale quite insufficient to generate the necessary resources to finance the research and marketing effort essential for undertaking product innovation and sales promotion, quite apart from being able to command economies of scale in actual manufacture.[1] The importance to the co-operative movement of the development of the groups is evident from the fact that even the largest co-operative had a turnover of no more than Fr 600 mn ($110 mn) in 1968, and the next two of between Fr 300 mn and Fr 400 mn. That of the thirty leading dairy co-operatives averaged about Fr 120 mn ($22 mn). Resources on this scale do not compare with those available, for instance, to the soft drinks/dairy products group Perrier-Sapiem, which has recently swallowed up Genvrain and Fromages Bel, giving it a combined turnover of Fr 3 bn ($550 mn), or to a company like Gervais-Danone. Yoplait, the largest, representing a throughput of 984,000 litres (216,000 gallons) a day, comprises ten im-

[1] The results of an analysis of the economics of dairy product processing in France by a research team under D. Hairy of the Institut National de la Recherche Agronomique (INRA) are expected to be published shortly.

portant regional co-operatives and unions, including such large enterprises as UCALM at Le Mans, Riches Monts at Clermont Ferrand, CLARA at Amiens, and the Coopérative Laitière Centrale de Paris. Over 80 per cent of GAMA's 876,000 litre (190,000 gallons) daily throughput is accounted for by Prospérité Fermière of Arras and Union Laitière du Poitou. Union Laitière Normande (over 500,000 litres—110,000 gallons) supplies 80 per cent of that of Fromançais.

Apart from numerous regional mergers between co-operatives, another recent development has been the acquisition by co-operatives (some of them members of the three major groups) of interests in private firms. Colarena of Nantes has a 34 per cent holding in Frigecrème, France's third manufacturer and distributor of ice-cream. At Lyons ORLAC, one of the Yoplait co-operatives, and France-Lait, which specialises in milk powder, condensed milk, and sterilised cream, have acquired shares in Vivalp & Martens, with a turnover of Fr 200 mn ($ 36 mn) and interests in a wide range of dairy products, including all types of liquid milk, as well as in animal feed. In the Centre region Centre-Lait and Grégoire & Fils are concentrating their production and marketing resources.[1] The co-operative groups have also embarked on the difficult task of developing transnational relationships, Yoplait with the Swiss Union Laitière Vaudoise for the manufacture and distribution of fresh products under its brand name, Fromançais with the BEZ-Nordmark German co-operative group.

Although it would be an exaggeration to suppose that French co-operatives had, during the space of five years, been purged of parochialism, there is no doubt that in the dairy sector they have managed to build up a substantial degree of countervailing power in face of a parallel trend towards the formation of increasingly large, and frequently transnational, units in the private sector. In addition to the pooling of resources achieved by mergers inside France a number of private firms have access to the research and development facilities and investment capital of the international corporations which have acquired shareholdings, sometimes majority shareholdings, in them. Nestlé Alimentana has a 20 per cent interest, for instance, through its French subsidiary SOPAD, in Chambourcy, whose fresh products are acquiring an international reputation. Nestlé also has an interest, whose extent remains unknown, in Roustang-Jaillon, and a controlling one in Grosjean, the third largest manufacturers in France of processed cheese. During 1968 and 1969 Unilever, through its subsidiary Astra-Calvé, also acquired control of three firms, mainly manufacturing fresh products, with a wide geographical spread, La-Roche-Aux-Fées of Nantes, Rousset of Lyons, and Cazajus in the South-West.

This growing concentration of manufacturing demand will exert an

[1] Acquisition by co-operatives of controlling interests in limited liability companies has given rise to a number of problems, not all of them yet by any means resolved. How far, for instance, should a parent co-operative become involved in the management of a subsidiary company? This question has been highlighted in two recent cases where companies (one of them controlled by ULN) have got into severe financial difficulties.

increasing pressure in favour of rationalisation of local collection and depoting of raw milk during the coming decade, which will inevitably be felt at the level of the producer as well. The degree of competition between co-operatives and the private sector varies a good deal from one part of the country to another. Producer prices are, however, usually the subject of an *accord professionnel* between the co-operatives, the private creameries and the producers, who are represented not by the co-operatives themselves, but by the *syndicat*, the local departmental branch of the farmers' union. A *prix de base*, pool price delivered dairy, is agreed, to which premia for quality, etc., and bonuses (reflecting in the case of members of co-operatives a share of the profits, may be added. The co-operatives frequently have a dominant voice, so that where a co-operative covers a wider area than a single department the basic price may run there as well. Both private and co-operative dairies have at times been inclined, where competition between them is keen, to take on too many customers, thus accumulating surpluses of butter or skim powder, which they would merely dispose of at intervention. FORMA has tried to discourage this by cutting off investment grants to enterprises which consistently sell large quantities at intervention. Efforts to persuade those with surplus milk to transfer it to others with deficits have not met with a great deal of success. In practice it has been difficult to agree a price for accommodation supplies that would fairly represent their opportunity cost to the vendor. Since deficits anyway tend to arise during the trough, those firms which have spare supplies are usually anxious to avoid any risk of causing their staff and plant to be under-employed by cutting their supplies too fine.

In Normandy transport is now fully pooled between the co-operative and private sectors. Where the two still exist side by side the co-operatives claim to have the lower collection costs per litre. It seems, however, that there is still scope for considerable rationalisation in areas like western France where the co-operatives are dominant. Producers tend to cling with excessive loyalty to societies whose throughput and radius of collection no longer has any economic reality. Second-stage collection, on the other hand, often yields considerable economies of scale. We visited one SICA,[1] Union Laitière des Deux-Sèvres et du Centre Ouest (Technolait), whose milk-drying plant with a daily throughput of between 70,000 and 90,000 gallons of skim, serves 18 constituent butter-making co-operatives within a radius of under 50 miles. The bulk of its output, denatured into calf feed, is marketed nationally through ULN, but a proportion is resold locally.

In an industry in which manufacturing interests are predominant, and being geared increasingly to export, satisfaction of liquid demand, which, including cream, absorbs only about 17 per cent of total production in France, presents problems. Very nearly half is still supplied by producer-retailers, far the highest proportion in any member country. The distribution system is thus ill-adapted to supplying the big cities, especially those remote from the main milk-producing areas. A certain stimulus to

[1] Socéité d'intérêt Collectif Agricole. See p. 236.

efficiency in retailing is however being provided by the supermarkets which are stocking an increasingly wide assortment of fresh dairy products, including milk; substantial discounts are offered, as well as special offers, such as a period of free delivery, and milk is even used as a loss leader. Although retail margins are not controlled, distributors claim that maximum retail prices fixed for each department by the local *préfêt* are set too low to provide any incentive to improve their efficiency. The prices do in fact reflect the distance of the consumption from the production areas, the lowest (in the West) being about 25 per cent below the highest (along the Mediterranean seaboard). Largely owing to the long distances involved there is no flourishing market for depot supplies such as exists in the Netherlands, and, for reasons already mentioned, those with surpluses find it less trouble to retain their entire intake and sell any surpluses to intervention as butter or skim powder.

The supply of Paris presents a major headache. At the time of the take-over by Perrier-Sapiem of Genvrain there appeared to be a risk that Société des Fermiers Réunis (SAFR), a Genvrain subsidiary, might disappear altogether in the course of the operation, leaving 60 per cent of the Paris market unsupplied. The balance of demand is at present met by the co-operatives. Paradoxically one of the main motives influencing the Crédit Agricole (CNCA) to take a 15 per cent share in the new private group was to help ensure the continued existence of SAFR. This would prevent a larger share of the unremunerative business of furnishing Paris with liquid milk from falling to the CNCA's client co-operatives, who might have been tempted to take it on. SAFR continue in the meantime to press for an increase in the maximum retail price. It is possible that, in conjunction with a determined effort on the part of distributors supplying the big cities to cut costs, the government may be persuaded to subsidise them for a period.

Between 50 and 75 per cent of the liquid demand is in the North and East of France. In the meantime a big merger in the co-operative sector is planned in order to co-ordinate liquid supplies in the Massif Central and the South-West. A so-called Société du Littoral, drawing on the production of four major French co-operative unions, as well as of others from Luxemburg, Germany and Switzerland, would retail 500,000 litres (110,000 gallons) a day (and attempt to establish a brand name for its milk), mainly along the French Mediterranean coast, where an increasing urban and tourist population could provide a growth market.

FORMA is the agency responsible for applying the EEC regulations in France. In practice its dairy products division, employing 10 persons, is mainly concerned with policy aspects, and also handles applications for restitutions. All intervention buying and connected procedures, including tendering for intervention stocks, and denaturing for animal feed, is delegated to Interlait.[1] In France minimum lots for offering to intervention are 5 tons for butter and 20 tons for skim powder for a price delivered in

[1] See p. 45.

store up to a maximum of 100 km. 500,000 tons have been purchased since 1968 and there were 53,000 tons in store on December 31st 1970.

Germany

The gradual rise in gross returns from milk production as prices were raised towards the common EEC level in the years preceding the unified market was one factor influencing the 7 per cent increase in national output of milk between 1965 and 1968. The incentive was mainly to better management. Average yields rose steadily until, at 3,771 litres (802 gallons) in 1968 they slightly exceeded the Belgian level, but cow numbers remained relatively stable. Deliveries to dairies went up by 15 per cent. Of the 83 per cent of total production being delivered in 1968 about a quarter was sold as liquid milk or cream. Some 15 per cent of the balance remaining at the farm was also retailed in liquid form. Total production, 21·1 mn tons in 1968, is expected to continue rising, despite the disappearance of small herds, as yields further improve. Projections of output for 1975 range between 22·5 mn and 23·6 mn tons.[1] The recent downward trend in per head consumption of liquid milk is expected to continue. There is a difference of opinion about the fall in butter consumption; OECD expect it to be substantial. It is, however, generally agreed that cheese consumption will rise, especially that of soft-paste cheese.

A greater proportion of cows is still in herds of 10 cows and under than in any other EEC country. In 1967 only 2 per cent of cows were in herds of over 20. But the recent rapid decline in the number of smaller herds, either under economic pressures or thanks to positive measures of encouragement, is expected to continue throughout the early seventies. By 1975 between 300,000 and 400,000 cows may have been eliminated from these herds, but there will still be some 600,000 herds of which over a quarter would contain fewer than 6 cows. About a third of the farms with fewer than 10 cows are believed to be part-time holdings, accounting for over a million cows, or more than 15 per cent of the national herd. A large number of these are 1, 2 or 3 cow herds, which could be given up without much hardship.

Production is mainly concentrated in Schleswig-Holstein, Lower Saxony, and North Rhine-Westphalia, with about 44 per cent of total output between them, in the North, and in Baden-Württemberg and Bavaria which account for another 44 per cent, in the South. Small collecting dairies and manufacturing units predominate in the South, medium-sized ones in Schleswig-Holstein and Lower Saxony. The very large enterprises are in the South and in North Rhine-Westphalia. The North accounts for about half of butter production and nearly 20 per cent of cheese; the South for 40 per cent of butter and 80 per cent of cheese. Over a third of production for the liquid market is concentrated, as would be expected, in the densely populated industrial area of North Rhine-Westphalia.

[1] See footnote 2, p. 86 for sources.

The number of dairies and cheese factories has been contracting rapidly during the sixties, by a fifth between 1960 and 1965, and by a further quarter since then. This rapid concentration is hardly surprising in view of the rather small scale of operation of most of them. In 1967, 40 per cent of dairies employed no more than 5 persons and only 8 per cent employed over 50. Over 70 per cent of all dairies had an annual throughput of under 10 mn litres (2·2 mn gallons) averaging just over half that volume. Eight per cent had a throughput of more than 30 mn litres. The outstanding feature of the German dairy industry is the predominance of the co-operatives, especially in the North, which account for 80 per cent of the total first-hand milk deliveries in the Federal Republic. The 1,350 co-operative dairies are organised into 14 *Centralen*, to which they are attached with rather stronger links of loyalty and discipline than in the case of the French *unions*, under overall control of the Milch- Fett- und Eier- Kontor (MFE) at Hamburg. The Kontor took over in 1948 from the Milchwirtschaftsverbände, part of the closely knit system of agricultural co-operatives established during the thirties. The private sector is concentrated geographically in Bavaria, where between 35 and 40 per cent of milk is delivered to private dairies. Although in the country as a whole 20 per cent of milk is delivered to private dairies, all but 5 per cent of it is marketed through the MFE. The four largest private firms, all subsidiaries of major international companies (Nestlé-Oursina, Carnation, and Libby), as well as two smaller subsidiaries of Unilever and Kraft, are all members of co-operative *Centralen*, partly because the MFE provides a useful outlet for their products on the German market, but mainly because the dairy zoning system has prevented them, until its recent abolition, from acquiring access to new sources of raw milk.

This system statutorily allotted exclusive collection areas to each dairy and gave it a monopoly of liquid sales within that area. Both producers and retailers were therefore tied to particular dairies, and could only with difficulty obtain authorisation to change to another one. Dairies were, however, allowed to assign farms to each other, and, as is apparent from the statistics, to amalgamate. The system, though rational from the point of view of first-stage transport, has tended to preserve inefficient firms and slow down the concentration of manufacturing into large units. It has often made arrangements for supplying the major cities with liquid milk unnecessarily complicated, involving a considerable amount of depoting, bulking, and other wholesaling activity on the way from rural collecting dairies to urban bottling plants. In many cases wholesaling co-operatives supplying cities have access to insufficient milk from their own affiliated co-operatives and are obliged to purchase balancing supplies of accommodation milk at a relatively high premium. Since the zoning arrangements ceased on April 1st 1970, however, a substantial degree of rationalisation has already got under way, with the urban dairies using their weight to improve their own chain of supply by forcing further amalgamations among local co-operatives. On the manufacturing side the MFE claims that so long as it is able to ensure that the *Centralen* offer producers a higher price for milk than that corresponding to the butter or skim-powder intervention price (which thanks to its efficient organisation it believes it will on the whole be able to do) most of them will be content to continue delivering to their old dairies. Certainly the MFE can rely on the inertia and general inclination to let well alone of the average small farmer. On the other hand the big private firms, which have already acquired substantial market weight even in a situation of rather restricted access to raw-milk supplies, are unlikely to spare their efforts to obtain a larger share of what is now a free market. Until now, it is claimed, the Kontor's financial strength has enabled it to ward off take-overs, but it has been taking no chances. Its members have been encouraged to diversify out of bulk production of 'intervention' products in anticipation of the end of zoning in order to assure to the co-operative sector a growing share of the market for new products. The MFE has one of the most important research and development organisations in the European dairy industry, and its brand name for a wide range of products, 'Delicado', is being intensively promoted both at home and in export markets.

The EEC dairy regulations are administered by the EVSt for oils and fats. Only quality butter (*Markenbutter*) is eligible for intervention. 140,000 tons were purchased in 1968/69 and 152,000 tons in 1969/70; with 51,000 tons left in store at the end of 1970. The EVSt deals almost exclusively with the Milch- Fett- und Eier-Kontor on behalf of the co-operatives, the Butterauffang- und Betriebsgesellschaft which represents the private sector, and representatives of the trade. These it regards as its three 'partners'. Most offers of butter for intervention are made by the MFE. A few dairies do offer direct. Sales out of store have been mainly as second quality butter. In 1970 between 8,000 and 10,000 tons were sold by tender each fortnight on completion of 8 months in store. Offers are received in Frankfurt by the EVSt, and passed on to Brussels by telex for acceptance or rejection.

IMPLICATIONS FOR THE BRITISH MARKET

It will be evident from all that has been said above that the pattern of consumption of dairy products in the EEC, and hence that of milk processing, manufacture, and distribution, differs radically from that which exists in the UK.[1] Any consideration of the effect on the dairy sector of

[1] The main features of the British dairy industry will be analysed in the course of the following pages. For a description of the structure of production, distribution and manufacture the reader is referred to Butterwick and Neville-Rolfe, *op cit*, pp. 110–15, and to the production map, *ibid*, p. 129; to Patrick O'Neill, *The pattern of dairying in Britain*, 'The Milk Industry', January 1970, pp. 26–9; and to *Economic aspects of the dairy manufacturing industry. A workshop report*, Agricultural Adjustment Unit, University of Newcastle upon Tyne, Bulletin No. 12, 1970, which also provides an invaluable analysis of current trends and possible future developments. For all statistical information see *Dairy Facts and Figures, 1969*, published by the Milk Marketing Board, Thames Ditton.

adopting the CAP therefore raises a number of major questions to which the answers are far from clear, all the more so since the common regulation for liquid milk, the most important outlet for UK domestic production, is still, after nearly three years, only in draft form. How far then will the present British system have to be changed? To what extent can the EEC regulations be adapted, or bent, to fit the different situation which exists on this side of the English Channel and in Northern Ireland?

It is worth at the outset considering what aspects of EEC dairy policy would without question be mandatory. First a price structure would have to be accepted which, whatever changes may have occurred in official intervention levels of individual products by the end of any transition period, values manufacturing milk much more highly in relation to liquid milk than is at present the case in Britain. The cost to manufacturers of raw milk would be similar throughout an enlarged Community and in the UK would no longer be related to that of manufactured products entering the country at 'world' prices, or at minimum import prices set not very far above them. Second, movement of milk and of dairy products between the UK and other member countries would, in principle at least, be entirely free.[1] Third, no subsidies to milk production in any part of the UK would be permitted. Fourth, national regulations for price pooling would not be allowed. The system which formerly operated in the Netherlands, for instance, whereby a levy on liquid sales was paid into a central fund for redistribution at a flat rate per litre among all producers regardless of the destination of their milk is now forbidden. Fifth, Community standards of quality and minimum fat content would have to be observed. Finally, zoning arrangements, such as have existed in Germany and Italy, whereby producers were obliged to deliver their supplies to a single designated dairy, would not be permitted.

This list of rules and prohibitions could appear at first sight to require major dismantling of the British milk marketing system as it has evolved over the past 35 or more years. Though some people might feel this to be opportune it seems more probable that in practice the Milk Marketing Boards would be permitted to continue functioning much as before, if only because the British system is already the envy of many milk producers in the existing Community, who so far from insisting on its abolition might even hope to persuade their governments and the Commission to allow them to adopt similar arrangements in their own countries. As producer organisations the Boards start *prima facie* in a favourable light in the perspective of Community philosophy. Largely owing to French insistence, the draft regulation on *groupements de producteurs* no longer restricts the extent of any such organisation to a specific

---

[1] How far this becomes a reality during the seventies remains to be seen. Movement may, in any case, still be impeded by differing public health regulations. These are unlikely to be harmonised before the beginning of the transition period. It must therefore be hoped that there would be an opportunity for expressing the British viewpoint during that period.

Milk and Dairy Products

maximum share of total Community turnover of a particular product or group of products.[1] Although Articles 85 and 86 of the Treaty of Rome may as a consequence be less generously interpreted in favour of organised agricultural producers than was originally the intention, these articles are directed against practices, cartels, etc., which 'are likely to affect trade between the Member States and which have as their object or result the prevention, restriction or distortion of competition within the Common Market'. Even in the absence of special exemption from these provisions for producer groups it might be difficult to prove that the activity of the Boards in Great Britain, as sole purchasers of milk off farms in England, Scotland and Wales, could be so described, as long as it were in theory open to producers in northern France or the Low Countries to deliver liquid milk into southern England. In practice at current sea-freight rates it seems unlikely that, even with an all-year-round roll-on/roll-off bulk tanker service, transport costs could be kept sufficiently low to make this a paying proposition. Estimates obtained a year or two ago for roll-on/roll-off Dunkirk–Harwich, and privately communicated to us, indicated that the cost of delivering milk in London from the closer continental ports would be between 5p and 6p a gallon. A channel tunnel might, however, alter the picture. In Ireland the physical obstacles to the movement of liquid milk across the intra-Community frontier between South and North would of course be minimal. The implications of this are discussed later.

Under French legislation,[2] which has not so far been challenged by the Commission, a majority of producers in a *département* or group of departments may vote in favour of channelling all sales of any single product through their own organisation, any dissident minority being then obliged to comply with such an arrangement. This may include the power to raise a compulsory levy on all producers for financing the producer organisation's marketing activities. In the event of such an *extension des règles de discipline* being conceded to producers in several departments a *comité économique* may be formed at regional level to co-ordinate their activity, the regional committees being in their turn federated, if desired, at national level. Since the MMBs satisfy the other main criterion for recognition by the Commission of producer groups, that their members should be engaged in first-stage production and marketing, there seems no reason to suppose that the Boards' position as sole purchasers of their members' output would contravene Community principles.

Certain aspects of the MMBs' present activities would, however, be clearly inadmissible, and others at least doubtfully admissible. Since it would be out of the question for manufacturers to have access to raw milk at a substantially lower price than their competitors in the rest of the Community the system of rebates would disappear completely, and with it the Boards' powers of dictating (or at any rate strongly influencing by means of the terms of their annual contracts

[1] See p. 238.
[2] Loi d'Orientation Agricole, 1962.

with manufacturers) the uses to which manufacturing milk should be put. Furthermore it seems doubtful whether the Boards would any longer be in a position to give absolute priority to sales of milk for liquid consumption. Supplies contracted to processing-only dairies[1] would of course be sure of finding their way to the liquid market, but processing firms with manufacturing capacity, as well as depots which also manufacture, would be free to put the milk which they purchased from the Boards to its most profitable use. Especially in the case of the big vertically integrated companies operating in the London area this might not necessarily prove to be the liquid market.[2] Average costs of manufacturing fall with increased throughput, which could reduce the attractiveness to firms with divided interests of such premium on liquid milk as might remain. On the other hand, some firms have substantial capital tied up in their retail side, and milk rounds might not in any case prove easily saleable. Firms manufacturing only butter and/or cheese, however, and with no interest in the liquid market, might be reluctant to surrender milk to that market during the winter trough except at a substantial premium. Given the much higher realisation price for manufacturing milk that would be assured by the EEC price structure (at 1970/71 EEC price levels, around 47·0d (19½p) per gallon compared with 20·99d (9p) per gallon averaged in England and Wales in 1969/70), producers might have to be satisfied with a somewhat lower return than at present from liquid sales, say 48·5d (20½p) a gallon. If their average return from both markets were unduly in excess of the Community target price (in 1970/71 equivalent to 45·6d (19p) ex-farm) there would be political pressure to which the government in a period of sharply rising food prices might be inclined to submit for a lowering of the retail price of liquid milk. This could be brought down by as much as ½p (1½d) per pint without reducing the present rate of return to producers, though some increase in the retail margin would probably also have to be conceded in the light of higher labour costs. Given the low price elasticity for liquid milk (sales hardly dropped when the price went up to 11d per pint in 1969) a fall to 4p (9½d) a pint would not normally increase sales by any great extent,[3] though at a time when other food prices were going up the effect might be greater than usual, especially if combined with vigorous publicity. There might prove to be a significant cross-elasticity with evaporated milk, however, which has a relatively high elasticity of demand and which would, like wholemilk powder, become more expensive.

It is necessary to consider at this point the question of how far it would remain permissible for receipts from milk sales to be pooled and averaged out to individual producers. Inside the Community pooling is freely

[1] Processing in the context of milk indicates heat treatment, not manufacture.

[2] The Prices and Incomes Board found costs to processing retailers to have been already in 1965 2s 4d per gallon higher in London than in the Provinces. *The Remuneration of Milk Distributors Final Report*, National Board for Prices and Incomes Report No. 46, HMSO, 1967, Cmnd 3477, p. 13.

[3] According to National Food Survey data the price elasticity of demand for liquid milk is −0·2; this would imply an increase in consumption of about 2 per cent.

practised at the level of the firm. It would be impossible and anyway inequitable, for the individual producer to be paid according to the particular use to which his raw milk has been put. In France, for instance, co-operatives whose catchment area covers two or three departments and which supply the liquid market as well as manufacturing dairy products, pay their members a pool price based on gross realisation. To the extent that the Milk Marketing Boards are recognisably producer organisations, even though not co-operatives, there would seem to be no obstacle to pooling being carried out at Board level. In no legal sense could any of the five Boards be said to be operating a 'national' pool equivalent to that formerly administered in Germany or the Netherlands. In Germany pooling was achieved with the aid of a federal tax levied on all sales of liquid milk. Returns from liquid and manufacturing milk were pooled in the Netherlands by means of the Dairy Fund, which was itself a section of the Agricultural Equalisation Fund, 'a general fund for agricultural price support constituting part of the State Budget'.[1] How far it is economically desirable for so large a producer monopoly as the MMB for England and Wales to operate pooling over the whole of its territory is of course another matter, but in doing so it would hardly be acting against EEC regulations.

The change of pricing system, including the disappearance of guaranteed prices and standard quantities, would involve the abolition of the UK Milk Fund.[2] In any case its balancing function would become superfluous. Producers in Scotland and Northern Ireland where an above-average proportion of milk is sold for manufacture would no longer be at a price disadvantage compared with those in England and Wales. Even in Northern Ireland, where under a third of milk produced goes to the liquid market, it should still be possible to lower retail prices and keep producer returns at or above target price levels.

There remains the problem of seasonal prices. The Boards would claim that their primary aim is to ensure an all-year-round supply of liquid milk sufficient to meet a demand which varies relatively little between summer

---

[1] *Agricultural Policies in 1966*, OECD, Paris, 1967, p. 390.

[2] Under present arrangements each Board is allotted a Standard Quantity of milk, based on the Board's liquid-milk sales in the previous year plus a margin for contingencies. The government-guaranteed price applies only to that Quantity. To the extent that a Board's net receipts from milk sales fall short of the amount guaranteed to it annually at the Price Review (that is, its allotted Standard Quantity multiplied by the Review price plus its producer deliveries in excess of the Standard Quantity multiplied by the average realisation price for manufactured milk), the Board may be compensated from the UK Milk Fund. Owing to the smaller proportion of milk produced that can be sold for liquid consumption in Scotland and Northern Ireland, gross receipts in these four Board areas are insufficient to ensure that average realised price per gallon reaches the level of the effective guarantee price. In England and Wales, on the other hand, with a high proportion of milk being sold on the liquid market, Board receipts are usually in excess of guaranteed price returns. This excess, which is paid into the Milk Fund, is, taking one year with another, sufficient to compensate the other Boards. There is thus no net subsidy from the Exchequer to UK producers as a whole.

and winter. At present this is achieved by two sets of incentives, to the producer through differential seasonal prices, and to the processor-manufacturer through the system of rebates. Under EEC conditions, however, the incentive to the processor-manufacturer would have to be in the form of a premium on liquid milk and no longer of a penalty on manufacturing milk. An earlier decision by the Council of Ministers limited such a premium to the equivalent of 2·3d per gallon. This was with difficulty reconcilable with the guidance to member governments on permissible maximum retail prices which should take into account not only the price for manufacturing milk and the cost of processing raw milk for human consumption, but also an additional amount sufficient to encourage dairies to undertake such processing. The proposed maximum premium seemed wholly insufficient for this purpose. It has been tactfully allowed to lapse.

Seasonal differentiation of prices at national level is frowned upon by the Commission, but there is nothing against it being operated by individual dairies. The practice is fairly widespread in the northern part of the Community where costs of milk production, as in the UK, tend to be higher in the winter. On the other hand, owing to the relatively small marginal quantities required to ensure satisfaction of the demand for liquid milk, the differentials can be left fairly narrow. In Federal Germany, for instance, the highest average monthly producer price for the country as a whole was about 13 per cent above the lowest in 1968,[1] compared with a difference of 45 per cent in England and Wales in 1968/9. There seems no reason why the Boards, as purchasers of first instance, should not continue to pay differential prices on this scale if they are necessary to elicit sufficient supplies during the trough to satisfy demand. A widespread switch into summer milk by UK producers, leading to large surpluses for manufacturing, is certainly not in the interests of an enlarged Community. At his meeting with the Council of Ministers at the end of October 1970 Mr Geoffrey Rippon is said to have stressed the importance of being able to 'supply liquid demand throughout the country and throughout the year'.[2] Although subsequent press reports suggest that the British delegation received certain assurances on the question of liquid-milk marketing, no details have been published of what these might be.

A final uncertainty about the adaptation of the UK system to that of the EEC concerns zoning. In the UK producers may only sell their milk to the dairy or depot to which their supplies are allotted by the local Board. Since these arrangements are made on their behalf by their own producer organisation this type of zoning, which has over the years helped to promote and maintain a low level of average transport costs per gallon, is not entirely analogous to that recently discontinued in Germany and due to cease in Italy by 1972. In both these countries zoning was imposed by

[1] Ranging from 24 per cent in Schleswig-Holstein to 9 per cent in Bavaria and Rhineland-Palatinate.
[2] *Farmer and Stockbreeder*, 3 November 1970.

Milk and Dairy Products

specific legislation.[1] Whilst it is true that zoning in the UK results from the provisions of the Agricultural Marketing Acts it does so only indirectly. To the extent that like all the Boards' activities they have the approval, implicit at least, of a majority of producers the present arrangements for milk collection seem likely to be acceptable to the Commission.

So far we have assumed a reasonably accommodating attitude on the part of the Commission to the present UK system, mainly on the score of the entrenched position which it affords to producers, the strengthening of whose influence on the market is one of the main objectives of the CAP in its second, post-1967, phase. Indeed, as some continental farmers are already aware, the Agricultural Marketing Acts designed to help British farmers, especially dairy farmers, in the thirties are in some respects tailor-made for their own situation today. It would, however, be a mistake to assume without question that the Commission's agreement to the retention of every feature of the milk marketing scheme not obviously contrary to EEC regulations was necessarily desirable. Entry into the EEC might on the contrary provide an opportune moment for amending the scheme in the light of some of the criticisms advanced against it over the past 35 years. Since these have been largely concentrated on the scheme as it operates in England and Wales it will be appropriate to deal with those two countries first and to consider separately any special implications of EEC membership for Scotland and Northern Ireland.

England and Wales

There is of course nothing fresh about the doubts that can be raised concerning the activities of the MMB for England and Wales. What is new is the sudden opportunity for resolving them that could be presented by the need for repealing, or radically amending, the Agricultural Marketing Act of 1958[2] during a transitional period accompanying entry into the EEC. This could be a more effective spur to change than any of the recommendations of the half dozen or more Commissions and Committees on milk marketing that have been published, argued about, and largely ignored, since 1935. There are a number of major questions which would arise during a basic reappraisal of the scheme. Should the Board continue to be the sole first-hand purchaser of raw milk? If so, should the cost of secondary movements of milk, as well as of primary transport, be shared by all producers? If, on the other hand, transport costs ought to be more sharply differentiated between regions, should not the actual returns from milk sales also cease to be pooled at Board level? Should distributive margins and retail prices for liquid milk remain under government control? Should membership of the Board be widened?

Two main arguments are advanced to justify the Board's privilege as

[1] See pp. 91 and 100.
[2] The 1958 Act repealed and consolidated earlier legislation, including the original Acts of 1931 and 1933.

sole purchaser: first that the Board is able to organise, generally through its regional offices, farm collection in such a way as to prevent overlapping transport and minimise costs; and second that the Board, as the sole seller of raw milk, is able to exercise countervailing power on behalf of producers in an oligopsonistic market. Cost per gallon of ex-farm collection of milk in England and Wales has risen steadily over the past twenty years, and by over 40 per cent since 1960, though much of this can be attributed to increases in costs of fuel and labour. The cost even today (1·45d per gallon in 1969/70) is admittedly fairly low in relation to the total cost (about 33d (14p) per gallon) of distributing milk from farm-gate to doorstep, and certainly competitive with the cost of primary transport in EEC countries. Nevertheless, the 'overall impression' of the Prices and Incomes Board of the transport as of other sectors of the milk industry is that its efficiency is less than it might be because of duplication'.[1] The Board's report found that neither the basic allocation of farms to depots and dairies nor the routing of vehicles on regular farm collection are carried out with reference to formal optimising techniques. It therefore recommended the immediate application of a model already developed by the MMB for planning milk movements on a 3-, 6- and 12-month basis. 'A total planning strategy which allowed individual contractors to work within more closely defined areas' such as the Incomes Board proposes would hardly be advanced by a dismantling of the present system and a return to the looser arrangement of contracts between individual producers and numerous first-hand purchasers of milk favoured by some opponents of the Board.[2]

To the extent that the number of potential first-hand purchasers of milk has been steadily falling[3] and the industry has become increasingly concentrated in the hands of a few larger processor/manufacturers, the Board's role in exercising countervailing power on behalf of producers may be seen as of growing importance. True, a situation where a producer organisation has absolute control over the allocation to processors and manufacturers of a product whose price is anyway guaranteed by the government prompts the question 'countervailing against what?' In an EEC situation, however, the notion would be more relevant. Assuming that as a producer organisation the Board, or its successor in title, were allowed to retain the right to sole first-hand purchase (producer-retailers always excepted), which it probably would be, its countervailing power would be exercised on behalf of producers in a virtually free market. In the absence of any strong or widespread co-operative organisation producers might otherwise find themselves at a considerable disadvantage in negotiating contracts with processing dairies and manufacturers.

[1] *Pay and conditions of workers in the milk industry*, Report No. 140, National Board for Prices and Incomes, January 1970, London, HMSO, Cmnd 4267, pp. 24.

[2] See, for instance, Linda Whetstone, *The Marketing of Milk*. Institute of Economic Affairs Research Monograph No. 21, London, 1970, pp. 40 *et seq.*

[3] In April 1965, 503 organisations in England and Wales received an average of 3·5 mn gallons per organisation. In April 1970 the number of organisations was 312 with an average gallonage of over 5·75 mn gallons.

The second main question, whether the cost of secondary movements of milk for liquid consumption[1] should, like that of primary transport of raw milk, be shared more or less equally between all producers throughout England and Wales, is from the MMB's point of view a false one. According to the Board the cost of secondary transport from depot to liquid dairy (or, if it is over 12 miles, from dairy to dairy), of balancing supplies of accommodation milk to ensure satisfaction of demand for liquid milk is the financial responsibility not of the Board (and thus a charge on the producer) but of the Ministry of Agriculture. Since there is no subsidy paid by the Ministry the cost is in effect passed on to the consumer by means of the transport allowances to distributors which are taken into account by the government in fixing the maximum retail price.[2] However, as was pointed out by the Committee of Investigation into a complaint by producers in the Board's South-Eastern region 'the only ultimate source of funds from which producers and secondary (transport) charges are paid is the proceeds of the sale of milk to consumers'.[3] This confirmed the opinion of the Prices and Incomes Board given a year earlier that the division of financial responsibility was artificial and should be abolished, the MMB accepting the whole cost of transport and of depot handling as a marketing expense.[4] Indirectly, therefore, the cost of secondary transport is borne by the producer, and the question posed above is not as false as the Board maintains. On milk produced on farms close to centres of population the cost is, however, likely to be lower than on milk produced in peripheral areas. In the South-East all liquid milk supplies are delivered direct to distributing dairies. There is no depoting. Whereas in the Far-West region, for instance, a relatively small proportion of the milk that reaches the liquid market undergoes primary transport only. Much of it has to be moved on, especially during the trough period, from depots to distant urban (mainly London) dairies. On the other hand most of the milk produced in the region goes for manufacture. Over the years the Board has

[1] The cost of moving any milk from depot to factory is borne by the Board, but most depots have manufacturing capacity.

[2] These transport allowances, at rates fixed according to distance, etc., by the Ministry on the basis of costings surveys, are in fact paid by the Board to distributors on behalf of the Ministry. They are then averaged over the total gallonage sold for liquid consumption, and recouped by the Board at a corresponding flat rate per gallon (3·32d, in 1969) on its sales.

[3] *Complaint by Messrs. G. Padfield, G. L. Brock and H. Steven, milk producers in the South-Eastern region, as to the operation of the Milk Marketing Scheme 1933 (as amended). Report of the Committee of Investigation for England and Wales, January 1969* (Chairman, Mr David Karmel, QC). Ministry of Agriculture, Fisheries and Food, 1969, p. 10. The complainants, Chairman, Vice-Chairman and immediate past Chairman respectively of the South-Eastern Regional Committee of the Milk Marketing Board, maintained on behalf of a large majority of producers in the region that the Board's regional transport rate of 0·66d per gallon charged to them insufficiently differentiated the price paid to them from that paid to producers in the Far Western region, who only suffered a corresponding deduction of 1·35d per gallon in respect of transport costs.

[4] *op cit*, Cmnd 3477, p. 20. It is possible that in 1971 the Board may in fact be made responsible for secondary transport.

pursued a logical policy of encouraging the location of manufacturing plant (including setting up its own) in peripheral regions so as to minimise the need for long-distance haulage of liquid supplies. But thanks to the pooling system producers in these regions continue to receive the same basic price for their milk as those in inner regions whose milk is sold mainly for liquid consumption. The Karmel Committee of Investigation concurred with the South-Eastern complainants' submission that as a *quid pro quo* the Board's deductions from Far-Western and other peripheral producers' basic price in respect of transport should reflect the notional cost of moving milk from their regions to a liquid market, or at least that proportion of the notional cost of reaching a liquid market which the total quantity of milk sent to that market bears to total sales of milk off farms in England and Wales (i.e. about two-thirds). The Committee found the present scale of regional differentials to be 'out of date and logically indefensible' and bearing no relation to either actual or notional costs.[1] However, while supporting the principle that producers in outer regions who get the benefit of the pool price should in their turn concede to those located closer to centres of population the benefit of the lower cost of moving their milk to the liquid market, the Committee declined to make specific recommendations, as being outside its terms of reference, about the actual range of differentials in regional transport rates to be adopted.[2] In any case no action was taken by the Board to implement the Karmel recommendations. These were not mandatory and were of course in direct opposition to the Board's own views.

To the next question on our list—should actual returns from the Board's milk sales no longer be pooled but be regionally differentiated?— the Board would also give a negative reply. Nor was it ever suggested by the South-Eastern complainants during the course of their dispute with the Board that pooling should be abandoned. Indeed, as has been seen, their case was based largely on its existence. On this issue expert opinion has generally supported the Board. In 1936 the Cutforth Commission concluded that 'a flat price as a final objective appears to us . . . to be unanswerable',[3] a view quoted with approval nearly thirty years later by the Davis Committee,[4] which recommended that even the vestigial

[1] Besides the differential in regional transport rates of 0·69d per gallon (see page 109, Note 3) the 'residual element' of 0·5d, a relic of the pre-war regional pooling system, raised the total differential between South Eastern and Far Western to 1·19d. per gallon.

[2] In 1966/7 South-Eastern region was contributing 5d per gallon to the pool and Far Western Region receiving a subsidy of 3d per gallon (Karmel, p. 45). The Davis Committee (Karmel, Appendix V, p. 23) recommended raising the transport differential between the two regions to 2·4d per gallon. 'Mr Camm's proof' (Karmel, Appendix 21), put forward on behalf of the South-Eastern region, came out with a range of 4·32d per gallon (p. 73).

[3] *Milk Report of the Reorganisation for Great Britain* (Chairman, A. E. Cutforth, Esq.). Ministry of Agriculture and Fisheries, Economic Series No. 44, London, HMSO, 1936, p. 135.

[4] *Area variations in producers' prices for Milk*. Report of an Independent Committee. Chairman, Sir Herbert Davis. Milk Marketing Board, Thames Ditton, 1963.

'residual element' should disappear, and also supported Cutforth's recommendation that the only permanent price differences should be those due to differences in services and in transport costs. In an EEC situation, however, with retail prices for liquid milk differentiated by regions and with the price of manufacturing milk much closer to that of milk for liquid consumption, the case for a flat price would become a good deal less convincing and the demand by producers in inner regions for a regional structure of pool prices increasingly vociferous. As has already been pointed out, the disappearance of the Board's powers of allocation of milk supplies would probably tend to a certain localisation of contracts between the Board and wholesale purchasers of milk, leading willy-nilly to a strengthening of its regional organisation. The difficulties involved in fixing regional price boundaries are considerable. The Board's present regions are drawn mainly from the point of view of administrative convenience; in its proposals for establishing zones for differential transport deductions the Davis Committee chose largely to ignore them. Even so it was hard entirely to eliminate anomalies as between producers on either side of regional boundaries. In this case the differentials were not in themselves large. Anomalies would be likely to be magnified where differentials not only in transport costs but in basic price were involved. It might be necessary to allow producers within a certain distance of a border to opt for inclusion in a neighbouring region; in some cases the pattern of local primary transport might indeed dictate this. As far as transport was concerned the Davis Committee concluded that payments to individual producers differentiated on grounds of accessibility would be impracticable. Camm's proof suggested that though practicable it would be fairly complicated.[1] Allocation of individual mileage ratings could involve much wrangling and grievance, and on the whole a flat regional pool price for all producers regardless of their accessibility would probably be found preferable. This would take into account not only the total value of milk sold and total transport costs incurred, but also seasonal differentials, which would tend to vary between one region and another according to the strength of the local demand for liquid milk.

Although we argued earlier that the England and Wales Milk Marketing Board's price pooling arrangements might be defended before the EEC Commission as being non-'national' and producer-, as opposed to government-operated, it looks as though once British entry into the EEC became a certainty a detailed re-examination of the present system by an independent body would be, if not essential, at least opportune. The disadvantage of price regionalisation to producers in remote and peripheral areas would probably be no greater in the UK than in other parts of an enlarged Community, and might well, given the better farm structure and marginally easier conditions for a switch to beef or lamb production, be somewhat less. The Davis Committee, while accepting that small milk producers in the West might be hard hit by wider transport differentials

[1] Karmel, *op cit*, pp. 68–71.

for lack of alternative products to which to turn, pointed out that 'not all milk producers in the more distant areas . . . are small farmers and we do not feel that this problem should be allowed to prevent what seems to us, on economic grounds, the proper pattern of milk prices to farmers generally'. The report concluded that while short-term transitional arrangements might be made to soften the impact of change for him, the long-term problem of the small farmer was a national one, not confined to milk. In the same context the Karmel Committee dismissed the argument that some farmers might be driven out of milk production if the differential were radically altered, on the grounds that 'if such a situation should arise it would be for the government to consider the resulting economic and social problems'. Within the EEC it would be not only for the government but for the Commission to consider them. Assistance for disadvantaged minorities should increasingly be available in future under the Community's co-ordinated regional policies from the Guidance Section of FEOGA and the European Social Fund.

The fourth question raised on p. 107 concerns the setting of maximum retail prices for liquid milk. Since this is practised in all EEC member countries[1] at present, and is allowed for in the draft regulation on liquid milk, it seems unlikely to be abandoned when the Community is enlarged. Although the Commission may succeed in establishing, either by regulation or by a formal 'decision' of the Council of Ministers, the basic principle of regionalised prices, local control by individual governments over actual price levels will probably be retained for some time to come and only disappear in the context of longer-term economic and monetary union. So long as retail prices for liquid milk are controlled and a target price for raw milk is offered to producers, control of distributive margins seems also bound to be permitted. On the other hand one of the arguments in favour of a fixed rather than a maximum price is that a maximum price enables supermarkets and chain stores to force wholesale prices down so far as seriously to affect producer returns, quite apart from encouraging a switch to manufacturing by processing dairies no longer able to compete on the liquid market. That milk out of the entire range of foodstuffs retailed should still be singled out for price control is an anachronism, the motives for whose continuance are of course political rather than economic. Given the existence of price control, however, the procedure for reviewing fixed or maximum distributive margins needs to be kept as finely tuned as possible to take account not only of distributors' changing costs and of return on their investment, but also of the potential encouragement to inertia inherent in the system. In Britain the most recent review, by the Prices and Incomes Board in 1967,[2] recommended an increase in existing margins for distributors in the London metropolitan area and a decrease for those in the provinces, though special delivery charges might continue to be made, at the government's discretion only, in remote rural areas.

[1] Except Germany, where they are fixed at dairy, but free at retail.
[2] *op cit*, Cmnd 3477.

To the extent that they involved differentiated retail prices these proposals would if adopted have meant a first step in the direction of a regionalised price structure. The PIB criticised the seven-day delivery system at a uniform price across the country which is enshrined in the present distributive system on the grounds of its high cost, mainly of labour, and its tendency to inhibit innovation, freedom of consumer choice and competitiveness. The Board hesitated, however, to recommend changes (e.g. different controlled prices for doorstep delivery and for sale in shops, incentives to 5- or 6-day delivery, discounts for bulk purchase) because of their unknown quantitative effect on the total market for liquid milk,[1] and 'because the total market for liquid milk is of great importance for the system of support for the farming industry'. In the EEC it would become relatively less important, given the much higher price of manufacturing milk and producer interests would not necessarily be harmed by greater freedom being given to distributors.

Another of the PIB's recommendations which seems to have aroused no official response, that the distributive trade should be represented on all MMBs, leads to a consideration of the last of the questions of principle meriting discussion in the context of UK entry into the EEC. Should Board membership be widened? There is a fairly widespread misapprehension among continental admirers of the British system that the marketing boards are 'interprofessional'. Association with producers of processors, distributors and consumers is in fact more strongly established in parts of the Community, notably the Netherlands but to some extent in France, than in Britain. Participation by the dairy industry and trade in the activities of the Marketing Boards is in fact limited to the Joint Committees set up under the Milk Marketing Scheme for England and Wales (as amended 1955) and for Northern Ireland (1954). No such Committees exist in Scotland. The England and Wales Committee includes eight representatives of the Board (the Chairman, who is chairman of the Committee, Vice-Chairman, Managing Director, and five of the elected Board members). The 17 members appointed by the Milk Distributive Council (MDC) are the Chairman of the Council, 4 representatives each of the National Dairymen's Association, the Creamery Proprietors' Association and the Co-operative Milk Trade Association, and the three Associations' secretaries, and a representative of the Amalgamated Master Dairymen (a grouping of small firms independent of the NDA). The Secretaries of the Board and of the MDC act as joint secretaries to the Committee. One would think that 25 members made a rather unwieldy Committee, but it only meets about twice a year and it seems that much of its basic work is carried out by small unofficial working groups. The Board is required to consult it on such matters as the terms and form of contracts of sales of milk by the Board or by authorised registered producers; amounts of and

---

[1] The government did not act on the PIB's concluding recommendation that it should sponsor experiments which would yield some of the necessary quantitative data on which to base a review of the present system.

criteria for the Board's allowances; the Board's method of allocating milk supplies; the description and composition of milk and milk products; hygiene and quality testing, and so forth. The Committee also deals with training, education and scientific research in the industry, and serves as a forum for the discussion of any matter, imports for instance, on which both sides might wish to make representations to the government. In reaching formal decisions the Board and the MDC each collectively have a single vote, any resolution on which the two fail to agree being referred for arbitration to an independent third person, usually, since acute differences tend to be on financial questions, a chartered accountant. In fact points of difference are usually referred to the working groups, consisting of Committee members and co-opted experts, for consideration, a system which discourages the taking up of entrenched positions in Committee and facilitates compromise. Only in the last resort is formal disagreement registered by means of a divided vote.

On the whole the idea of interprofessional co-operation has not flourished in Britain. Even those who have from time to time recommended the abandonment or modification of the marketing board system have tended to propose setting up, in lieu of or above the Boards, statutory bodies entirely independent of sectional interests, some of them with wide powers of direction.[1] The concept of an organisation representing and reconciling the interests of farmers, industry and trade has never been widely canvassed, and the Boards have continued, in the spirit in which they were originally conceived, primarily to serve the interests of producers. The Milk Board can, and does, claim to have promoted the public interest as well, to the extent that, for instance, milk is cleaner, the pattern of its collection more rational, and its manufacture more economically located than was the case 35 years ago. It has of course been argued that these and other benefits could have been realised without the Board's formidable apparatus of regulatory powers. A certain self-satisfaction characteristic of established organisations has not always made for smooth relations between the Board and other sectors of the dairy industry. A recent report submitted to the Ministry of Agriculture deplored the 'nervous, not to say hysterical, attitude' of the Milk Distributive Council to the activities of the Board.[2] The Council, representing the buyers of milk, was objecting to the raising of further capital by the Board by means of increasing their producer levy from 0·25d to 0·5d per gallon in order to finance, amongst other things, the construction of further manufacturing capacity, mainly for butter, in peripheral areas, and the purchase of additional bulk collection and transport material. The report concluded that the Board

[1] cf. proposals for a Central Milk Authority by the Cutforth Commission (1935), for a Milk Commission by the Williams Committee (1946), for Commodity Commissions by the Lucas Committee (1946), for a Fatstock and Meat Authority by the Verdon-Smith Committee (1964) and for an Egg Authority by the Wright Commission (1968).
[2] *Proposed amendment to the Milk Marketing Scheme 1933 (as amended)*. Report by David J. Stinson, Esq., on the Public Inquiry held on June 4th and 5th 1969. London. Ministry of Agriculture, Fisheries and Food, p. 11.

Milk and Dairy Products

would be legitimately exercising the countervailing power at its disposal in raising the capital in this way and the objection was not sustained.[1] The case is worth quoting as an example of the poor interprofessional relations arising out of the present system.

On other occasions the Board's activities have been less well viewed by independent observers. In the Padfield case, as has already been seen, the Karmel Committee considered the absence of adequate regional transport differentials to be contrary to the public interest. In its evidence to the Committee the Board had made the rather naïve claim that 'the present system is in the public interest because it works well in practice and is acceptable to the great majority of producers'. The changes proposed by the complainants would in its view, by causing discord among producers, impair the efficient marketing of milk. 'It must be in the public interest to maintain the *status quo*', concluded the Board blandly, 'if to change it in the manner sought by the complainants would be contrary to the public interest.' Another argument advanced in favour of retaining the present system was that neither the Board members appointed by the Minister nor the Minister himself had ever objected to the Board's price differentials —'cogent evidence that the present system of determining producers' prices is in the public interest'.[2] To this the complainants had replied that the appointed members were believed to have 'abstained on every occasion from voting on the issue'. As for the Minister 'he adopted and persisted in the view that it was entirely a matter for the Board'.[3] It was not until the complainants had fought all the way to the House of Lords for and obtained a writ of Mandamus directed to the Minister, that he was forced to consider their complaint and refer it to a Committee of Investigation. The complainants' victory was a Pyrrhic one since the Minister was in no way obliged under the terms of the 1958 Agricultural Act to act upon the Committee's recommendations, nor did he do so. In the absence of ministerial intervention the Board thus remains effectively insulated against such complaints in the future, and free to ignore the views of its own registered producers and even of the Board members appointed by the Minister.

Entry into the EEC could provide an opportunity for improving these relations inasmuch as the Board of Management of the intervention agency

[1] 'No complaint is made of the Board's activities except in relation to their encroachment into the distributive and manufacturing sector. The Board's share of distribution is 3·2 per cent of total sales. Although in 1955 the Board's share of distribution was only 0·9 per cent, so that it is now some 3½ times as great, 96·8 per cent of distribution remains in private hands. The Board's proportion of the manufacture of butter, the product of lowest realisation, has increased since 1960 from 18·6 per cent to 25·1 per cent, doubling the gallonage of milk so used. But the private manufacturers, other than the combines, have also doubled their gallonage and the changed proportions in butter manufacture seem to me to be as likely to reflect the combines pulling out of the manufacture of an unprofitable product as the effect of competition by the Board.' *ibid*, p. 10.
[2] *op cit*, Karmel, p. 109.
[3] *ibid*, p. 109.

for dairy products would include, besides producers, representatives of processors, manufacturers, distributors and consumers, maybe one or two independents as well, and officials from the Ministry of Agriculture, Fisheries and Food (and possibly of the Treasury and Trade Ministry). As we have already pointed out, the influence of an interprofessional body of this kind, meeting in plenary session, varies a good deal from country to country, and is in some cases negligible. But during the early stages of adapting to the CAP at any rate it could provide a useful bridge between producers and users of milk at a time of uncertainty and change. There is no obviously suitable existing body which could take on the role of intervention agency for dairy products in the UK, as there is for cereals, livestock and sugar. The MMB for England and Wales is debarred in its present form on several counts. Apart from the three ministerial nominees it only represents producer interests. It has substantial manufacturing interests of its own, and could therefore seem to be a not wholly disinterested party in, for instance, receiving tenders for restitutions or the disposal of intervention stocks. Third the Board, although *primus inter pares*, has no jurisdiction over the other four Boards. The intervention agency—which might perhaps be known as the Dairy Commission—would be operating for the whole UK.

Clearly none of these objections are insuperable. Since acceptance of tenders depends entirely on Brussels this is not a decisive point. If it were thought desirable for the Board to form the nucleus of a Dairy Commission, however, it would be possible to divest it of its manufacturing interests by handing them over to what are at the moment its Regional Offices. It is arguable that with the regionalisation of the milk price structure greater devolution to the regions would anyway be desirable. Free market conditions would require the development of a system of contracts between producers and processing dairies and producers and manufacturers. Negotiations for these might be better conducted at local level by Regional Boards, though these need not necessarily be as numerous as the present Regional Offices of the England and Wales Board. Their administrative boundaries would coincide as far as possible with one or more of the regionalised retail price zones. In each region a wholesale pool price for each zone would be paid to producers out of the Regional Board's gross returns from sales. These sales would not be confined, especially in the case of areas peripheral to the liquid milk market, to the regions in which the milk being sold was produced. Contracts would be entered into with distant buyers. At present the Board's powers to switch liquid supplies from surplus to deficit regions enable it to prevent local shortages of liquid milk in deficit regions, especially during the winter trough. Under a freer system processors in these regions might well fail from time to time to secure adequate supplies on contract from Regional Boards, either because of faulty forecasting of demand when the contract was drawn up or through unanticipated interference with supplies by natural causes. The Dairy Commission could usefully continue to act as a clearing-house for requests for accommodation milk when such breakdowns occurred. Balancing supplies would normally be available only from manufacturers, who would release it at a premium.[1] The Commission could also continue, to the extent that central control of them seemed administratively desirable and economically justified, to exercise the Board's present activities in the fields of milk recording and costing, business recording, AI services, publicity, and hygienic and other technical supervision and research. It would also of course replace the Joint Committee as a forum for negotiations between producers, industry, trade, and government about retail prices, margins and allowances (assuming that control over retail margins were retained as well as maximum retail prices), and between producers and industry about levels of regional price differentials in respect of transport and seasonality.

One objection to the setting up of Regional Boards is that staff would be unnecessarily duplicated. It is not the Board's policy to divulge the way in which its present staff of between 6,000 and 7,000 persons is deployed. This figure includes all those working in its technical and milk recording services, AI centres, and so forth, as well as in its factories. The staffs of the Regional Offices vary in size from region to region, but, being mainly concerned with first-hand transport arrangements, are not large. Negotiations on behalf of producers with the Creamery Proprietors' Association about the level of rebates are, under the present system, conducted centrally by the Director of Marketing and his assistant, backed with a small research staff. In the EEC situation this aspect of the Board's (or Regional Boards') work would be more complicated and extensive since it would involve entering into contracts with all bulk users of milk, not only the manufacturers. Even the Board's own factories would be bidding for supplies.[2] At present there is no need for formal negotiation of supplies to processing dairies. The Board is able to guarantee them their full requirements of milk for liquid consumption whatever they may turn out to be, and uniform margins are fixed in advance for the whole Board area by the government. On the other hand there would not necessarily be any increase in the number of manufacturing outlets. Indeed, further concentration is likely to result from the freer market. This would certainly be a strong argument in favour of centralising contracts. Since it would undoubtedly be necessary for Regional Boards to maintain close contact with each other when negotiating with purchasers, their usefulness as separate negotiating bodies might also be questioned.

A closer examination of the circumstances to be expected in a free-market situation could, therefore, show it to be in the interests of pro-

---

[1] It would be up to Regional Boards to negotiate that producers supplying these manufacturers had a built-in right to a share in any such premium.

[2] The Board's factories are not parties to negotiations at the moment, but the negotiated rebates are applied to them in the same way as to private manufacturers. In fact they tend to be treated less favourably in the matter of supplies, often being residual recipients of marginal quantities of raw milk.

ducers, consumers, and general economic efficiency for the centralised decision-making of the MMB for England and Wales to be maintained. In that case an intervention agency would have to be set up *ab initio*. We believe that, however much its activities would be governed by decisions taken in Brussels, the agency should, for reasons already given, have a Board of Management that was interprofessional in the generally accepted continental sense, though its administrative staff might be largely recruited from among persons at present employed by the five Milk Marketing Boards.

Scotland and Northern Ireland

As far as the transition to the EEC system is concerned fewer of the problems arising in the case of the MMB for England and Wales would apply in Scotland. The two northern Boards' areas are sufficiently homogeneous not to require sub-division for pricing purposes. The same, owing to the central location of the main liquid markets, is also true of the Scottish Board's area. Thanks to the relatively small demand for liquid milk in proportion to total supplies (only 54 per cent for Scotland as a whole in 1969–70,[1] including the trough, compared with 66 per cent in England and Wales) the problem of switching accommodation milk scarcely arises. Indeed, seasonal differentials in producer prices, especially in the North, are generally smaller than in England and Wales. Standard transport deductions for primary transport are related directly to distance. Largely as a result of the high proportion of milk collected in bulk (rising to over 99 per cent in the Aberdeen and District Board's area) depoting has been entirely eliminated, and the problem of secondary transport costs is less significant, producers close to liquid markets tending *ipso facto* to obtain more price advantage from their location than in England and Wales. Nevertheless, reduction in the total number of first-hand purchasers of milk since World War II has, owing largely to their wide geographical dispersion, been less marked in Scotland. The amalgamations, prompted in England and Wales by the system of wholesale allowances that was introduced as an incentive to the purchase of large-scale heat-treating equipment after the war, have not been so widespread. In Scotland there are still some 380 first-hand organisations buying 250 mn gallons a year compared with 312 in England and Wales buying 2,100 mn gallons. In the Scottish Board area the three major purchasing companies, whose largest dairy, in Glasgow, processes 30,000 to 40,000 gallons a day, account between them for less than half of the milk sold by the Board. The Board's own factories take 20 per cent.

In the remoter Western Isles milk sales are not subject to any Board scheme. As in England and Wales there are country districts in Scotland

[1] Fifty-nine per cent in the North of Scotland Board area (the proportion on the mainland is as high as 80 per cent, but in Orkney it is only about 10 per cent); 48 per cent in the Aberdeen & District Board area; and 55 per cent in the Scottish Board area).

where pasteurisation is not carried out by producer retailers. The draft EEC regulation permits unprocessed milk to be sold direct by producer to consumer. It would seem, however, that in principle all milk passing through dairies in the EEC would have to be processed since dairies are by definition places where milk is heat-treated. In the UK some 30 mn gallons a year of farm-bottled non-processed milk is still sold by dairies. It looks as if this practice will have to be discontinued.

The disadvantages and compensations of adopting the EEC system in Northern Ireland would be similar to those in Scotland. With under 30 per cent of milk going to the liquid market the province presents the closest approximation to EEC conditions of any part of the UK. A levy system will protect producers from the price fluctuations for dairy products on world markets to which they have long been exposed. The Northern Ireland Board realised 18·06d per gallon in 1969/70 for the 72 per cent of total milk supplies that were sold for manufacture. This was $\frac{1}{2}$d a gallon more than in 1968/69, but the year before there had been a drop of 1$\frac{1}{2}$d. Under the EEC price structure pooled producer returns in the Board's area should increase more than enough to make up for the loss of payment from the UK Milk Fund (7·09d per gallon in 1969/70). A higher pool price (perhaps a shilling (5p) or more above the 1969 level) would inevitably stimulate supply, even allowing for the rise in feed costs (though this would be proportionately smaller than in England in view of the present relatively high price of feed grains in the province). Production of butter, which already accounts for 40 per cent of usage of manufacturing milk but only satisfies a third of local demand, could well rise to a level sufficient to meet that demand (anyway, demand as reduced by the price effect) in full. The co-operative creameries in the west of the province, conscious of the safety net provided by the EEC intervention price, would tend especially to step up their production. Absence of intervention arrangements, coupled with a fairly high-price elasticity of demand, for condensed milk and sterilised cream would tend to set a limit on the expansion of those products, which in 1969/70 accounted for 13 per cent and 14 per cent of usage of manufacturing milk respectively. Almost 100 per cent of the sterilised cream and nearly 60 per cent of the condensed milk is exported to Great Britain and beyond the UK (with aid from transport rebates paid to manufacturers[1]), as well as 90 per cent of cheese (mainly Cheddar and Cheshire). In the EEC this would cease to enjoy its privileged entry in preference to exports from the Irish Republic and the EEC into Great Britain under the present 'voluntary' limitation arrangements. Competition from Commonwealth countries would, on the other hand, be reduced by the Community levies. Nor, obviously, would any butter surpluses which might arise in the province benefit from priority on the British market.

A significant aspect of entry into the EEC for Northern Ireland's milk

[1] Effectively about half the cost of these is borne by producers in the form of a lower realisation price, and the rest falls on the UK Milk Fund. If continued in the EEC their entire cost would therefore be borne by Northern Ireland producers.

producers will be the eventual disappearance, economically speaking, of the border with the South. The eradication of brucellosis, shortly be to achieved in the province, will give them short- or even medium-term protection against imports destined for the liquid market. Whether manufacturing milk would be free to cross the border by the end of any transition period would depend on how far common standards of dairy hygiene had been agreed, and put into practice, in the Community. At present standards in Southern dairies are not acceptable in the North. The Northern Ireland MMB, however acceptable to the EEC Commission as a producer organisation with monopoly powers as sole first-hand purchaser of raw milk in its own area, could one day be obliged to compete with imported supplies in its sales to manufacturers. It might even find itself accepting registered producers from the northern areas of the Republic. The efficiency of the Board's own collection system, giving average transport costs as low as 1·6d per gallon, would ensure some protection against imports. On the other hand producers in the South accustomed to much lower rates of return might be prepared to absorb quite a proportion of any higher transport costs of exports to the North and still compete with the Board in supplying manufacturers in the Six Counties, obtaining higher return than they could get from Southern creameries which were selling butter at intervention. But, generally speaking, the longer imports are, for one reason or another, delayed the narrower the advantage to producers in the South is likely to become.

The dairy processing and manufacturing industry in Northern Ireland is, considering the small size of the country, by no means concentrated, and the advent of a free market in milk, including free imports from the South, seems bound to lead eventually to some rationalisation. At present there are forty-three dairy enterprises working in the province. Of the major private factories four, all condenseries, belong to Nestlé, and one each to Ambrosia, the CWS, Pickerings (a Heinz subsidiary), and Antrim Creameries (making territorial cheeses). The five processing dairies belonging to Northern Dairies (based on Hull) also manufacture fresh products. Ten smaller independent firms engaged mainly in the liquid milk market also do some manufacturing. The thirteen producer co-operatives in the West are, as already mentioned, mainly engaged in butter making. Finally, the Northern Ireland MMB itself has six factories producing butter and milk powder, and a seventh, at Bangor, processing and distributing liquid milk, ice-cream, and special products.

In anticipating the situation in which all Ireland finds itself within a common market for milk the Board has a number of choices of action, not all of them mutually exclusive. It could, of course, plan to divest itself of its manufacturing interests altogether and concentrate on using its monopoly of first-hand milk collection in the province (which we assume it would be the wish of a majority of producers to continue) to obtain the best possible prices and conditions of sale for producers in what would be, considering the number of potential manufacturing buyers and the possibility of bulk imports from the Republic, a fairly competitive market. Alternatively, the Board could itself remain in the market, possibly in association with the Western co-operatives, and consolidate a strong direct-producer interest in manufacturing. Another possibility would be for it to engage in partnership, either by formally acquiring a shareholding or on some sort of contracting basis that would make use of the equipment and expertise of its existing plants, or both, with one or more of the private firms in the province. The Board could also establish co-operative marketing links with An Bord Bainne, the Milk Marketing Board in Dublin[1], or, if that Board were to become the intervention agency for the Republic, direct with the co-operatives in the South, a number of which operate fairly close to the border. Producers' organisations on both sides of the border may in any case be obliged eventually to reach some sort of working arrangement over supplies to guard against excessive price cutting—down as far as intervention level at any rate—that could in the end only damage their members' interest.

In view of the recent strictures of the Ashton Committee on the commercial activities of another Marketing Board in Northern Ireland,[2] the first option—to concentrate on selling milk—might appear to be the safest, and softest. The second is certainly more hazardous, unless it were merely the intention of the co-operative group (the Board plus the co-ops) to manufacture mainly for the intervention agency. Otherwise it is questionable whether a joint co-operative enterprise on this scale would have sufficient access to resources of finance and commercial know-how to mount the sort of research and development and promotional effort necessary for entering the highly competitive common market for the more sophisticated type of dairy product. It would after all be competing not only with major British companies, but with Gervais-Danone, MFE, ULN, Yoplait and the rest. These handicaps could perhaps be overcome through a partnership with private industry, especially if it were with a firm to which the Board had something to offer in return in the way of technical know-how based on its own experience. The Ashton Report has stressed the difficulty which may arise of reconciling producer interests with those of partnerships of this kind in the pig-processing industry. There are obvious conflicts of interest, to which reference recurs several times in this study, between agricultural producers and processors, which have not been satisfactorily resolved even between producer co-operatives and manufacturing/wholesaling consumer co-operatives. For this reason the presence of the CWS in the Northern Ireland dairy industry probably provides little scope, despite first appearances, for partnership with producer interests.

We would not presume, without much closer acquaintance with the operation of the NIMMB's factories, to suggest which, if any, of these alternative courses should be adopted by the Board once a transitional

[1] See pp. 261-2.
[2] See p. 130.

period had begun. The dilemma that they represent does, however, have a wider application than to the particular Northern Ireland context. On the Continent, as has been seen, dairy co-operatives are in big business. It cannot of course be assumed unreservedly that because of this they are both economically and commercially efficient and that they always act in the best interests of the producer. But the presumption must be that in general the countervailing power which they exercise in an increasingly concentrated market has considerable effectiveness at least compared with the atomistic nature of the production of the primary product which they are handling. In Britain the co-operatives are weak, and countervailing power of a different kind has been exercised on producers' behalf by the MMBs. The nature and extent of this power would be modified by entry into the EEC. Since it does not lie, as it does mainly on the Continent, because of the very different demand situation, in the sphere of manufacturing, some consideration would have to be given to the future role and policy objectives of factories owned by Boards in other parts of the United Kingdom. The history of milk marketing during the past 40 years in Great Britain and the structure of the dairy industry, dominated as it is by a few large enterprises (including the CWS), hardly suggest that producers are well placed to exercise much direct leverage either in manufacturing or retailing. The recent withdrawal of two major international food groups from marketing yoghurt may be cited as an indication of the hazards of innovation in a competitive market where technical development costs are very high. On the other hand, it may be argued that so long as this island remains deficitary in butter and cheese (which it is likely to do even at EEC retail price levels) there is not much risk attached to the Boards' concentration on manufacturing those products, and that this would continue to be the best means of maximising returns.

CHAPTER 6

Livestock and Meat

This chapter is concerned with cattle, sheep and pigs, and the carcase meat derived from them, that is to say beef and veal, mutton and lamb and pigmeat. Poultry-meat is included in Chapter 7. These products have far the most complicated marketing system of all agricultural commodities in both Britain and the member countries of the EEC. The reasons why this subject is so complex, and even forbidding, will be apparent: the numbers and varieties of breeds of animals, the lack of conformity within these breeds, the many different forms that meat can take, the bewildering list of by-products (who can be certain what is the activity of a fellmonger?), and the problems associated with an exceptionally perishable product. It seems probable that very little is known by consumers about the marketing system that lies behind the meat that they buy. Perhaps people do not want to know about it, to be forced to associate meat with the live animal that produced it.

So far as the British market is concerned, the report issued in 1964 of the Verdon-Smith Committee of Inquiry[1] provides much detailed and valuable information. The main objects of this chapter are to summarise the principal features of the existing British marketing system, so as to provide a basis for comparison with practices in EEC member countries, to highlight the changes that have occurred since the work of the Verdon-Smith Committee, and to identify the main current trends in the development of livestock and meat marketing in Britain. Considering the economic importance of the subject, and particularly the significance of meat in total consumers' expenditure (about 7 per cent), it is surprising that more follow-up work has not been done on this report. This is one of the important roles that the Meat and Livestock Commission (effectively in operation only since October 1968) is beginning to fill.

Meat supplies in Britain, both home produced and imported, were estimated to amount to about 3·6 mn tons in 1969/70. Of this total a little over two-thirds (2·5 mn tons) was home produced, and the rest imported. Exports were very small: about 60,000 tons of meat, plus live animals (some 212,000 cattle, 50,000 sheep, and 25,000 pigs) whose meat equivalent

[1] *Report of the Committee of Inquiry into fatstock and carcase meat marketing and distribution* (Chairman, W. R. Verdon-Smith, Esq.). HMSO, London, 1964, Cmnd 2282.

was roughly as much again. Self-sufficiency has greatly increased since the war, though not to the extent of realising fully the expectations of government policy. In 1953/54 when government control of the trade was being relaxed, imports were at about the same level as at present but home-produced supplies were approximately 600,000 tons less than are available now.

There are two basic marketing choices open to the British livestock producer. He can sell by auction, or he can by-pass auctions and sell by private treaty, on the hoof or to deadweight centres, including bacon factories. The proportions of all stock that go through auctions have been falling, the trend being particularly noticeable in pigs. Detailed information is limited to the number of certifications made under the Fatstock Guarantee Scheme which does not cover all stock sold, but the following table gives a fair indication of the trend (Fatstock Guarantee years April–March).

Auctions as percentage of total certifications in the UK in selected years 1956/57 to 1969/70.

	Cattle	Sheep	Pigs
1956/57	71·7	66·8	33·0
1959/60	77·3	66·3	28·0
1962/63	69·6	63·6	20·6
1965/66	65·7	60·4	16·5
1968/69	55·0	58·0	13·9
1969/70	53·4	60·0	14·6

Source: Meat & Livestock Commission

Selling livestock, whether finished beasts or stores, by auction is a straightforward matter. The producer instructs the auctioneer and pays for the transport to the market. The auctioneer pays to the producer the prices realised, less commission, generally without delay. Any additional payment under the Fatstock Guarantee Scheme is obtained on the basis of a certificate, provided either by the auctioneer, acting as certifying officer on behalf of the Ministry of Agriculture, or more recently, by fatstock officers of the Meat and Livestock Commission, which now administers the scheme for the Ministry.[1] All sales are, of course, made on a liveweight basis. Buyers, who include retail butchers, meat wholesalers (with or without slaughterhouse facilities of their own), meat processors and dealers move the livestock immediately either to the slaughterhouse or, in the case of stores, to the place where they will be further fattened.

The growing proportion of livestock that is sold outside auctions can be valued either through visual inspection of the live animal after weighing or through various kinds of examination of the carcase of the dead animal. The latter method permits far more accurate assessment of the value of the animal. The closer that the price-fixing point gets to the condition at retail of the meat, the more accurate can be the value assessment. Most non-

---

[1] For a description of the British support system, see Butterwick and Neville-Rolfe, *op cit*, pp. 131–2 (beef and veal), p. 143 (mutton and lamb) and p. 150 (pigmeat).

auction sales are done on a deadweight basis. Nearly all direct sales of pigs are deadweight and about 90 per cent of direct sales of cattle and sheep. There are several other advantages to direct sales (either liveweight or deadweight), for instance, lower transport costs and less risk of disease. Direct selling would undoubtedly have made further progress in Britain at the expense of the auctions if it were not for the Fatstock Guarantee Scheme. If an animal fails to qualify for certification at auction, the producer has the option of trying again either at another auction or offering to a deadweight buyer. For livestock which are borderline cases under the Scheme, the producer has lost these options if he goes straight for a direct deadweight sale.

Fatstock leave the producers' premises in a live form but their value, whether the price is fixed live or dead, is in the carcase. Problems of relating the two together still present difficulties despite efforts that are being made to show the farmer how his product turns out as a carcase, and to explain to him what the buyer is particularly looking for. Changes in the marketing methods for livestock are closely connected with progress towards an agreed basis for carcase classification. This is inevitably a very slow process particularly as it is influenced by many developments outside marketing itself which are tending to result in a greater volume of uniform carcases. Among these are improvements in livestock breeding, more detailed knowledge of the best use of animal feedingstuffs, and the increasing standardisation of demand, associated with the expansion of multiple meat-retailing organisations and the growth of self-service.[1] In Britain the livestock and meat industry seems to be on the verge of being able to agree classification standards in which all parties would have confidence. Such an agreement could greatly influence both marketing and production. It is expected that recommendations for a classification system for cattle on a voluntary basis will go out to the trade in the near future. The most important feature of any scheme of this kind is that it should be kept as simple and straightforward as possible so that the maximum number of producers and buyers use it. On the other hand, the scheme must be clearcut about such carcase characteristics as can be precisely described and are of real importance. The only essential features appear to be weight, age and a reliable back-fat measurement, with some extremes of conformation excluded. Least progress in Britain has been made on mutton and lamb classification, to the great benefit of the New Zealand producer who has worked to carefully supervised grades for many years. When classification is finally introduced and accepted by the trade, it will make possible important changes in meat and livestock marketing in Britain. The EEC countries have made very little progress in classification on a national level. France with its strong livestock markets would like a livestock classification system first. Germany is more interested in pressing its own carcase classification. There has been even less progress in harmonisation on a Community basis.

[1] See also Chapter 2.

A large number of developments are currently influencing the British livestock and meat industries. So far as marketing is concerned, there appear to be five factors of particular importance. First, there is a very strong trend towards concentration of production on fewer farms. This concentration, which has affected most types of agricultural production, has been strongest in the pig industry, in which the number of producers has fallen by about a third over the past five years. A similar, though less marked, trend in concentration has affected cattle and sheep. For all three there is a marked tendency for the average size of enterprise to increase year by year.

Thus, even a large buyer need now deal with comparatively few producers. This is well illustrated from the case of Wall's which buys about 75 per cent of its pigs on contract. In 1960 Wall's had 3,500 producers on contract. By 1968 the number of producers had fallen to under 1,000, and the average number of pigs delivered per producer had increased by six times. Concentration of production not only eases the procurement problems of buyers but also makes possible closer links between producers and buyers.

There is a second trend in livestock marketing that is also exemplified by Wall's. As both the number of livestock sold deadweight by private treaty and the average delivery per producer increase, there is a tendency for producer and buyer to deal regularly with each other and for each side to expect to renew a contract at its termination. Livestock producers who prefer to sell without contracts, which are anyway uncommon for cattle and sheep, also tend to work closely with one or two buyers. Several large buyers now favour close links with a limited number of producers, including Sainsbury's and the Co-operative Wholesale Society Meat Group. Traditionally farmers have established regular outlets for their stock through local butchers with slaughtering facilities. Now these links are being developed between the larger independent producers and some of the important buyers of livestock. The foundation of the relationship is the knowledge that the producer can acquire of the buyer's needs. This gives the existing partner an advantage over other producers who may wish to secure a similar outlet, and may also enable him to obtain a premium price for his product.

Trends in the pattern of meat retailing in Britain are also significant. The multiples have continued to erode the share of the market enjoyed by the family butcher. Now the supermarkets are competing very actively for consumers' expenditure on meat. Various estimates have been made of the proportion of the trade that the supermarkets may have in the future. In reality these can be little more than well-informed guesses, as so much depends on changes in consumers' buying habits. The successful operation of a self-service meat department involves the offering of pre-packed cuts of standardised quality. There are problems associated with the supply of these products, including the preservation of the meat, the accurate estimation of demand, and the need to change slaughterhouse techniques so that much of the cutting is done at this point rather than by the retailer. All these are problems which the retailer and the slaughterhouse/meat wholesaler are now in process of solving. How many consumers will be prepared in the near future to desert their family butcher in favour of the self-service store can only be a matter for conjecture. There is no more recent statistical evidence of changes in the pattern of retail butchering than that supplied by the 1966 Census of Distribution. This showed that the number of butchers' shops, just over 38,000 in 1966, had declined by nearly 10 per cent during the five years since the previous Census. This was rather less than in the case of most other retail establishments. Average turnover had also gone up proportionately less. On the other hand the proportion of butchers' establishments with a turnover of under £10,000 a year, or even of under £20,000 a year, all small or medium-sized businesses, is substantially smaller than that of all types of food shops taken together. It is possible that independent butchers have stayed in business to a greater extent than other independent retailers in the face of competition from multiples and supermarkets by being able to afford a lower profit margin on their higher turnover. This would be quite apart from the protection afforded them by a special expertise (or alleged expertise) not expected from mere purveyors of foodstuffs like grocers or greengrocers, whose numbers declined much more rapidly between 1961 and 1966. Certainly in the butchery trade there has been no trend comparable to that in grocery towards self-protection by centralised buying through voluntary and co-operative retailing chains.

A fourth factor is the application of sales promotion to meat. The large retailing organisations in Britain, whose turnover of meat has become increasingly important, are intent on developing their public image as suppliers of products of good value and/or good quality. The chief difference between them lies in the relative emphasis laid on these two product characteristics. In this fierce competition 'own brands' play a large part. The speed with which some organisations have moved into 'own brands' is remarkable. The technique is already used for bacon and some meat products such as sausages and meat pies. In these products the retailers' brands have in some cases been successfully promoted against the national brands of the large meat processors. Some attempts have also been made to establish brand names for cuts from carcase meat. With the present trend in supermarket retailing, however, it seems unlikely that meat processor-wholesalers will be successful in launching new brands.

Finally, individual producers of livestock have been increasing their scale of operations and therefore acquiring a more advantageous position from which to negotiate with the big wholesale or retail buyers. At the same time there has been a considerable increase in recent years in the number and activity of livestock producers' marketing groups. The total number of groups which are members of the Association of Livestock Producers' Marketing Organisation, an affiliate of the NFU, now amounts to 125. There are, however, considerable variations among these groups in turnover, commercial organisation, discipline and range of activity. They have had far more success in pigs than in cattle and sheep.

Livestock groups in Britain have yet to prove themselves as a permanent effective force in agricultural marketing. Many of them are very young. Few have as yet established commercial links with outlets for their members' products on a notably better basis than the members could obtain on their own and without the cost of running the group. Apart from problems of overhead costs, there are difficulties over capital or credit and management which government assistance through the Central Council for Agricultural and Horticultural Co-operation can no more than ease. Only a handful of groups have as yet grappled effectively with the delicate problem of supplies of feedingstuffs for their members. It is not at all easy for a group to create a commercial relationship with a feedingstuffs supplier (which may be a useful source of credit) and still retain its independence and sense of identity.

The attitude of livestock buyers to the formation of producer groups for marketing is clearly of great importance. In Britain this attitude takes various forms, but enthusiasm is a rarity. The most obvious reason for this—that buyers are reluctant to see producers obtaining greater bargaining strength—is by no means a full explanation. Some have had poor experiences in the past through groups failing to supply according to their undertakings, though allowance should be made for the possibility that buyers may exaggerate these failures. Others fear that the existence of an intermediary between producer and buyer in the form of the group may inhibit the development of the close relationship which they particularly want. The question is whether such a relationship is really of mutual advantage and can be of as much benefit in the long-term to the producer, even though he is necessarily the weaker partner. The best structure for group marketing would allow buyers to have access to producers, so that exchange of technical information on quality requirements continued, with the group retaining responsibility for price negotiations and for fulfilment of delivery obligations.

Looking to the future, there may be three main elements in the development of livestock marketing in Britain. First there will be an increasing concentration of supplies due partly to higher average size of herds and flocks, and partly to the growth of group marketing. Some of the groups may retain responsibility for marketing members' produce beyond the point of slaughter and thus integrate forwards into the meat trade, but the majority may well consider that they would do better to avoid these specialised functions. On the demand side there will also be further concentration. Part of this will be at the expense of the independent family butcher, but it would be a mistake to write off the smaller retailer who could benefit from the availability of packaged wholesale cuts and might be able, through co-operative buying, to compete effectively with the larger organisations. The relationships between sellers and buyers are likely to continue to be complex and varied. The use of contracts will grow as classification schemes are accepted, but informal arrangements, which seem to suit the livestock and meat traders, are likely to remain the most important links between the various interests for many years to come.

What has been said above applies in general to bacon as much as to other forms of meat. Bacon curing is a feature of the British livestock market which distinguishes it very clearly from that of the EEC, where bacon, especially the Wiltshire cure, is not a widely used form of pigmeat. The Netherlands have traditionally exported some bacon to the UK, but under the current Bacon Understanding[1] enjoy a rather limited share (about 2 per cent) of what is the world's largest single market (639,000 tons in 1969/70. Just over a third of this is supplied from the UK itself, including about 10 per cent from Northern Ireland). Bacon factories absorb some 40 per cent of all pigs marketed in Britain. Of these about 60 per cent are procured on a grade and deadweight basis, generally on contract. Over the past decade there has been a marked move away from the practice of curing whole carcases; the proportion is now less than 30 per cent. The reasons for this are mainly economic. Most factories have found it more profitable to sell part of the carcase as fresh pork, or use it for processing. This in its turn has increased the use of heavy hogs and of cures other than Wiltshire, such as the Midland, better suited to the middles or joints of the larger carcase. The economic pressures towards concentration in the bacon industry have been considerable. Of the 170 factories in production in 1967, 32 accounted for more than 80 per cent of the bacon produced in England, Scotland and Wales during the first nine months of the year, well over half of it coming from seven factories. Ownership is even more concentrated, being largely in the hands of about a dozen companies, including two major ones. The main companies do their own wholesaling, and some have retail outlets as well.[2]

There is a similar degree of concentration in Northern Ireland, where the four largest factories currently account for over 50 per cent of output, and only nine out of the province's 21 factories even have slaughtering facilities. Some of them are very small. Four out of the six largest are unusual enterprises in that they are jointly owned by the Northern Ireland Pigs Marketing Board (which through a wholly owned subsidiary PMB (Investments) Ltd, holds a controlling interest in them ranging from 51 per cent to 66⅔ per cent of the share capital) and four different private firms with interests in meat processing. The Board's four companies are: Northern Ireland Farmers' Bacon Co., Cookstown (with R. H. Thompson), Producers' Bacon Co., Belfast (with Smithfield and Zwanenberg), Ulster Farmers' Bacon Co., Newry (with H. Denny, a local firm who also have a factory of their own, and W. P. Anderson), and Ulster-Swift Ltd,

---

[1] *Understanding on the Supply of Bacon to the United Kingdom Market*, 1969. HMSO, London, Cmnd 3957.

[2] For a fuller description see *The bacon curing industry*. Report of the committee of enquiry set up by the Economic Development Committee for Food Processing, National Economic Development Office, London, December 1967.

Enniskillen (with Swift). Of the five directors of PMB Investments three are Board members, one is a local business man whose appointment is subject to the approval of the Northern Ireland Minister of Agriculture, and the fifth an executive director who is on the board of each of the subsidiary companies. The Pigs Marketing Board itself, originally set up in 1933 under the Northern Ireland Agricultural Marketing Act of that year, was re-established in 1954 after the period of war-time government control. Eleven of the Board's members including the Chairman are elected by registered producers. Three, all local business men, including the Vice-Chairman, are appointed by the Minister. There is a total administrative staff of 119, of whom 30 are field men dealing with the reception of pigs at factories.[1]

The Board is statutorily the sole purchaser of bacon pigs but in practice 99·5 per cent of all pigs are marketed through it. Under the Centralised Pork Scheme any pigs surplus to factories' curing requirements are sold to the Board, which disposes of them as whole carcases or sides of pork. Though optional the scheme has offered advantages sufficient to induce most curers to take part in it. Only registered producers may sell bacon pigs or vote in Board elections. Non-bacon pig producers may also qualify for a vote by registering. Any producer who has not marketed any bacon pigs during the previous six months is obliged at the end of the year to apply for renewal of registration. Out of 15,000 registered producers fewer than half regularly finish pigs, the remainder being mainly engaged in producing weaners. Although 36 per cent of herds still contain under 20 pigs, the structure of production is becoming more concentrated and 54 per cent of pigs are now in herds of 200 pigs and over. Between 10 and 15 per cent of marketings are accounted for by co-operatives or producer groups, a trend which has emerged effectively only during the past five years. Owners of breeding herds have also formed weaner groups. These groups have been actively promoted by compounders. The Board has in principle been reluctant to give too much encouragement to anything which might lead to extreme forms of vertical integration, but is prepared to pay feed firms direct for pigs delivered to it where a producer or group specifically authorises it. This practice is, however, still very limited.

A government subsidy, equivalent to that paid to producers in Great Britain, enables the Board to pay producers the guaranteed prices fixed at the Annual Review. Otherwise its activities are entirely financed by means of a producer levy, which has until recently been 4s 6d (22½p) per pig delivered. This included an element for capital investment of 2s 6d (12½p), now discontinued, which has enabled extensive improvements to the Board's factories to be carried out and ammortised over the past twelve years. Apart from satisfying local demand for pig-meat the Board's main

[1] A detailed account of the Board's functioning and activities is to be found in the *Report of a Committee of Inquiry set up to examine the marketing of pigs in Northern Ireland* (Chairman, Professor John Ashton). HMSO, Belfast, June 1970, Cmnd 545. The Report has been published since our own visit to Northern Ireland.

outlet is in the form of bacon on the GB market, though recently some EEC countries have purchased pork sides. All Wiltshire bacon is marketed in GB by the Ulster Bacon Agency, in which the Board has a minority shareholding, but parity of directorships with independent curing and processing interests. All pigs are bought by the Board on a grade and deadweight basis, penalty prices being paid to encourage bacon weights and high quality. A summer bonus for June and July, announced a year ahead, has reduced the natural seasonal fluctuation in supply by up to a half. Otherwise the Board operates a level price policy, changing producer prices as infrequently as possible, perhaps four or five times a year. This is achieved by means of a stabilising fund operated through a Special Account. This benefits from the provisions of the 1952 Finance Act in favour of the Wool Marketing Board which exempt from tax any end-of-year surplus. A maximum of £0·75 mn may be held in the fund at the end of any one quarter. In fixing its prices the Board has to take account of the state of the market, the level of the fund, and the government guarantee. Monthly forecasts are calculated for the twelve months ahead on the basis of these factors as well as of the foreign market situation and of the effect on supply of import quotas under the Bacon Sharing Understanding. Allocation of pigs to factories is by quotas fixed by the Ministry of Agriculture on the basis of 1963/65 throughput. Since the quotas are adjustable to some extent it is said that they have tended over the years to promote rationalisation rather than fossilising the structure of the industry. The Board charges a uniform price for pigs to all factories regardless of location. This price is related to factories' costs and realisations. An acceptable level of curing margin is negotiated[1] annually between the Board and the factories of the independent sector, which controls about 57 per cent of output, having regard to the known costs of the Board's own factories. The second element of the price paid by the Board to the independents consists of course of the price of Ulster bacon on the London Provision Exchange. This is fixed in consultation with the Ulster Bacon Agency.

Despite the fact that 90 per cent of Northern Irish bacon is marketed outside the province, thus incurring relatively high transport costs, producer prices are said by the PMB to have exceeded those obtained in Great Britain. That production has nevertheless not greatly expanded is attributed to the higher cost of feed, minimum import prices for cereals and the tendency of GB to become a net exporter of barley to third countries having accentuated Northern Ireland's disadvantageous geographical position. The Ashton Committee, however, too a sceptical view of the Board's price comparisons, which it found 'entirely misleading'. Nor did it accept that a contributory factor to the Northern Irish pig producers' better return from the market has been the relatively greater efficiency of the local bacon processors. On the contrary it considered that the Board's monopoly, by preventing the diversification essential to the

[1] Effectively it is the 'balance', providing for production costs and profit on bacon, which is negotiable and currently accounts for over 40 per cent of the final applied margin.

growth of the pig-processing industry, had given producers a lower return than they might otherwise have obtained.

It seems appropriate at this point to refer to the province's other main livestock export. In terms of net output beef is Northern Ireland's most important commodity, input costs being relatively low. There is a suckler herd of 190,000 cows (though this only represents an average of about six per holding), and up to 150,000 store cattle are imported every year from the Republic. Since 1960 a decreasing proportion of finished cattle surplus to domestic needs has been exported at high cost on the hoof. Increasing competition from the South, both on the GB market and for stores, has also led to a considerable rationalisation of slaughtering facilities. There will soon be a single abattoir only, at Belfast, and one each at the five major processing plants, which are large by GB standards. Between them British Beef, Lonsdale (Spillers), Moy Meats, Mid-Ulster Meats and FMC had an average weekly throughput of nearly 2,100 head during the 52 weeks ending March 1970. FMC has recently taken over its Newry plant from an Anglo-Danish firm which had failed to establish a large-scale retail pre-pack enterprise. Nevertheless there would appear to be some scope for reducing the proportion of sides exported and carrying out more boning and processing on the Irish side of the Channel. Although seasonality of production, especially on the many small farms, inhibits any extensive development of contracts between producers and processors, there has been, judging from reduced business at livestock auctions, some increase in direct sales.

The EEC system[1]

For beef and veal the support system, for which the basic regulation is 805/1968, revolves round a guide price. This both sets the actual level of protection against imports and provides a trip for internal market intervention. Import levies are calculated by substracting from the guide price, which is fixed annually for a period of a year, the current duty-paid import price. These are estimated weekly by the Commission, without reference to the Management Committee, on the basis of quotations on 64 UK markets, on Dublin market, and on Vienna market, and of information received from the Danish livestock export organisation.[2] For each country an arithmetical mean price of all qualities of beast is reached, to which is added a fixed charge for freight and the *ad valorem* duty of 16 per cent. A weighted average of the resulting four country prices then becomes the official import price on which the levy on live cattle is based for the

[1] A brief summary only is given here. For full details the reader is referred to R. C. Rickard, *Beef and veal in the Common Market: an examination of the EEC market regulations for beef and veal, effective from July 1968* and *A common market for pigs: an examination of the EEC regulations for pigs and pigmeat effective from 1 July 1967* (Exeter University, Department of Agricultural Economics) and subsequent circulars.

[2] When the Community is enlarged a new basis for calculating the import price will obviously have to be devised.

coming week. The proportion of the levy actually charged (100, 75, 50, 25 per cent or nil) depends on the current level of market prices within the Community for fat cattle (*gros bovins*), excluding those of manufacturing quality, and for calves, in relation to the guide prices for beef and veal. The market price is estimated by means of a weighted average of prices on designated markets in each member country. When the market price falls to 106 per cent of the guide price 25 per cent of the levy is applied. As the price falls further the level of the levy is progressively raised. When the market price reaches the actual guide price the full levy is applicable.

For fresh and chilled meat the levies fixed for live cattle and calves are applied to sides and cuts by means of conversion co-efficients, the basic *ad valorem* duty being 20 per cent. For frozen meat, levies, which are in this case fixed only monthly, are calculated in a similar way, the guide prices of sides and cuts being derived from the guide price for live cattle. The c.i.f. price for sides is based on reports from member countries and other sources, with co-efficients for calculating, for levy purposes, c.i.f. prices for fores, hinds and cuts of different quality. Unlike those for live cattle and for fresh and chilled meat, levies on frozen meat are applied in full with certain exceptions. In order to enable Community manufacturers to compete with imports of corned-beef, meat destined to that end is levy free. A levy-free (but not duty-free) quota of 22,000 tons a year is bound in GATT. Meat for other processed products may be imported at a reduced levy, which varies from quarter to quarter, being higher in the autumn, up to a given quota fixed quarterly in the light of the internal supply situation.

There are two types of intervention, optional and mandatory. Intervention is optional for national governments (acting through their respective agencies) when the representative market price for the Community falls below 98 per cent of the guide price, or when prices fall below derived intervention prices for certain qualities of cattle in certain regions. The object of this is to prevent local prices having a disproportionate effect on the Community average and thus making necessary more generalised intervention. Intervention becomes mandatory once the market price has fallen below 93 per cent of the guide price. The purchase price (delivered store) paid by the intervention agency may not be above that laid down for local voluntary intervention, and may be below. In all cases the prices at which the agencies intervene are determined by the Commission in consultation with the Management Committee. Normally refrigerated storage space is hired by intervention agencies, but provision is made in the regulations for subsidies to be paid to private firms for holding intervention stocks if necessary. Sales out of store are subject to either a price fixed by the Commission (in consultation with Management Committee) or to a minimum price above which tenders are invited.

Restitutions, for beef only, are limited to exports to certain traditional markets, including that of forequarters to the UK. About 20,000 tons a year on average is involved.

Official EEC market arrangements for pigs (Regulation 121/67) differ in certain important respects from those for beef and veal. The guide price is replaced by a basic price, for slaughtered pigmeat of a standard quality, fixed at a level 'at which it contributes towards stabilising market prices without leading to the formation of structural surpluses'. Intervention buying may occur when the arithmetical mean of the price of pigmeat in the Community is, 'and is likely to remain', below the basic price.[1] The purchase price may be not higher than 92 per cent nor lower than 85 per cent of the basic price. Protection at the common frontier is achieved by a complicated system of levies combined with sluice-gate (minimum import) prices. The sluice-gate price per kg of pigmeat of standard quality (from which are derived corresponding prices for cuts, processed products, etc., by means of co-efficients) is composed of three elements: the current value on world markets of the feed grain required to produce one kg of pigmeat in third countries; a standard amount corresponding to the value of the non-feedgrain element; and a standard amount representing general production and marketing costs. Sluice-gate prices are fixed quarterly on the basis of feedgrain prices over the previous six months. The levy per kg of imported pigmeat consists of two components: first, the difference between the price in the Community and on world markets of the amount of feedgrain required to produce one kg of pigmeat in the community; and second, 7 per cent of the average of the sluice-gate price over the preceding four quarters (10 per cent in the case of processed meat). In the event of a free-at-frontier offer price being lower than the sluice-gate price the levy is increased by a supplementary amount equivalent to the difference between the offer price and the sluice-gate price.

The market structure in the EEC

There are considerable variations in consumption of meat between the member countries of the EEC. The highest consumption per head is in France and the lowest in Italy. The average for the whole Community is about the same as for Britain. The most striking difference is that consumption has been increasing in all the member countries while it has been falling

[1] There has been a good deal of dissatisfaction among the trade, especially in France, at the alleged inflexibility of the present intervention process for pigmeat. Prior to 1967 intervention buying by SIBEV was automatically tripped off as market prices fell towards the intervention level, and much of French opinion is strongly in favour of this type of preventive intervention. In the unified market, on the other hand, intervention can only occur when the average price for all Community markets falls to a certain level. This, in the critics' view, penalises a country where the price cycle may happen to be a week or two ahead of that in the rest of the Community, by delaying intervention there. It also tends to extend unnecessarily the trough of the cycle, and thus the length of the intervention period, for the Community as a whole.

in Britain. To meet this growth in consumption farmers in the EEC member countries have steadily increased their production of livestock, particularly of pigs. Taking the Community as a whole, the level of self-sufficiency has risen. By contrast there has been a marked expansion of trade between member countries in live cattle, mostly from France and Germany to Italy, and in live pigs. Intra-Community trade in meat has also risen substantially, France being the main exporter of beef and veal to member countries and Belgium and the Netherlands the leading exporters of pigmeat.

In each of the member countries the livestock and meat market systems share several of the characteristics of the British system. The trends in marketing that can be identified are very similar to those that have already been noted in Britain: concentration in the trade, including a certain amount in retailing; the growth of producer groups; the rationalisation of the structure of slaughtering; links between processors, wholesalers and producers; and a gradual movement towards integration, loose in the case of beef and veal, closer for pigmeat.

In France there are about 3,000 firms engaged in the meat trade, employing some 25,000 people. The 1966 census revealed that many of these firms were very small, over 900 having only one or two employees. At the other end of the scale the businesses employing more than 50 people numbered 51, but accounted for over a quarter of the total employment in the trade. In addition the census showed that there were 8,000 firms of livestock dealers. Most of these are very small businesses; between them they only employ 16,000 persons. There are no livestock auctions. Traditionally French country livestock markets are conducted on the basis of the individually concluded bargain. There has, however, been an increasing trend, originally set off by war-time restrictions, for dealers to buy direct from farms. Since production is in general still very fragmented this has tended to work against the interest of the small farmer who is then selling without much awareness of current price trends. Though in theory producer groups provide the best way out of this situation, the psychological difficulties of forming these, quite apart from the shortage of farmers with adequate education or organisational ability to get them off the ground, has led the authorities in some areas to encourage the establishment, or revival, of local markets instead. These at least restore a measure of transparency to the trade, even if not as much as would be secured by setting up auctions. While firms in the French livestock and meat trades remain small and based on on-farm deals, local markets and local (often municipal) slaughtering facilities, there are indications that the structure of the marketing system is altering. The changes are of three kinds. First, the large meat-processing companies are now buying, sometimes on contract, direct from producers, or producer marketing organisations, rather than from the wholesalers. Second, the co-operatives after a slow start in meat marketing are now beginning to develop more effectively. The Groupe Lafayette's meat marketing is being regionalised. Some of these regional co-operatives appear to be prospering. For instance, SOCOPA (based on Angers) has built up a direct trade on contract with some supermarkets, and SICA Centre-Sud (covering Auvergne, Aquitaine and Languedoc) after a shaky start is doing likewise. Third, there has been a fairly rapid growth over the past few years in producer marketing groups. By 1970 the number of these groups had risen to about 250, dealing mostly with pigs, but 90 specialising in cattle and 20 in sheep. There are no reliable statistics of the share of the total market controlled by groups, but a fair estimation might be that up to 12 per cent of total French output of pigs and beef cattle is in their hands, with a much smaller proportion (under 5 per cent) of the output of sheep. While no group exactly resembles another, in general the livestock marketing groups have two principal problems, to decide how far forward to market their members' production, and to persuade potential members that they really will benefit from joining a group. So far some of the successful groups have in fact been those involved in activities strictly outside marketing, such as providing their members with advice on production and improved breeding stock.

French producer organisations in meat and livestock marketing are already of some importance. The current trends—a reduction in the importance of livestock markets in the large towns, growing sales ex-farm rather than at markets, and the absence of much direct business between producers and meat processors—should work to their advantage. Visits were therefore made to some of these organisations in order to study their development and prospects. One of these was SICAV-21, a regional organisation based in Dijon which includes some producer groups in its membership. SICAV-21 (Société d'Intérêt Collectif Agricole[1] pour la Viande. 21 is the departmental code-number of the Côte d'Or) was started up in 1962 by local farmers at a time when there was a glut on the beef market owing to a drought. It covered the department only, and had some financial and moral support from the local dairy and AI co-operatives. Some members were convinced enthusiasts from the start, others joined from convenience or haphazardly. Turnover of sales (all meat) progressed from 1,400 tons in 1962 by steady annual increases to 8,000 tons in 1969 (including *viande foraine*, i.e. imported from other departments, 1,600 tons). From the beginning direct sale to retail or to institutions was a primary policy objective. Some other SICAs got into difficulties through making contracts with wholesalers, often small upstart butchers who thought they were on to a good thing, who were '*pas sérieux*', and then went bust. In the case of SICAV-21 the financial risk of unsettled accounts has been well spread. Although the SICA started by marketing only beef it soon became apparent that both suppliers and purchasers wanted it to deal with the whole range of meat. This diversification also has the advantage of preventing the underemployment of staff and plant and of reducing overheads. It was also found that the seasonality of traditional methods of beef production did not match demand, which tends to peak between

[1] For a definition of the SICA see p. 236.

April and September. The SICA uses, and its offices are located next to, the Dijon municipal abattoir.

The 4,400 members of the SICA represent about 50 per cent of producers in the department, but only about 1,100 of them market exclusively through the SICA. These include the four producer groups which make long-term contracts with the SICA: beef (470 members), pigmeat (150), veal (100), and sheepmeat (100). As officially recognised producer groups they get financial assistance from FORMA for paying technical advisers. The SICA thus has two types of supplier, exclusive (*sociétaires adhérents*) and casual (*sociétaires usagers*). Since the groups do not produce enough to satisfy the demand of the SICA's customers the *usagers* are in no way discouraged, and there is always the hope that they may eventually become full *adhérents*. In 1969 the groups provided 13,000 out of 18,000 pigs, but only 3,400 out of 12,300 cattle, beef production being still much more small-scale than that of pork. In addition they produced 6,900 sheep and 7,000 calves. The groups are not yet well enough organised to provide an all-year-round full range of meat. Most of the *viande foraine* is pigmeat, either imported from the Netherlands or from other departments of France (where producers prefer to have their pigs slaughtered in local abattoirs). There is in general a shortage of pigs in East and South-East France, and a growing demand for pigmeat, especially of pork loin, by supermarkets. Thanks to the influence of groups, producers are becoming better informed about, and attuned to, consumer demand.

SICAV-21 is a *société civile* (private company), the Board of Directors (*conseil d'administration*) of eighteen members being elected by 'A' shareholders, who are farmers. 'B' non-voting shares are held by the Chambre d'Agriculture of the *département* and by a few dealers. The shares are Fr 30, each 'A' shareholder being entitled to a minimum holding equivalent to 3 per cent of the value of the sales of his stock through the SICA. Besides a central Annual General Meeting, at which company officials are present, there are annual meetings of each of the SICA's five geographical sections. No officials being present, these meetings give members more of an opportunity for letting off steam than at the Annual General Meeting.

A third of the Board is re-elected annually. Each of the four producer groups has elected a Commission of between eight and twelve group members (in the case of the pig group there are two Commissions, one for fatteners and one for breeders). These have an advisory role in the working out of terms of contracts made by the groups with the SICA, and one member of each Commission (usually the chairman) is a member of the Board. Any profit made by the SICA is distributed as a *complément de prix* to group members. *Usagers* do not share in this distribution.

The SICA uses four municipal abattoirs, at Dijon, Vesoul, Beaune and Les Laumes. It has its own processing plant at Dijon next to the abattoir. It is planned to form a GIE (Groupement d'Intérêt Economique) in conjunction with co-operatives or SICAs in the adjoining departments of

Yonne and Saône-et-Loire, and others in the South of France, as well as a co-operative at Dijon which has just taken over a private *salaisonnerie* (pork butchery/curing plant) and a private *salaisonnier* in Paris. The Groupement is designed to market pigmeat products (*charcuterie*) over a sales area covering about half the country. The association with the private sector is prompted by the need for special expertise in this field. A loan from the Crédit Agricole will be obained, at 7 per cent.

The SICA has horizontal contacts with other SICAs but no structural or contractual links. An inter-regional structure (Centre-Est/Bourgogne/Franche-Comté) was attempted in 1964, but it proved to be insufficiently closely integrated for effective action. Vertically, links have been established with a cereal co-operative, giving group members some price incentive to purchase its compounds. Only in the case of weaner production is purchase of feed from co-operative mills obligatory. Integration towards the market has developed very little. In the case of one supermarket only (where contracts for poultry are based on weekly quotations on Dijon market) does a *contrat juridique*, as opposed to a short-term *contrat moral*, exist. It seems that in a situation of potential glut buyers are unwilling to enter into long-term agreements.

Another SICA visited was the Société 'Beef-grill' at Châlons-sur-Marne. In contrast to those of SICAV-21 the members of 'Beef-grill', as its name implies, believe very strongly in concentrating on a single type of livestock production. This reflects the predominantly arable nature of the region in which it operates. This SICA had its origins in 1963 in an experimental feed lot of 30 cattle being fattened on lucerne meal and dried beet-pulp. Numbers increased up to 1968 when the SICA was formally set up. Throughput was 3,000 head of fat cattle in 1969. In 1970 it will be nearly 10,000. Originally lucerne production arose out of the need for a break-crop in a mainly cereal-producing region, and cattle production from a need to make use of the lucerne. Now, however, it is no longer an essential factor in the enterprise. 'Beef-grill' is a SICA *anonyme* (one share one vote) whose shareholders are three co-operatives and seven GAECs (*groupements agricoles pour exploitation en commun*), groups of between two and five farmers who have pooled their resources of land and stock, each of the members having either one or two feed-lots of 180 cattle each. They are mainly located in the Marne department, but a few are outside. One of the three co-operative members is Copaluz, which has three sections, engaged in drying lucerne and beet-pulp, feeding cattle, and purchasing farm supplies. Not all members belong to all three sections. Copaluz markets its dried feed through France Luzerne.

The SICA provides store cattle, feed (through France Luzerne)—members using their own stocks of cereals—technical advice and supervision, and marketing service. Five thousand stores, mainly Salers breed, are purchased under contract in the Massif Central (departments of Cantal, Lozère and Aveyron). About 2,000 Charollais are bought from a dealer in the Allier department and some from a SICA in the Indre. Stores are also imported from Poland through Cofanimex, the Polish state livestock trading organisation, which is responsible for the transit of the cattle right up to the French frontier. The SICA has its own buyers (*techniciens*) for vetting the cattle both in Poland and in France. It has also just set up its own *section maigre* for the production of stores in the Brie region, southeast of Paris, and should purchase about 500 in 1970. Output, mainly of 300 kg-plus carcases, is gradually being approximated to demand. This is tending to revert to the heavy beast with a certain amount of fat, public taste having moved away from very lean meat, especially as beef is increasingly required for grilling.

It has been found that regular supplies to the market are essential, and so therefore is a regular influx of stores. Although the SICA's suppliers are reliable and loyal their output tends to be strongly seasonal. Artificially reared calves from dual-purpose dairy cows have to be purchased as well as single-suckled calves of beef breed. Dairy co-operatives in the West are keen to supply these, but the SICA is at the moment trying to organise more local sources of supply. When throughput was small, selling was rather haphazard, but the SICA has now managed to build up a certain reputation, nearly half being sold direct to supermarket chains, and another 30 to 40 per cent to wholesalers, in both cases on the basis of annual contracts. The aim is to sell each lot in advance at the same moment as the stores for it are being purchased. In 1970 65 per cent of sales will be in other EEC countries, especially in Germany, where there is a big demand for bull-beef. One German chain takes 200 beasts a week. Except in the Netherlands the cattle are sold mainly on the hoof. Even where sales are made on a liveweight basis the SICA always obtains the deadweight from the purchaser and pays its members on a deadweight basis.

Some of the French regional agricultural co-operatives play an important part in meat and livestock marketing. One of these is the Union Départmentale des Coopératives Agricoles (UDCA) at Bourg-en-Bresse, which covers not only its own department (Ain) but has also penetrated a number of neighbouring departments. Its main meat and livestock activity is in pigs. There are about 250 producers in *groupements* in the Union's region, about half in weaner groups and half in fattener groups. The weaner groups contain anything from 5 to 60 sows; the aim is that all groups should average between 30 and 50. Fattener groups at present average about 100 pigs being fattened at a time, the largest having 700. The average size rather than the number of enterprises is increasing. It is intended that in a year or two all weaner groups should be buying their breeding stock through the co-operatives. Breeding trials are being geared to French demand for the 95–110 kg liveweight pig, mainly of a local type of Large White. The Union marketed 103,000 weaners and 5,000 tons of meat in 1969 for producer groups. It has its own abattoir and pork butchery (*atelier de charcuterie*) at Bourg.

There are a number of government or semi-government organisations involved in livestock and meat marketing in France. At the centre is

FORMA, whose constitution and principal activities have already been described (Chapter 3). In the meat sector FORMA gives financial incentives to the making of contracts between producer groups and their members, and may, under certain conditions, contribute to the development of co-operatives and SICAs. It has also provided grants towards converting farms from milk to meat production. FORMA has made direct investments in meat-processing factories, and in the development of foreign marketing organisations. FORMA's three affiliated bodies are all to some extent involved in meat marketing. SOPEXA has a responsibility for market expansion and export promotion; CENECA is active in trade shows; and COFREDA provides technical and managerial advice to producer groups. SIBEV, which acts on behalf of FORMA as the intervention agency for beef and veal as well as having general responsibilities in the meat trade, including work on livestock and carcase classification, is a separately constituted company.[1] Intervention in France in 1968–9 amounted to 17,159 tons of meat, of which only 31 tons were in the form of live cattle. There was no intervention buying in 1969/70.

In Germany the post-war political division of the country has severely disrupted the balance of the livestock and meat industries. The pre-war German market was shared between farmers in the East specialising in winter-fattening based on root crops, and farmers in the western part of the country who traditionally specialised in summer-fattening on pasture. Imports were controlled and the Reichstelle für Tiere und Tiererzeugnisse, whose activities are further described below, often intervened in markets in the autumn. However, the two types of production normally preserved a balance through the year of livestock supplies with demand for meat. With the division of Germany and following the end of the food shortage, the problem of surpluses of livestock in the autumn had, by about 1957, become much more severe. Recently there have been important changes in the structure of livestock markets associated with improvements in cold-storage transports, the need to supply West Berlin with meat rather than livestock, and the economies of operating slaughterhouses away from crowded urban centres. Slaughterhouses have moved into the producing areas, about 70 or 80 being built between the Danish and Belgian frontiers. Of the 27 to 28 mn pigs slaughtered in Germany, 7 to 8 mn come from these so-called 'despatch' establishments. Very few are sold on contract. Most are traded on a liveweight basis and middlemen, agents or merchants are frequently involved. The co-operatives are doing 25 to 30 per cent of the business. 80 per cent of pigs are now sold direct, to the very considerable loss of the livestock markets. Hamburg, which ten years ago saw 15,000 pigs on the Tuesday market, now has 3,000–4,000. The downward trend in the South has been slightly less severe. In 1960 Munich's throughput of pigs was 10,000 weekly, but it has now fallen to about 4,000. These changes are all the more extreme because total slaughterings have greatly increased over this period.

[1] See p. 46.

Much the same has happened in the cattle markets. In the whole Federal Republic about 30 per cent of cattle pass through livestock markets (about 44 per cent for instance in Bavaria and 24 per cent in north Germany). The despatch abattoirs are of more recent date, but the trend is occurring at as fast a rate as for pigs. Husum market may well be closed after next year. In general, there is a movement towards selling on a deadweight basis. One of the problems of livestock marketing in Germany is that there is at present no independent quality assessment for grading, such as exists in Britain through the MLC's fatstock officers (for deficiency payments) at markets. The German inspectors, though ostensibly independent, are in fact employees of the slaughterhouse. The activities of the Bundesforschungsinstitut für Fleisch (in Bavaria) might eventually result in more independent grading standards for meat.

The German co-operatives are relatively weak in meat and livestock marketing. There are four principal reasons for this. First, specialisation of function between weaner producers and fatteners has made less progress in Germany than in Britain, largely because of the greater risk of disease in Germany through the movement of pigs between farms. The operation of weaner schemes, the most simple form of co-operative activity in livestock marketing, is therefore less available to the co-operatives. Second, there is a very strong tradition in Germany of making a deal on a 'there and then' basis when selling livestock. German farmers like to sell their livestock themselves, clapping hands in the process. Auctions are confined to store cattle. This attitude makes co-operative or group marketing very difficult to arrange. In fact the activities of the German co-operatives in livestock are very little different from those of the private trade. Third, until recently the co-operatives have not owned many slaughterhouses or meat-processing factories. The position is changing through the development of co-operatives like Südfleisch and Nordfleisch which are moving towards vertical integration linked with supplies of co-operatively produced feed. Fourth, the demand for meat in Germany has been until recently very fragmented, and consequently there has been no pressing need for the development of countervailing power on the part of producers. The large chain stores have now invaded the retail meat market at the expense of the independent butchers, who immediately after the war were responsible for almost all retail sales of meat. Their share has now dropped to less than half the total. The advent of large buyers, some of which have links with livestock enterprises and feed mills, has presented the co-operatives with a real opportunity of negotiating improved terms for their members. In Germany about half the total number of livestock is sold direct to butchers, processors, etc. Of the remainder, that sold through intermediaries, the co-operative sector is responsible for about 30 per cent, or 15 per cent of total livestock supplies. This proportion could greatly increase in the future.

In Germany the problem exists to a fairly acute extent of reconciling the interests of the old-established co-operatives operating in the livestock/meat trade with those of the newer producer marketing organisations.

This needs some further explanation. The Raiffeisen livestock organisation consists of about 250 local co-operatives which are ostensibly grouped under 12 regional co-operatives. In effect, however, the regional structure which counts is the *Viehverwertung* (five in number), which in turn is linked with the central organisation, the Deutsche Vieh- und Fleischzentral. The *Viehverwertung* is responsible for much of the initiative in producer livestock and meat marketing. It provides finance for slaughterhouses, has aided the development of the *Erzeugerringen*, local associations largely concentrating on weight recording, and has taken a part in establishing the new producer groups (*Erzeugergemeinschaften*). Under the marketing law (*Marktstrukturgesetz*) these must consist of not less than seven members, and have an annual throughput of a minimum volume of meat or livestock, in order to qualify for subsidy: either 2,000 beef cattle, 2,000 calves, 5,000 sheep, 20,000 fat pigs, or, in the case of mixed stock, the equivalent of at least 4,000 livestock units. Weaner groups, which have to be separately constituted, must market at least 20,000 weaners a year. Groups have been promoted by both the Raiffeisen co-operatives (there is some overlap in membership) and the private trade. The trouble is that there is no necessary identity of interest between the producer groups (which have the advantage of disciplined membership) and the Raiffeissen slaughterhouses (which have capital and outlets for meat, but lack undisputed claims for loyalty from their members).

The present intervention agency for livestock and meat, the Einfuhr- und Vorratstelle, is the successor to the Reichstelle. The latter had a monopoly on imports as well as powers to intervene on domestic markets. These were used with the object of preventing farmers from being exploited by merchants in times of surplus supplies. It was argued that on the main livestock markets, Hamburg, Munich, Cologne and Frankfurt, merchants had been able to buy up summer-fattened cattle very cheaply in the autumn and then use their ownership of cold stores to rig the meat market between then and the spring when the winter-fattened cattle appeared on the market. The Reichstelle's intervention kept up prices for livestock in the autumn and tended to equalise meat prices during the winter. The EVSt's activities have been very similar. Since 1952, when the EVSt began to buy at autumn markets, notably at Husum, Bremen, Oldenburg, Bremerhaven and Hamburg, its purchases have mostly been in the period from mid-September to mid-November.

Germany is the only member country where intervention buying of live cattle has occurred on any scale. Most of this has occurred in Region I, the North and North-West, Germany being divided into three regions for intervention purposes. There some 16,600 fat cattle, equivalent to about 4,800 tons of meat, were bought in the autumn of 1968. The obvious difficulty of defining quality standards for live cattle has not been resolved, and the EVSt is not likely in future to press the Commission for the use of this type of intervention. Intervention for meat has been on a fairly small scale so far, about 9,000 tons in 1968/69 and about 7,500 tons in 1969/70.

The procedure has been to retain about a quarter of these purchases, process the meat, and add it to emergency stocks, some of which are held in Berlin. The remaining three-quarters are disposed of by inviting tenders from the trade in the spring. Import licences are dealt with by EVSt; export licensing, fixing of restitutions and their payment by the Zollamt in Hamburg. The EVSt employs about 100 people.

In both Belgium and the Netherlands there is some tendency towards vertical integration in the pig industry, the movement being much stronger in the Netherlands, where over half the pigs produced are the subject of contracts which generally cover marketing as well as the supply of feed. In Belgium there is much less integration, probably about 10 per cent of total production. The Boerenbond has organised one marketing group (Covavee) near Antwerp, which also handles beef cattle, but in the main the trade is still in the hands of private merchants, who sometimes take the responsibility for organising supplies to factories. Auctioning (at co-operative *veilingen*) is limited to pigs, generally on a deadweight basis, but, as in the case of fruit and vegetables, lots tend to be inconveniently small for the larger buyers. Most Belgian slaughterhouses are owned by the local authorities. Producers of beef cattle have found themselves in a sellers' market (prices tending to be rather higher in Belgium than elsewhere in the EEC), and there has been little incentive for producers to form themselves into marketing groups.

The intervention agency in Belgium for livestock and meat is the OBEA, whose structure has already been described (Chapter 3). Intervention buying has been on a nominal scale, none for pigs, and only about 40 tons of beef in 1968/69 and none in 1969–70. There are two intervention points in Belgium, at Antwerp and Gambes near Namur, at both of which Régie Frigorifique Belge (Refribel), a state-owned organisation, has cold stores. Private cold storage capacity is also available. The Belgian market demands very lean beef. Even Charollais tends to be too fat. Demand is mainly for dual-purpose Moyenne et Haute Belgique (white and blue cattle). Refrigeration facilities at the public abattoirs, including the one at Anderlecht (the main meat market), are poor. The large users employ their own procurement staff (*ramasseurs*), who mostly buy from the bigger rearing units, but all beasts pass through the markets. Some contracts have been made with producers, but these have been few in number and buyers have not yet gained confidence that producers will honour their contracts.

In the Netherlands meat and livestock marketing is, as one might expect, more closely organised than in the other member countries. The extent of integration in the pig industry has already been mentioned. There is a considerable variety in the contracts used. Some involve a complete integration, the farmer becoming virtually an employee of the integrator, whereas in others the marketing is left entirely to the farmers' discretion. Price guarantees and loss-sharing arrangements are becoming more common, both being practised by the co-operatives as well as the private trade. Strict quality standards are enforced, partly in order to promote the important export trade for fresh and canned pigmeat. The Dutch canning industry is highly concentrated, more than half being in the hands of three companies. The private canning industry makes contracts with farmers and has integrated back into the ownership of slaughterhouses.

Beef production in the Netherlands is much less important, the country having a large deficit which is made up by supplies of fresh meat from France, Denmark and Belgium, and of frozen meat from Argentina. Beef cattle are largely by-products of the dairy industry. There are a few producers with about 50 to 100 cattle, but generally rearing is on a very small scale. Sales are mostly made at markets, of which Rotterdam is the largest, the methods of sale being bargaining rather than auctions. Veal production, however, is done in an entirely different manner, consisting of large specialised enterprises, usually integrated with feed companies or meat wholesalers, producing on contract often for the export trade.

The Dutch intervention agency is VIB, the organisation of which has already been described. In fact to date there has been no intervention buying.

Luxemburg has a small surplus of pigmeat and lower-quality beef. Veal is imported mostly from the Netherlands. Slaughterhouses are municipally owned with the exception of one recently constructed by the co-operative organisation (CPL) at Mersch with a modern meat-processing and packing plant. Livestock are marketed by small groups of farmers, smaller than the normal EEC *groupements de producteurs*. Retailing of meat is still largely in the hands of individual butchers, though there are a few chain operations, including the consumer co-operative. Owing to the Luxemburg Protocol, there has to date been no intervention activity. This would be the responsibility of SER (Section Cheptel et Viande).

Italy has a very substantial deficit in meat. About 45 per cent of total supplies are imported. In 1969 imports consisted of 1·19 mn head of cattle and 216,000 tons of meat, EEC countries, Denmark and Eastern Europe being the main livestock suppliers and Argentina the principal shipper of meat. The import trade is dominated by about a dozen large firms which also operate on the home market. Processors, concentrated in the North, sometimes import direct, but more often buy from the importers. In the whole country there are about 5,000 meat traders, some of whom combine trading with a butcher's business. The Italian livestock and meat trades are notably fragmented. Producers' organisations are beginning to make progress in group activities for trading in store cattle, but in general the co-operative grip on the market is still very weak. Pig production in the North is closely linked with dairying.[1] Consumption per head of pigmeat has been rising during the past decade, by 15 per cent between 1961 and 1966 alone. Italian producers have, however, been slow to adapt their output to the growing demand for lean pork, and butchers, who until quite

[1] See p. 92 .

recently were forbidden to sell it alongside other forms of fresh meat, lack the expertise to cut the smaller carcase.[1] Traditional heavy hogs, for processing into ham and *salami*, continue, therefore, to constitute the main supply, and technical progress in breeding and feeding tends to be slow.

Perhaps the most interesting feature of the Italian market from the British point of view is the substantial import of Yugoslav meat and livestock. As a result of a special agreement between Yugoslavia and the EEC which came into force from early 1970, limited quantities of both livestock and meat of specified qualities are admitted at a reduced levy. The period of the agreement is three years, the quantities permitted in any one year being linked to shipments in the previous year. There are two rates of levy rebate, one appliacble from August 15th to January 31st and the other from February 1st to August 14th.

IMPLICATIONS FOR THE BRITISH MARKET

To a large extent the more important trends in livestock production and in livestock and meat marketing are common to both Britain and the Community. In both, production has increased in recent years, though in the EEC countries, notably Italy, consumption has risen still faster, leading to a considerable rise in Italy's imports and to a rather lower degree of self-sufficiency for the EEC as a whole than in the case of most of the temperate products. In both, governments have shown a good deal of concern about the marketing of meat, provoked by a desire to introduce greater stability into markets, characterised by erratic supplies[2] and fluctuations in prices, as well as by the need to control standards of hygiene on behalf of consumers. In both, despite efforts extending over many years to secure improvements, the marketing system remains generally confused and disorderly. An official of the Commission generalising about the meat trade in the EEC described it to us as being 'like playing billiards on board a leaking ship in a storm', a phrase which might equally be applied to the situation in Britain. In both, improvement to marketing mainly depends on grading and classification schemes, better market intelligence, increased direct selling on contract, and the development of effectively disciplined producer marketing organisations. These are all being introduced but progress in both Britain and the EEC is slow.

The change in British government agricultural policy following the 1969 election will bring Britain more closely into line with the EEC in the livestock and meat sector as in cereals. The new policy involves the use of frontier controls in order to bring the level of market prices closer to farmers' guaranteed prices and thus reduce the Treasury's liability for deficiency payments. Access to the British market for meat has in fact

[1] M. Valdinocci, *Zootecnia Italiana 1969*, US Feed Grains Council, Rome, pp. 59–60.
[2] See *Stability and the Beef Market*. Agricultural Adjustment Unit, University of Newcastle, Bulletin No. 9, 1970.

already become less free than is sometimes supposed. Bilateral arrangements such as the Anglo-Irish Free Trade Agreement and the agreements with Australia and New Zealand hold open to certain suppliers a market which is otherwise regulated through controls imposed for animal health reasons (associated with foot-and-mouth disease) and by quotas and other restrictions on imports. In recent years price policy for beef cattle has been deliberately employed to increase home production, on import-saving grounds, at the expense of traditional suppliers.

British policy for livestock and meat has thus become more protectionist. Nevertheless, adoption of the CAP will have important effects on markets other than those due to changes in relative prices of the various meats. Grass will become even more attractive as a feed compared with concentrates based on higher-priced cereals. This will increase the autumn flush of fat cattle, and alter the balance of supplies of fresh meat, particularly as Ireland will be similarly affected. Britain is already giving financial assistance to producer groups engaged in livestock marketing, but harmonisation of these aids with those of the EEC will eventually be necessary. Since under the EEC system the Bacon Understanding will have to be terminated, more active competition for the British domestic market will result between British farmers and pig producers in the Irish Republic and Denmark. The Understanding would presumably start to be phased out during the transitional period. By the time that this occurs the pig-processing industry will have had some 10 years of protection against unlimited imports of bacon during which to put its house in order. The exchequer support which factories receive in respect of that part of their output which is cured, under the Bacon Curing Industry Stabilisation Scheme, would also be contrary to Community rules of fair competition. Notice is therefore served on the industry that by the time British entry into the EEC were achieved, towards the end of the current decade, the process of rationalising and modernising of production and marketing, and above all of diversifying out of bacon, which has been slowly reducing unit costs and raising gross returns per pig processed to an economic level, would have to be complete.[1] These developments are likely to have the effect of giving Britain a smaller share of the domestic market for bacon than it now obtains thanks to the Understanding.

[1] In this connection it is appropriate to quote from the conclusions of the food manufacturing 'Little Neddy's' report already referred to: 'It appears to us that greater profitability is associated with more diversified activities; taken with the evidence on curing costs we have obtained and the obvious inference to be drawn from the increasing use of pigs partly for bacon, the relative unprofitability of bacon curing to the first-hand stage is apparent. But this is not the entire answer. The more successful companies undertook diversification as a deliberate act of company policy, and it appears to us that clear objectives, formulated and executed by good management and aggressive marketing, are as important in their success as diversification of product. Other companies, while technically competent, have been less far-sighted and have tended to seek political rather than commercial remedies for their financial difficulties. We believe that fundamental rethinking of policy is necessary collectively at industry level and by individual companies if the industry is to be effective in the future.' NEDO, *op cit*, p. 40.

The Northern Ireland industry hopes to retain a relatively greater proportion of its share because of superior quality and skilful promotion, but, as the Ashton Report has concluded, much the same considerations apply to its future as apply in Great Britain. It is no part of our brief to speculate what compensation the Community's regional policy might provide for the eventual disappearance of such special government assistance to agriculture and to the food-processing industries in Northern Ireland as has up to now been available in the form of Remoteness Grants and other subsidies. But it is clear that competition for processors of all forms of meat in the province will be intensified.

The Ashton Report does not only draw attention to the need for a fundamental diversification by the Northern Ireland curing industry out of its present overdependence on specialised Wiltshire bacon production into the growing market for pork and other pig products, especially that in Great Britain. The Committee also recommends a radical reconstitution—the Board's partisans would perhaps call it emasculation—of the Pigs Marketing Board. Since the past record of the Board as a mainly elected body has to some extent shown it to be unsuited to conducting commercial operations[1], these should, in the Committee's opinion, be wound up and its partnership interests in the processing industry sold off to private buyers. If the Board retains any interest in processing it should be confined to a single, wholly owned, factory. However, the report is generally unfavourable to any producer participation in the processing and selling of pigmeat products, believing that the Board should concentrate its activities on organising production and marketing, of weaners as well as of finished pigs, and conducting research and development in these spheres. As part of this package the Board's purchasing monopoly of bacon pigs, the factory quota system, and the negotiated curing margin would all be discontinued in favour of a system of contracts for all types of pigs between producers and processors (no longer to be viewed as simply 'curers'). The contracts would be registered with, but not necessarily negotiated by, the Board.

The Minister of Agriculture, while accepting that there were 'cogent reasons' for the Committee's recommendation that the Board should dispose of its investments, decided that the present moment was inopportune for such a change. Greater independence of action is, however, to be given to PMB (Investments) Ltd, whose relations with the Board are recognised to have been 'less than harmonious'. The subsidiary company will 'assume in effect the role of Trustees independent of but periodically accountable to the PMB', with the Minister acting as arbiter in the event of disagreement between the two. The Board will remain the sole purchaser of bacon pigs. The quota system will also be retained, but the government goes part of the way to meeting the Ashton Committee's recommendation

[1] Belfast Producers Ltd made continuous annual losses between 1957, when the Board acquired a majority holding in the company, and 1967, when it was obliged to go into liquidation.

by making the system more flexible and encouraging the Board to offer an increasing number of pigs outside quota for sale to processors on a contract basis. The government evidently hopes that these changes of emphasis will prove sufficient to ensure more effective assertion of the interests of producers in the processing business. The day-to-day running of the factories will of course remain in the hands of the minority shareholders, all of whom have expertise in this field. The Ashton Committee took the view that the lack of ultimate financial responsibility of the partner firms and their position as sole agents for the sale of the factories' output tended to conflict with what should be the Board's interest of maximising profits on behalf of producers.

Inside the EEC the factories would be facing increased competition in a less protected market. With the retail price of Wiltshire bacon likely to rise (and demand for it therefore to fall) relatively more than that of other processed forms of pigmeat as a result of the change in support system, an efficiently conducted programme of diversification becomes all the more urgent. Producer participation in processing is of course quite common in the EEC. PMB (Investments) Ltd would present no problems therefore—other than the familiar one of securing its efficient management. But it seems probable that the factory quota system would not be considered compatible with Community rules on competition. The Stabilisation Scheme would, as already noted, have to be discontinued. The PMB, being a producer organisation, could continue to function as at present, but minus its ministerial appointees. The Board's administrative costs are already financed out of a producer levy. As a producer organisation its monopoly over bacon pigs would probably be acceptable, in Community terms, as complying with the wishes of a majority of producers. But once there were no quotas or stabilising arrangements and the importance of diversifying out of bacon were accepted, as any sort of economic realism suggests it must be, the monopoly would in any case have lost much of its point. Even if it were extended to purchases of all pigs, as it could be under the Marketing Act if an appropriate majority of producers were in favour, its value to them in terms of price stability would, in an EEC situation of free imports of pigs from the Republic, be questionable. Indeed, it seems doubtful whether the Board's present price stabilisation fund (the Special Account) could continue to function unless it could be linked to similar arrangements in the South on an all-Ireland basis.

Processing of other forms of meat in Northern Ireland will also have to be adapted to changing circumstances. Further development of sales of jointed and pre-packed meat and of new types of manufactured products can help to overcome the disadvantage of the province's remoteness by reducing sea-transport costs per pound of meat exported. Indeed, in an enlarged Community all parts of the UK will have access to a bigger protected market, and thus an opportunity for expanding livestock and meat exports which are at present negligible. To achieve this an effective organisation for sales promotion will be required in order to exploit, for instance, the limited demand already created for spring lamb on the Continent.

Little mention has been made of sheep meat since it is not at present subject to a common EEC regulation.[1] But COPA is known to be pressing for one which would involve target and threshold prices, import levies, and a basic price governing intervention buying. About UA 130·50 kg (25 p/lb) was mentioned in 1968 as a possible basic price. The French Government is dissatisfied with the present situation under which free entry of sheep meat and livestock from other member countries is combined with a duty under the CET on imports from third countries (20 per cent on fresh and chilled meat; 16 per cent on live beasts). Although French national arrangements exclude imports from third countries when prices on French markets fall to a certain level, it is alleged that many of the sheep continuing to enter France from Belgium and the Netherlands while other imports are suspended have been heard baa-ing with strong Irish or Scots accents. Finally, the Commission itself is interested in the possibilities of sheep as an alternative source of income to milk in upland areas, as well as in prospects for combined sheep and beef cattle raising, a form of husbandry virtually unknown in the Community. Both could form the object of reconversion grants for farmers who were giving up dairying.

Another aspect of the Community meat regulations which could closely affect Britain concerns imports of frozen beef. EEC arrangements for these are adapted to a somewhat different pattern of demand from that existing in Britain, where much of it has traditionally been used for catering, or even purchased by the housewife for consumption at home. In the EEC 80 per cent of imports go for manufacture. The small proportion for direct consumption is unevenly distributed among member countries. In Italy, for instance, frozen meat may not be sold in shops retailing fresh or chilled meat. Regulations for frozen beef relate mainly to supplies for the canning industry. The annual levy-free quota of 22,000 tons bound in the GATT is redistributed each year between member countries according to arrangements worked out in Management Committee. Although imports for manufacture into corned beef enter free of levy, those destined for other forms of processing are subject to quotas. These are fixed quarterly by the Commission in consultation with the Management Committee and enter at a reduced rate (which varies from quarter to quarter according to the internal supply situation) of current levy. Britain's imports of frozen meat have averaged 51,000 tons in the three years 1967/69, mainly from Australia and New Zealand.[2] Since any share of this present GATT quota would be negligible when divided among 10 member

---

[1] For an outline of the situation for mutton and lamb in the Community see Butterwick and Neville-Rolfe, *op cit*, Chapter 8.

[2] This average conceals a steep upward trend. No information is available as to what proportion is manufactured, but the restrictions on imports of boned chilled meat from the Argentine have probably led to some increase in consumption of boneless frozen meat by caterers and housewives.

countries, new arrangements will have to be negotiated having due regard to the UK industry's traditional requirements and suppliers. It is improbable that any more than a small proportion of manufacturers' needs could be satisfied from Community sources.[1] The quarterly quotas of imports at reduced rates of levy are therefore likely to have to be increased in an enlarged Community.

An intervention agency will be required for Britain. As already noted, intervention in EEC meat markets has been on a small scale in the past two years and livestock intervention has almost come to an end. Such intervention as occurs is likely to continue to be seasonal, consisting of buying up fairly small quantities of fresh meat in the autumn and selling it frozen at a lower price in the early spring. In Britain the organisation best suited to carry this out is the Meat and Livestock Commission, established under the 1967 Agriculture Act with 'the general duty of promoting efficiency in the livestock industry and the livestock products industry'. Unlike the HGCA, the Commission does not at present possess trading powers. It consists of nine members (including the Chairman and Deputy Chairman) all independent and all appointed by the agricultural Ministers. Members' salaries are paid direct by the Treasury from the Consolidated Fund. The various interests in the livestock and meat industries (listed in the Schedule to the Act) are represented on three Advisory Committees (Production, 19 members; Distribution, 25 members; and Consumers, 7 members), the Chairman of each being appointed by the government. The Commission is statutorily obliged to consult these Committees. In addition the Commission is assisted by other smaller committees and panels, for instance, that for economics which do not have the same statutory position. During its brief existence (a little over two years) the Commission has been chiefly engaged in carrying on the work of the Pig Industry Development Authority, developing beef- and sheep-recording schemes, negotiating with the meat trade about standards for carcase classification, promoting home-produced meat, and starting an auction-market price intelligence service. The small head office in London has a staff of about 30, the remainder (about 600 people) being divided between the main headquarters at Bletchley and the regional offices. The Commission's income, amounting to about £1·8 mn, is derived from levies that are collected at the point of slaughter and still much resented by the meat trade.

An examination of the work and organisation of the existing EEC intervention agencies for livestock and meat suggests that the Commission would be well placed to act as the agency in Britain. It possesses unrivalled knowledge of the complexities and obscurities of British livestock and meat marketing and has developed its own price-intelligence service. Through its work on carcase classification it has experience of

[1] In 1970 it was estimated that about 470,000 tons of meat of manufacturing quality would be available within the present Community, of which 34,400 represented half of the total yield of the Community's subsidised cow-slaughter policy.

quality control of meat, which is important in market-intervention activity. In its constitution it possesses a suitable degree of interprofessionalism. Although it does not own any cold stores, there should be no problem in leasing the small amount of capacity which intervention buying would be likely to involve. Finally the Commission already has on its staff people with the type of experience required to run an intervention agency. For the amount of intervention buying that we anticipate the number of additional staff needed should certainly not exceed half a dozen.

Intervention, particularly of pigmeat, may prove necessary from time to time in Northern Ireland since the main means of mitigating price cycles in the whole of Ireland will consist of intervention buying on both sides of the border. In the North this would be carried out under instructions from the central UK agency, either by a local office of the agency or by the Northern Ireland Ministry of Agriculture if, as seems probable, it is considered more appropriate for intervention for all products in the province to be administered centrally on behalf of the UK agencies by the Ministry.

CHAPTER 7

Eggs and Poultry-meat

The eggs and poultry-meat sector is one in which the patterns of production and marketing in Britain and in the member countries of the EEC have been converging so rapidly during the past three or four years that by the end of any transition period for British entry into the Community they are likely to be almost indistinguishable. Production on the Continent of table chicken and other poultry has been moving towards the large-scale integrated type of businesses established in Britain, on the transatlantic model, over the past 15 years. The same trend, though much less pronounced, even in Britain, is also observable on both sides of the Channel in the case of egg production. As far as official price support is concerned the phasing out of the egg subsidy, to be completed by the end of March 1974, and the introduction of minimum import prices will put the British egg producer on a similar footing to his EEC counterpart. There are no target or intervention prices for eggs or poultry-meat in the Community, and imports are restrained by a system of levies and sluice-gate prices. The fact that the protection at the frontier given to the British broiler producer arises largely from veterinary restrictions makes it no less effective than the Community system. In coming under the Common Market regulations, therefore, British producers of eggs and poultry-meat will find themselves on fairly familiar ground. Even the new Egg Authority due to start operating on April 1st 1971 could in many respects prove to be more compatible with existing EEC rules about producer organisations than the Egg Marketing Board which it replaces. Producers should not be too much troubled by the EEC regulations governing eggs and poultry-meat. The effect of the cereals regulations, pushing up feed costs, will be much more serious. Even more so will be the competition of free imports from the rest of the enlarged Community.

The pace of the technical advance which has revolutionised the pattern of egg and poultry-meat production in large areas of the world has been particularly rapid in the EEC during the past five years. Breeding, feeding and management practices originally imported into Europe from the USA via Britain and Scandinavia are now widespread in all member countries, even if the average size of production unit is still considerably smaller than in Britain. As a result the Community, which five years ago still imported

Eggs and Poultry-meat

5 per cent of its requirements of eggs and 6 per cent of that of poultry-meat, is now virtually self-sufficient in eggs and broiler meat and 99 per cent self-sufficient in poultry-meat as a whole. Egg products, and some shell eggs as well, continue to be imported from third countries mainly for use by the Italian *pasta* industry. Consumption of eggs, in 1967/68 over 14·0 kg per head in Germany and in the BLEU and 12·2 kg per head in France, is expected to rise relatively slowly. Dutch and Italian consumption actually fell between 1963 and 1968, and in Italy even at its peak never reached 10·0 kg per head. Rising standards of living in the South of Italy are, however, likely to give some boost to consumption in the future. OECD projections forecast a rise in average per capita consumption in the Community as a whole from 12·5 kg to 13·0 kg, to absorb an anticipated total output of 2·6 mn tons by 1957, an increase of about 9 per cent over its expected level in 1970. The demand for poultry-meat, on the other hand, will continue to increase a good deal more rapidly between 1970 and 1975, by 17 per cent, to 1·95 mn tons (of which 0·28 tons would be from culled hens). OECD also forecasts a further 30 per cent expansion during the subsequent decade, whereas demand for eggs would increase by less than 1 per cent per year.[1]

Since average yields of eggs per hen (now about 170 a year) are expected to continue to rise far more steeply than are average levels of consumption (by nearly a third between 1970 and 1975 and by a further 20 per cent during the ensuing decade), a steady reduction in the size of the EEC's laying flock is bound to occur. It is notable that since 1967 the price trend in all member countries has been a gradual downward one, with seasonal fluctuations also becoming less pronounced and periods of shortage increasingly infrequent. The consequent squeezing of profit margins will tend through the seventies to eliminate all but the small producer with a local retail outlet, the largest commercial enterprise, whether operating single or multiple units, and the co-operatively organised group of medium-sized flocks capable of negotiating contracts with chains and supermarkets. All experience suggests that concentration of poultry-meat production, especially of broilers, will occur even more rapidly and decisively than that of eggs. Some small-scale production of turkeys, ducks, capons, etc., will continue to meet local specialised demand.

Despite its present situation of near self-sufficiency there is still movement of both eggs and poultry-meat within the Community. All six countries are, however, expected to become fully self-sufficient in eggs before 1975. In 1970 surpluses from the Netherlands (118 per cent self-sufficient) and the BLEU (113 per cent) were still finding an outlet in Germany (40,000 tons) and Italy (14,000 tons), respectively still only 96 per cent and 98 per cent self-sufficient. But by 1975 net imports into both countries could be virtually nil. In the case of poultry-meat, however, the present much more fluid market situation seems likely to persist thanks to

[1] OECD, *Agricultural projections for 1975 and 1985, op cit, passim.*

154   The Principal Farm Products

more rapidly rising demand and to the fact that Germany will remain an net importer for the foreseeable future. Although the level of prices has shown a certain general downward trend on the key German market since the disappearance of intra-Community levies in July 1967 it has not been anything like so pronounced as in the case of eggs. Germany may, according to the Ifo-Institut, have achieved no greater degree of self-sufficiency by 1975 than the 55 per cent already reached in 1970.[1] Professor Strecker, on the other hand, believes that Germany could be at least 60 per cent, and possibly as much as 75 per cent, self-sufficient in chicken by 1975.[2] In any case the German market seems likely to remain open for some many years to come, a factor of which Danish broiler producers will be quick to take advantage in an enlarged Community.

The EEC system

The basic EEC regulation for shell eggs and egg products (122/67), and for poultry-meat (123/67) and derived products (199/67), deal with external trade only, making provision for a system of levies on imports, supplementary levies based on minimum import (so-called sluice-gate) prices, and restitutions on exports and re-exports. A supplementary regulation (1619/68), for eggs only, lays down standards of quality, grading, packaging, labelling, etc. These regulations have been described elsewhere[3], and brief comment will here suffice. All, whether for eggs, poultry-meat or their derivatives, are based on the principle of raising the price of imports to a level at which moderately efficient Community producers will be able to compete with them, and of preventing the entry of any produce at abnormally low prices. The difference between average costs of production of eggs (including hatching eggs) and poultry-meat in third countries and in the Community due to lower cereal prices outside is established. Allowance is then made for these and other fixed costs in fixing levies and minimum import prices. Those for egg products and for joints and offals of the different types of poultry are derived by means of fixed coefficients.[4]

Under the influence of these restrictions imports from third countries have been steadily declining. Between 1962 and 1969 those of hen eggs went down by 88 per cent, of poultry-meat by 72 per cent. The protection given by the poultry-meat regulation to the average producer in the Community is now rather more generous than that for eggs. The feed-conversion ratio allowed for in calculating comparative costs of production

[1] H. Schmidt et al, op cit, Tables 6–14.
[2] O. Strecker, *Der Eier- und Schlachtgeflügelmarkt von morgen*, 'Deutsche Geflügelwirtschaft', No. 21, July 1969.
[3] Butterwick and Neville-Rolfe, *op cit*, pp. 167–9, provides a brief summary. For an exhaustive account of the regulations for shell eggs and egg products see Betty J. Roscoe and R. C. Rickard, *Eggs in the Common Market*, prepared for the British Egg Marketing Board, University of Exeter, Department of Agricultural Economics, March 1968, and since brought regularly up to date in a series of supplements.
[4] To illustrate the method of calculating sluice-gate prices, etc., an example for broilers is given in an extended footnote at the end of this section, on pp. 156–70.

in the EEC and third countries for the purpose of fixing minimum import prices and levies (see note pp. 156–7) has remained fixed at 2·5 since 1962. Broiler production being concentrated almost entirely in the hands of specialised producers, average performance in the Community is now a good deal better than this, ratios of as low as 2·0 and 2·1 being claimed in some countries, notably the Netherlands. In the case of eggs standard production costs are calculated on the basis of an annual average yield per laying bird of 210. Although production figures of 225 and above are obtained in the most efficient laying units, average yields, even excluding backyard hens, are still well below 210. The ratios are fixed by the Council. Moves to lower that set for broilers, now quite unrealistic, have been blocked, mainly in deference to the interests of French producers, though even they generally achieve conversion ratios of between 2·3 and 2·4. To provide some idea of how the regulations work out in practice, minimum import prices applied during each year since 1967 are given below for selected products.

EEC: Average minimum import prices for selected products

		1968	1969	1970
Shell eggs[1]	(p per doz)	14·34	13.32	14·34
Liquid egg yolks	(p per lb)	21·53	20·82	21·09
Broilers (70 per cent[2])	(p per lb)	13·29	13·26	13·26
Turkeys[3]	(p per lb)	15·61	15·08	16·13
Ducks (70 per cent[2])	(p per lb)	13·12	11·75	13·03

[1] Standard.
[2] Plucked, eviscerated, without head or feet, but with heart, liver and gizzard.
[3] Deadweight.

Source: Marchés Agricoles, EEC Directorate-General of Agriculture, Brussels.

Official regulation of the internal market is confined in the case of eggs to the application of grading and other standards.[1] Producer organisations are to be encouraged to help 'adjust the volume of supply to the requirements of the market', by improving their marketing arrangements, improving egg quality, analysing production trends, and providing their members with market intelligence. Although it is intended in principle to make funds available from FEOGA for getting these activities started, a regulation on the subject is still awaited, as is one on the grading of poultry-meat and operation of poultry packing stations (*abattoirs*). Any buying-in and breaking out of eggs during periods of glut would also have to be organised by producers, but financed entirely from their own resources. Opinion as to the desirability of such action is very divided. As buying-in would, to be effective, need to take place on a Community-wide basis no scheme is likely to emerge in the near future, if ever. It might be provoked by a prolonged period of low prices in all member countries, but since the main effect of this would be a still greater concentration of production in the hands of large units, the medium-sized producers who stood most to gain from a buying-in scheme would probably have gone out of business long before it could be organised.[2]

[1] For details see Roscoe and Rickard, *op cit*, Supplement No. 12.
[2] See also p. 165 below.

Note: The method of calculating the sluice-gate (minimum import) price, levy and supplementary levy on broilers is given here as an illustration of the EEC system. The figures are those applicable in July 1969. The only variable element, however, is the grain price. The calculations apply to chicken (70 per cent)—plucked, eviscerated, without head or feet, with heart, liver and gizzard.

1. *Sluice-gate price*

   (i) Feedgrain prices on world market for six months previous to quarter during which sluice-gate price is fixed (i.e. 1 November 1968 to 1 May 1969)

Cereal	per cent of cereal ration		Price UA/100 kg		Cost UA/100 kg
Maize	78	×	5·469	=	4·2658
Barley	19	×	4·996	=	0·9492
Oats	3	×	4·853	=	0·1456
					5·3606
Unloading charge					0·4750
Cost of cereal ration					5·8356

   (ii) *Basic criteria*
   Liveweight: 1,500 gr
   Conversion ratio: 2·5 kg of compound feed per kg of growth
   Deadweight: 70 per cent of liveweight
   Proportion of cereals in feed ration: 65 per cent
   Conversion ratio (cereal element) per bird deadweight:
   $$2·5 \times \frac{65}{100} \times \frac{100}{70} = 2·321$$
   Non-cereal feed and additives: 2·5 kg − 65 per cent = 0·875 kg
   Price of non-cereal ration: UA 16·68/100 kg

   (iii) *Calculation of sluice-gate price*

   UA/kg
   (a) cereal ration (*variable element*) 0·058356 × 2·321 = 0·1354
   (b) flat rate amount (*fixed element*)
   includes allowance for:
   non-cereal ration (0·8750 kg)
   day-old chick
   farm production costs
   slaughtering and marketing costs   0·5586

   Sluice-gate price ((a)+(b))   0·6940

2. *Levy*

   (i) *Element (variable) (a)*: difference between cost of feedgrain ration at Community threshold prices and at world market prices

Cereal	per cent of cereal ration	Threshold price UA/100 kg	Cost at threshold price UA/100 kg	Cost at world market price UA/100 kg
Maize	78	9·694	7·5613	4·2658
Barley	19	9·644	1·8324	0·9492
Oats	3	9·085	0·2726	0·1456
			9·6663	5·3606

   Difference UA 9·6663 − UA 5·8356 = UA 3·8307/100 kg

Basic criteria as for calculation of sluice-gate price (see above) except for:

Cereal element of ration: $2 \cdot 5 \times \dfrac{65}{100} = 1 \cdot 625$ kg

Allowance for 200 gr for day-old chick: $1 \cdot 625 + 0 \cdot 200 = 1 \cdot 825$ kg

Conversion ratio (cereal element) for deadweight bird: $1{,}825 \times \dfrac{100}{70} = 2 \cdot 61$

Calculation of *variable element* (a): $2 \cdot 61 \times \text{UA } 0 \cdot 038307 = \text{UA } 0 \cdot 1124$ kg

(ii) *Element (b) fixed* 7 per cent of average of sluice-gate prices of the four preceding quarters (May 1968–May 1969)

$$\dfrac{7}{100} \times \text{UA } 0 \cdot 6955 = \text{UA } 0 \cdot 0487 \text{ kg}$$

(iii) *Levy*

Element (a)   UA 0·1124 kg
Element (b)   UA 0·0487 kg

Total levy*   UA 0·1611 kg

Analagous calculations are applied for broilers plus head and feet (83 per cent), griller (65 per cent), geese, ducks, turkeys, and guinea-fowl.

* This is payable on all imports. For offers below the sluice-gate level a supplementary levy equivalent to the difference between the offer and the sluice-gate price is chargeable.

The market structure in the EEC

Belgium became the EEC's largest exporter of eggs in 1969, but the structure of production is still relatively small in scale. Flocks of 2,000 and 3,000 birds have recently multiplied in the Antwerp area under the influence of the port's grain imports and of feed firms which have been promoting a fairly advanced stage of integration in the interests of expanding their sales. Although the firms provide finance, technical advice, and a guaranteed market outlet, the producers (many of them part-time) supplying family labour and bearing the depreciation costs of building and equipment, insufficient attention is probably being given to the longer-term implications of market, either in the event of the growth of much larger scale production in Belgium or of difficulties on the export market, or both. The position is somewhat hazardous in that Belgian supplies tend to have both a marginal and cyclical effect on the Community market—effectively the German market—where Dutch exporters are much more securely established. However, 80 per cent of exports are now marketed by the Chambre Syndicale, grouping some 35 wholesalers who co-ordinate prices and supplies.

Domestic sales are dominated by the Kruishouten market, through which pass 17,000 cases a week. The co-operative sector is weak, accounting for about 5 per cent of national throughput through its clock auctions. As in the case of fruit and vegetables these have a limited appeal to the big buyer. We were told that no single packing station is sufficiently large to supply Delhaize Le Lion, the biggest of the food chains. Only the 15 to 20 largest out of 817 registered packing stations have an annual throughput of as many as 150,000 cases a year, and 200 of them sell fewer than 200 cases a week. The median station would be processing perhaps 900 cases a week, and selling mainly to exporters. The EEC regulations are said to have resulted in a considerable raising of the level of egg quality. Poor quality was also a contributory cause to a steady decline in consumption of chicken-meat in Belgium during the sixties, from being in 1961/62 nearly 40 per cent higher than the Community average, it was by 1964/65 4 per cent below.

The five difficult years between the inception of the common agricultural policy for livestock and the beginning of the unified market in eggs and poultry-meat in 1968, when high intra-Community levies considerably limited access of Dutch eggs and chicken to their traditional German market, have left the poultry industry in the Netherlands in a rather strong position among the present member countries and give it good prospects in an enlarged Community. Production is mostly within a 60-mile radius of Rotterdam, whose efficiency as a port for discharging grain imports is a vital factor. The main German poultry-farming area to some extent shares a similar advantage, through its proximity to Bremen, but much of French production, notably that of Brittany and the South-East, lies further away from the main grain ports and areas of domestic cereal production.

In the Netherlands a high degree of technical efficiency and lower unit costs of production have not been achieved, of course, without considerable concentration, though the average size of unit is still a good deal smaller than in Britain. There are now 57,000 commercial egg producers, compared with 200,000 in 1958. About half of total output is due to between 3 and 4 per cent of them. The pace has notably quickened in the past three years. In 1968 there were 388 producers with flocks of 5,000 or more layers, comprising 3·8 mn birds. In 1969 the number had risen to 530, with 4·6 mn birds or just under a third of the national flock, including 16 units of over 25,000 (10 in 1968). There are no producer groups or very large private concerns. Only 30 per cent of production passes through co-operative packing stations, but the key to their success lies in the fact that they have formed themselves into 10 export groups which between them account for 70 per cent of all egg exports. They also have 30 per cent of the domestic market, including contracts with the four principal supermarket chains.

All but about 5 per cent of broiler output (200,000 tons deadweight in 1969) is in the hands of some 3,000 producers formed into a dozen groups, which are all integrated, to a greater or lesser extent, with the compound-feed industry. Generally speaking, the integrators do not own the birds, nor are they engaged in production on their own account. Co-operatively produced birds are marketed under the brand name Friki, and there are a number of private brand names. Ninety-six per cent of broilers are frozen. The *Produktschap* for eggs and poultry runs a stabilisation fund for the domestic market. An annual target price is agreed. Any difference between selling price and target price is paid into the fund, by buyers when the selling price is lower, and by producers when it is higher, than the target price.

Turkey production is highly concentrated and integrated, and 75 per cent of output (12,000 tons in 1969) passes through co-operative packing stations. For ducks the proportion is nearly 90 per cent. Duck production (8 mn head a year) has been promoted by the government for social reasons in the former Zuider Zee area as an alternative to fishing.

In Italy, as in the case of milk, both production and consumption of poultry-meat and eggs is largely concentrated in the North, which has 76 per cent of total incubator capacity (Centre, 15 per cent, and South 9 per cent). Egg production has risen steadily during the sixties, from 6·8 bn in 1962, to between 9·5 bn and 10 bn during the last years of the decade. Only just over a quarter of this total is believed to be at present subject to any form of grading. The advent of the EEC regulations means that at least those who wish to export to other parts of the Community must put their house in order. But in general orderliness will only come very gradually to the domestic market. Something between 1,000 and 2,000 packing-stations are said to be applying for accreditation. There are four very large production units, Pollo Arena, Cipzoo (in which Bibby's holds a controlling interest) both in the Brescia-Verona area, Rossignoli, which has close links with both of them, and Gandolfi. Although the latter's own flock is no more than 100,000 birds, it has a network of contracted producers, enabling it to market some 3 bn to 4 bn eggs a year. With two other firms it effectively controls 95 per cent of the Italian wholesale trade, as well as the important import trade on behalf of the *pasta* industry in egg products and low-priced medium and small shell eggs from Eastern Europe. In these circumstances co-operatives have not made much headway in egg marketing.

Consumption per head of poultry-meat is believed to be at or approaching the 10 kg mark, and thus the next highest after France in the Community. Production of broiler meat, which constitutes 85 per cent of that of all poultry-meat, fluctuated between 470,000 tons and 580,000 tons during the second half of the last decade. Yellow fleshed birds are preferred. Broilers are appreciated as being the cheapest form of meat, and frozen birds are generally not in demand because of their higher cost. Production is still only partially concentrated into big units, which account for about 30 per cent of total output. Of this two-thirds are produced by Pollo Arena, which has its own feed plant, and Cipzoo. Both distribute, even as far as the South, in their own chilled transport. Another 30 per cent of the industry is in course of concentration. There is some co-operative production in the Forlì area. One of the major supermarket chains, whose headquarters we visited, Standa, purchases only fresh birds, all on contract. Contracts for non-eviscerated birds are based on week-to-week market prices, but dressed poultry is purchased on 12- or 6-month contracts at a previously negotiated price.

In France the level of national output of eggs and poultry-meat and the way in which that output is marketed are still strongly influenced by the haphazard production of tens of thousands of small farmers. It is estimated that 50 per cent even of broilers come from this source. At the beginning of 1968 there were under 600 units with a capacity of more than 10,000 broilers[1] per crop, accounting between them for about a quarter of national sales. Only about a dozen of them had a capacity of over 50,000. The level of efficiency on farms and at packing stations is generally lower than in the Netherlands. Average conversion ratios established by random sampling have recently been in the 2·35–2·37 range.[2] In 1969 only 134 packing stations out of more than 2,700 were processing over 500 tons of poultry-meat a year.[3] Neither the structure of production nor of processing lends itself to vigorous market promotion or the establishment of brand names. The unequivocal refusal so far of the French housewife to buy frozen chicken is a further complicating factor in the development of large-scale production and marketing. The proportion of output of eggs from non-specialist flocks is about 60 per cent, and even specialist commercial flocks are still operating on a relatively small scale. In 1968 there were just under 900 units of 5,000 layers and above, accounting for about a third of the output of all commercial flocks.[4] Shortage of capital has inhibited the development of very large units, loans from the Crédit Agricole being only available for those of 10,000 birds and under. Although Article 21 of the Agricultural Law of 1962 which laid down maximum limits for the size of livestock units had been quietly ignored for some time before it was formally repealed at the beginning of 1970, its existence undoubtedly helped to slow up the pace of modernisation of the poultry sector in France. The large injections of outside capital which have been a notable feature of the poultry industry in some other countries has also been prevented by the rule barring 'non-professionals' from engaging in this form (as in all other forms) of farming. But even this may in future become more honoured in the breach than in the observance.

Owing to the absence of regional markets of any importance Paris (Rungis) market still establishes the general internal price level for eggs and poultry in France, although not much more than 10 per cent of production passes, on average, through it. With the development of contract production and direct sales to supermarkets and chains by the bigger producers it has increasingly become a residual market for surplus supplies. The marginal, and often seasonal, production of the 50 to 60 per cent of non-specialised producers therefore has a quite disproportionate

---

[1] C. Adjiman and F. Nicolas, *Les grands élevages avicoles en France*, INRA/CERDIA, Massy, 1969, p. 16.

[2] *Le prix de revient du poulet de chair en France*, 'Nouvelles de l'Aviculture', Special Number, July 1970, Institut Technique de l'Aviculture, Paris.

[3] *Structures et activités des abattoirs de volailles*, 'Nouvelles de l'Aviculture', Supplement to No. 114, March 1970.

[4] Adjiman and Nicolas, *op cit*, p. 6.

impact on prices at Rungis, thus affecting prices received by the specialist commercial sector as well. More energetic application of the EEC regulations on grades and standards at all marketing stages may gradually eliminate the baneful effect of the *'oeuf fermier'* and the casually produced broiler unloaded on the market, but in the meantime the price system remains absurd. As far as the large-scale egg producer is concerned Adjiman and Nicolas identified three forms of market outlet, independent wholesalers (used by just over two-thirds of producers), producer groups (16 per cent of producers), and direct to retail, including supermarkets and chains (another 16 per cent). This pattern varies, however, with scale of production. Fifty-seven per cent of eggs marketed by the first method came from units of 10,000 and over; the proportion was 28 per cent only in the case of members of producer groups; and two-thirds of the eggs packed by producers on their own premises came from the biggest units. The greater capacity of the large producer to establish direct contracts with users is evident.

There are currently 125 recognised *groupements de producteurs*, of which 50 specialise in egg production and 55 in broilers, including 15 doing both. The remainder are engaged in miscellaneous activities, producing large chicken (e.g. *poulet de Bresse* (a type of intensively fattened milk chicken)), turkeys, guinea-fowl, *foie gras*, rabbits, and hatching eggs. The egg and broiler groups are organised in four *comités régionaux économiques* covering the whole of France and centred on the four main production areas, the majority of groups in each case being the North-West (Brittany and Pays de la Loire). The largest, which we visited, is in fact a union of local co-operatives of the Ain *département* (UDCA) in the South-East, representing 300 producers with a total laying flock of only 1·4 mn. Its sales network covers twenty-two departments. It is currently supplying, amongst other buyers, 430 supermarkets from its two packing stations, one of which, with an annual throughput of over 700,000 cases, is said to be the largest in France. Contracts with the French supermarkets are based on time's price at Rungis, but in the case of its Swiss customers two previously negotiated seasonal prices form the basis for payment. For its broiler group, consisting of 30 producers mainly with 10,000 bird crops, UDCA is associated with SICA-Bresse, whose packing station processes up to 5 mn broilers and between 0·8 and 1·0 mn *poulets de Bresse* a year.

Marketing of eggs and broilers in France has been marked recently by the failure of producers to establish their own intervention arrangements. The producer organisations sponsoring the scheme at national level, SIPA-Oeuf and SIPA-Volaille,[1] had fulfilled all statutory procedures under the 1962 Law for obtaining an *extension des règles de discipline* to all producers of above a certain minimum scale, including the minority opposed to the scheme. This authorised the raising of a compulsory levy at hatcheries and packing stations. The levy would have financed some seasonal buying-in, as well as market intelligence, sales promotion, and technical

[1] See Butterwick and Neville-Rolfe, *op cit*, pp. 163–4.

research. The working of the scheme was, however, frustrated by a minority of packing stations which refused to collect the levy. After about six months FORMA was obliged to intervene on behalf of the SIPAs to help with refunding those levies that had been duly paid, in order that the scheme could be wound up. Broadly speaking, the split in opinion was between those remote from markets, who favoured it, and those with easier access who felt it to be unnecessary, and the line of division also ran, inevitably, between the owners of smaller and medium-sized units, mostly grouped in the *comités régionaux*, and a few large-scale producers, usually operating their own packing stations, some in the Paris area, though the opposition also included at least one big co-operative union in the South-West and a group in Brittany integrated with a leading compound feed manufacturer. The co-operative sector as a whole will probably have to build up a much greater weight in the egg and poultry market before any renewed effort of this kind can be made, and then it is unlikely to include any provision for intervention. This will depend on a rather long-term attrition of the volume of the volatile non-commercial production, elimination of the smaller commercial units and an increase in the average size of those staying in business, and, above all, a much higher general level of efficiency on the part of packing-stations, especially those in the western part of the country, in order to overcome their geographical disadvantage in relation to the main centres of population.

If it had not been for the five years during which egg and poultry-meat producers in Germany enjoyed the protection of intra-Community levies against Dutch imports, the structure of production there would have changed more rapidly. Although the number of farmers with laying hens fell by nearly a million between 1961 and 1967, 90 per cent of the 1·6 mn still left in production kept fewer than 50 birds, and most of those kept under 20. There were only 1,800 units of 3,000 birds and over. The first two years of the unified EEC market have obviously accelerated the process. There are now some 50 units of over 30,000 layers. One of 2 mn birds, and another of 1·5 mn, belonging to a publishing company and to a firm of nylon spinners respectively, have overtaken the 0·5 mn bird unit established a few years ago in West Berlin at the top of the table. Nevertheless production remains essentially small in scale. Layers in units of 3,000 birds and over still constitute only 22 per cent of the national flock. Well over half of all eggs are still marketed direct by farmers, either from door to door or at farm-gate, or to travelling dealers, or to shops and restaurants. Sales to packing stations only predominate in the main production areas of the North-West and in regions that are remote from large centres of population. The relatively higher cost of transporting eggs (and poultry-meat) than of transporting the bulk ingredients of the feed required to produce them works in favour of producers closer to these centres. Of course the western parts of Lower Saxony and the north-eastern areas of North Rhine-Westphalia, which are easily accessible both to the Rhine and the North Sea and to the Ruhr, enjoy a double benefit. Remoteness has, however, proved a spur to at least some producers in Schleswig-Holstein and Bavaria, the one with access to imported, the other to local, sources of cereals, to lower unit costs by achieving greater efficiency in production and marketing. Integration has tended to be stronger in these areas, but it has also been gathering momentum in less remote areas which are still too far from the Rhineland conurbations for the traditional direct trade. Already in 1967 it was estimated that 90 per cent of egg production in Lower Saxony was from the Weser-Ems region, which is supplied from Bremen, and half of it from three *Kreise* alone.[1] In one of them, Vechta, the integrating activities of a single-feed company, owning its own hatchery, have built up a group of units, including one of over 200,000 layers, with a combined flock of 4 mn birds within a radius of 15 miles.[2]

Rationalisation of the non-traditional sector will also be encouraged by concentration in the pattern of demand. Even four years ago a large consumer co-operative buying group like GEG had a weekly requirement of 10,000 cases. A co-operative organisation such as the Milch- Fett- und Eier-Kontor is able to supply eggs on this scale. MEF still has under 10 per cent of the federal market, but it is continuing to develop a policy of integration with packing stations and the larger producers, in association with feed firms (to which it is supplying its own dried skim and other additives), and with manufacturers of egg products, which provide an outlet for breaking out surplus eggs if the market situation demands. In this way producers will increasingly be trying to by-pass the traditional wholesale packers by developing co-operative packing arrangements of their own, and ensuring to the consumer the fresh and well-graded produce that he demands. In this respect even the producer with the large laying unit finds himself competing, through his co-operative, not only with other wholesalers but also with the traditional small farmer, who is likely to remain, in Germany, a persistent feature of the urban retailing scene for many years to come. Indeed, as they become less numerous they are likely to be more efficient and competitive. They will also provoke less violent cyclical and seasonal oscillations of prices as the volume of their marginal supplies declines.[3]

As in most other countries poultry-meat production in Germany is already more concentrated than that of eggs. Though the non-integrated producers remain numerous (about 10,000, supplying a local trade), there are only 2,000 producers of any importance of broiler meat, some of them grouped into companies with a crop capacity of 100,000 birds or more. About 70 per cent of total output is marketed through the co-operative Geflügelkontor GmbH, which acts as agent for its members, who may be either co-operatives or private individuals or companies.

---

[1] F. Hülsemeyer and H. Wigger, *Strukturen der Eiererzeugung und - vermarktung in der BR Deutschland*, 'Deutsche Geflügelwirtschaft', No. 34, 1969, p. 1522.

[2] P. Sauner, *L'organisation de la production en Allemagne*, 'Nouvelles de l'Aviculture', No. 121, June 1970.

[3] See O. Strecker, *op cit*.

They are not obliged to sell through GFK so long as they notify it of their intention not to do so. Integration is often looser than in some countries, producers generally having no financial links with packing stations, though they do to some extent with feed firms. Nor are the feed firms themselves involved in production. It has been government policy to keep the broiler industry in the hands of farmers. In Germany the private banks have provided a good deal of finance for the poultry industry, though this has become less readily available as the damaging effects on an infant export trade in table poultry following revaluation begin to have their effect, and imports from the Low Countries become even more competitive.

Whether the industry will benefit from the new law on producer groups remains to be seen. As with other products, the minimum quantities having to be marketed by a group for it to qualify for the starting-up subsidies have been set fairly high: 2,000 tons a year of meat in the case of broilers, 750 tons for other forms of poultry-meat, 18 mn eggs (say, from 80,000 hens), between 3·6 mn and 5 mn hatching eggs.

IMPLICATIONS FOR THE BRITISH MARKET

As has already been pointed out, official support measures for poultry-meat, eggs and egg products in Britain will by the late seventies be by no means dissimilar to those in the EEC. As far as market intervention is concerned the future is, it is true, still obscure on both sides of the Channel. In Britain, at the time of writing, the new Egg Authority has yet to announce its plans, and it is not clear whether the government intends to provide exchequer support for any support buying which the Authority might eventually decide upon. As things stand this would have to be financed entirely from the levy which the Authority is entitled, under Part I of the Agriculture Act 1970, which defines its powers and responsibilities, to raise. This is likely to be applied on sales of day-old chicks. There is no provision in the Act for an exchequer subsidy. In either case if intervention is decided on the Authority is likely to follow the recommendations of the Wright Commission's report[1] in limiting buying-in to the post-Christmas period when egg prices traditionally fall to a low level. The Committee anticipated that after the disappearance of the British Egg Marketing Board contracts between producers and packing stations would become the normal method of sale of eggs from commercial flocks whose owners did not wish to do their own wholesaling or retailing, or had no convenient access to that type of outlet. Even if contracts tend to be the main basis for sales, the level of prices on the relatively small residual market will be particularly sensitive to marginal supplies. Since it is inevitable that contract prices will be linked to prices on this free market, intervention should be seasonal just in order to avoid such fluctuations. The report considered that it was therefore desirable that contracts should be based on the Authority's reports of 'the tone of the market as a whole'.

[1] Cmnd 3669, *op cit*, pp. 82–4.

Support buying in a 'normal' January–February period might apply to between 200,000 and 300,000 cases, involving expenditure of £400,000 a year. Otherwise intervention should, in the Commission's view, be confined to periods when in the judgement of the Authority, 'the long-term stability of the industry made this desirable'. In most years it would not be necessary, and, if carried out, it would only be for 'comparatively short periods'. It would 'involve pitching the intervention price certainly no higher than, and possibly lower than, the bare costs of production, depending on the amount of over-supply, and therefore the degree of "discipline" required'. The Commission estimates that £150,000 a year would suffice, and also provide for a reserve fund. Disposal of intervention stocks would probably be by open general tender to processors.

If the Egg Authority does receive Treasury assistance this would, in present circumstances at least, have to be discontinued in the case of entry into the EEC. Even allowing for the political pressure that can still be exercised on behalf of the small family farmer, it seems fairly unlikely that any intervention buying for eggs will have been introduced into the Community by then, not at any rate intervention conducted by official agencies. The possibility cannot be entirely excluded that some contribution from FEOGA might become available for producer groups towards the cost of buying-in operations that were mainly financed out of a levy on production. First-stage intervention for fruit and vegetables provides some sort of precedent, but in the case of eggs it would, in order to be effective, have to be conducted on a nation-wide, and not simply a local, basis and co-ordinated at Community level so as to operate simultaneously in all member countries, the price cycle being now fairly closely synchronised throughout the EEC. The difficulty of ever achieving such a co-ordinated action is underlined by the recent failure to establish a levy-financed market intervention scheme in France. In any case there has so far been little enthusiasm for it in other member countries.

There is, however, a good measure of agreement on the desirability of establishing reliable market information and forecasting at Community level. Tentative steps have been taken in this direction by the major interprofessional organisations.[1] These also have informal links with some of their opposite numbers in Britain. Their main contacts would eventually be with the Egg Authority, which is to some extent interprofessional, and one of whose main tasks will be to provide a market information service for the British egg industry. A degree of market transparency is aimed at which might even in the long run lead to the establishment of a futures market of the kind operated at Chicago.[2] This could help to produce a

---

[1] Produktschap voor Pluimvee en Eieren, Boerenbond Belge, Unione Nazionale de l'Avicoltura, Confédération Française Avicole, and Zentralverband der Deutschen Geflügelwirtschaft.

[2] At present there is no agreed basis for domestic market quotations. Community levies are fixed per kg. In the Netherlands prices are usually given per 100 eggs and in Belgium and France per egg. In Germany at retail the weight range of the grades being

more rational structure not only of the market for shell eggs, but of that for egg products, on which the shell egg market depends for absorbing surpluses.

The abolition of the BEMB at the end of March 1971 and the disappearance of the egg subsidy by 1974 will between them give fresh impetus to trends in the structure of production and distribution of eggs in Britain which have been apparent for some time. There will be a further reduction in the number of packing stations. Some of the smaller ones have undoubtedly been kept going thanks largely to the flat-rate allowances on throughput which they received as agents of the Board regardless of whether they had any outlets of their own for the eggs which they collected. It is believed that, apart from Thames Valley Eggs and Yorkshire Egg Producers, which with their associated co-operatives claim between them not far short of half of total packing station throughput, few other egg-collecting enterprises (possibly as few as three) in Great Britain have been buying back from the Board the totality of eggs collected by them. The great majority of the 300-odd packing stations have been in the habit of 'declaring' some proportion of their throughput and off-loading it on to the Board. These eggs have constituted the bulk of the surplus first-grade eggs which the Board has been obliged from time to time to remove from the market for breaking out. In the free market situation that will emerge during 1971 producers will have a limited choice of action. They can enter into contracts with packing stations to sell a minimum number of cases a week, which would normally correspond to the whole of their current output, but could also be limited to a maximum. The minimum size of pick-up would depend on the relative geographical situation of producer and packing station, but in many areas could easily be not less than 10 cases (of 360 eggs each) per week, which represents the lowest level of production likely to be profitable (say 60 per cent) of about 850 layers (or about 70 per cent of 750). Second, producers, depending on their scale of operation, and their location, can sell direct to wholesalers (usually by contract or exchange of letters), to retailers or to consumers. This category will also include the few wholesaler/retailers who have their own production units. Third, they may enter into exclusive contracts with hatcheries as multipliers.

The removal of the Board will greatly intensify competition between the co-operative packers, the largest private packers (including one co-op that 'went public' a year or two ago), and the major producers, for a gradually shrinking number of wholesale or wholesale/retail buyers. These include buying groups, both voluntary and co-operative, the Co-operative Wholesale Society, the food and variety store multiples, a dwindling number of traditional food wholesalers, and the cash-and-carry groups, most of which have some connection with one of the other categories. This concentration of demand will inevitably lead to further

sold is stated. This gives a clearer idea of their relative value than the grade number alone or descriptions such as 'large', 'standard', etc.

Eggs and Poultry-meat

changes in the structure of egg production on the lines which occurred during the sixties. Whereas in 1960 89 per cent of the laying flock in England and Wales were in units of under 1,000 birds, the proportion had fallen to 39 per cent by 1969. By that time 55 per cent of the flock was in units of 5,000 birds and above, concentrated on 1,723 holdings (and in rather fewer business enterprises, though the exact number is not known). In the immediate future there will still be enough small producers to exercise a good deal of marginal pressure on the market, though not as disruptively as in France. On the other hand the agreement recently entered into between the two leading egg co-operatives, TVE and YEP, YEP's associated co-operative, West Cumberland Farmers, and Warsop Egg Farms, the egg-marketing organisation of J. B. Eastwood and Co., which has an average throughput of 15 mn eggs a week, will remove what could have been a major source of cut-throat competition in the free-market conditions of the post-BEMB period. The new company, Egg Farms Ltd, which expects to have some 20 per cent of the total UK market for shell eggs and will have an annual sales turnover of well over £70 mn ($1,680 mn), intends to pursue a policy of 'planned market expansion coupled with insistence on a high quality product' and hopes thereby to prevent excessive price fluctuations for both producers and consumers. These are, however, scarcely to be avoided altogether, and the next year or two is likely to see a further concentraion of packing-station throughput by large-scale producers along the lines of what has already occurred in the broiler industry.

Nearly 60 per cent of broiler output is now accounted for by units with a capacity of 50,000 birds or over, of which about two-thirds comes from units of 100,000 and over. Six firms now account for about 76 per cent of supplies, the leaders, Ross and Buxted Chicken, recently acquired by the Imperial Tobacco Group, having about 28 per cent of the market, and the next two largest, Eastwood and Sun Valley, some 14 per cent each. Another belongs to an important food-wholesaling group. There are no independent packers. All are wholly owned by producers. Most packing stations, therefore, process not less than 60 per cent of their owners' produce, the balance being made up by supplies produced under contract by so-called independents. In some cases packing stations process 100 per cent of their own produce (e.g. those owned by Eastwood). One major feed company with international connections has a majority shareholding in three of the six leading producer firms. Imperial Tobacco includes a feed firm amongst its subsidiaries. Financial links also exist between other well-known British provender millers and some of the smaller broiler companies. Only four firms of any importance are engaged in producing broiler chicks, one of which, an American firm, claimed three years ago to supplying 60 per cent of the market. Since then, a new breed developed in Britain by Sterlings has made a considerable dent in this claim. The market leader has interests in feed processing, but no major stake in production. Sterlings are part of the Ross group. There are 27 broiler hatcheries in Britain, mainly belonging to the big four, but also including some supplying their own group only with no sales to outside producers.

Production of other forms of poultry-meat, especially ducks and turkeys, is also becoming increasingly concentrated. Flocks of 10,000 or more turkeys now account for nearly 60 per cent of all birds. Owing to the heavy seasonal demand at Christmas, there is still room in the turkey industry, unlike the broiler industry, for a considerable number of small independent producers, whose marginal supplies tend to cause market price variations between one year and another. There are, however, a few large-scale producers, including Ross and Buxted, which between them account for about 27 per cent of the market. Eastwoods, who were originally turkey breeders, are said to be moving into production again after a long absence from the market. The small turkey is tending to replace the heavy chicken, though, retailing at 120p to 125p, it is particularly vulnerable to any marginal reduction in consumer spending on food.

Despite the rationalisation and contract system on which broiler production is based, there still seems to be sufficient marginal capacity for a four-year cycle to be discernible, even after all the shake-ups which have occurred since the first disastrous collapse of the five-year-old market in 1956. Consumption of chicken will, however, continue to rise, and should receive a boost from entry into the EEC, when it would provide relatively an even cheaper alternative form of animal protein to red meat than it does now. The present distributive set-up is, however, by no means as finely tuned as it might be to an increasingly discriminating demand. By the time entry into the EEC becomes a reality the British broiler industry should be reasonably well placed to meet competition from the Continent (assuming veterinary obstacles to imports are removed). The Netherlands industry, though organised in smaller units, is on present showing likely to present the most serious challenge owing to the very high degree of rationalisation achieved there in both breeding and feeding. A single standard broiler mash has been developed in which technical efficiency and cost have been optimised in accordance with a price structure of the cereal ingredients very different from that currently obtaining in Britain.

By the end of any transition period the British egg industry should also be in a slimmer and more vigorous condition to deal with the marginal supplies of eggs from the most competitive Continental producers, mainly in the Netherlands and Denmark, which will disturb the domestic market. There is, on the other hand, likely to be a strong demand in other parts of the Community for large eggs which, at the new ruling higher prices, may be less attractive to the British housewife. No new market outlet for medium and small eggs for breaking out will arise from joining the EEC owing to the relatively small number of plant bakeries in the Community as a whole. Equally, the high cost of freight on refrigerated products will work to the disadvantage of continental breakers who might hope to increase their exports of the frozen liquid yolks and whites used in

Britain for the industrial production of mayonnaise and certain types of cakes.

Certain aspects of the Regulation on grading and packing-station standards for eggs (and probably of that yet to be issued for poultry-meat) will require modification of present arrangements in Britain. From the egg producer's point of view the most onerous is likely to be that subjecting all persons who sell eggs (other than up to five dozen at a time at farm-gate) to the full rigour of grading and packing regulations operative for packing stations. The switch from five to seven weight grades will present substantial, but not insuperable, difficulties of adapting older types of grading equipment. The weight grades would no longer be known descriptively ('large', 'standard', etc.). Besides the three quality grades, A, B, & C (of which only the first two may be retailed for direct human consumption), an 'extra fresh' category was introduced at the request of France. Psychologically this will tend to downgrade grade A eggs in the eyes of the housewife. The EEC regulation requires, in theory at least, inspection of eggs for both weight and quality, at either packing-station or retail stage, or both. Eggs imported from member countries may not be inspected at frontier. This is to forestall any temptation to reject complete consignments on dubiously tenable grounds of quality. Responsibility for ensuring the quality of 'extra-fresh' eggs, for instance, rests with the government of the export country at packing station, and with that of the importing government at retail only. Nor can eggs imported from member countries be obliged to be stamped with the name of the country of origin. Some adaptation of present British regulations will probably be necessary to satisfy Community rules on inspection. The Egg Authority will be under no obligation, as was the Board, to supervise packing stations. Although local government inspectors of weights and measures check egg weights at retail they do not at present handle them for quality.

Finally, brief mention should be made of the special situation of Northern Ireland, whose egg producers have received a measure of subsidy to compensate for their geographical isolation. This has been partly direct support under the system of Remoteness Grants, and partly indirect through the possibility open to local packing stations to off-load their surplus supplies on to the BEMB, and at the same price as that paid by the Board throughout the UK regardless of transport cost.[1] Only 30 per cent of local production is consumed in the province. Medium-sized flocks predominate, three-quarters of all birds being in units of over 1,000 birds. Only 266 units (comprising a quarter of all birds) out of the total of 28,600 have over 5,000 layers. The end of the Board is likely to cause a

[1] Between February 21st 1970 and May 22nd 1970 Northern Ireland accounted for 28 per cent of all surpluses removed by the Board. After the demise of the Board, some part of transport costs will continue to be borne by the Treasury as recommended in the Wright Report. Whatever other aid might be available to the province through the Community's regional policy, a subsidy of this kind would not be permitted under the CAP. The same would apply to Orkney, subsidised transport of whose egg exports was also recommended by the Report.

substantial number of the province's 65 packing stations to disappear. The largest accounts for 60 per cent of total throughput. Two others process a further 20 per cent between them. Nearly half have a weekly throughput of under 500 cases. In anticipation of the Board's disappearance one firm, one of the four main poultry packers, is said to be establishing a depot in Lancashire. Egg producers are likely to undergo rather severe difficulties long before there is any question of entry into the EEC. The industry will therefore be in all the stronger position than it would now be if confronted with a completely free market in eggs. On the other hand the passage of time may well have eroded the advantage, according to one estimate now worth around 1p a dozen, which greater technical efficiency gives it over producers in the Republic, but to which its exports are unfortunately at present closed.

The structure of the Northern Ireland broiler industry would also give it an advantage in the South if exports were permitted. Eighty per cent of total output is produced on the 57 holdings with a capacity of 10,000 birds and over. However, the industry itself enjoys protection, for veterinary reasons, from all imports even from Great Britain. Ninety per cent of total output, less than half of which is consumed in the province, is accounted for by four groups, Moy Park, O'Kane, Ross and Amalgamated Poultry and Eggs.

CHAPTER 8

Sugar

The marketing policies adopted for sugar in both Britain and the EEC are, largely for historical reasons, unlike those for any other commodity. Until the middle of the 19th century cane sugar accounted for most of the world supplies of sugar. According to a British Board of Trade Report, world production of sugar in 1853 amounted to about 1·5 mn tons and of this 84 per cent originated from sugar cane. Beet sugar production in Western Europe developed rapidly during the second half of the century, and was centred in France and Germany, particularly the latter, where the domestic refining industry and beet producers were given extensive protection. The German crop of 1871 produced 186,000 tons of sugar. Ten years later production had risen to 600,000 tons and by 1884 exceeded a million tons. At the turn of the century Germany was producing about 2 mn tons of sugar from domestic sugar beet, of which about half was exported, usually at very low prices. Much of the excess production was shipped to Britain. In 1900 total British imports amounted to around 1·6 mn tons, of which less than 10 per cent was cane sugar. The dominance by Germany of the British market is illustrated by the fact that in the year preceding the outbreak of World War I, Britain imported over 900,000 tons of raw and refined sugar from Germany, representing roughly half its requirements.

During World War I extensive damage occurred to the beet-growing areas of Western Europe, particularly in northern France. Post-war policies in both Britain and France consisted of building up, largely for strategic reasons, their domestic and colonial sources of supply for sugar. In Britain sugar beet came to be regarded, as it had for many decades in northern France, as a useful break-crop on arable farms and a valuable adjunct to the fattening of beef cattle. Germany, which had lost some of its beet-growing territory in the East, re-established its production behind high tariff barriers on imports. During the thirties quotas were introduced in many European countries, including France, Germany and Italy. These quotas (and the contracts associated with them) were applied to both beet growers and sugar producers, and had the effect of drawing the whole industry together into 'interprofessional' organisations. During World War II Germany occupied much of the best beet-growing areas of Europe.

Despite a fairly large war-time increase in the beet acreage in Britain, sugar had to be strictly rationed.

This brief account of the development of the sugar sector in Western Europe indicates that many of its present characteristics have been in existence for some time: an ability to achieve rapid expansion in production of both beet and refined sugar, a tendency to move quickly into a condition of over-supply and hence some experience of quota and cartel arrangements among sugar refiners, and a long history of close government involvement in the sugar industry. So far as the last point is concerned, there has been a clear difference of policy between those European countries having political ties with sugar-producing regions overseas and countries lacking them, and therefore able to pursue national policies with less consideration for the problems of exporting countries. Two other points should be noted here. First, there are large variations in consumption of sugar per head in Western Europe, Britain and the Netherlands finding common ground at the head of the table. Secondly, the by-products of sugar refining, notably molasses and beet pulp, have been used for many years as feed for livestock. It is only the denaturating of refined sugar for this purpose under EEC regulations that has been a novelty.

The close involvement between the producers and the processors of sugar beet has already been mentioned. This involvement is necessarily closer than in the case of other agricultural commodities (for instance, egg producers with their packing station) because of the high transport costs of beets in relation to their value. Whether the sugar beet is transported by the farmer or by the factory, costs rise steeply if the distance is more than about twenty or thirty miles.[1] A farmer can only economically produce sugar beet if he has a processing factory in his neighbourhood through which he can ensure an outlet for his production. Likewise, in view of its high capital cost, which for a modern installation capable of processing about 5,000 tons of beets a day might amount to up to £10 mn, a new factory would only be established where reliable contracted supplies can be obtained. A tight relationship is necessary between the producer and processor in their mutual interest.

The increasingly large throughput required for an economic sugar factory influences the location of beet production as well as the structure of the sugar industry. In Britain, for instance, where the number of beet producers has fallen by half over the past twenty years while production has risen, the British Sugar Corporation, the sole processor of beets, is in process of closing down its only Scottish factory. The localised nature of beet production in Britain is equalled elsewhere in Europe. In France 62 of the 78 sugar factories working in 1967 were located in the four northern regions (Nord, Picardie, Haute Normandie and Région Parisienne), 30 being in the Nord alone. In Belgium there are three areas where beet-growing and the beet factories are concentrated, and in Ger-

[1] Nevertheless, beet is often moved further than this. Growers in the Netherlands sometimes move their crop up to 100 miles to the factory.

many effectively two, the Ruhr and the vicinity of Hanover. Concentration of production is at least equalled by industrial concentration among the refiners. This has important effects on sugar marketing and requires further comment.

In Britain a market-sharing agreement approved by the Minister of Agriculture (Statutory Instrument 839 of 1957) exists between the British Sugar Corporation, which refines most of the beet sugar, and the two private refiners, Tate & Lyle Ltd, and Manbré and Garton Ltd, which refine all the imported raw sugar and most of the BSC's output of raws.[1] The industry is similarly concentrated in the Netherlands and Belgium, both of which have a basic EEC quota of 550,000 tons. The Dutch sugar industry consists of six centrally controlled co-operative factores, Suiker Unie, accounting for 60 per cent of production, and six factories belonging to a private company, the Central Sugar Co., producing the balance. The two organisations appear to work together on the marketing of sugar. In Belgium the market leader, Tirlemont, effectively controls about three-quarters of national production, the remainder being accounted for by about a dozen small independents. In Germany where there are about 50 factories, several of the companies are owned by farmers, though remaining outside the agricultural co-operative movement. Farmer control of factories is particularly strong in the Hanover region, where there is a joint selling organisation in Braunschweiger Zücker AG, and in Bavaria/Württemberg where Süddeutscher Zücker AG has about 10 factories, and, including its associated companies, about a third of the market. Roughly half of German production is in the hands of companies controlled by producers. The largest private company, Pfeiffer & Langen (in total about one-sixth of the market) dominates the Rhineland area. In Italy Eridania with more than 20 factories is the most important producer, with about 35 per cent of the market on its own, and about 45 per cent including its associates. The French industry is somewhat difficult to disentangle owing to overlapping shareholdings. The three largest companies (Say, Béghin and Générale Sucrière) which market their sugar separately, control about 30 per cent of national production. The co-operative factories account for about 12 per cent. These, and a number of small companies producing about 13 per cent of the total, market their sugar through Sucre-Union which is therefore the single largest organisation in the French sugar market. Concentration in the industry is not confined within national frontiers. Through European Sugars (France) and the Compagnie Européenne de l'Industrie Sucrière most of the largest refiners in Europe are grouped together. The companies involved in these two organisations, which date from 1967, are Tate & Lyle, Béghin, Tirlemont, Eridania and Südzücker. Concentration on both a national and an international level is expected to continue.

---

[1] Manbré and Garton Ltd, which joined the agreement in 1970, at present only refines imported raw sugar. There is a separate agreement in respect of Scotland.

The EEC system

In forming a common policy for the sugar sector the EEC had to deal with three principal problems, the differences between member countries in self-sufficiency, the established price levels for sugar and sugar beet, and the existence of the French sugar-producing overseas departments (*départements d'outre-mer*), Martinique, Guadeloupe and Réunion, and some of the ex-French colonies in Africa. France, including the DOMs, and Belgium had fairly large surpluses which in the five years to 1967/68 averaged about 735,000 tons a year in France and 85,000 tons in Belgium. The other member countries ran small deficits during most of this period. There were considerable differences in prices to be overcome. In the five seasons preceding the introduction of a common price, the member countries' minimum prices for sugar beet (16 per cent sugar content) were as follows (no adjustment being made for contract differences):

UA per ton

	1963/64	1964/65	1965/66	1966/67	1967/68
Germany	16·88	18·13	18·13	18·13	18·13
France	12·91	13·09	13·09	13·79	13·79
Italy	16·68	19·05	19·91	19·65	19·68
Netherlands	13·22	16·26	16·26	16·26	16·26
Belgium	15·76	16·86	16·86	16·86	16·86

Source: EEC Commission

The Commission originally proposed (March 1964) the formation of a common market for sugar within the Community with free competition among producers of sugar beet and also between the processing and refining factories. In fact the Council of Ministers finally decided to postpone the establishment of such a free market until July 1st 1975, and to adopt meanwhile a policy based on common prices for a certain quota of sugar allocated to each member country. In arriving at this decision the Community must have been as much influenced by the existence of quota systems in each member country, which permitted controls on production, as by the need to take account of the special circumstances of the sugar industry, including the overseas interests of France. The regulations for setting up a market organisation to implement these decisions were concluded at the end of 1967. Regulation 1009/67, which covers beet and cane sugar, sugar beet, sugar cane, molasses, syrups, etc., came into force for the 1968/69 campaign. At the time of writing therefore the Community has the experience of two seasons of the operation of this modified common market for sugar.

The key to the market organisation for sugar is the quota system. The regulation lays down basic quotas for production of white sugar for each member country, the quotas to come into force from the 1968/69 season. Although ostensibly based on average production during the years 1961/62 to 1965/66 the quotas were in each case fixed higher, exceeding average production during this period by only about 4 per cent in the case of France, by about 9 per cent for Germany, but by as much as 44 per cent for Belgium. The agreed quotas were Germany 1,750,000 tons of white sugar, France (including DOMs) 2,400,000 tons, Italy 1,230,000 tons and the Netherlands and Belgium/Luxemburg 550,000 tons each, a total of 6,480,000 tons. At the time when the quota decisions were made it was expected that this total would exceed consumption of sugar in the Community by about 200,000 tons. In fact, consumption in this year was less than had been estimated by the Commission (about 6 mn tons) and the quota for which the maximum price applies (see below) exceeded consumption by about half a million tons.

National quotas are then divided out among factories (or enterprises of more than one factory) within each member country. The method of allocation is laid down by Regulation 1027/67, with some discretion being left to individual governments. It is based on the factories' (or companies') average production during the period 1961/62 to 1965/66. The factory quotas are divided up among producers of sugar beet by means of national or regional interprofessional agreements. In these agreements provision is usually made for the reservation of some part of the quota for new entrants to beet farming. The Netherlands uses a different system without quotas to producers as an average intervention price is used.

The regulations provide for the establishment of guide and intervention prices for white sugar and a minimum price for sugar beet by August 1st of each year to apply to the following year. For 1968/69 and 1969/70 these were respectively UA 22·35 and UA 21·23 per 100 kg and UA 17·00 per ton. A comparison with the figures already given for the beet prices in member countries prior to harmonisation shows the extent of the rise in French producer prices. These will have been further accentuated by the currency changes of 1969. The full intervention price applies to sugar produced up to 100 per cent of each factory's quota (or company's quota). Over 100 per cent and up to 135 per cent of the quota a lower intervention price applies, this being reflected in a lower price to producers. Over 135 per cent there is no provision for intervention and the factory must sell this excess production outside Community markets. The basic intervention price applies to sugar of standard quality (No. 3), although only an unimportant quantity of this type is produced, and is applied to the main surplus area of the Community (northern France). The same price is currently used elsewhere in the Community with the exception of Italy, which has a derived intervention price, plus a degressive subsidy, and of the French overseas departments which also have derived prices, though the method of derivation is not directly related to transport costs.

The purpose of the guide price for sugar (currently UA 22·35 per 100 kg for standard quality sugar), which is fixed at about 105 per cent of the intervention price, is largely concerned with the control of imports, though it also represents (theoretically) the price level the Commission would like to see. A threshold price is established consisting of the guide price, plus transport costs from the main surplus area (northern France) to the most remote deficit area (Palermo). These transport costs (including handling, insurance, etc.) currently amount to UA 2·59 per 100 kg, to give a threshold price of 24·95 per 100 kg. The threshold price is implemented by a levy charged on the difference between the world price and the threshold price. As the market price in the EEC has so far always been below the guide price, this arrangement effectively keeps out all imports of white sugar. A threshold price is also established for raw sugar, derived from the white sugar price, and for molasses, the price of which is lower, the Community having a small deficit. There is a complicated tariff to provide for levies on products containing sugar. Import licences for these and for white and raw sugars are necessary, applications for which have to be accompanied by a deposit.

The sugar factories contract with the producers in two ways. So-called A contracts are used for quantities of sugar up to the basic quota. For these the beet producer receives a guaranteed minimum price of UA 17·00 per ton, basis 16 per cent. Contracts for quantities in excess of the basic quantity are called B contracts. For sugar manufactured by the factory against these contracts the factory has to pay a production levy. The level of this levy depends upon the total production of the EEC and also the price level in the Community compared with world markets. The object of the levy is to make up some of the loss that the Community sustains as a result of production of sugar in excess of the 105 per cent of consumption. The factory is allowed to charge 60 per cent of this levy to the beet producer, who cannot depend on receiving for contract B quantities a price in excess of UA 10·00 per ton. Contracts at the full price are described as being for 'fat beets'. Those for quantities between 100 per cent and 135 per cent of the basic quota (minimum price UA 10·00 per ton) are described as 'demi-fat beets'. Quantities in excess of this, for which there is no price guarantee whatever, are described as 'thin beets'. Originally it had been envisaged that factories might have a profit-sharing arrangement with producers, the so-called *règle de partage*. This has so far not been implemented in any of the member countries except Germany, and there the arrangement is confined to the co-operative sector.

In order to reduce their theoretical surplus position each member country is permitted to 'carry forward' into the next year up to 10 per cent of the basic quota. This amount is then added to the surplus calculation in the following year. The Netherlands which, as already mentioned, have a fixed price for sugar, do not operate this system, but instead work on the basis of a three-year period for which 350 per cent of the basic annual quota is applied. The reason for this difference is that Dutch farmers often grow beet only one year in four or five.

The relationship between the guaranteed price for sugar beet and the intervention price for white sugar is calculated as follows:

Sugar

	UA per 100 kg
Cost of sugar beet UA 17·00 per ton on a yield of 130 kg per ton	13·08
Add: Transportation cost to factory	1·60
Factory cost including profit	7·50
	22·18
Less: Return on sale of molasses	0·95
Intervention Price for Quality 3	21·23

The pulp from the sliced sugar beet does not figure in the above calculations as it is regarded as the property of the producer and either returned to him or sold on his behalf.

The original intention of the Commission had been to operate restitutions (and denaturing subsidies) for sugar in much the same way as for cereals. That is to say, the restitutions would have been varied frequently to reflect differences between world and EEC prices and the changing pattern of supply and demand in the Community. In fact the international market is so volatile that this would anyway be difficult to arrange satisfactorily and since the rather disastrous experiences of 1968/69, when a flood of exports followed an excessively generous setting of the restitution, the Commission has increasingly relied on another method. During 1969/70 both the permanent restitution and the denaturing premium[1] remained in force, but they were deliberately set so low that virtually no use was made of them. Instead tenders have been used. In the case of export restitutions, the tendering takes place regularly once a week. The tenders are made every Wednesday to the national intervention agency which passes them on to Brussels. The numbers of firms competing vary, but it is normally about a dozen to a score for the whole Community. The tenders can be made by either factories or the sugar trade. The Commission then notifies the agencies which tenders have been accepted. Successful tenders are available for the current month plus three months. There is no obligation on the Commission to accept any restitution tenders however low. In fact, in some weeks no tenders are accepted. This method, therefore, permits a close control of export business. Tenders for denaturing have been done at irregular intervals, but the procedure is much the same. The possibilities of abuse of the restitution and denaturing system are well recognised. It would be possible for traders through collusion to 'rig' the market to their advantage. It would even be theoretically possible for a single trader to combine dumping a few cargoes on the London or Paris markets, and thus temporarily depressing the price, with making a restitution offer which reflected this temporary price situation. But the financial risks involved in conducting operations of this kind are very great.

Generally speaking the EEC sugar marketing system is regarded as satisfactory by both beet producers and crusher-refiners. The former have a

[1] The denaturing premium was suspended in the autumn of 1970, but could be brought into use again if necessary.

generous guaranteed price for a limited quantity. In some parts of the Community, notably northern France, farmers can supply marginal tonnages in excess of their basic quotas at prices which comfortably cover marginal costs. In other words, B contracts at UA 10·00 per ton of sugar beet can be remunerative to efficient beet producers. So far it appears that these contracts are more attractive to the producer than to the crusher-refiner. The latter is liable to have to pay to the Fund 40 per cent of the maximum levy, or UA 4·67 per ton of beet. Payment of this sum reduces the margin on processing to under UA 3·00 per ton. Other things being equal, marginal quantities of beet can be worked profitably on this basis. But the refiners find that the extra quantities they take on B contracts bring other difficulties. The campaign has to be stretched into late January, by which time weather conditions may be adverse. Contracts normally include settlement on the basis of beets sampled and stored in field clamps. If these are left for a long time there is likely to be some deterioration as well as a loss of sugar content, which is for the factory's account. At the end of the season tare may be lower, but both the quantity and the quality of the beets may be adversely affected and transport costs may be higher. Consequently there may be increasing reluctance on the part of the factories to conclude B contracts on a large scale, though they may be forced to do so in order to preserve their farmer custom. It may be that failure to agree about quota reductions to check the growth of surpluses (e.g. at the meetings of the Council of Ministers in February 1970) is less important than might be supposed, and that the economic squeeze on refiners on tonnages in excess of the basic quotas will turn out to be a more significant inhibition.

In most other respects the factories in the EEC, like the farmers, are satisfied by the Community's transitional marketing arrangements. The margins permitted on the basic quotas to cover transport and processing of the beets are generally regarded as fair. The quota system suits the industry very well though there are complaints about the quantities. While the system tends to make rigid the structure of the industry, it must be remembered that one company which buys out another also acquires the latter's quota. Indeed, the acquisition of additional quotas through take-overs has become so attractive to expanding sugar companies in France that a number of smaller refineries have grouped themselves together round Sucre Union in an effort to protect themselves from marauding companies. This is not, of course, the only reason for the concentration that has occurred in the French sugar industry, where mergers have been effected largely in order to increase marketing strength.

Some complaints are expressed by refiners and by the trade about the use of the permanent tenders for restitutions in preference to a more realistic level of normal (i.e. freely available) restitution. It is felt that export business is lost or done at lower levels than might otherwise be obtained because of the uncertainties of this system. But in fact it seems to work. A more important complaint is concerned with the actual operation of intervention buying. Because of the high costs involved for FEOGA, the Commission is, in general, reluctant to make purchases at intervention, though it can be argued that intervention buying has sometimes suited its political objectives. A balance between supply and demand can, it is felt, be established more economically by juggling the quantities accepted at tenders for export restitutions and denaturating premiums without removing the sugar from trade channels. Consequently, the Commission, working through the intervention agencies, tends to make selling at intervention as unattractive as it can within the framework of the regulations, for instance through extremely strict quality control, insistence on storage arrangements which may not suit the refiners, or setting the *prime de stockage* unrealistically low and thus creating selling pressure early in the season. It is this fact, as much as the reluctance of the refiners to sell large quantities of their sugar to a state-trading organisation (and therefore risk having it sold on to their customers) that provides the explanation for the tendency for sugar prices to oscillate around the intervention price level and occasionally fall below it.

The EEC refiners evidently have somewhat mixed feelings about intervention in the sugar market, but they would certainly like to keep it as a safety net. They would also like to see the basic quotas preserved, or if possible increased, higher and more permanent export restitutions, world agreement on sugar designed to stabilise world prices at higher levels than have prevailed recently and, of course, the entry of Britain into the EEC with the minimum of safeguards for the Commonwealth Sugar Agreement. Within these general objectives which, if realised, would produce an ideal situation for the EEC sugar industry, one can detect national differences. Germany and Italy, for instance, are more anxious to increase prices than is France.

The market structure in the EEC

Each of the member countries has an intervention agency for sugar. In the Netherlands and Belgium the work is done by the 'umbrella' organisations already described, respectively VIB and OBEA. Exceptionally there is no Dutch Commodity Board (*Produktschap*) for sugar, the co-operative and private sectors of the industry being unable to agree about the establishment of a Board. The Dutch single price system permits the co-operatives to let farmers have the right to deliver to the factory quantities corresponding to their shareholding in the factory. Suiker-Unie makes annual contracts with producers. There has been no intervention buying as yet in the Netherlands where there is an approximate balance between supply and demand. Despite the large surplus position in Belgium, intervention buying has been on a nominal scale. In the one test case that has occurred so far Tirlemont was both seller and buyer. The reluctance to sell to OBEA is largely explained by a fear that the agency will sell back through the market to Tirlemont's own customers.

The largest surpluses, actual and potential, are in France. There is a special agency for sugar, FIRS (Fonds d'Intervention et de Régularisation du Marché du Sucre) established in July 1968, barely in time for the first season under harmonised regulations. This organisation, which is described in detail in Chapter 3,[1] took over most of the work of the interprofessional GNIBC (Groupement Interprofessionnel de la Betterave, de la Canne et du Sucre). Careful thought was evidently given to the possibility of including sugar under the responsibility of FORMA. The decision to create a special organisation for sugar was no doubt prompted by the particular problems of the sugar sector and the unusual marketing arrangement.

The German intervention agency for sugar, the EVSt for sugar in Frankfurt, is rather similarly constituted to the other German agencies, but with a smaller staff. The EVSt for sugar is a semi-governmental organisation established under public law (*Anstalt des öffentlichen Rechts*) by the Sugar Act of 1951. The Board, which meets twice a year, consists of 24 members representing the relevant Ministries, the sugar trade producers and consumers (four members each). The Chairman is from the Ministry of Agriculture. The number of staff (currently about 25 against a permitted complement of 36) is rather smaller than that of FIRS. The explanation of this appears to be that quality control is farmed out to independent licensing officials specialising in sugar grading. Otherwise the organisation and type of work performed is comparable to those of FIRS. Prices for sugar in Germany have tended to fluctuate slightly above the intervention price. The EVSt price reports show that in 1968/69 selling prices for sugar (category No 2) were in the bracket UA 21·73–UA 22·20 per 100 kg, the intervention price being UA 21·73. In that year the EVSt bought about 85,000 tons of sugar, roughly half raw and half white. In 1969/70 about 27,000 tons were acquired, all white. German imports some 50,000 tons of sugar levy-free from East Germany under a special arrangement, this being destined for West Berlin.

Italy is the only EEC member country with a regular deficit in sugar. Consumption, which is rising steadily, amounts to about 1·5 mn tons compared with the quota of 1·23 mn tons. The quota is lower than the slicing capacity of the Italian sugar industry,[2] which may be closer to the current level of consumption. Imports, mostly from France and Germany, are made under government regulation by tender from the trade. Eridania, which dominates the market, has formed with two other large companies (Societá Italiana Zuccheri, with 24 per cent of the market, and Montesi with about 13 per cent) Asso-Zuccheri, an association representing over 80 per cent of total production. The Italian sugar industry is therefore very highly concentrated, the only competition to Asso-Zuccheri coming from a number of small private firms and from the co-operatives, which are

[1] pp. 48–9.
[2] The length of the campaign, which has an important effect on capacity, could probably be extended, though in Italy, as elsewhere, an extension raises problems for both growers and factories.

latecomers to the business and now have about 7 per cent of the market. Four of the co-operative factories operate in former land-reform areas under the aegis of the state development agencies (*Enti di zviluppo*). The fifth, in Tuscany, belongs to the Federconsorzi.

Until 1958, when the co-operatives started up, farmers had complete freedom in theory to make contracts with any of their local factories. Effectively the factories carved up the territory between themselves. The basis for the present factory quotas under the EEC system is the 1962/67 production. Quotas are fixed annually, supposedly to take account of changes in production. Recently, considerably less than the permitted margin has, in fact, been switched. Switching has tended to be from the private sector in the North to the private sector in the South, and no further switching may now occur until 1975, except such as may be effected by closing old factories and opening new ones. This disadvantages the co-operatives, which have none suitable for closing, and prevents them from expanding away from the traditional beet-sick areas.

No clear statistics exist of the proportion of sugar being used for industrial purposes and for retail, since figures for production of crystallised and powdered sugar are no longer published separately. Consumption for industrial purposes can be estimated at about 150–200,000 tons. Differential rates of tax are maintained on the two types of sugar, but statistics of tax receipts do not distinguish the two. Very little (about 0·2 per cent) sugar is actually sold direct to the sugar-utilising industries.

There is no demand from farmers for fresh pulp, which, owing to high transport costs and the generally high proportion of tare in beet deliveries, is unsaleable. All pulp is therefore dried, a proportion being returned free to producers and the rest sold off.

IMPLICATIONS FOR THE BRITISH MARKET

The bulk of British imported supplies of sugar, which themselves represent some two-thirds of total supplies, enter under the preferential (and fixed) price of the Commonwealth Sugar Agreement. In 1968, when the Agreement was made of indefinite length, the following clause was added: 'The provisions of this Article are subject to the understanding that the UK Government, if it successfully completes negotiations for the accession of the UK to the European Economic Community (i) cannot be committed to continuing contractual obligations under the Agreement after December 31st, 1974; (ii) shall, in the event that it does not accept such contractual obligations after December 31st, 1974, consult with the other Parties to the Agreement with a view to seeking means of fulfilling the objectives which those obligations would otherwise fulfil'. Britain is therefore contractually bound until the end of 1974, which coincides with the end of the EEC's own transition period for sugar. The British Government is also bound to make some arrangements for the sugar-exporting countries of the Commonwealth after 1974, though this commitment is necessarily less specific.

Solutions to the problem of the future of Commonwealth sugar in the UK market could take several forms. Negotiations over British entry so far as sugar is concerned must take account of two main points. First, as the UK has virtually no freedom of manœuvre for the period up to the end of 1974, any settlement for this period must include in the package some provisions for post-1974. Second, it is difficult to envisage any compromise over either pre-1974 or post-1974 Commonwealth sugar supplies which would be so adverse to the exporting countries in the agreement as to provide any major solution to EEC surpluses for at least a decade. Representatives of the EEC sugar refiners sometimes give the impression that they regard the UK deficit not only as 'theirs for the taking', but also the answer to the problem of what to do with between one and two million tons of surplus sugar. No doubt these expressions of opinion represent in large part the establishment of a negotiating position. Clearly account has to be taken of the likely expansion of low-cost UK production[1] at EEC prices. Any calculation of the extent of this expansion, which would, of course, be greatly influenced by the extent of the basic quota attracting the full price, is extremely hazardous. It has to take account of developments in other crops which can be both competing and complementary. But at the least British growers could be expected to expand production by the end of 1974 to fill the gap which might be left by dropping out the sugar supplies from developed Commonwealth countries. Such an expansion would present, as things stand at present, considerable problems over crushing capacity.

The British Sugar Board which administers the pricing mechanism of the British sugar market in relation to both home and Commonwealth supplies, is the obvious organisation to act as the intervention agency. It has long experience of international trade and quality control of the product. The present staff of the Board consists of about 22 people in all, including the full-time Chairman. In addition there is a part-time Vice-Chairman and three other part-time independent members of the Board. None of the members of the Board represent refining or trade interests, nor are there any consultative committees of the interprofessional type. Despite its large shareholding in the British Sugar Corporation (BSC), amounting to 25 per cent of the equity, the Sugar Board is not represented on the Corporation's board. It appears that the Board has been successful in avoiding conflicts of interests and in keeping out of the 'politics' of sugar.

Basically, there are three elements in the work of the Sugar Board.[2] First, it is responsible for buying at the fixed Commonwealth Sugar Agreement price the quotas of the signatories to the Agreement in f.o.b. terms, programming the offerings and then selling to the UK refiners and

[1] See F. G. Sturrock, *Alternative sources of supplies for British sugar*, 'The National Westminster Bank Review', August 1969 and February 1970.

[2] A fuller description of the Board's work is provided in Appendix VII of the Board's 1969 Report.

trade on the f.o.b. basis equivalent of the London Daily Price, a c.i.f. price calculated daily by a committee of the London terminal market. On these transactions it usually makes a loss, as the fixed CSA price has been above the world price since the Sugar Board came into existence with the exception of two periods in 1957 and 1963–4. Consequently, its second activity is to raise a levy (called the surcharge) on all sugar imported into the UK, including sugar contained in other products such as confectionery. Proceeds of this levy are also required to finance the third part of the Board's work. This consists of making up to the BSC the difference between the price that the Corporation pays to farmers for sugar beet, that is to say the guaranteed price as decided by the Government at the Annual Review, and the price obtained by the Corporation for its raw and refined sugars sold in the open market. These payments take account of the so-called Incentive Agreement between the government and the Corporation, which is designed to provide the latter with rewards for increased efficiency.

In carrying out these three principal functions (there are others, including dealing with sugar under the Anglo-Irish Sugar Agreement)[1] the Board handles large sums of money. Over the past few years it has bought about 1·7 mn tons of sugar every year at a cost of some £80 mn. Proceeds of sales and the surcharge vary inversely to the level of world prices. Net receipts from the surcharge totalled £54·7 mn in 1969 compared with about £85 mn in each of the two previous years. In 1969 the actual payment to the British Sugar Corporation was £7·3 mn, and the estimated liability at the end of the year £8·5 mn, both considerably lower than in previous years, as a result of higher world prices, partly brought about by the International Sugar Agreement. At first sight, the staff seems very small in relation to these large sums. That the Board is able to keep its administrative costs so low (under £100,000 a year, exclusive of payments to the Customs and Excise for work carried out on the Board's behalf) is due to two reasons. First, much of its work is regulated by fairly simple and predetermined formulae. In particular, the buying is done at prices fixed for a period of three years. The principal area of discretion for the Board is over marketing, where the Sugar Act lays down that it should sell at 'the best price reasonably obtainable for the sugar having regard to the date of delivery and the other terms and conditions of the sale'. In arriving at this price the Board is greatly assisted by the existence on its doorstep of an international market for sugar. The activity of this market is sustained by the operations of merchants and brokers, the latter being largely kept afloat by selling commissions paid by Commonwealth producers, the scale of which seems generous considering that prices are fixed. Second, the Board is able to farm out some of its work. The Customs and Excise collects the surcharge payments, including those on processed products, deals with claims for repayments on exports, supervises sugar imported free of surcharge for denaturating for animal feed, certain chemical purposes and for export, and remits the balance on these transactions to

[1] See p. 263 footnote 1.

the Board. The fact that the British refining industry, consisting of BSC, Tate & Lyle Ltd, and Manbré and Garton Ltd, is even more concentrated than in the Common Market countries, further facilitates the work of the Board. By working closely with the Ministry of Agriculture, the Board is also able to operate its economics and statistics section without a large staff.

With Britain a member of the EEC the Sugar Board's role would be modified but not greatly changed. It already acts in a general advisory capacity to the government on sugar questions, particularly on the Incentive Agreement with the BSC. Its advisory work would be extended as the Board would be likely to contribute a member to the government's team for the Management Committee for sugar in Brussels. Its principal task at present, the purchase at special prices and sale of Commonwealth sugar, would continue, but the form this ought to take would, of course, depend on the terms negotiated for the CSA signatories after 1974. Here the problem is whether Britain retains sole responsibility for implementing the CSA prices or the Community shares in the responsibility—in other words, how the surcharge/levy system for Commonwealth sugar is dealt with in an enlarged Community. The Board would become responsible for applications for exports with restitutions and for denaturing with premia. As Britain has a large deficit in home-produced sugar, it seems unlikely that the former could become as important as for other member countries, though it must be remembered that the British refiners already have a sizable export trade. More important than this is the value of exports of products containing sugar. Even if the Customs and Excise continued to handle claims for restitutions on the sugar content of these exports, the Sugar Board might be expected by the Commission to take on a more direct responsibility for their supervision. Some 10,000 tons of raw sugar currently enters Britain free of surcharge and is denatured for use as animal feed. Under the EEC system this sugar would be subject to import levy. But refined sugar, either based on imported raw sugar or domestic sugar beet, would be eligible for subsidy for denaturing to bring the cost down approximately to a levy-free basis. As other ingredients for compound feeds would become more expensive in Britain, it is to be expected that a considerably larger quantity of sugar would be used for animal feeds.

If the common policy for sugar is applied to Britain, the BSC would no longer require subsidisation via the Sugar Board from the surcharge on imports. The domestic market for refined sugars would be sustained at a level sufficient for refiners to pay producers the required minimum prices described earlier. While the BSC's monopolistic position as the sole beet-crusher in Britain might be ended, it is difficult to argue that this would make much practical difference, as the Corporation would be the only refiner eligible for a quota under the EEC system. If the British quota were set at substantially more than the present tonnage of about 850,000 tons, it is possible that some other organisation might apply to crush and refine the balance. The only difference to the Sugar Board that the change in the status of the BSC might bring could be that the Board would be likely to divest itself of its shareholding in the Corporation.

Finally, there is the question of intervention buying of sugar in Britain. This could become a possibility if the CSA signatories retain access rights comparable to those at present, if the British quota is set at a high level, if sugar is exported to Britain from other member countries, perhaps including Ireland, and if the normal demand, plus exports with restitution and denaturing for animal feed, fails to keep in step with these supplies. If intervention buying became necessary, the Sugar Board would require extra staff to deal with the buying operation and the supervision of stocks. Allowing for some redeployment of existing staff the Board might require up to a dozen new staff to deal with the extra work, including price reporting to Brussels, that could arise as a result of Britain adopting the common policy for sugar.

CHAPTER 9

Horticulture

1. FRUIT AND VEGETABLES

In 1967, the latest year for which data are available, fruit and vegetable production accounted for 14 per cent of the gross value of agricultural output in the EEC as a whole. In Italy the share was nearly a quarter, and in France, the Community's second most important producer, just under 10 per cent. Proportionately in Belgium (16 per cent) and in the Netherlands (12 per cent) fruit and vegetables account for a larger share of gross output than in Germany (8 per cent), which takes third place in the Community, some way behind France, in the total value and volume of horticultural production. Much of German production, about 20 per cent of vegetables and almost half of fruit, is, however, not marketed. The high level of import demand of the large urban population in Germany is therefore a dominant feature of the Community's market structure for this sector, the country being less than 60 per cent self-sufficient in both fruit and vegetables. Germany accounts for some 60 per cent of EEC imports, including those from third countries, of vegetables and fresh fruit. Italy, the Community's largest exporter and Germany's main supplier, also has the highest per capita consumption of fruit and vegetables, so that exports represent only about 12 per cent of total vegetable and 7 per cent of total fruit production, compared with the Netherlands which export nearly half their vegetables, and with France, between 15 and 20 per cent of whose fruit production is exported.

The sixties have seen a considerable expansion of horticultural production in the Community, total output of vegetables and of fruit increasing by about 8 per cent and 16 per cent respectively between 1964 and 1969.[1]

[1] These and subsequent figures are based on the most recently available data published, in 'Statistique Agricole' 1969, No. 8, by the Statistical Office of the European Communities. In order to reduce the effect of year-to-year climatic variations, a three-year-running average has been adopted, the years referred to in this and subsequent paragraphs being the central year of each three-year period, with the exception of 1969, which is an average of 1969 and 1968. Figures for 1969 are in any case mostly provisional. For more detailed information about production of individual crops and varieties in each member country since 1960, the reader is referred to 'Statistique Agricole'. Community statistics in this sector should, however, as is stressed by the Statistical Office, be treated with considerable reserve. There is still an absence of comparability between member

The main stimulus to vegetable production occurred, in all member countries except Germany (where it has not greatly developed at all), in the middle years of the decade. Since 1966 total production has tended to level off. The share of the market represented by the five main crops, tomatoes, cauliflowers, carrots, onions and lettuces, has, however, risen steadily to about 45 per cent of the Community total. Fruit production has everywhere been rising steadily each year since 1964 and will continue its upward trend as orchards of top fruit planted during the past five years come into bearing. In the southern half of France, especially, plantings of top fruit received much official encouragement during the early sixties, at least in part because it provided a convenient form of resettlement to those obliged to leave Algeria. While peaches in the Rhône Valley and Provence have proved quite competitive with those grown in Italy, many people have doubted the wisdom of encouraging apple production south of the Loire. Climatic conditions—strong drying winds, low rainfall, hail, and spring frosts—and the irrigation, special insurance policies, and air-heating systems which these demand, have all added so much to unit costs that Grade I fruit (sometimes no more than 60 per cent of output) from the south of France competes with difficulty with apples produced in the more benign climate of northern Italy, or closer to the main markets in northern France and the Netherlands. Output of apples in the Community rose by 21 per cent between 1965 and 1969, mainly as the result of expanded production in Italy (now with 25 to 30 per cent of EEC output) and France (20 to 25 per cent). Although Germany still accounts for over a third of the apple crop much of it is of poor market quality. Pear production went up by 29 per cent during the same period, but has been levelling off somewhat since 1967. Italy accounts for between 50 and 60 per cent of the pear crop, France and Germany for about 15 per cent each. Though total output of peaches has not greatly increased, the proportion reaching the market has steadily risen, especially with the development of the new orchards in France, whose share of the Community production has risen to nearly one-third, compared with a quarter in the early part of the decade. Italy accounts for virtually the whole of the balance. Seventy-five per cent of the table-grape crop also comes from Italy, where a big expansion of production has occurred since 1966.

Italy is also the Community's largest producer of cauliflowers (over 50 per cent), onions (45 per cent), lettuces (35 per cent) and tomatoes (75 per cent). Cauliflower production, of which France accounts for between a quarter and a third, increased by about 10 per cent over the period 1967/68 in all member countries except Belgium and Luxemburg. In the same two years a similar expansion occurred of onion production, of which France accounts for 25 per cent and the Netherlands for 20 per cent. Although total output of lettuces (of which France, with 30 per cent, is the

countries' statistics. The figures presented here are intended to provide a very broad order of magnitude of production trends as a background to recent developments in EEC policy.

second producer) has not greatly risen, the Netherlands have steadily increased their share to nearly 15 per cent. Tomato production, which went up sharply in the middle of the decade, by about 5 per cent, is shared between Italy, France (12 per cent) and the Netherlands (8 per cent). France (45 per cent of total) is the largest producer of carrots, followed by the Netherlands with 20 per cent. France and Italy share about equally 80 per cent of output of peas and haricot beans.

Recent years have seen increasing specialisation among vegetable growers throughout the EEC, even in Italy where production is traditionally mixed (*coltivazione promiscua*). This has involved higher yields and growing independence, by means of heat in the north of the Community and irrigation in the south, of weather conditions. Area under glass in the EEC, 17,400 ha in 1968, has more than doubled since 1956, and even in Sicily costs per kg of tomato production can be reduced by as much as 40 per cent by use of plastic cloches.[1] Although any increase in total demand for vegetables is likely to be a function of population rather than of income, one effect of rising incomes will be a steady shift to consumption of higher quality and processed, especially deep-frozen, produce. Dutch exporters are expected to continue to expand their sales on the important German market, but more slowly than in the mid-sixties in the face of increasing competition from France and third countries, including the southern hemisphere. Competition from South-Eastern Europe may well be a serious obstacle to increased exports by Italy in the EEC.

A similar trend towards demand for processed forms of fruit, including juices, may also be expected, but without any marked rise in the overall per capita level of fruit consumption. At over 100 kg a year this is already high in Germany and Italy. In other member countries consumption has customarily fluctuated from year to year with supply, marginal increases being largely a function of low prices caused by seasonal glut.[2] A permanent inroad into the market will therefore tend to be made only by growers whose produce still retains, by reason of high quality or unseasonability, a high income elasticity. To some extent the CAP for fruit and vegetables with its stress on grading has been designed to show growers the way. The limited extent of officially financed intervention and the relatively low levels of protection at the common frontier should also, in theory at least, do something in the long run to discourage a flood of poor quality fruit from reaching the market. Unfortunately, it is often in practice the efficient producer who, with a relatively large investment at risk, suffers most from the climatic factors to which fruit and vegetable production is so peculiarly subject. Even more than the market for eggs, that for fruit is vulnerable to sudden increases in marginal supplies from haphazard

[1] R. Vandervaeren, *Le développement quantitatif probable de la production et de la consommation de fruits et légumes dans la prochaine décennie*, Louvain, Fédération des coopératives horticoles, Report No. 61 (French version), undated, p. 16.

[2] H. Schmidt *et al*, *Aggregation of future demand and supply for agricultural products in the EEC 1970–1975*, Munich, Ifo-Institut für Wirtschaftsforschung, 1969, pp. 190–2.

producers. But there is also a long-term trend to commercial overproduction in the Community. Between 1967 and 1969 (calendar years) the area of non-specialised apple orchards in Italy fell by 25 per cent. Sixty-two thousand ha in specialised apple production produced about two-thirds of the Italian crop in 1969, yielding an average of 25 tons, compared with 1·5 tons/ha from the 292,000 ha of primitive orchards. Production surplus to internal needs is expected to reach about 700,000 tons in 1970 though it may not rise above 750,000 in 1975. The situation in France is potentially even more serious. In 1969 apart from the 97,000 ha of apple orchards in production, of which over half were planted to Golden Delicious, there were a further 15,000 ha not yet in bearing (of which over 9,000 ha to Golden Delicious). Total French output of apples, 1·8 mn tons in both 1968 and 1969, may reach 2·3 mn tons by 1975, giving an export surplus estimated at between 570,000 tons and 650,000 tons in 1970, and one as high as 950,000 tons by 1975. German import demand could be about 625,000 and 700,000 tons in the same two years, but this could still leave the Community with a surplus of approaching 1 mn tons by 1975.[1] Substantial surpluses of pears and peaches too are anticipated during the early seventies, also well exceeding the likely import demand of Germany, Belgium and Luxemburg.

The EEC system

The CAP for fruit and vegetables incorporates protection against low priced and low quality imports as well as intervention on internal markets. Besides duties, most of them seasonal, applicable under the common external tariff,[2] provision is also made for additional countervailing charges (*taxes compensatoires*) to be imposed in the case of abnormally low offers. For this purpose reference prices for all products are fixed by the Commission corresponding to the lowest market prices in the area of greatest surplus for each product. If on two consecutive days import prices[3] are at least UC 0·50 below the reference price, the Commission may, without consulting the Management Committee, at once impose a countervailing charge equivalent to the difference between the reference price for the particular product and the import price. Due consideration is given to the quality of the imported product and the charge appropriately adjusted by means of *coéfficients d'adaptation* to the nearest equivalent quality of the product for which a reference price has been fixed. This closes

---

[1] See R. Vandervaeren, *op cit*, and C. Bonato *et al, Proiezioni della domanda e dell' offerta al 1970 e 1975 dei principali prodotti ortofrutticoli nei paesi della CEE e dell'area Mediterranea*, extract from proceedings of the National Horticultural Conference, Milan, March 1968.
[2] For a list of the duties applicable to the main crops see M. Butterwick and E. Neville-Rolfe, *op cit, Market*, Appendix K.
[3] In respect of at least 30 per cent of total imports offered on the Community's 14 representative markets.

a loophole which until 1969 enabled exporters to dodge countervailing duties on the grounds that their products were not of exactly equivalent quality to those to which official reference prices had been allocated. It should be noted that import prices are not actually established at the frontier itself, but are calculated on the basis of wholesale prices paid by importers at internal markets with due allowance made for transport costs from the frontier and for all Customs duties currently applicable. Consultation of the Management Committee, although no longer required for the application of countervailing duties, so as to ensure that they are applied with the least possible delay, is laid down for the fixing of coefficients, and for the establishment of criteria for altering rates of duty.[1]

Quality control, based on standards (Class I and Class II) established by Regulations 23/62 and 158/66 and mostly identical with those laid down in the Geneva Protocol,[2] is also applied inland, either at wholesale or retail level, and not at the common frontier. Regulation 158/66 (as amended by Regulation 2516/69) also permits these standards to be adjusted downwards or upwards in the event of a serious internal shortage or glut by the introduction or suppression of an additional Class III (*catégorie de qualité supplémentaire*). Formerly at the discretion of individual member countries, such a step may now be taken only for the Community as a whole by Management Committee decision. Class III goods may at all times be freely supplied internally by producers to consumers 'for their personal needs' and to the processing industry.

Member countries may, in the event of a threat of 'serious disruption to the market', request the imposition of quantitative restrictions on imports from third countries during certain periods of the year of lettuces, endives, haricot beans, melons, table grapes, tomatoes, artichokes and apricots. The Commission is bound to act on such a request within twenty-four hours, without consultation of the Management Committee. Any other member country objecting to the Commission's action has the right of appeal to the Council of Ministers, which must meet without delay. These arrangements (prolonged from 1969 under Regulation 2513/69) are due for review by the Council not later than January, 1973.[3] Regulation 2514/69 lays down more detailed criteria than had been established by Regulation 159/66 for identifying a situation under which the above safeguard measures may be taken in conformity with Article 19

---

[1] Countervailing charges have been applied on about ten occasions since 1962, for between one and two weeks at a time, and generally on imports of tomatoes and table grapes from Eastern Europe.

[2] Drawn up by the United Nations Economic Commission for Europe's Working Party on the standardisation of perishable foodstuffs.

[3] They apply to, amongst others, the 'Perpignan' products, so-called from the Spanish earlies competing with growers in that district, to South African grapes competing with Belgian, and to certain fruit entering Germany from Poland. None are likely to be renewed. Imports from Spain will become subject to arrangements (possibly minimum export prices) to be negotiated as part of the proposed Association Treaty between Spain and the EEC.

of the GATT.[1] Account must be taken of the following: the volume of imports (or exports) both current and foreseeable; availability of supplies on the internal market; actual or foreseeable prices for Community produce on that market and whether the trend is sharply upwards or downwards relative to the basic price (or for products with no basic price-to-price levels during recent years); market prices of imports from third countries; and quantities of internal produce likely to be subject to buying-in operations. Safeguard measures, which may be confined to products of particular sources, destination, quality or size, may be imposed only 'to an extent and for a period that are strictly necessary'.

Remedial action on Community markets for fruit and vegetables takes place in two distinct stages.[2] In the first instance growers' organisations may themselves at any time or in any locality withdraw produce from the market. Member governments are obliged to pay them full compensation (reimbursable out of FEOGA) for such withdrawals[3] provided that the withdrawal price (*prix de retrait*) does not exceed the purchase—or intervention—price (*prix d'achat*) plus 10 per cent of the basic price (*prix de base*) of the product in question. Amounts realised by growers'

---

[1] It should be noted that provision is made in both Regulations 2513/69 and 2514/69 for restriction of exports (or imposition of an export tax), should this be necessary to safeguard internal supplies to consumers, as well as of imports.

[2] The intervention system laid down by Regulation 159/66 was altered in a number of important respects by Regulation 2515/69. The system applicable from June 1st 1970, is here described. The alterations were based on recommendations made by a committee set up by the Commission in 1968 to enquire into a number of serious shortcomings in the 1966 Regulation revealed during 1967/68, its first season of operation. This happened to coincide with a massive apple crop, especially in Germany, where the predominantly old orchards gave unusually heavy yields, as well as in Switzerland and Austria. The consequent destruction, in accordance with the Regulation, of large quantities of surplus apples in other parts of the Community received a great deal of press and TV publicity. Apart from this result of exceptional circumstances, there were also a number of basic defects in the EEC system which it did not need emotive criticism to bring to light. Three waiting days of low prices had to pass before a state of 'crisis' could be declared and intervention take place. Producer organisations, which were required to finance 10 per cent of intervention costs, ran out of funds. The fixing of buying-in prices for Class II produce, on the low side in order to avoid excessive intervention costs, made it more advantageous for growers to turn in their first-quality produce for destruction, thus bringing relief to the market and pushing prices for second-quality produce above buying-in level. Finally, the system was not mandatory on member governments (Germany and Luxemburg opted out altogether) and the degree of intervention and the level of intervention prices was permitted to vary from country to country, as will be apparent from Appendix B. It should be stressed that intervention buying was not originally intended to form part of the system at all. It was introduced largely on the insistence of Italy as a *quid pro quo* for the disadvantages which the high level of Community cereal prices brought to Italian livestock producers. The original Regulation 23/62 envisaged Customs duties and application of quality standards to imports as the main methods of protecting the EEC grower. Since 1963 considerable progress has been made in imposing standards on all Community markets, but neither achievements nor shortcomings in this field have made the headlines in the same way as the intervention measures.

[3] On cauliflowers, tomatoes, table grapes, apples, pears, peaches, and citrus only.

organisations from the resale of produce withdrawn from the market (see below) are, of course, deducted from the compensation payable. The three types of prices are fixed by the Commission with monthly variations, before the beginning of each year in consultation with the Management Committee. The basic price, of which withdrawal price and intervention price are a function, is calculated for a number of pilot products on the basis of average market quotations on designated markets in areas of surplus production representing between 20 and 30 per cent of total Community production over the previous three years, exceptionally high or low quotations being left out of account. Basic prices for secondary pilot products or non-pilot products or varieties are derived by means of fixed coefficients. Withdrawal prices payable out of Community funds are those appropriate to Class II and Class III produce only.[1] No higher price may be paid for any Class I produce withdrawn. Growers' organisations are of course at liberty to finance withdrawal at a higher level out of their own funds.

The second type of remedial action may occur if prices for a given product (or derived product) on any one representative market remain for three days below the purchase price fixed for that product. A state of 'serious crisis' may then be declared by the Commission on demand of a member country. The purchase, or intervention, price is in each case 90 per cent of the basic price. Again only prices for Class II and Class III produce are payable. The two principal differences between the intervention and withdrawal procedures are first that the former is carried out by (or at any rate on behalf of) the official intervention agency of the country in question, and second that intervention is optional. Germany and Luxemburg have already let it be understood that they do not intend to operate it, and the other governments, except the Italian, are believed to be reluctant to do so.

Under either procedure disposal of stocks, whether in fresh or processed form, may be free to charitable institutions, or by resale by open tender for animal feed or other non-human utilisation, including, in the case of apples and pears, distillation into alcohol of not less than 80 per cent proof. Alternatively, a proportion may be retained, with compensation paid, by growers for consumption on their own holdings. No reimbursement from FEOGA is now available for produce deliberately destroyed. In exceptional cases the Management Committee may authorise sales to the food-processing industry where no distortion of Community trade is thereby involved.

Finally, Regulation 2515/66 amends earlier arrangements for export restitutions. Restitutions for any product are identical throughout the Community, but may vary according to the destination of the produce being exported. They are fixed from time to time (after consultation with Management Committee) having due regard to the most favourable

---

[1] There is a view that this is still too generous and that aid should be available only for a strictly limited number of approved varieties of each product.

export price currently obtainable, to quotations on third country markets, to the most favourable current price for imports in third countries, to producer prices in exporting third countries, and to current c.i.f. prices at the common frontier. So far restitutions have been granted on exports of citrus from Italy, of dried fruit from France, and of some apples to specific destinations (Eastern Europe, Northern and black Africa).

The CAP for fruit also involves certain so-called structural measures. Regulation 2511/69 makes special provision for citrus.[1] Regulation 2517/69 lays down conditions for Community grants for grubbing apple, pear and peach orchards to replace those hitherto made by national governments in Belgium, the Netherlands and Germany, which were no longer permissible after May 1st 1970. Applications for the grant must be submitted not later than March 1st 1971 accompanied by a written undertaking by the applicant to complete grubbing of the trees by March 1st 1973 and not to undertake any new planting on his holding of the fruit in question for a period of five years from the date of grubbing. Originally a grant of UA 500 per hectare, of which half may be recovered by member governments from FEOGA, was to be payable in two equal instalments, the first on effective completion of grubbing and the second three years later on the evidence that no new plantings have taken place in the meantime. In view of the rather poor response, involving 4,500 ha for the entire Community, the grant has been stepped up to UA 800, payable in a single lump sum.[2] Growers who fail to meet the undertaking not to replant within five years will be obliged to repay the grant in full. It is hoped that these arrangements will encourage the disappearance of old unproductive orchards.

Although the 1969 package of amendments to the basic regulations should bring about some improvement in the working of the CAP for fruit and vegetables, it seems doubtful whether a rational market structure for the sector will be achieved in the Community much before the end of the current decade. In any case, horticulture will always by its nature be more subject to disturbances due to marginal changes in supply, both between and within years, than other sectors. Technical progress seems unlikely ever to make more than a proportion of growers completely independent of weather conditions. The education of the urban consumer will continue to be assisted by more regular contact with better quality produce, but this will be achieved more through the spread of the retailing revolution than by the application of official quality standards, however useful these may be as an initial stimulus. Policing of these is in any case all

[1] Subsidies are to be granted to Italian producers towards improving the quality and market image of their oranges. In their present condition these meet a rather poor demand in the EEC outside Italy, despite the high level of protection against imports from third countries not enjoying preferential arrangements with the Community.

[2] About £132 an acre. In the UK the subsidy for grubbing which is available under the Agriculture and Horticulture Act 1964, involving payment of one-third of standard costs, currently amounts to between £35 and £45 an acre, depending on the quantity and girth of the trees to be removed.

the more difficult in countries such as Italy and France with a multiplicity of small rural markets and a much fragmented retail trade. An increase in the volume of demand for large, uniform and regular supplies will in itself improve the market effectiveness, still very feeble in large areas of the Community, of the producer organisations whose creation was, after the establishment of quality standards, the second major object of the CAP for fruit and vegetables. The policy's third main aspect, market intervention, was, significantly, the result of an afterthought. It has been much inspired by Dutch thinking and experience not always relevant to larger countries than the Netherlands or to the less immediately perishable forms of produce such as apples. Withdrawal from the market may only receive Community financial aid for a limited range of products. Though producer organisations will be free to finance such operations from their own funds (i.e. levies on their members) on any product, it seems unlikely that there will be any widespread adoption of *veiling*-type sales outside the Low Countries. During the coming decade producers will tend rather to use their (hopefully) newly acquired countervailing power in direct confrontation with wholesalers, and especially wholesaler/retailers. The *veiling*, even in the country of its birth, is beginning to seem out of touch with the future.[1] As far as the CAP is concerned the principle of officially financed withdrawal of produce from the market is to be confined to nine products of which only two, cauliflowers and tomatoes, could be said to involve surpluses that were due to purely seasonal and not partly to structural factors. And, to the extent that tomatoes are grown under glass, between-harvest or longer-term shifts out of their production are also subject to structural constraints.

As has already been noted, structural surpluses of apples, pears and peaches are likely to increase during the next few years. It does not seem, therefore, as if this aspect of Community policy will of itself bring about much long-term market stability. The decision to prohibit the destruction of surpluses, however attractive ethically, also lessens the effectiveness of buying-in in relieving the current market situation, since produce donated to charitable institutions or sold to distillers is still bound to be competing to some extent with that left on the open market. Nor, since Class II or Class III stuff will be given away, is it conducive to creating a desirable 'image' for the particular fruit or vegetable amongst its recipients.

THE MARKET STRUCTURE IN THE EEC

Belgium

Co-operative organisations operating clock auctions (*veilingen*) have provided the obvious mechanism for applying the EEC regulations in Belgium. Ninety-five per cent of Belgian fruit and vegetable production is sold on the domestic market. Apart from a few tomatoes and lettuces, the

[1] See p. 196.

main export crop is chicory (*witloof*). In 1968 and 1969 withdrawal from the market of cauliflowers became necessary, owing mainly to the effect of sudden changes in the weather, though relatively small amounts were destroyed. The warm autumn of 1969 added large numbers of outdoor lettuces to normal glasshouse supplies, necessitating the removal of 100,000 boxes from market. Otherwise consumption of vegetables is in general keeping pace with rising supply. About 10,000 tons of apples were taken off the market in 1969. Domestic supplies of fruit meet competition, especially from February onwards, from imports, mainly of apples, from third countries. The small size of Belgian orchards (80 per cent of fruit holdings are of 1 ha or less) makes for inefficient marketing and rather poor quality. Grubbing grants from the national budget had up to the end of 1969, when they were superseded by the new EEC regulation, resulted in the disappearance of some 9,000 holdings of about 1 ha each, accounting for perhaps 10 per cent of the country's apple production. Competition from imports, both EEC and third country, will give further impetus to this structural trend, and arable farmers too will give up their traditional plots of top-fruit. Producers of table grapes, a traditional Belgian product, are on the whole an ageing community. The probable disappearance of a third of the surviving 30,000 glasshouses, mostly located in the Brussels area, should still leave sufficient supplies for what is essentially a luxury market. With Cape grapes admitted in the country from 1 March, forced production for the April market is now seriously hit by imports.

Further streamlining of Belgium's rather antiquated retail system during the seventies will also influence the pattern of horticultural production and marketing. At present only some 30 per cent of supplies are subject to centralised purchasing by chains and supermarkets, a proportion expected to more than double by 1980. As a consequence nearly half of the country's 45,000 greengrocer shops and half of the 20,000 wholesalers dealing in fruit and vegetables will probably go out of business, although the short distances involved will continue to benefit the efficient small operator in Belgium for many years yet. The clock auction system, with each producer passing individually past the clock and often offering lots so small as to be of little interest to large buyers, is proving increasingly inadequate to cope with these changes in the demand pattern. Of the 21 auctions, mostly started during and after the last war (only one dates back to before World War I), 16 are run as co-operatives. The Boerenbond, to which these are affiliated, is faced with a considerable task in persuading its members to concentrate their supply into large lots of uniform quality. Even where some auctions have managed to organise a common brand name for their produce, they still have little discipline over the timing of their members' sales. Significantly it was the wish to extend their selling season to a maximum length as well as to reduce unit costs of production by introducing uniform packaging, palletisation, etc., which originally caused the members of the only successful co-operative independent group of any note to break away from the *veiling* system. Consisting of 10 large top-fruit producers, each with orchards of between 20 and 40 ha, in the Gorsen area, Hesbania has also broken with Belgian tradition by entering the export market for apples. Based on its central refrigerated storage with a capacity of 8,000 tons of apples and 2,000 tons of pears, it exports not only to the nearby German market but to a number of non-EEC countries with a demand for high-quality fruit.

The Netherlands

The even greater effects of the retailing revolution on clock auctions in the Netherlands, their fount and origin, have been noted by Ellis and Kirk.[1] Since the auctions there are geared primarily to export, the influence has come mainly from foreign buyers. UK and German chains and supermarkets have come to occupy a dominating position, with 80 per cent of trade with the UK by 1968 concentrated in the hands of five firms. Dutch growers are evidently better organised than are those in Belgium to present uniform lots of fruit and vegetables of a size acceptable to large buying organisations. It is ironical that this should be resulting in a loss of market transparency. As the structure of domestic demand also becomes more concentrated, the clock auction, whose benefits by the grower is already being questioned in the case of exports, may prove to have had its day. Indeed, as Ellis and Kirk point out, even in the present situation of fragmented retail demand, some loss of freshness and quality may result from retailers having to visit several different markets in the course of a day in order to obtain a full range of homegrown and imported produce. On the other hand the EEC regulations are tailor-made to the situation in the Netherlands. Ninety-five per cent of output is accounted for by recognised producer groups. Buying-in has presented no problems, and has been carried out entirely by producer organisations through the medium of their clock auctions.

Luxemburg

In Luxemburg two co-operatives, Centralfruit and Luxfruit, are the officially recognised producer groups. Horticultural production is relatively small. The Luxemburg Government does not intend to exercise its option under Regulation 2515/69 to intervene in the case of a state of 'grave crisis'.

Germany

Virtual absence of exports and the traditionally large import content in German consumption of fruit and vegetables has tended, as in the UK,

[1] P. G. Ellis and J. H. Kirk, *The selling of fruit and vegetables: a comparative study of commission trading*, Wye College Marketing Series No. 4, University of London, 1968, pp. 18–19.

to leave domestic growers poorly organised on the home market. The influence of German buyers in EEC markets, already noted in the Netherlands, also extends to Italy, and to some extent to France and Belgium as well. While supplies from other member countries have in recent years energetically adapted production, packaging, and marketing methods to the demand of their most important EEC customers, German growers have themselves been left far behind in grading, production under glass (the area of which has slightly fallen), and adaptation of supplies to modern techniques such as deep-freezing which are particularly suited to the rapidly expanding and highly income elastic demand of the West German economy. Whereas in Germany the output of the vegetable-preserving industry hardly expanded at all during the sixties, in France, where there was a 70 per cent increase between 1961 and 1967, production is now about double the German. Imports into Germany of preserved vegetables of all types in 1968/69 were 51 per cent higher than in 1967/68, the share of domestic produce in consumption falling from 64 per cent to 50 per cent.[1] With the home market largely by-passed or ignored by the supermarkets, associations of independent retailers and other centralised buyers, auctions (some 60 of which are organised by co-operatives for their members) are the main marketing channel for domestic growers, especially in the large consuming and market-gardening area of North Rhine-Westphalia. But commission selling is prevalent in certain urban centres, notably Munich.[2]

The unsatisfactory situation can to a great extent be attributed to the very fragmented nature of production, divided among tens of thousands of smallholdings, many of them run by industrial workers on a part-time basis. The climate has not been propitious to the development of effective cost-conscious co-operative production and marketing in Germany. Nor does the Bauernverband leadership appear to have greatly interested itself in pressing the claims of horticulture. As yet, only about 35 per cent of total output comes from recognised producer groups. A recent investigation[3] located only two second-tier co-operatives, both of them in the middle Rhine Valley and each comprising five co-operatives (out of a probable total for the whole country of over 200). Expenses of marketing, through central auctions, tend to be inflated by lavish staffing, as well as by the large number of consignors (one had 17,000, the other 13,000) whose produce has to be collected. Some start has been made in organising groups of producer groups to carry out subsidised market withdrawal under the EEC regulations. The first of these, comprising nine groups in the North Rhine area, Vereinigung der Rheinischer Erzeugerorganisationen für Obst und Gemüse, is also carrying out publicity, providing

[1] 'Ifo-Schnelldienst', Munich, 30 January 1970, p. 20.
[2] Ellis and Kirk, *op cit*, p. 17.
[3] J. H. Kirk and P. G. Ellis, *Horticultural marketing co-operatives: the scope for large-scale organisation*, Wye College Marketing Series No. 5, University of London, December 1969, p. 27.

technical advice, and setting up a market intelligence service in the manner encouraged by the Commission's policy.

Italy

Until recently, the growth of Italian export sales in the EEC could be largely attributed to private enterprise. Despite the importance of fruit and vegetable production in the agricultural economy, co-operative marketing has developed only slowly, and recognised producer groups still account for only 15 per cent of total output. This proportion is expected to double by 1972, but for some time to come it must be expected that only in a few areas will there be producer organisations capable of carrying out the Community buying-in policy, which has up to now been administered almost entirely by the official intervention agency, AIMA. This absence of producer participation, though partly attributable to the temperament of the Italian grower (more independent even than in most countries), is also due to a hitherto unresolved philosophical discussion between the Italian authorities and the Commission about the status of some 20-odd producer associations (*associazioni prodottori*), all but two of which have been formed since 1966. Between them they account for about 30,500 growers, cultivating 130,000 ha of orchards and market gardens. Since all except two of these associations comprise two or more, and in one case as many as 40, separate co-operatives, their status as first-stage co-operatives (*co-opératives de base*), which would alone make reimbursement from FEOGA of their buying-in costs possible, is in dispute. According to the Commission they are not *bona fide* producer organisations in the sense of Regulation 156/66. The main the inspiration behind their creation has indeed been avowedly political, four of them being under Communist sponsorship, one Democratic Socialist, and most of the rest organised either by the Christian Democratic co-operatives, or by the joint committee (*comitato d'intesa*) of the Federconsorzi and the two farmers' unions. Only one is sponsored by a regional development agency (*ente di sviluppo*) and therefore, in principle at least, apolitical. They are distributed throughout the main horticultural areas of the mainland and Sicily. It seems unlikely that some compromise will not eventually be reached enabling these associations to participate in applying the Community intervention measures.

Apart from the political implications, which lie outside the scope of this study, there may well be some organisational advantage in grouping co-operatives in this way in the interests of concentrating managerial and marketing talent, always scarce resources. There is certainly a risk of fragmentation. Producer co-operatives in Italy are divided into three main organisations, the Communist Lega Nazionale Co-operativa e Mutue with 6,000 constituent co-operatives, the Democratic Socialist Associazione Nazionale Cooperativa with 1,000 and the largest, with 11,000, the Confederazione Cooperativa Italiana. Of this last the Federazione

Nazionale Ortofrutticole forms one of the 10 constituent national federations. It comprises some 400 co-operatives specialising in fruit and vegetable production, about a third of them in pears and peaches, 60 or 70 in citrus (Sicily), and the remaining 30 or 40 in table grapes (Apulia and Abruzzi) and other fruit and vegetables (including artichokes in Sardinia). In size they vary between 30 members and 1,000, 100 being the median. Co-operative loyalty is strongest in the North. There are relatively few horticultural co-operatives in central Italy. Besides these three groups there are about 150 independent co-operatives of Liberal (Conservative) complexion, and perhaps 100 co-operatives organised by (in the Federazione's view imposed by) the regional development agencies which have not affiliated to any of the political groupings.

The Federazione Nazionale now claims that over a third of all Italian export sales, about half of them within the EEC, are made by its members. Sales promotion abroad will increasingly be taken over by the Istituto di Comercio Esterno (ICE). For export purposes co-operatives are grouped into about half a dozen, generally regional, consortia. At home contracts are made with both supermarkets and industrial processors, usually on a seasonal or annual basis. The Federation owns only one processing plant, at Piacenza. The canning industry is still very fragmented, the five largest firms, including Cirio, having less than 25 per cent of the market.

France

As with other products, fruit and vegetable marketing is becoming more extensively co-ordinated (*organisé*) in France than in any other member country except the Netherlands. Although only some 40 per cent of horticultural output is accounted for by officially recognised producer groups, the volume involved is nevertheless substantial. Almost 100 per cent of cauliflower and artichoke production, 50 to 60 per cent of apples, nearly half the output of peaches, 30 to 40 per cent of apricots and pears, and an appreciable proportion of the table-grape, artichoke, melon, canning pea and tomato crops is already marketed through groups. Growers of early crops, round Perpignan in the South-West, previously in a sufficiently sellers' market for them not to consider it necessary to organise themselves, are now being forced to do so in the face of free entry of imports from other member countries. In 1970 there were 265 groups marketing fruit and vegetables, and another 90 specialising in potatoes, of which 20 in earlies. Most groups deal in a single product only.

The groups tend to be of three types. There are co-operatives of very small growers who have found it increasingly difficult to sell their produce individually in local markets and afford to grade their output. However good technically (and even here they are of uneven quality) they are often not very effective commercially. In this category may be included a certain number of producers that joined or formed groups as a result of hasty concessions made immediately following the events of May 1968.

Many were keen to obtain the benefits of the withdrawal prices reimbursed out of FEOGA via FORMA, without bothering much about the corresponding obligations. They may represent as much as 15 to 20 per cent of groups in the case of products in which around 50 per cent is marketed through groups, but efforts are being made to bring their activities up to the appropriate standard.

The second category consists of growers operating middle-sized holdings of up to 20 ha, technically go-ahead in production and storage methods and often not bad at marketing. They are mainly located in the Garonne, Loire, and Gard Valleys and include many former Algerian settlers, who tend to be hardworking and clannish. Finally, there are the low-cost large-scale growers of efficiently graded produce, especially apples, pears, and peaches. Even they are finding profit margins squeezed by Italian competitors.

As far as qualifying for FEOGA finance is concerned, the legal status of the groups is immaterial. They may be co-operatives, SICAs, syndicates, or associations[1] (though not *groupements d'intérêt economique*). All are associated vertically with the economic committees for their particular product (through which they are free to market their produce or not as they wish) and generally with a co-ordinating committee at national level as well. Where there is more than one group in an area the regional committee will lay down which is to carry out withdrawal operations. The Association Française des Comités Economiques Agricoles des Fruits et Légumes in Paris co-ordinates market information for its members, but has no marketing role.

Growers' organisations receiving Community aid for withdrawing produce from the market are, surprisingly, not obliged to market their produce collectively, except for co-operatives, whose statutes anyway forbid members to sell their produce individually. Only in the case of cauliflowers and artichokes have producer groups, owing to the geographical concentration of production in Brittany, acquired such a preponderant place on the national market as to obtain an *extension des règles de discipline* over non-members as well. Although the right to individual sales is preserved (other than in the circumstances just mentioned) it is, in fact, rarely exercised since, after all, the main purpose for which groups are formed is to co-ordinate supply on the market. Nevertheless, very few groups as yet are in the habit, except in the case of year-to-year contracts with canneries by vegetable growers, of entering into contracts with purchasers. Perhaps 15 per cent of total output is subject to contract. The co-operative cannery (Conserve Gard) set up by producers of cling-stone peaches in the Nîmes area is one isolated example of an attempt at vertical integration. It has been experiencing difficulties in marketing, especially in establishing a brand image. This is partly due to the slow development until recently of any interest in fruit and vegetables by supermarkets and chains in France, and partly to the distance of many groups from the main

[1] For definition of all these see p. 236.

consumption centres. The canning industry operates on a correspondingly small scale. In 1967 only 21 canning and jamming firms had an annual output exceeding 2,500 tons. There are only three major French enterprises, including the co-operatively owned Compagnie Générale des Conserves. Quick-freezing of vegetables is highly concentrated, but in the hands of the usual international companies. Some of the smaller cannery firms established in the main production areas have acquired a certain expertise in taking advantage of temporary local gluts of all types of fruit and vegetables that are surplus to the demand of the fresh market. The larger enterprises, on the other hand, are of their nature obliged to rely on supplies of a limited range of products contracted with more important growers. In any case only the big firms have the resources for providing the necessary technical assistance and supervision.

SICAs and co-operatives are sometimes poorly served by their selling staffs, which are either inexperienced or a refuge for failed dealers. They tend not to assert their countervailing power against wholesalers, the main channel for disposal of produce, who are inclined to be more aggressive in their buying than in their selling. Owing to the great distances separating the main producing areas in Brittany and the Mediterranean region from the main consumption area round Paris, growers, whether grouped or individual, have little choice but to sell firm, rather than on commission, at local markets, leaving the wholesaler to carry the risk of transport to the terminal market, which may be anything up to 700 miles away. By the time the produce reaches Paris (Rungis) the wholesaler himself tends inevitably to be more of a price-taker than a price-maker. In these circumstances the little influence of producers over, or knowledge of, prices in the terminal market has been a big spur to official encouragement to co-operation among growers in France in order to co-ordinate their supplies on the primary market in large uniform lots. The construction since the war in production areas of some 20 so-called *marchés d'intérêt national* (markets of national importance), with rail and telex communications with the capital, to receive these supplies is another aspect of the same policy. It has come in for much criticism, partly because of the palatial nature of many of the buildings, but also because of an already perceptible, if not yet widespread, tendency to sell by telephone on description and so by-pass physical markets altogether. The imposition of quality standards and the encouragement of producer groups by EEC regulations since 1962 have both given considerable impulse to all these developments.[1]

No description of vegetable marketing in France is complete without a reference to the SICA of St Pol de Léon in the department of Nord-Finistère founded in 1962, which operates some nine auction markets for virtually the entire supply of cauliflowers in Brittany. The SICA, consisting originally of 4,000 producers and 65 merchants who controlled

---

[1] For further description of French marketing methods see Ellis and Kirk, *op cit*, pp. 14–16 and 37–43, R. C. Rickard, *Regional Planning and Horticulture in France*, London, PEP, 1968, *passim*, and Kirk and Ellis, *op cit*, pp. 23–6.

60 to 65 per cent of production, is linked through a *comité économique* with a union of co-operatives which accounts for a further 20 per cent. The remaining opters-out have recently been incorporated compulsorily into the scheme by means of a poll of all producers. The auctions enable produce to be withdrawn, Dutch fashion, if prices fail to reach a fixed level, and up to the withdrawal price fixed by the Commission the SICA is reimbursed from FEOGA, via FORMA, for its outlay. As in the Netherlands, however, the auction system does lead to delay in the despatch of produce to its final destination, all the more so in France given the remoteness of the production area from Paris, and to a consequent loss of freshness and lowering of the price received by growers. In the long run, the St Pol de Léon growers may also find it more profitable to use their substantial countervailing power to sell on description to wholesalers at Rungis rather than to local wholesalers obliged when bidding at auction to discount the substantial risks of price fluctuations on the terminal market.[1]

Some of the small local co-operatives have indeed already formed a union specially for the purpose of marketing that 20 per cent or so of their output of cauliflowers which is purchased direct on description by multiples, supermarkets, and the Comptoir Agricole Français (the 'MacMahon' co-operatives' central marketing agency), which opened a large depot at Rungis in 1969. CAF itself sells almost entirely to central buying organisations of various kinds, not all of them in France, and to a few distributing wholesalers. The 'Lafayette' Group also has depot facilities at Rungis, organised through SICA Entrepôts Rungis (SICAER) formed in 1970. The move of the Paris market to Rungis (just off the Autoroute du Sud near Orly airport) from the traditional Les Halles in the centre of the city may slow down, but is unlikely to reverse, the tendency observed during the market's last five years on its old site, for a growing proportion of the capital's fruit and vegetable supplies to by-pass the central market altogether. By 1967 about 30 per cent of these (23 per cent of vegetables and 39 per cent of fruit) were being delivered direct to retail, including 11 per cent to multiples and consumer co-operatives (a proportion which has certainly increased during the past three years).[2]

IMPLICATIONS FOR THE BRITISH MARKET

Though entry into the EEC will face British growers with serious problems of readjustment to the free entry of produce from other member countries,[3] adoption of the regulations for fruit and vegetables on the whole presents fewer difficulties of adaptation than is the case for other products. In the matter of grading standards, for instance, although the British Government

---

[1] See Ellis and Kirk, *op cit*, p. 42.

[2] *L'assortiment complet des fruits et légumes aux Halles Centrales de Paris*, Paris, Centre technique interprofessionel des fruits et légumes (CTIFL), 1970.

[3] See Butterwick and Neville-Rolfe, *op cit*, pp. 202–6.

has never formally signed the Geneva Protocol, standards already fixed for produce in the UK are broadly in line with it, the main difference being that whereas British standards are applicable at wholesale stage those laid down in the Protocol refer to point of despatch. In the Community, whose standards are those of the Protocol, control is, of course, also imposed at the wholesale stage, but is supposed to take into account the 'nature of the journey' from the point of despatch. Changes of administrative procedure involved in both acceptance and policing of EEC grades should therefore prove minimal. Nor would selection of 'representative markets' in connection with the fixing of reference prices from which to calculate countervailing charges present any problem. London would clearly be one of them, and Liverpool, as a main fruit-importing centre, another. These alone should ensure that any price quotation for imports would relate to at least 30 per cent of total imports.

The main issue over adopting the EEC system is linked to growers' own organisation of their marketing, which will in any case have to be intensified in the face of the challenge of freer imports. This is likely to be necessary for all major products, whether by means of specialist or multi-product co-operatives or groups. But in the case of apples, pears, tomatoes and cauliflowers organised marketing would become obligatory for producers wishing to take advantage of financial assistance from FEOGA, whether in the form of starting-up subsidies or reimbursement of the cost of buying-in operations. This could prove an important incentive to those not already organised in any kind of marketing group to form new groups, or at any rate join existing ones. A recent estimate[1] suggests that there are at present some 130 co-operatives and producer groups of various kinds in England[2] engaged in fruit and vegetable production and marketing, accounting for perhaps 13 per cent of total national sales. In the case of apples and pears two organisations accounting for over half of co-operative sales, Home Grown Fruits and East Kent Packers, would be quite capable of undertaking buying-in, as would some smaller ones like Waveney Growers. They already possess the necessary administrative set-up and are reasonably well concentrated geographically, mainly in Kent and East Anglia. Though some of HGF's constituent co-operatives and growers are located in Somerset and the West Midlands (accounting for about 10 per cent of the group's throughput) their packhouses are in daily communication with headquarters, which markets all members' output centrally. It seems probable that independent growers in East Anglia or the West Midlands would prefer to join HGF, or one of the other existing viable groups, than set up new separate organisations answering to the criteria

[1] Kirk and Ellis, *op cit*, p. 5.
[2] The numbers in the other countries of the UK are fewer relative to their agricultural area, but considerations affecting the situation in England apply *pari passu* to Scotland, Wales and Northern Ireland. In the case of Northern Ireland competition from across the border would, on present showing at least, be weak compared with that to be expected for livestock products.

laid down in Regulation 159/1966. One of the disincentives to establishing market withdrawal schemes is the relatively high cost of maintaining the administrative superstructure required to carry out an operation that may only become necessary at infrequent intervals. The fact that the net cost of the actual buying-in and disposal would be reimbursed from FEOGA does not in itself make it worthwhile for a small group to carry the year-to-year overheads involved.

The same considerations apply in the case of cauliflowers, where the three organisations controlling about half of co-operative throughput would be likely to act as a catalyst to growers who do not at present belong to them, at least where the geographical situation allowed. The three, East Lincs Growers, Western Growers in Cornwall, and Vegetable Growers in Kent, are in fact all geographically concentrated. For tomatoes there is no co-ordinated selling of the 60 per cent of total co-operative output attributable to the Land Settlement Association. The Association's smallholdings, originally allotted to former coalminers and industrial workers between the two world wars, and more recently to ex-farmworkers, are widely scattered geographically. It may therefore prove more practical for the LSA, which has acquired considerable knowhow in uniform packaging, provision of market information, etc., to encourage its constituent estates of smallholdings to act as nuclei for local groups of tomato producers formed *ad hoc* for the purposes of the EEC regulations, while itself continuing to play its present, non-selling role. No other specialist tomato-growing organisation (other than the Guernsey Tomato Marketing Board, which lies outside our terms of reference) seems at present in a position to operate buying-in. The above list leaves out of account a number of flourishing multi-product co-operatives, in the West Midlands for instance, or Humber Growers, or Nursery Traders (Lea Valley), which would clearly have the necessary organisation to conduct subsidised buying-in on behalf of members producing the relevant products. The same applies, of course, to the larger regional general-purpose co-operatives, like East Anglian Farmers or Southern Counties (SCATS).

Government assistance in the form of grants towards capital investment in buildings and plant under the 1960 Horticulture Act was extended by the 1964 Agriculture and Horticulture Act (later amended by the 1967 Act) to cover, amongst other aspects of marketing, the improvement or initial operation of co-operative marketing businesses. The terms on which grants are available for the latter could without difficulty be adapted to conform with those laid down for fruit and vegetable producer groups in Regulation 159/1966, i.e. a sum not exceeding 3 per cent, 2 per cent and 1 per cent respectively of average turnover[1] for the first three years of operation. Under the EEC system, however, outright capital grants are inadmissible. It therefore seems likely that these would have to be phased out during the transition period for British entry, and growers will be well advised to make

[1] Calculated on the basis of members' aggregate turnover during the three calendar years preceding the formation of the group.

all possible use of them—regardless of whether their group is eventually to be engaged in buying-in operations or not—in order to equip themselves for the moment when Britain becomes a full member of the Community. If the Commission's present proposals on producer groups[1] are accepted by the Council, assistance other than that for starting off would be exclusively in the form of low-interest loans.

It may fairly be concluded, therefore, that competition from abroad and the continuing concentration of demand at wholesale level (which will, of course, happen whether or not Britain joins the EEC) will constitute more pressing motives for producers to organise themselves collectively than will of itself the possibility of operating subsidised market intervention, which is in any case likely to occur only sporadically. Disposal of any bought-in surpluses might also, incidentally, prove a problem in Britain if quantities were so large, localised and perishable as to exhaust rapidly the possibility of donating them to charitable institutions. The rule which now forbids the destruction of surpluses that are withdrawn from the market—or, rather, disallows grants from FEOGA in respect of surpluses destroyed—might prove somewhat anomalous. It seems doubtful whether an industry so concentrated and sophisticated as is that for animal feed in Britain would have any use at all for random lots of fruit or vegetables for processing. Nor are there any facilities for the distillation of surpluses into industrial alcohol such as exist on the Continent, where agricultural produce still competes (usually with the help of subsidies) with synthetics as a major source of alcohol. Apart from some imported molasses the British industry is geared entirely to the use of synthetics. Whilst cider makers might be persuaded to undertake the initial fermenting process of surplus apples, for instance, distillation of apple wash would, though technically feasible, present a wholly uneconomic prospect to distillers. The cost of disposing of the effluent alone would be prohibitive.

2. NON-EDIBLE PRODUCTS

Bulbs and flowers for cutting are grown commercially in all EEC member countries, the Netherlands being the largest producer, with about 40 per cent of total area, including over 1,500 ha under glass in 1969. Italy, with nearly 1,700 ha of glass in 1968, and France account for another 20 per cent each. The total area under glass in the Community, which rose by 150 per cent between 1960 and 1966, has gone up again substantially during the past five years, by a further 50 per cent in the Netherlands and by over 40 per cent in Italy. In addition there are some 45,000 ha of plant nurseries in the EEC. About 35 per cent of this area is in France, 30 per cent in Germany and 25 per cent in Italy.[2]

[1] See p. 238 et seq.
[2] The most recent figures are given in EEC Agricultural Statistics No. 9, 1969. National statistics are not, however, always comparable in detail and in some cases are far from complete.

The market organisation for non-edible horticultural products, introduced in 1968 (Regulation 234/68), differs from that for other products covered by the CAP in that it is exempt from pursuing two of the objectives enshrined in Article 39 of the Rome Treaty, to which the basic regulations for edible products are said to be dedicated, i.e. assurance of regular supplies and reasonable prices [sic] to consumers.[1] The system consists basically of a series of minimum quality standards to be observed for bulbs, cut flowers, fresh ornamental foliage, and live plants.

Since it is normal for commercial growers to purchase from other growers for purposes of multiplication bulbs that are below the standards laid down in the Regulation on bulbs (315/68), control of bulbs is to be established at retail level. Exports of sub-standard bulbs from Belgium and from the Netherlands (which account for 95 per cent of EEC bulb production) were formerly forbidden. They may now circulate freely at wholesale level within the Community, to the benefit of commercial growers in the other member countries, but the former Dutch size standards are still applied to all exports beyond the common frontier.

Uniform minimum export prices are also applied to prevent cutthroat competition and protect customers in third countries from loss of quality which this might involve, though it might have been expected that quality control of exports would of itself have been sufficient to achieve this. Minimum export prices are fixed in consultation with the Management Committee for inedible horticultural products.

Fresh cut flowers and fresh foliage are subject to control at wholesale level (Regulation 316/68). No agreement has yet been reached on standards for pot and other plants.

Only in the Netherlands is control really effective at present, thanks largely to the predominant clock auction system. Commission trading is the normal method of marketing in other member countries. In France a training scheme for inspectors has been operating for nearly two years, but in Italy arrangements for control are still very sketchy. Whilst the main object of the bulb regulation is to protect the consumer, that for cut flowers is of more direct value to the trade. The common standards help to promote sale by description, particularly in intra-Community trade, facilitate the exchange of market information by teleprinter, and generally contribute to market transparency.

The common external tariff (CET) applies to all imports from third countries, and some quotas have been maintained, temporarily at least. Despite pressure from the French Government for minimum import prices on roses and carnations, mainly as a protection against non-EEC Mediterranean producers, the Commission has taken the view that the emergency measures against low-priced imports allowed by the safeguard clause of Regulation 234/68 are adequate.

---

[1] 'Newsletter on the Common Agricultural Policy', No. 6, Brussels, April 1968, p. 2.

IMPLICATIONS FOR THE BRITISH MARKET

As in other branches of horticulture entry into the Common Market will expose British growers to fierce competition from imports. As far as the actual regulations are concerned, bulb grades are in line with the voluntary BIS standards already adopted by most growers. It will be a source of satisfaction to the daffodil section of the trade in Britain, probably now more important even than that of the Netherlands, that Dutch views on bulb standards have not prevailed in intra-Community trade. Standards for daffodil bulbs are based on traditional description ('double-nose', etc., implying a minimum size of bulb which will throw a flower; and a maximum number of bulbs in a basket of given capacity) and not, as in the original draft regulation, on the actual measurement of each bulb. This is important to English growers, especially those in the South-West, where climatic and soil conditions enable a smaller bulb to throw a satisfactory flower than would normally be the case in the Netherlands. This could sometimes involve 15 per cent more blooms per ton of bulbs. Standards adopted for tulips appear to present no problems, though this sector will be in a much less strong competitive position than will daffodil growers. Production of hyacinth bulbs in Britain is unimportant.

To some British observers the flower grades seem unnecessarily complicated. On the one hand assessment of visual characteristics is bound to involve an element of subjective judgement. Coding by stem length, on the other hand, appears to be unduly arbitrary, not to say irrelevant.

Dutch growers would probably hope to obtain British support for the principle of a Community fund, financed by a levy on growers and the trade, which would take surplus bulbs off the market in a season of glut and destroy them. German growers, who are not numerous, have objected to the existence of such a fund in the Netherlands, which has been in operation for some years, on grounds of distortion of competition. In addition the Dutch have proposed a central fund for publicity, on the lines of that already operated by the *Produktschap* for ornamental plants, that would also be financed by means of a levy. One per mil of turnover of growers, wholesalers and retailers has been suggested. The publicity would be neutral as to firms, but would promote member countries' particular specialities.

CHAPTER 10

Vegetable Oils and Oilseeds

The EEC is far from being self-sufficient in vegetable oils, though a distinction should be made between olive oil whose commercial production, confined virtually to Italy, covers between 70 and 80 per cent of demand, and other oils, of which Community production covers only about 10 per cent of demand. Olive oil, accounting for 20 per cent of total consumption of vegetable oils in the EEC, is subject to a common Regulation, No. 136 of 1966. Of other sources of oil in the Community only rapeseed and colza (the two are vitually indistinguishable), sunflower seed, and raisin seed are at present regulated, also by Regulation 136/66. Linseed, for whose production national subsidies are still permitted, may eventually be added to the list.

Olives, the oil from which is a relatively unimportant product of French Mediterranean agriculture, remain, despite increasing harvesting difficulties of what is essentially a labour-intensive crop, of major economic and social importance to Italy's agriculture. The main relevance of olive oil to the present study is the deficiency payment type of price support which constitutes one element of the EEC market regulation. This is discussed below. Until the common market came into force in November 1966, Italian producers of olive oil had been protected by a duty on imported olive oil and by a tax on margarine and on substitutable vegetable oils which raised the retail price of these to a level comparable with that of olive oil.

One or more of the four types of oilseed covered by Regulation 136/66 are produced in each of the member countries. Sunflower seed and raisin seeds, a by-product of wine-making, are crushed commercially only in Italy and France (a negligible quantity in Italy in 1969, where output has been steadily declining, but still 30,000 tons in France). Of the 643,000 tons of colza and rapeseed produced in the Community in 1968/69 just over two-thirds was grown in France, just over a quarter in Germany (mainly in Schleswig-Holstein and Bavaria), and the balance in the Netherlands, Italy and Belgium. Guaranteed prices operated for a number of years prior to 1966 in France and Germany, where production received a boost at the time of the Korean War whose impetus was never lost. In the Low Countries, where no subsidy previously existed, the common market regulation has stimulated production. The Belgian acreage increased from 43 ha in 1966 to 646 ha in 1968, that of the Netherlands from 5,000 ha to 6,700 ha. The stimulus to production has been equally great in France, where the acreage rose from 179,000 ha to 248,000 ha over the same three years, and in Germany where the acreage increased by two-thirds and yields by a third. Only in Italy has production continued to decline.[1] The 1969/70 harvest in the Community is expected to reach 750,000 tons, compared with 439,000 tons in 1966, the last harvest before the common regulation came into force. Whereas a case for support for production of oilseeds, often on smaller holdings, is argued mainly on farm-income grounds, rapeseed and sunflower seed also provides cereal farmers, large and small, with a useful break-crop in their rotation. Since so little of the EEC's requirements of vegetable oils can be produced from its own resources the common regulation has been framed with more regard to the interests of consumers within the Community and of exporting producers in third countries (mainly developing countries with associated status) than is the case with other temperate products. Oilseeds may be imported duty-free and their products at a low or nil tariff.[2] Internal market price levels have not been jacked up above those of substitutable products on the world market by means of import levies. A deficiency payment type of support (*aide directe au producteur*), whose working is described below, backed by a minimum intervention price has been adopted for the protection of Community producers and processors.

The oilseed crushing industry, including that part of it processing seed produced in the Community, is becoming increasingly concentrated in all member countries. In Belgium there are only two crushing plants. No oilseeds are grown in Luxemburg. In the Netherlands of 15 crushing plants only three use rapeseed, including Unilever, the national leader, whose activities are integrated with refining and margarine manufacture, and Duyvis. In Germany seven out of 18 crushers purchase rapeseed. In Italy there are a large number of small plants, but the two largest, at Genoa and Ravenna, purchase over 50 per cent of the domestic crop. France has the largest number of crushing plants using rapeseed and sunflower seed, but of the 62 still operating only 15 do so on an industrial scale, with Lesieur as the outstanding leader.

Imports of oilseeds and other raw materials for crushing as well as of oilcakes and meals, including soya, enter the Community duty-free. But vegetable and fish oils bear duty under the CET: those for technical and industrial use of between 3 and 8 per cent *ad valorem* and those for

[1] Commission of the European Communities, *Rapport sur la situation de l'agriculture et des Marchés Agricoles présenté par la Commission au Conseil*, Brussels, June 11th 1969, p. 168.

[2] Provision is also made for the imposition of a countervailing charge (*montant compensatoire*) in the case of excessively low offers from third countries 'which threaten seriously to prejudice' producers' interests in the Community. This has so far been involved only in the case of certain imports of sunflower-seed oil from Eastern Europe and of castor oil from Brazil and the Chinese People's Republic.

human consumption of between 9 and 15 per cent. There is a 25 per cent duty on margarine. The possibility of extending and increasing these duties has been discussed recently as a means of raising the price of margarine in the Community and encouraging butter consumption. Alternatively a straight tax on vegetable oils whose yield would be used by FEOGA to subsidise the retail price of butter has been suggested. Ideas of this kind have been circulating mainly among dairy farmers' organisations. Among a number of subsidiary proposals in the package presented by the Commission in December 1968 (the Mansholt Plan), was one to apply taxes of between UA 20 and 60 per ton on a wide range of vegetable oil products.[1] It has not, however, so far been considered officially by the Council of Ministers. There might in any case be practical difficulties in the way of implementing any of these proposals since the duties are all bound in GATT and protective taxes might also prove contrary to that agreement.

THE EEC SYSTEM

Olive oil

The regulation for olive oil operates in a manner similar to that for cereals, with a system of target, intervention and threshold prices, seasonal increments, import levies and export restitutions. There is, however, one important difference in that there are two target prices, fixed annually not later than October 1st and effective from November: a producer target price (*prix indicatif producteur*), or norm price, fixed at a level 'fair to producers and with due regard to the need of maintaining the required volume of production' and a market target price (*prix indicatif du marché*) fixed at a level 'permitting a normal market flow of home production having regard to the prices of competing products'. An intervention price, with no regional variations, is designed to guarantee producers a price as close as possible to the producer target price, due account taken of transport costs to intervention centre. Intervention price and market target price are subject to ten equal monthly increments. Olive yields being by nature highly variable between one year and another,[2] provision is also made for the operation of an official buffer stock to help reduce excessive price fluctuations. If, despite this, the producer target price should have to be fixed (as it normally has to be at the beginning of a season of above-average yields) at a level above that of the market target price, a subsidy (*integrazione di prezzo*) equivalent to the difference between the two is payable to producers. This is, in effect, a deficiency payment. It is fixed in advance for the entire harvest year.

[1] Commission des Communautés Européennes, *Memorandum sur la reforme de l'Agriculture dans la CEE, Partie C IV, Mesures de mettre en oeuvre pour réaliser une meilleure stabilisation du marché des matières grasses*.

[2] This is reflected in annual levels of intervention purchases of oil in Italy: 1966/67 nil; 1967/68 13,000 tons; 1968/69 nil.

Import levies on olive oil are fixed weekly, or more frequently if necessary, the threshold price (also subject to ten equal monthly increments) being derived from the market target price, and the lowest c.i.f. price being established on the basis of reports received by the Commission from the main producing and importing countries. Criteria for fixing the levies are established in Management Committee, but the Commission is free to fix the levies themselves without the Committee's approval. Reduced or nil rates of levy may be granted on imports by fish and vegetable canneries. Levies on imports of refined products are made up of two elements: a variable one pro rata of the virgin oil employed, and a fixed one designed to protect Community refiners. Special provision is also made for levies on imports of fresh or preserved olives. Restitutions are not automatic and are granted only on exports, mainly bottled and not in bulk and amounting to some 18,000 tons a year, to traditional markets. Olive oil for re-export may either be imported free of levy, subject to deposit, or levy-paid, in which case a restitution may be claimed on the re-export. Since both levies and restitutions may be pre-fixed, the latter arrangement gives processors some opportunity for speculation. The quantities involved are not, however, large: of 24,000 tons imported into France in 1969, mainly from Spain and Tunisia, 2,000 tons were re-exported.

It is worth giving some account of the method adopted in Italy for administering deficiency payments, if only as an indication of the relative complexity, compared with the UK, of working a deficiency payment system in a country of numerous tiny smallholdings. For each of the first three olive harvests in which Regulation 136/66 was applied an average of 1·18 mn claims, each in respect of an average of just over a third of a ton of oil and of Lit. 75,000 (£50) was dealt with. Responsibility for vetting claims is delegated by AIMA, the intervention agency, to the provincial (roughly equivalent to county) offices of the Inspectorate of Food (Inspettorato Provinciale dell' Alimentazione), or in some provinces to local offices of the regional development agencies. Producers, singly or co-operatively, must submit three forms to their local inspectorate: first by April 15th of each year a declaration of the area of olives and number of olive trees on their holdings located in the province, and second, by May 15th, a declaration of olives harvested in the previous season and a claim for deficiency payment on oil extracted from them. A third form, claiming deficiency payment on oil extracted from the secondary pressing of the olive marc, must be submitted by August 31st. Each claim is checked against the previous year's corresponding declaration of olives under cultivation, against records submitted by each press to their local inspectorate of olives delivered and oil extracted, and against target yields of olives and oil established for the local area by the provincial commission (see below). All claims exceeding one ton of oil are checked *ipso facto*. Of smaller claims only those exceeding by more than 10 per cent the expected quantity, having regard to the local target yield, for the holding are subject to further scrutiny. The inspecting office may amend any claims whose falsity it deems to be due to genuine error, but claims suspected of being fraudulent must be passed to the local provincial commission. This consists of five officials, including a public accountant, and five representatives of producers, including the president of the local co-operative oil press, if any, under the chairmanship of the provincial inspector for agriculture. In a number of provinces where there is little olive production the inspector acts in place of a commission. The commissions are also required to exercise general supervision of the scheme, watch for abuses, and propose to AIMA measures to prevent their repetition. Claims are settled by the food inspectorates, which are empowered to make a payment on account of up to 70 per cent of the amount due. There have been widespread complaints of delay in payment. This is due in part at least to AIMA's difficulty in obtaining cash from the Treasury, but also to the relative inefficiency of the inspectorates, a relic of post-war food rationing whose activities over the previous decade had been almost entirely nominal. Deficiency payments are now normally settled in August (that is seven or eight months after harvest), allowing a month from May 15th for the commissions to establish the target yields and an average of two months for payment. Disputed claims obviously take longer. A few are even still outstanding from 1966/67. About 4·5 per cent, or 75,000, of claims for the 1967/68 season had not been settled by May 1969. The number of outright rejections seems to be small, about 0·5 per cent, and of prosecutions for fraud even fewer.

Oilseeds

As had already been made clear there are at present no levies or duties on imported oilseeds. Restitutions are, however, granted on certain traditional exports, such as those from the Netherlands to the UK and Denmark (3,000 to 4,000 tons a year) and from Germany to the UK, Ireland and Algeria (about 7,000 tons). Since the restitution is set somewhat lower than the subsidy, exports are discouraged and presumably continue only in cases where the actual price obtainable offsets this disadvantage. The level of restitution is also influenced by the expected state of supply on the internal market.

Prices for intervention buying, set a little below the target price, are derived for a number of centres from a basic price at Genoa, Italy being reckoned as the most deficitary zone. Intervention has, however, so far occurred rarely, and only twice in the case of sunflower seed. In the first case, on a parcel of 400 tons in 1968/69, tenders for purchase of the intervention stock proved below the floor price and were rejected by the Commission. A second tendering was therefore opened and the renewed offer had to be accepted by special regulation. In the second case (700 tons in 1969/70) a single tender was received, satisfactory only because of an accidental miscalculation by the crusher concerned of the effects of changes in French and German exchange-rate parities.

The deficiency payment type of subsidy payable on oilseeds consists in principle of the difference between a Community target price and the lowest offer c.i.f. EEC ports as determined weekly (or more frequently if there is much fluctuation on the world market) by the Commission. Regulation 136/66 lays down that target prices for Community-produced oilseeds should be fixed 'at a level fair to producers, having due regard to the need of maintaining the necessary volume of output in the Community'. Since there is no prospect of self-sufficiency the definition of 'necessary' would appear to be somewhat elastic, nor is any definition attempted in the preamble to Regulation 136/66. C.i.f. prices are determined by the Commission without reference to or need for confirmation by Management Committee, which, as in the case of olive oil, is only competent to discuss basic criteria for their determination. Price reports are received by the Commission from the relevant national intervention agencies (see below) and from other sources such as Comtel-Reuter. Prices of soya, being the main competing product, are also taken into account and their effect calculated by means of co-efficients laid down in the regulations. At times of the year when quotations on world markets for oilseeds are nil or unrepresentative a seed price is reconstituted, again according to fixed coefficients, on the basis of current offers of oil and oilcake. Deficiency payments due to them may alternatively be pre-fixed by applicants for a period of three months following the current month (the subsidy for any unexpired period of current month being the same as for the following week). The pre-fixed subsidy is calculated by simply adding to the current subsidy appropriate monthly increments. The pre-fixing takes no account, as it does in the cereals regulation, of indications of price changes on a futures market. The target prices are subject to identical monthly increments (*majorations mensuelles*), seven in the case of rapeseed, starting from September 1st, and five in the case of sunflower seed, starting from December 1st.

The subsidy or deficiency payment may be paid to the producer of the seed, to a wholesaler, or to a crusher. For reasons mentioned below the majority of applications are made by crushers and few if any by producers. Upon delivery of a parcel of seed at a crushing plant the local representative of the national intervention agency issues a certificate for the amount delivered. The subsidy is only payable in full on completion of crushing since it relates not only to the quality of the seed delivered (based on a standard—*qualité type*—of 10 per cent moisture content and other criteria) but also on that of the oil extracted (based on a standard of 2 per cent impurity). The preliminary analysis made at the moment at which the seed is delivered and comes under official scrutiny (*mise sous contrôle*) may occur as long as three weeks before crushing takes place. An advance payment may, however, be made on the basis of provisional quality in return for a deposited cheque or bank guarantee.

In view of the relatively complicated procedure involved in claiming the subsidy and of the inevitable delay in its payment, producers generally prefer to leave merchants or crushers to put in the claim. They may reasonably reckon that the price which they receive does include the amount of deficiency payment due to them, less some deduction by the purchaser for his trouble in claiming it and for the interest cost of awaiting official settlement of the claim. The trade is also in a better position than the individual producer to take any advantage there may be in pre-fixing the subsidy. How much the producer loses on balance from not claiming direct is difficult to calculate, but the advantage of prompt payment is evident. Ignoring monthly increments the basic Community target price is currently UA 202·50 per ton, giving a deficiency payment (at a world price of, say, UA 100·00) of UA 102·50. Producers are guaranteed a minimum return by means of a basic intervention price (at Genoa) of UA 196·50 per ton (with derived prices ranging down to UA 176·00). The purpose of the subsidy is to coax producer returns upwards from this basic minimum in the direction of the target price. Buying at something above intervention price the crusher (supposing he were to claim the subsidy and pass it on in full to the producer) would be getting his seeds at a net price below that ruling on the world market, say, UA 198·00 minus subsidy of UA 102·50 equals UA 95·50. In this example the crusher would be paying UA 100·00 on the world market. In setting a price with his crusher or merchant it must therefore be the producer's objective to obtain for himself as large a proportion as he can of the margin of UA 4·50, pushing the crusher's purchase price as far as possible towards the target price of UA 202·50, which is of course the crusher's break-even point, leaving aside transport costs, between home-grown and imported seeds.

As in the case of other products the mechanics of intervention vary somewhat from country to country. In Belgium it would be carried out by OBEA, which despite the substantial increase in national acreage, has so far not been required to intervene. Deficiency payments and restitutions are also dealt with by OBEA. In the Netherlands the *Produktschap* for margarine, fats and oils is responsible, on behalf of the Ministry of Agriculture, for making the deficiency payments. Since these are made in all cases to crushers, of whom there are only three in the country, their administration is no problem. The Board, on which there is no producer representative, consists of 26 representatives of crushers, refiners and the trade under a full-time chairman nominated by the government. It employs about 50 persons, but EEC work constitutes only a relatively small part of its activities and no new staff have been taken on as a result of the Community regulations. The *Produktschap* supervises the import and re-export of oils and acts as a channel with the Commission for applications for restitutions. The collection and administration of import duties is, however, in the hands of the Ministry of Finance.

In Germany intervention is carried out and deficiency payments administered by the Einführ- und Vorratsstelle for oils and fats. Few farmers make direct contracts with crushing mills so that as far as deficiency payments are concerned the EVSt is dealing either with producer co-operatives, which handle three-quarters of the crop, with the crushers themselves, or with one particular wholesaler, a leading international shipper, which purchases from both producers and co-operatives. The EVSt, besides administering deficiency payments, issues import licences for olive oil and acts as a channel for fixing of restitutions on oilseed exports. These are, however, paid by Hauptzollamt Jonas in Hamburg.

In Italy deficiency payments are dealt with by AIMA. There has been no intervention. There is a special financial arrangement whereby the French Government punctually pays to wholesalers in France deficiency payments due on some 140,000 tons of rapeseed exported annually to Italy for crushing there. Owing to the Italian system of public accounting it has often not been possible for disbursements to be made until the necessary funds have been received by the Treasury from FEOGA, sometimes involving the French trade in payment delays of up to eighteen months.

French arrangements are analagous to those for other products subject to EEC regulations. Of the 1,530 claims for deficiency payments on rapeseed dealt with by SIDO (Societé Interprofessionnelle des Oléagineux) for the 1968/69 harvest, nearly two-thirds were submitted by sixty crushers for a total of 176,000 tons. The remaining 550 claims totalling 21,000 tons came from ten merchants (including CNTA—see below). Each claim may relate to more than one parcel of seed placed under official scrutiny. There were no direct claims from producers, even from producer co-operatives, but the agricultural co-operatives are shareholders in the Comptoir National Technique Agricole (CNTA), a private merchanting organisation with a dominant position on the French market for oilseeds. This is responsible for the 50,000 to 60,000 tons of exports a year to Algeria and, together with two other major shippers, for the 140,000 tons exported to Italy. SIDO has not so far made any intervention purchases. There are no authorised stockists (*stockeurs agréés*) such as exist for cereals, and it might have difficulty in finding storage space for any large quantities of seeds. Unlike ONIC in the case of cereals SIDO becomes the legal owner of intervention stocks.

IMPLICATIONS FOR THE BRITISH MARKET

Oilseed rape has only been introduced on any appreciable scale into arable rotations as a break crop since the mid-sixties, mainly in southern parts of England where continuous barley growing had become fairly common, and where sugar beet and potatoes have not traditionally provided a profitable alternative to cereals. There is no government price support. At present yields (averaging between 15 and 20 cwt/acre—19 and 25 qls/ha—depending on whether it is spring or winter sown) and prices, based on those of competing imports, of about £40 a ton, rapeseed does not give a gross margin comparable to that obtainable from wheat or barley. On the other hand it provides a safe means of switching from barley to wheat by avoiding the virtually assured loss of wheat yield from disease entailed in growing it directly after several barley crops. Given current prices and yields of all three types of crop this rotation is reasonably sure of giving a higher gross margin over, say, four years than continuous barley growing. At EEC cereal and rapeseed prices the degree of certainty would be much greater. The present gross return per ton to EEC producers on a crop of rapeseed lies somewhere between a minimum intervention price of just over £73 and a target price of £84. There is a point in this price range at which yields of close on 20 cwt an acre, which are not uncommon for winter-sown crops, could make it at least as profitable to British producers as wheat or barley, even at their likely EEC price levels. Indeed, being fairly well adapted to less good soils and to a high rainfall, rapeseed could even in some areas prove, for farmers wanting to increase their arable acreage, a more profitable cash crop than cereals. British entry into the EEC might therefore have an explosive effect on the area sown to rapeseed, which is at present between 7,000 and 10,000 acres.

Of this acreage about 600 are in East Anglia and almost all the rest in Hampshire, Wiltshire and Berkshire. About three-quarters of the crop is at present marketed by a single consortium of producers in Wessex. The need for a joint marketing arrangement has arisen out of the absence of any forward demand for home-grown oilseeds on a domestic market which is wholly influenced by the price and volume of imported seeds of all kinds. Farmers individually are therefore at the time of sowing unable to obtain any firm quotation from British crushers for their seeds due to be harvested and offered on the market six months or so later. By maintaining a close relationship with a well-known firm of oilseed merchant-brokers Wessex Agricultural Producers Ltd are, however, able to secure a minimum forward price for their members. Once within the EEC, of course, the deficiency-payment system would protect producers from low market prices after harvest, and the intervention price provide them with an assured minimum return.

Most of the seed is at present purchased by British crushers, but occasional sales are made to the Continent if local crushing capacity happens to be fully booked with imported seeds. There are only three crushers purchasing rapeseed in Britain, at Glasgow, Liverpool and Hull. The first, geared mainly to soya beans, is too distant to be of interest to present domestic producers. The one at Hull has, thanks to the improved margins on crushing soya, recently come back into operation after having dismantled its plant. Oil from home-grown seed currently amounts to about 4,000 tons a year, which must be seen against a total national consumption of all vegetable oils of some three-quarters of a million tons. Even at the sort of increased level of output to be expected under EEC conditions domestic supplies will continue to be of little significance compared with imports both of rapeseed itself (mainly from Canada and Poland) and of other substitutable seeds.

Though the present reasons for group marketing might become less important as a result of joining the EEC, consortia like the Wessex one would be likely to continue and others become established in areas where rapeseed production is encouraged by the new price structure. Since, as has already been explained, there is some scope for speculation in the pre-fixing of the deficiency payment type of subsidy, a consortium with access to information about world markets may well prefer to apply for this direct, which it is entitled to do, rather than leave it to the crusher to take whatever advantage there may be to be gained from pre-fixing.

Administration of the deficiency payments would clearly present no problems in Britain. They would be handled by the Ministry of Agriculture in the way to which it has been accustomed in the case or cereals. There would be no need to set up a special intervention agency. In the fairly unlikely event of any seed being offered to intervention its purchase, storage and eventual resale could be carried out by the trade under the direction of the Ministry.

CHAPTER 11

Other Farm Products

The previous chapters in this Part have described the marketing problems of the seven principal groups of agricultural commodities. There are a number of other products which can be briefly noted. The list includes those which are produced in one or more of the existing member countries but not (or only to a negligible extent) in Britain, such as wine, tobacco and rice, those for which Community regulations have not as yet been made, such as peas, beans, hops and potatoes, and wool which is classified as an industrial product in the EEC and is therefore not included under the CAP. For the purposes of this study it seems appropriate to confine comment to the three products for which Marketing Boards exist in Britain, hops, potatoes and wool.

Hops

Germany is the main producer of hops in the Community, with about 80 per cent of total output. This is shared among 9,500 producers averaging 1·5 ha each. In France and Belgium 700 producers account in each country for about half of the remaining 20 per cent. Most of the Belgian output is marketed by two co-operatives. All imports from third countries are subject to the CET, and Belgium in addition imposes quota restrictions on non-Community imports.

A draft resolution was due to be considered by the Council of Ministers at the end of 1970. This has not been published up to the time of writing. It is not expected to involve either import levies or a system of intervention buying. Its main aim will be to establish quality standards and introduce compulsory certificates of origin for all hops, hop powders, and possibly hop extracts, produced in the Community. The same criteria would presumably be applied to imports as well. Second, the regulation will encourage the formation of producer groups, more, it seems, as a means of promoting quality and improved production techniques than of encouraging co-operative marketing. Third, some degree of income support on a flat rate per hectare may be proposed that would raise producers' returns up to the level of a rather low norm. However the criteria for this are arrived at, it would be in line with current thinking in the Commission to restrict grants of this kind to members of recognised producer groups. Finally, there seems likely to be some safeguard clause against abnormally low-priced imports. The reason for having a regulation for hops at all is not altogether clear, though considerations of political balance and national advantage can never be entirely excluded. It is known that there has been some French pressure, for instance, to establish a regulation for flax and linseed.[1] The hops regulation, on the other hand, is likely to be mainly of benefit to German growers, both in safeguarding their own quality standards from the risk of inferior imports by means of certificates of origin, and, through income support of a number of very small producers, providing aid from FEOGA that may be more socially than economically justified.

Since neither the details of the proposal, nor its likely fate at the hands of the Council, is known, the effect of an EEC regulation on Britiain's 530 hop growers is difficult to assess. It is in any case certain that imports from the other member countries of an enlarged Community would be free. In 1969/70 these amounted to some 46 per cent of total permitted imports. The volume of imports, just under 8 per cent of that of the domestic crop in 1969/70, is limited by agreement between the Brewers' Society and the Hops Marketing Board through the medium of the Permanent Joint Hops Committee. This consists of three independent ministerial appointees and equal representation of brewers and the Board. The Board generally accepts the brewers' view of what will be a tolerable level of imports during the coming year, taking account of domestic production forecasts, brewers' stocks, and the overriding need to maintain price stability in which both parties have a mutual interest. Individual production quotas, measured in centals of 100 lbs, are adjusted annually in the light of brewers' forecasts of their requirements, and the basic quota for England is revised every five years. Prices are fixed annually by a method which is broadly as follows. Variable and fixed costs per acre plus a 'reasonable' margin of profit are evaluated by the Board's economists, in conjunction with the Brewers' Society's resident auditor, in order to arrive at an estimate of the aggregate value of the crop, whose acreage is, of course, known. This aggregate divided by total consignments gives the average price per cental payable to the producer. Differential payments for quality are weighted according to the amounts of each quality forthcoming. The higher the anticipated brewers' demand (and hence the higher the level of the annual quota) the bigger the divisor, and the lower, paradoxically, the basic average price. But producers' gross returns are of course higher.

As far as hop-marketing arrangements in an EEC context are concerned, there is a likelihood of the present quota system being continued.

[1] This French proposal is believed to involve a system of acreage payments. A regulation of this kind would be of considerable interest in Northern Ireland, where the Agricultural Trust has been pioneering new techniques of growing and harvesting flax, with a view to its possible reintroduction as a subsidised crop in the province.

It would probably have to be shown to be no longer statutory, but rather a form of discipline imposed by a majority of producers through their own organisation. In any case it is unlikely that there would be many potential new entrants into hop-growing. Its current profitability, indicated by the rather high value attached to the quotas (which are transferable), would undoubtedly be less in the absence of the quota system. The capital cost of starting from scratch is extremely high. There are, moreover, constraints of soil and climate.[1] Nor, since they require two or three years to reach full bearing, are hops suitable as a catch-crop or break-crop. Inside the Community, hops may in any case seem a much less financially attractive alternative to those farmers now excluded by the system from growing them, in view of the much higher gross margins than at present that will be obtainable, at EEC price levels, for cereals and oilseed rape. If the number of would-be new entrants (or of present quota-holders wanting to increase their production) were relatively small, the present marketing system could probably be maintained without too much difficulty, the Board, *qua* producer organisation on the French model, remaining sole statutory purchaser of hops and operating a pool price. Its success would, however, depend a great deal on the willingness of the Brewers' Society to continue voluntarily to restrict imports (or at any rate on its ability to persuade its members to do so) from other parts of an enlarged EEC. What is known of the draft regulation does not suggest that its provisions will result to any great extent in a modification of the present cyclical trends in prices and production of hops on the Continent. The cycle is, broadly speaking, an eight-year one, with three years of buoyant prices and a five-year trough. Whether British brewers would be prepared to forgo the possible advantages of buying in the free market in favour of the more stable negotiated prices that might emerge from the present system as adapted to conform to EEC rules, is a matter for speculation.

Alternatively it might be possible for producers and brewers to set up a stabilisation fund on the lines of that operating in the Netherlands for broilers. An annual target price is agreed. The difference between this and the market price paid to producers is paid into the fund by buyers when the producer price is below the target price and by producers when it exceeds it.

Potatoes

In general, marketing arrangements for potatoes in Britain are similar to those in the EEC. In both the trade is divided between private merchants, often specialising in potatoes, and co-operative organisations; frontier controls are mostly used to protect producers of early varieties and an increasing quantity of potatoes is being marketed on contract by producers direct to processors for the manufacture of potato crisps, for canning, and

[1] Early frosts, for instance, are considered too great a risk to harvesting further north than 53°N.

for various types of instant foods. The major difference in the two markets consists in the quantities used for animal feed and industrial purposes. These uses are comparatively unimportant in Britain. Over two-thirds of the domestic crop is sold for human consumption, compared with only about one-third in the EEC.

The activities of the Potato Marketing Board have been described elsewhere.[1] In 1970 the Board submitted a new scheme designed to increase its future income while providing assurances that the increase would be limited to what was patently reasonable. The suggested formula provided for annual recalculation of the maximum rate of ordinary contribution (at present £3 per acre) according to the variations in the guaranteed price and average yield. Objections were made to the proposals by producers and at the time of writing final decisions had not been made.

Perhaps the most striking recent feature of potato marketing in Britain has been the growth of producer-controlled potato groups. Fears have, however, been expressed that some of these groups might be too small, that packing-house facilities might be inadequate, and that there might be problems caused by producers being members of more than one group. The findings of a recently published enquiry[2] do indeed suggest that where the managerial resources, office staff, and sophisticated equipment of a co-operative trading society (at any rate those of the efficient modernised society studied in the enquiry) are available, the outlook for producer marketing may be more assured than it is in the case of smaller groups, especially those not employing full-time managers. Of the 30 co-operative-type organisations marketing potatoes in 1967 ten were run by traditional trading societies. Of the groups five were multi-product, and 15 single-product, of which seven were operated by voluntary managers drawn from among the membership and by part-time staff. These all marketed seed. Of the eight with full-time managers and staff, two marketed mainly seed and earlies, and the rest maincrop potatoes. Between them the 30 organisations handled 220,000 tons of potatoes in 1967, or nearly 6 per cent of total recorded English sales.

One of the aims of a co-operative producing maincrop potatoes would be to achieve regular loadings of graded supplies in quantities large enough to enable it to bargain satisfactorily with large wholesalers and/or processors. The processing industry still relies largely, however, on direct contracts with individual growers for supplies grown to the specification of each factory. Contracts are sometimes unduly biased in the processors' favour, and, in the case of canning, specifications are especially exacting. The structure of potato production in Great Britain is being much influenced by the concentration and specialisation of demand. A decline of over 25 per cent in the number of producers registered with the Potato Marketing Board between 1965 and 1969, and a decline in total acreage of

[1] Butterwick and Neville-Rolfe, *op cit*, pp. 208–10.

[2] E. T. Gibbons, *Co-operation and the potato market*, University of Newcastle upon Tyne. Department of Agricultural Marketing Report No. 14, 1970.

only 17 per cent, confirms a continuing rapid rate of disappearance of the small acreage grown by the general farmer. The number of wholesalers has been declining much more slowly. In 1967 there was still one licensed merchant to every 12 producers. Only a minority of wholesalers will, however, be capable in future of catering for the requirements, increasingly specialised in quality and large in quantity, of the processing industry and the big retail food chains. The three leading firms of crisps manufacturers, for instance, use, between them, well over 300,000 tons of potatoes a year.[1] The annual usage of potatoes for freezing is expected before long to be well over 100,000 tons, a large proportion of which will be shared between three firms. Concentration of this type of demand inevitably increases the scale of operations of wholesaling firms. Gibbons estimates that the eight largest merchanting enterprises now handle more than 1 mn tons of potatoes a year, or over 20 per cent of total recorded sales. Between 1946 and 1968 the biggest, Ross Group (now a subsidiary of Imperial Tobacco), is believed to have absorbed 30 companies concerned in the wholesaling of potatoes. It also owns Britain's biggest chain of greengrocers.

Owing largely to the development of potato-based convenience foods, per head consumption of maincrop potatoes in Britain remained remarkably steady during the late sixties. On the other hand, in Germany, as in the other EEC countries (except Italy, where potatoes are of little importance), consumption continues steadily to fall. Despite the development of modern retailing, housewives, including urban ones, still attach great importance to the once-a-year bulk purchase of main-crop for storage in the cellar. A recent Attwood survey of 4,400 retail food shops showed that in less than a quarter of them were two forms of potato sold, and only 3 per cent had three or more forms in their assortment.[2] As a result young housewives tend to regard potatoes as something bought only by the old, the conservative, and the parsimonious, and substitute other forms of starch foods. Development of potato convenience foods does not seem to be far advanced. Advocates of better potato marketing are still thinking mainly in terms of improved quality, grading, packaging and branding of tubers for retail consumption. This is the main aim of the producer groups (*Erzeugergemeinschaften*) whose spread is being promoted by the new Marketing Law. This lays down as a minimum throughput for new groups qualifying for starting-up subsidies, 2,000 tons a year of maincrop, 5,000 tons of earlies or 3,000 tons of potatoes for starch. Groups specialising in supplying the food industry (minimum 2,000 tons) are, however, also specified. The producer group idea is still regarded with considerable scepticism in Germany, but potatoes are a crop for whose production and marketing groups have already existed for a number of

---

[1] Gibbons describes recent developments in processing and wholesaling, *op cit*, pp. 26–45.

[2] O. Strecker, *Entwicklungslinien auf dem Markt für Speisekartoffeln bis 1980*, offprint from 'Ernährungsdienst' (undated).

years, especially in the North. Two co-operatives mainly supply Hanover, which have been pursuing an energetic policy of market promotion, including establishing a brand name, since the mid-sixties, draw the bulk of their supplies from producer groups in the surrounding potato-growing region. At Wankum on the Lower Rhine a group of 130 producers, successfully competing with their Dutch neighbours' exports of earlies, have one of the largest automated packing stations in the Community.

In France potato growers formed some of the earliest *groupements de producteurs* from 1963 onwards. There are now 90. Twenty-five specialise in seed and 20 (seven in Brittany, 10 in the West and South-West, and three in the Rhône Valley) in earlies. Such a large share of total production of seed and earlies was acquired by the groups that they were able to secure an *extension des règles de discipline*, giving their *comités économiques* control of the marketing of virtually the whole of the national crop of both.[1] The other 55 groups are far from dominating the maincrop sector, but the development of group marketing seems to have occurred *pari passu* with that of the potato-processing industry in France. Although currently using only 200,000 tons its demand is expected to reach 1 mn tons (over 10 per cent of the national crop) during the seventies. One factory in the Aisne is already absorbing nearly 100,000 tons a year.

France has official support arrangements different from those in the Netherlands, where a *Produktschap* operates partly subsidised intervention buying of ware potatoes and exporting of surplus of seed. SNIPOT (Société Nationale Interprofessionnelle pour les Pommes de Terre) has an almost identical constitution to that of SIBEV and Interlait.[2] It is a limited liability company with restricted share capital that is divided equally between producers and the trade. Each has equal representation on the Board, and holds the Chairmanship for alternating periods of three years. Its main task is to improve the quality of marketed potatoes, promote mechanisation of grading and packing, and so forth. It also operates a buffer stock (*stock de manœuvre*) under the direction of FORMA, to ensure adequate end-of-season commercial supplies. Premia (*primes de stockage*), of Fr 15 per ton in 1970, are offered for potatoes of appropriate quality kept in store, by growers or merchants, until the last months of the maincrop season. This scheme covers some 450,000 tons annually (about 5 per cent of total production).

There is no immediate prospect of any common EEC regulation for potatoes being introduced. In such preliminary discussions as have taken place among member countries, however, two points of view seem to have emerged. The Dutch would favour a regulation without levies or restitutions, but with normal protection by the CET, whose main purpose would be the enforcement of quality standards for all types of potatoes both for imports and intra-Community trade. The French, though gener-

[1] Gibbons, *op cit*, p. 94, has urged the merits of establishing a second-tier co-operative in England.
[2] See pp. 45–6.

ally in agreement with this, would also like buffer-stock schemes to be introduced in all grower countries and co-ordinated at Community level. Any quality standards adopted would be likely to conform to those agreed from time to time by a special working party at FAO/ECE in Geneva, of which the Comité Européen du Commerce Intereuropéen des Pommes de Terre is a member. The Comité represents the private and co-operative wholesale trades of the Six, Denmark, Spain and Switzerland. Its rule book, *Règles et usages du commerce intereuropéen des pommes de terre* (*RUCIP*), laying down standards of quality, trading, arbitration and professional conduct, is now accepted by 95 per cent of the trade in those countries. Though Britain is not a member of the Comité, representatives of the Ministry of Agriculture and the Potato Marketing Board have recently started to participate in the Geneva working party.

In the absence of any draft regulation the implications for the PMB of entering the EEC remain much as they were three years ago.[1] The Board does not operate in Northern Ireland, where the Ulster Government supports the ware price at £1 a ton below the level of that guaranteed in Great Britain. There is no acreage or other levy. To compensate for the removal of this support, which would not be permitted under any common market regulation that might eventually be agreed upon, the province's growers should be able to draw some advantage from the quality of their seed. Provided varieties could be adapted to continental demand there might be a promising future for exports. Seed is not only produced under aphis-free conditions but is, thanks to a rule forbidding potatoes to be grown more than once in any five years in the same ground, virtually free of eel-worm as well. The monopoly role of the Seed Potato Board, which acts as the sole intermediary between growers (other than merchant/growers) and the trade, could no doubt be made quite as acceptable to Community rules as is that of the *groupements de producteurs* in France.

Wool

The marketing arrangements for wool in Britain and the EEC member countries reveal more significant differences and raise some interesting problems for Britain as an applicant for membership of the Common Market. Wool is quite an important item in British farm sales, amounting to £13·5 mn in 1969/70, including deficiency payments of £5 mn. These figures can be compared with £86 mn from production of mutton and lamb (deficiency payments of £1·7 mn). In addition the hill-sheep subsidy cost about £6·5 mn.

Wool production in Britain has been falling recently (69 mn lb in 1969 against 75 mn lb in the previous year) and the number of producers registered with the Board has also declined (106,000 compared with 114,000 in 1968).

For twenty years the British Wool Marketing Board has exercised a

[1] See Butterwick and Neville-Rolfe, *op cit*, pp. 211–13.

monopoly on the marketing of all wool produced by sheep farmers in the United Kingdom. The Board consists of 10 members elected by producers and representing each of the regional organisations, two elected by producers but drawn from the trades and industries with interests in wool, and three appointed by the agricultural Ministers. These three are not civil servants and do not have a responsibility to report back to the government. At present the three members appointed by Ministers consist of a chartered accountant, a trades unionist and a member of the House of Lords. In addition to its marketing responsibilities the Board runs educational courses, sponsors research, conducts a limited amount of promotion, and administers the deficiency payments paid to implement the guaranteed price for wool ($53\frac{1}{4}$d in 1970–1).

Wool production is a much less important activity in the EEC countries than in Britain. The total number of sheep in the whole Common Market (20·2 mn in 1969) is fewer than in Britain (26·6 mn in 1969). The difference in wool production is less as more sheep are kept mainly for their wool and their milk than for sheep-meat. Total EEC production of both fleece and skin wool is estimated to have amounted to 92 mn lb in 1969 compared with the United Kingdom's production of 106 mn lb (both greasy basis). Wool is classified as an industrial product and therefore is not included in the CAP. In general, marketing is rather disorganised, but under the pressure of economic adversity leading wool growers in the six countries are beginning to join together for marketing purposes. The British Board is generally regarded as the model for a marketing organisation which growers hope could be applied in other European countries.

France has the largest number of sheep in the Community (about 10 mn) and the largest production of wool. As in Britain there is a very large number of breeds of sheep, over thirty in all. Some sheep are kept primarily for wool production and others primarily for their milk, which is used for Roquefort and other cheeses. The wide range of types and qualities of wool present problems for its marketing, which is made more difficult by the fact that there are some 300,000 producers, the average flock being less than thirty-five ewes. Most farmers sell their wool to merchants who go round from farm to farm buying ungraded clips. In the last ten years, however, the government, acting in conjunction with the Fédération Nationale Ovine, has provided financial assistance through FORMA to encourage producers to form marketing groups which undertake the collection, grading and selling of the wool. This has taken the form of a subsidy paid to groups (since 1969 through the eight regional wool co-operatives). When the scheme started the subsidy was sufficient to cover the cost of collecting and grading (about 4d per lb), but it has since been reduced and now amounts to about 0·54p per lb. The scheme is due to end in 1971. In addition grants can be obtained from the Fonds de Développement Economique et Social for building warehouses for grading wool, up to 20 per cent of the total cost, and interest-free loans are also available from the Crédit Agricole. Despite this assistance French wool marketing still largely remains in its traditional form. The co-operatives' share of the market, which now stands at about one-third of total production, has somewhat declined in recent years.

In Germany, where there are about 1·1 mn sheep, wool marketing is concentrated in the hands of the Deutsche Wollverwertung (DWV) which was founded in 1934 to market the wool produced by members of the regional sheep-breeding societies. DWV handles about 97 per cent of all wool produced in Germany. It receives wool from producers at its two grading centres in a very roughly graded form, makes up lots of the appropriate size, and then sells the wool by auction. Producers are paid the sales proceeds less a service commission. In addition they receive a government subsidy in the form of a quality premium, varying according to the quality of the wool. In 1969 the first-quality premium (11·3d per lb) was applied to 30 per cent of production, and the second-quality premium (7·5d per lb) to 60 per cent of production. The remaining 10 per cent received no premium. These subsidies can be compared with an average market price of wool in 1969 of about 34d per lb.

Wool marketing in Germany is well organised compared with France, but producers, who number about 48,000, are looking for further improvement. Grading is very haphazard. The method of selling by auction can be criticised on the grounds that normally no reserves are placed on the wool. Total marketing costs, consisting of DWV's commission plus warehouse charges, plus the producers' time spent in grading, appear to be higher than in Britain.

In Italy there are some 8 mn sheep, most of which are kept for their milk. There are ten main breeds producing, as elsewhere in Western Europe, a great variety of types of wool. Most producers sell to dealers who then grade the wool, and sometimes scour and comb it. About a quarter of total wool production is marketed by the regional syndicates associated with the Federconsorzi. The syndicates receive the wool and grade and value it. The producer is normally paid 80 per cent of this value immediately. Selling is arranged either by private treaty or by auction, at the discretion of the syndicate, the producer being paid the sales proceeds less the advance payment and less a commission charge. A government subsidy on marketing expenses is available to the syndicates amounting to just under 1p per lb. There is no central marketing organisation for wool.

Since wool is not classified by the EEC as an agricultural product it can be argued that no implications would arise as a result of British membership. On the other hand sheep farmers in the EEC are pressing for a change in this classification and are receiving the support of COPA. It is possible that wool might be included in future regulations for sheep and sheep-meat. In this case the level of support to producers in an enlarged Community including Britain would be harmonised. It seems inconceivable that frontier controls would be imposed. The support would therefore have to be in the form of deficiency payments related to target prices, or varying quality premiums as practised in Germany. From the British producers' point of view it would probably be more advantageous if wool remained classified as an industrial product, since the returns from wool, including deficiency payments, are so much higher than in any of the EEC countries.

Whatever decision is made regarding the classification of wool, the future of the British Wool Board should be secure. There are very evident benefits from operating a central marketing organisation for this product. Indeed the farm organisations in the EEC wool-producing countries would like to emulate the Board. Even if exception were taken to its monopoly (which seems unlikely) most producers might prefer to continue to deal with it. The composition of the Board itself might require some slight changes, particularly in order to remove any doubts about the independence of the three members at present appointed by the government.

PART THREE

The Future for Regulated Agricultural Markets

CHAPTER 12

EEC Farmers' Marketing Organisations and their Future

Earlier chapters have contained frequent references to producer organisations engaged in the marketing of farm products in the Community. It will be apparent that these are both numerous and varied. Some idea of the number of organisations that is involved in marketing can be obtained from examining the publications of the various federations or central co-operative institutions that exist in the member countries, or an excellent booklet recently prepared on this subject by the Central Council for Agricultural and Horticultural Co-operation.[1] The latter, in addition to containing much detailed information, includes comments on the reasons for the variety of organisations that exist in agricultural co-operation and for the absence in the EEC countries of a simple pyramid structure embracing all types of co-operation with a single powerful body at the head.

For the benefit of the outside observer who might well feel some irritation at the failure of EEC farmers to achieve better results with their marketing, it is worth mentioning certain fundamental issues that have kept co-operation divided. First, there are the religious and political differences between farmers which, however misguidedly, greatly influence their commercial loyalties. The two main unions in France orginated in the traditional French division between Catholic and secular. In the Netherlands there is a clear distinction between the two principal organisations corresponding roughly to the religious differences of the country. In Belgium the main division is linguistic, and in Italy political. Relatively few French-speaking farmers belong to the Belgian Boerenbond, and it would be difficult, to say the least, to envisage a Communist farmer being happy as a member of a group sponsored by the Federconsorzi. Second, one must take account of a lack of identity of interest among farmers in commercial terms. What is good for one farmer is not necessarily good for his neighbour, which is, incidentally, one of the reasons why farmers' unions' attitudes to co-operation have tended to be somewhat equivocal. A

[1] *Agricultural Co-operative Organisations in the EEC.* The Central Council for Agricultural and Horticultural Co-operation, London, June 1970.

rise in grain prices acts to the disadvantage of the livestock producer. The difference of interest applies even to farmers engaged in similar production. Measures to promote sales of, for instance, cheese or wine are of interest to all farmers concerned in their production. At the same time there is competition in a limited market between the producers of the various cheeses and of the different types of wine. These differences of commercial interest become more acute in an economic Community covering a large area. Tomato growers in Italy have very different marketing problems from those of the glasshouse producers of the Netherlands.

A further factor leading to disunity is provided by differences of viewpoint about the appropriate form of structure for agricultural co-operation, particularly so far as the strength of the central organisation is concerned. This more than any other reason has caused the division between co-operatives in France. It need not be due entirely to doctrinaire considerations. There is plenty of scope for disagreement based on sensible differences of opinion as to what structure will lead to greater efficiency. Finally, there are the problems which arise as a result of the unique feature of co-operatives, that they are owned, and to some extent run, by the people using their services. Any commercial organisation has to pay close attention to what its customers, and to some extent its shareholders, require, but a co-operative is under far more direct pressures of this kind. Under these circumstances it may be difficult for a co-operative fully to satisfy all its members. At the very least there will always be strong differences of opinion between the old members who have been closely involved in the development of the co-operative or even in its creation and new members who can take a more detached and objective view of what the organisation is doing.

Perhaps the greatest problem facing agricultural co-operation is how to ensure that members are informed about the activities, developments and objectives of their organisation. In Western Europe membership of a co-operative is, at least in principle, voluntary. Good communication with members is, of course, vital to any voluntary body. Improvements here could ease some of the problems and difficulties of co-operatives already mentioned. But good communications may not of themselves solve the difficulty of reconciling religious or political differences with commercial objectives. Divisions of this kind between farmers are likely to remain. The key to this, as to many of the other problems associated with co-operatives, lies in good management, the average standard being far below that of the best-run co-operatives. Unfortunately the boards of directors of farmers' co-operatives are too often unaware of the need for high quality of management, of the remuneration required, and of the career structure in which it should operate.

Whatever their views on other aspects of co-operation in agricultural marketing all observers agree on the paramount need for discipline among members. Members must sell what they produce to, or through, their co-operative, or at least observe agreements to sell a specified quantity or proportion of production. The marketing co-operative cannot function effectively without being able to depend on members honouring these agreements. Regrettably farmers very frequently do not. If they receive favourable offers they may well accept them even if this means breaking a commitment to the co-operative. Examples can be found in all countries of farmers behaving incorrectly to their organisations. If the market is right, they may deliver only second-grade qualities to the co-operative and sell the better produce elsewhere. In time of over-supply they unload all they can on to it.

Despite these various inadequacies of co-operation as a method of improving marketing structures, EEC member governments have tended to retain faith in it, and have therefore, over the years and to a varying extent, provided assistance to co-operatives, both in the form of direct grants and by fiscal exemptions.[1] This help has been greatest in France, where co-operatives enjoy a number of important fiscal advantages including exemption from corporation tax on all profits other than those from retailing and from processing agricultural produce for non-human consumption, from local business taxes, and from property tax on buildings with an agricultural purpose (e.g. silos). Although receiving the same investment grants (*primes d'orientation*) as private firms in the food industry, agricultural co-operatives are entitled to a special subsidy (*subvention à la coopération*) as well. In Germany they receive no subsidies other than those to which their constituent members may be entitled, and fiscal privileges are more circumscribed. Profits are taxable on any activity not confined to a co-operative's own membership and on any non-agricultural activity. This excludes from exemption many dairy co-operatives, for instance, producing ice-cream, milk drinks, etc., not classified as farm products. In Belgium and Luxemburg tax concessions are limited to very small co-operatives not engaged in processing, but in Luxemburg subsidies are paid on new investments. Rather limited investment subsidies are available to Italian co-operatives, which also enjoy some minor tax concessions; those with very small capital assets are exempt from tax on their profits. In the Netherlands co-operatives enjoy no fiscal exemptions or privileges and receive no subsidies.

The scope, and success, of other types of incentive to farmers to organise the supply of their produce on the market has also varied considerably from country to country. In Germany, where the post-war political climate has been inimical to *dirigisme* of all kinds, co-operatives have received little direct official encouragement since 1945. Their regional organisation had, however, been greatly strengthened by pre-war legislation.[2] In the dairy sector especially, the co-operatives' position was reinforced by the rigid structure of milk deliveries inherited from before

[1] See *Agricultural Co-operation in the EEC*. Agricultural Series No. 21, EEC Commission, Brussels, 1967.

[2] Particularly the law imposing audit conditions which brought about the federalisation of co-operatives.

the war. During the early sixties an attempt to encourage cereal growers to form specialist producer groups (*Erzeugergemeinschaften*) for growing and marketing quality wheat met with very modest success despite the financial incentives offered. Under the Marketing Law (*Marktstrukturgesetz*) of 1969, however, the principle was extended to livestock enterprises, and starting-up grants will be payable to producer groups, subject to a minimum annual throughput, which varies from product to product and is often quite substantial. It is perhaps significant that at least as much emphasis was laid in the 1969 legislation on the setting up of sales promotion agencies for farm produce on the home market, to compete with imports, and on export markets, and on the further development of a central price reporting organisation. Although initial grants will also be available, the main source of finance for this will be a fund (*Absatzfonds*) based on a levy on all produce at the point of processing and on a charge on the value of agricultural land.

In the Netherlands membership of the fruit and vegetable clock auctions was originally made compulsory by law, but the compulsion was eventually withdrawn once the *veiling* principle had become firmly established. Recently neither the Netherlands nor the Belgium government has shown a great deal of enthusiasm for directly encouraging producer groups, believing this to be the role of the already flourishing co-operative movements in those countries. In Italy too co-operatives, except for those sponsored by the Land Reform Agencies, have largely been left to develop their own organisation. Only the need for producer groups that are capable of carrying out buying-in arrangements within the framework of the fruit and vegetable market regulations has stimulated government action to encourage their formation. A number of these groups are sponsored by the Federazione Italiana dei Consorzi Agrari (Federconsorzi), generally in association with the two main (non-Communist) farmers' unions.[1] The *consorzi agrari* are not, however, despite their name, co-operatives in the sense that they are financed mainly by their members' shareholdings. Indeed their paid-up membership has not in most cases increased at all during the past ten years. Although shareholders have the right to elect the council of their local (provincial) *consorzio*, which in turn has some say in the election of the central council in Rome, producer control of the organisation is tenuous, to say the least. Directors and managers of the provincial *consorzi* are nominated from Rome in agreement with the local councils, whose compliance with the wishes of the central body tends to vary in inverse ratio to their financial strength and stability. Effectively the Federconsorzi are a highly centralised buying group of farm requirements, handling just over half the country's sales of tractors, tractor fuel, and fertilisers. As such they have built up massive reserves over the past twenty-five years and constitute a powerful autonomous economic and political force exercised in the name of all

[1] Confederazione Generale dell' Agricoltura and Conferazione Nazionale degli Coltivatori Diretti.

Italian farmers. Only to the extent that the Federconsorzi are closely linked with the political party that has led all the post-war governments could it be said that government policy had up to the time of the introduction of the draft law on groups in 1969 actively promoted organised producers in Italy.

France, on the other hand, presents a picture of official encouragement to co-operative producer action so extensive and elaborate that it deserves a closer look. To the outside observer there is a bewildering proliferation of alternative forms of association, each known by its inevitable acronym, CUMA, SICA, SETA, SIPA, GAEC, SMIA, and so forth. Many of them derive their legal existence from the *loi complémentaire d'orientation agricole* of 1962, since whose promulgation new initiatives to persuade farmers to organise their production and marketing have succeeded each other every few years. Each, launched with high hopes and its own special statute, usually a set of meticulous regulations, has made no more than a marginal dent in the mass of unorganised—perhaps unorganisable— individualistic peasant farmers.[1] It has been said, by a Frenchman, that 'France is the land of impressive, bold and penetrating declarations but also of laborious and half-hearted attempts to put theory into practice.'[2] The history of French agricultural policy during the past decade suggests that there is some truth in this. All the same it would be unfair to underestimate what has been achieved, in the face of considerable inertia, by a few dedicated officials and energetic producers. It is worth briefly assessing how far the encouragement given to *groupements de producteurs* has been successful. The main concept behind them, as spelled out by the 1962 Law, is to introduce discipline into both production and marketing by their members: into production, by observing proper methods of husbandry and adopting up-to-date techniques under the guidance of qualified extension workers, so as to lower costs per unit of output; into marketing, by regulating the quantity and quality of produce going for sale, either through the group or individually under conditions of timing, grading, and price laid down by the group. Recognised groups receive grants and loans, spread over a number of years and degressive over time towards their operating costs and investments in plant and equipment. Where members of a group (or of a *comité économique regional* comprising a number of groups in a region) are in a substantial majority ('*largement majoritaire*') among producers of the commodity whose production and marketing the group undertakes, the minority of non-members may be required, after a public enquiry, to submit to group discipline (*extension des règles*). In this way market withdrawal arrangements and a compensation fund may be organised and financed from a compulsory levy on all

[1] A recent enquiry by Caen University on behalf of Lait-Viande Basse-Normandie established three categories of farmer in the three departments of Lower Normandy: 13 per cent of *innovateurs*; 32 per cent of *evolutifs*, who were capable of changing their attitudes; and 55 per cent of *traditionnels* characterised by their immobility. *Le Figaro*, November 10th 1970.

[2] Charles Morazé, quoted in P. Pinchemel, *France, a geographical survey* (Bell, London, 1969, translated by Christine Trollope and A. J. Hunt), p. 149.

producers, whether in the group or not. This has been achieved, for instance, in the case of Breton cauliflower production.[1]

The law permits a variety of associations to qualify as groups: co-operatives, often acting in the name of only those of its members who are forming the group, and their unions; SICAs (*sociétés d'intérêt commun agricole*), which, unlike co-operatives, may have a minority of non-farming shareholders[2] and operate on the principle of one share one vote;[3] *syndicats*, whose members do not subscribe any capital and who have usually come together for production purposes only; and simple *associations*. These last two categories constitute a basic form of producer group, which often develops later, for marketing purposes, into a SICA or co-operative. A GAEC (*groupement agricole d'exploitation en commun*), consisting of farmers who have pooled their land and assets to work it in common, may become a member of a producer group in the same way as any individual farmer.

The development of producer groups between 1964 and 1967, under the aegis of FORMA and its promotional subsidiary COFREDA, made relatively slow progress despite the enthusiastic support of M. Pisani during his time as Minister of Agriculture. The whole concept seems to have come up against a number of entrenched interests: of the co-operatives, which saw little reason to develop new types of association outside the agricultural co-operative movement; of the FNSEA, the principal farmers' union, which also viewed with some suspicion the direct contacts being established between producers and FORMA, through COFREDA; and, curiously enough, of local officials of the Ministry of Agriculture, not only out of jealousy of FORMA, it seems, but also because of the ingrained suspicion which the average *fonctionnaire* is supposed to entertain for anything that could be construed as monopolistic privileges of any kind (in this case for farmers). The boost given to producer groups by the introduction of the common regulation for fruit and vegetables in 1967 accelerated their development, so that by the middle of 1970 some 850 had been officially recognised, 112 of them since the previous year. Just over half of them had received financial aid from FORMA, to a total

[1] See p. 201.

[2] In the case of SMIA (*société mixte d'intérêt agricole*) up to 70 per cent of shares may be held by non-farming firms. The participation of outsiders would, incidentally, make SMIAs and SICAs ineligible for the Community-financed aids envisaged by the Commission's proposals for producer groups (see pp. 303–9 below). These, as their name implies, must consist exclusively of producers. Groups that are corporate shareholders in SICAs would, however, themselves be eligible for aids.

[3] That is, a SICA *anonyme*. In a *SICA civil*, a form of partnership, it is one man one vote, as in a co-operative. A co-operative may not buy or sell produce outside its membership unless it is a *co-opérative anonyme*, in which case it may buy up to 20 per cent of its produce from non-members in any one year. The proportion was originally 49 per cent, but SICAs formed since 1968 have been obliged to follow the same 20 per cent rule as co-operatives. SICAs are, however, permitted to give tax-free rebates to their members to compensate for this restriction and as an inducement to non-member suppliers to join. The right to buy at least a proportion of produce from outside the membership is especially important to meat SICAs in order to ensure regular supplies to their customers.

value, including that given to regional committees, of nearly $10 mn, of which $2 mn was granted during the financial year 1969–70. Of this the largest share, $3·2 mn, had gone to meat groups (including $2 mn to pig groups). Poultry groups received $2·9 mn. There were 248 livestock groups, 123 egg and poultry-meat groups, 370 fruit, vegetable and potato groups. The remainder deal in miscellaneous products like honey, lavender and hops, and seven in the overseas departments in tropical products.

Rough estimates suggest that producer groups now account for between 10 and 12 per cent of beef output, 15 per cent of pigs, and just over 5 per cent of sheep; 10 per cent of eggs; anything between a quarter and a half of all poultry-meat; and a proportion of fruit and vegetables varying a good deal from product to product, 55 per cent or less in the case of top fruit, but reaching 95 per cent for artichokes, cauliflowers, and early potatoes. Despite the recent acceleration, the results, eight years after the passing of the *loi d'orientation*, are certainly not spectacular. Amongst a number of proposals now being considered is one that would put the screw on farmers to join or form groups by making them the exclusive channel for all official aid. Those remaining outside would of course continue to enjoy the general benefits of the CAP provided by target and intervention prices, if any, as well as recourse to low-interest borrowing from the Crédit Agricole statutorily available to all farmers. First-stage groups, formed for the purpose of contract production, for instance, would be entitled to the advisory services of ANDA (Association Nationale pour le Développement Agricole).[1] It would scarcely be possible for these to be provided in any discriminatory fashion. On the other hand ANDA's 3,600 extension workers would in future be at the immediate disposal of COFREDA to strengthen their own advisory services to the groups, with special stress being laid on economic as well as purely technical advice. All other forms of government aid not forbidden by EEC regulations, especially investment grants for buildings and other farm improvements, would be reserved to duly recognised producer groups capable of submitting viable long-term development plans. One particular attraction still remains for those not joining groups, for which all these incentives or disincentives cannot perhaps fully compensate and which presents an intractable problem. That is the built-in ability of the independent producer to evade taxation, especially value-added tax, not open to the member of a group maintaining properly audited accounts.

However modest the success of their policies French governments have led the way on producer groups. Encouragement of groups was also part of the Commission's long-term policy for the Community as a whole even before mounting surpluses highlighted the need for a common approach to structural problems. The Commission's point of view was obviously influenced by certain aspects of French legislation. In 1967 it submitted a

[1] ANDA is financed by a producer levy (*taxe parafiscale*) raised through normal tax channels.

draft regulation on the subject. Although both the European Parliament and the Economic and Social Committee have expressed their views on this draft, it has never been examined by the Council. A revised proposal was therefore submitted in the spring of 1970 as part of the Commission's elaboration of the Mansholt Plan of December 1968.[1] Estimating that some 14 per cent of the Community's total agricultural output is at present produced by groups, the Commission intends that over a period of ten years this proportion should be increased to 63 per cent.[2] The new draft therefore covers a wider range of products[3] and differs in several other important respects from the earlier version. Group members are no longer to be obliged to market their produce centrally. They may deal directly with purchasers so long as they conform to the standards, prices, etc. laid down for the group. Groups must constitute a minimum acreage or volume of production to be determined. The proposed rule whereby any one group was prohibited from marketing more than 5 per cent of the Community's production has, however, been dropped. On the other hand groups are no longer to be exempted from the provisions of Article 85 of the Treaty of Rome concerned with restricting competition. Aid is to be extended to unions of producer groups at regional (sometimes national) level. Groups would be entitled to starting-up subsidies (*aides de démarrage*) spread over the first three years of trading up to the equivalent respectively of 3 per cent, 2 per cent and 1 per cent of the value of produce marketed[4] (5, 4 and 3 per cent in the case of cattle, pigs and sheep). In addition they would receive over their first five years of existence loans at reduced rates of interest towards investments in storage, grading, packing, etc. In certain regions with special social and economic problems capital grants would be payable in lieu. Every union of groups would qualify for low-interest loans and for a once-for-all grant of up to UA 50,000. Apart from this one concession the substitution of loans for grants represents a fundamental change in policy from the original draft regulation. It is proposed that 30 per cent of all sums due to groups which have been approved by the Commission (after consultation with the Standing Committee on agricultural structure, and, where appropriate, with that on regional development) should be paid

[1] *Réforme de l'agriculture* (*propositions de la Commission au Conseil*), COM (70) 500 EEC Commission, Brussels, 29 April 1970, Part VI.

[2] As far as individual groups of products are concerned, in the case of only 6 out of 15 would less than this average proportion be marketed through groups by 1980: poultry, milk and wine (60 per cent); miscellaneous (sheep, honey) (60 per cent); cereals (25 per cent); and sugar (nil). The maximum target is 80 per cent for fruit and vegetables. Fruit and vegetable groups already set up under Regulation 159/66 (but not SICAs—see p. 236, footnote 2) would be assimilated to the proposed new Regulation while retaining, where appropriate, their right to aid from FEOGA for financing buying-in.

[3] Meat as well as live cattle, pigs and sheep; all fruit and vegetables covered by the common regulation (23/62); rapeseed and sunflower seed; linseed, flax, and hops; and various types of fish.

[4] Not based on actual marketings, but on the sum of the average volume marketed by each group member over the previous three calendar years times the average price received over the same period.

from the Guidance Section of FEOGA. The balance would be paid out of national budgets. Member governments would remain free to make additional grants of a similar nature, or larger grants of the same nature, provided they did not contravene Articles 92 to 94 of the Rome Treaty on aids by distorting competition.

While generally welcoming the changes, COPA and COGECA[1] have stressed the need to assist co-operative processing of agricultural products where farmers' organisations are competing against private industry. Mainly in this context both organisations regret the proposed withdrawal of the exemption from Article 85 of the Rome Treaty. Regulation 26/62 already gives agricultural producers' associations a certain latitude in favour of restrictive agreements or practices which are necessary for the attainment of the objectives set out in Article 39 of the Treaty (this defines the aims of the CAP). It would be for the Commission to rule whether Regulation 26/62 was being infringed in a particular case, which could also be tested in the European Court of Justice. COGECA considers the Regulation would be an inadequate safeguard if exemption from Article 85 were not conceded.

In the absence of debate, let alone decisions, by the Council, the Commission can only bide its time and observe what is happening in this field in member countries as a result of national policies. It is evident that to the Commission's regret on the Council's failure to respond to its initiative has been added some disappointment about the speed and form of development in the member countries. Only in France has official action been at all energetic, but even there many, perhaps about three-quarters, of the producer groups now established consist of already existing co-operatives which have made minor changes in their constitutions in order to become eligible for state aid. The same may have occurred, if to a somewhat lesser extent, in Germany. Some experienced observers there consider that many newly formed groups which are not co-operatives may not survive far beyond their first honeymoon period of three years, when they benefit from subsidisation.

The Commission's proposals also raise a number of legal problems. German law does not permit co-operatives to become producer groups, as they may in France. It has therefore been suggested that any EEC regulation on the subject should include a clause specifically stating that co-operatives may be recognised as groups in member countries. In France a co-operative may even be recognised as a producer group on behalf of only a section of its membership. French law, on the other hand, presents problems for transnational co-operatives or producer groups. The Commission has proposed that these, whose formation in an economic community seems desirable, should become limited companies. However, co-operatives may not according to French law be limited companies. The solution may be to set up separate European co-operative

[1] Comité des Organisations Professionnelles Agricoles. Comité Général de la Coopération Agricole des Pays de la Communauté.

companies. Indeed, COGECA has been engaged in drafting a statute for a supranational co-operative.

Given the importance attached in Brussels to the organisation of marketing by producers themselves, the farmers' sense of frustration over the little that has so far been achieved can be readily understood.[1] The long-term objectives of the Mansholt proposals include the principle of delegation to producer organisations of a far greater share of responsibility for the marketing of their members' products, including the responsibility for adjusting supply to demand and disposing of surpluses. As yet, the means of achieving this are vague and undefined, but at least it is clear that the Commission's viewpoint is influenced by the success of the horticultural organisations of the Netherlands, the model which—clock auctions apart— it has started to apply to horticulture in the other member countries. This involves the principle of producer responsibility for dealing with surpluses, even if in the case of certain products they are to receive financial assistance from FEOGA.

If the objective of greater producer responsibility appears over-ambitious, this goes to show how deeply imbued most people have become with the necessity for direct interference in agricultural markets. To say to farmers 'This is your problem. You are producing too much. Do something about it yourselves and we will help to pay your costs', now seems in political terms almost shocking, though it amounts to no more than treating agriculture like any other industry going through adjustment problems. Unfortunately, farmers' organisations can plausibly argue that it would be impossible for them to take on these responsibilities without receiving powers which governments would be unlikely to wish to make over to them, especially as these should logically include some in the field of foreign trade policy as well.

We believe that the Commission is correct in the emphasis that it is placing on the development of producer groups in marketing but unreasonably optimistic in thinking that these organisations could possibly play much part in overall market 'responsibility' for the foreseeable future.[2] In holding this view we are not so much influenced by the reluctance that farmers may well show in taking on such responsibility, involving as it will implications for farm incomes, the structure of production, the level of farm population and other matters which could face producers' organisations with grave problems. This reluctance might indeed inhibit adoption of

[1] Anyone with experience of work on establishing any sort of producer marketing organisation will be aware of the difficulties and frustrations, which, if for no other reason, can be said to justify the various 'starting-up' aids granted in both Britain and the EEC countries.

[2] As already noted the Commission has expressed the hope that nearly two-thirds of the Community's agricultural production might be accounted for by groups at the end of ten years. For the first five years it estimates that the total cost of its proposals for the support of groups, rising steeply from UA 7 mn in the first year to UA 160 mn in the fifth, would be UA 407 mn, of which UA 122 mn would be a charge on the Guidance Section of FEOGA.

the Commission's policy. A much more fundamental difficulty is the lack of organisations capable of fulfilling this role. Their growth is likely to be slow. Meanwhile, more study is required of the changes that are now occurring in farmers' marketing organisations, of factors which may be impeding their development and of the appropriate economic and other criteria which should be applied to them. In the present state of knowledge of this subject one can reasonably feel sympathetic to the 'go-slow' policy of the Council of Ministers. But the Commission's proposals have at least had the important merit of focussing critical attention on these problems.

The issues are of particular interest to Britain and the other three applicant countries. Although their co-operative organisations differ in various ways from those in the present member countries, they also share most of their problems. This applies even to Denmark where co-operative marketing is most strongly developed. The current issues of greatest importance in both the EEC and the applicant countries are vertical integration, the structure of co-operation, monopoly powers for producers' organisations, and assessment of the economic efficiency of such organisations.

The effects on agricultural marketing co-operatives of the pressures of vertical integration is a wide-ranging subject.[1] Here discussion will be limited to the single issue of how far forward in the marketing and processing chain it is necessary for a farmers' organisation to advance. The word 'necessary' must be stressed because it may sometimes be economically desirable for the organisation to engage in grading, processing, etc., simply because at the time such facilities are either not available or are yielding an exceptional profit. Under normal circumstances it is seldom compellingly necessary for a farmers' organisation to integrate forward, provided that it has complete control of its members' output and clear knowledge of the market situation. It appears that farmers' marketing groups are often tempted to move forward into another (and unaccustomed) stage because they do not exercise this degree of control. This is frequently because they have failed to reach the right size, to obtain the right outlets or to comprehend their existing market opportunities. Solutions can usually be obtained to most marketing problems which involve no need to integrate forward into the next stage.

Likewise, the problem of the right structure of marketing co-operation is extremely complex. In many of the EEC countries, as well as in the applicant countries, the principal aspect of the problem is how to accommodate the old with the new. The old consists of the large, long-established, sometimes well-entrenched and often wealthy organisations such as the Raiffeisenverband in Germany, the Belgian Boerenbond, the Federconsorzi in Italy, or some of the larger requirements/marketing societies in Britain. The new are typified by producer groups, which may or may not be associated with traditional co-operatives. The main advantage of the more recently formed groups, often consisting of younger

[1] See M. W. Butterwick, *op cit*, p. 38.

farmers, is that they may more readily be able to command their members' loyalty on a voluntary basis. In practice the problem of how to reconcile the interests of the two can only be dealt with case by case. Provided each organisation has a clearly defined view of its own role as well as that of the other, a viable working relationship can be established between the two. For instance, a co-operative slaughterhouse can collaborate with the livestock marketing groups in its area, the latter carrying out all or part of the slaughterhouse's procurement.[1]

The monopolistic character of co-operation in agricultural marketing raises a number of issues. At the local level co-operatives normally set geographical boundaries between each other with a view to avoiding 'wasteful' competition. For some products, including cereals, competition may be preserved through the activities of private merchants. For others, for example for the more specialised crops and for milk, an aggressive co-operative may rapidly achieve its policy objective of obtaining an effective monopoly of the market. French legislation, as already noted, permits a minority of recalcitrant producers to be forced by a substantial majority of all producers to market through a producer group. Finally, in areas where private merchants are few in number it is not uncommon for unwritten agreements to be made between the co-operative and the private sector in order to restrain competition for farmers' business.

One of the main objects of co-operative marketing is to channel supplies through a limited number of points, and thus to gain market strength. Consequently competition in the marketing sector is reduced. The intention must be to lower marketing costs, but excessive restriction of competition could in fact result in a loss of efficiency, especially if encouragement to co-operation were to lead to the total exclusion of private merchants and dealers. As already noted the Commission's earlier view, which favoured the development of organisations controlling no more than 5 per cent of total supplies, has now been dropped. The implication is that provided producers' organisations do not operate against the public interest, there is no objection to them developing complete control of the Community market for their product. We have already argued that in the present circumstances it is unrealistic to think that producers' organisations could take on such responsibilities for the major farm products in the near future. Apart from this the disappearance of the private sector could hardly be thought to be in the general interest of agricultural marketing. The fact that a co-operative is owned by those who use it may impose some restraints on the efficiency of its operation, since in practice managers will often find it difficult to cut out services demanded by a minority of members, deliveries of small orders of farm requirements, and collection of uneconomic quantities of produce. As things stand at present, a Community network of co-operatives would be unlikely to operate efficiently without the spur of competition from private merchants.

[1] The establishment by a co-operative of subsidiary organisations presents legal problems in Britain. A method of circumventing these is suggested in a booklet *Marketing Groups within existing agricultural co-operatives*, published by the Central Council for Agricultural and Horticultural Co-operation.

CHAPTER 13

The Future for Intervention

It must be apparent from the previous chapter that both the national governments of the member countries and the Commission are aware of the defects of agricultural marketing in the Community. The principal means of correcting them is to be a policy of giving encouragement to producer groups. But this and other policies, for instance those directed towards obtaining greater market transparency, better price intelligence, more detailed information about market developments, or more intensive sales promotion of agricultural products, cannot do much to alleviate the central problem of agricultural marketing in the Community: the tendency of the agriculture of the member countries to produce more than can be absorbed by the Community market plus world markets, other than at concessional prices.

The surpluses of some farm products which have bedevilled the Community in recent years are to a large extent due to farm prices being kept at unduly high levels in relation to overall demand. Frequent recourse to the tools of market support—intervention, export restitution, and denaturing premium—has been necessary because prices are too high. If prices received by producers were boldly lowered, high-cost farming would become unprofitable, more farmers would move into other occupations, and the problem of surplus supplies would be eased. The Commission's price proposals which accompanied its original memorandum for structural reform implied some attempt to face up to this issue. It was also forcibly stated in the Vedel Report,[1] and examined in some depth by a study group convened by the Federal Trust in London, at the end of 1969.[2] Clearly if the Community were really determined to avoid the trouble and expense of dealing with surpluses, threshold and intervention prices would be drastically lowered. Unfortunately, there are plenty of reasons for not doing this: problems of depopulating country areas, problems of retraining and resettling farmers, problems even, in some countries, of defence. Furthermore, farmers have votes and constitute often the largest single electoral

[1] *op cit*, Part 2, pp. 31–2.
[2] *A new agricultural policy for Europe. Proposals submitted by the Agricultural Study Group of the Federal Trust (rapporteur,* John Marsh), Federal Trust for Education and Research, London, January 1970.

bloc. To obtain agreement on firm measures of agricultural policy is difficult enough in any one country, but in a Community of six, in which one member or another seems in most years to be involved in an election, the difficulty is greatly increased.

Will future prices for agricultural products in the EEC be held at levels that will yield surpluses and therefore create a need for disposal policies? Any answer to this question is bound to contain a good measure of political guesswork. Account has to be taken of greater awareness of the growing cost of the Community's agricultural support policies. It is estimated[1] that the total cost of domestic market intervention in 1970 will have been UA 2,517 mn compared with an estimated UA 951 mn in 1969 and actual expenditure of UA 411 mn in 1968. On top of these prodigious sums there is the cost to national governments of a very wide range of aids to agriculture. At the same time the political strength of farmers must be declining as the proportion of the working population engaged in agriculture falls year by year. All this might indicate the possibility of the Commission standing a better chance in future of forcing through its proposals to reduce prices at least of the farm products in surplus. Our own view is that this is unlikely. At the best the present price structure will be maintained with only very minor downward amendments, inflation (including the inflationary effects on farm costs) being left to exercise a progressive squeeze on the profitability of marginal farms. But few in Brussels are optimistic that there will not in fact be some price increases during the next few years.

Faced with the apparent impossibility of using the pricing mechanism as the main tool for adjusting supply to demand, the Commission has turned to its structural policy. Recently structural policy, which used to consist mainly of such uncontroversial matters as land consolidation and regional development programmes for predominantly rural areas, has started to become more directly concerned with methods of restraining agricultural production. This in itself provides an illustration of a change in the political climate affecting agricultural policy and indicates some weakening of farmers' influence. It is easy to imagine the almost hysterical reception that would have been given to measures to encourage the removal of land from agricultural use, or the slaughter of milk cows, ten, or even five, years ago.

The Mansholt Plan's proposals are a good deal better than nothing. Unfortunately the Commission's various proposals for structural reform can only be expected to work rather slowly. Meanwhile the advances in the agricultural sciences and husbandry techniques are working in the opposite direction. The dairy industry provides a graphic example. Slaughtering premiums have resulted in the disappearance of some 250,000 cows. Proposed new payments to encourage farmers to cease production of milk may eliminate a further 250,000. Despite the large expenditure involved, the total will represent only some $2\frac{1}{2}$ per cent of the Community

[1] Commission of the EEC COM (70) 810 of July 29th 1970.

herd. As a German expert[1] has recently pointed out, it would require a reduction of no less than 650,000 cows per year simply in order to offset the current increases in annual yields per cow.

The recent easing of the pressures of supplies in the dairy sector has given some encouragement to the view that the worst is over. Hopefully this is so, but average yields continue to go up and the present lull may be largely due to two relatively dry summers. At all events it must be recognised that there are very limited possibilities for disposing of *any* increase in production. Consumption of dairy products as a whole within the present Community is rising at little more than the same rate as the population increase, despite promotional efforts to stimulate demand. Milk powder can be used as a substitute for fishmeal by the compound-feed manufacturers (at a considerable subsidy cost), and there are limited possibilities of disposing of butterfat in milk replacers for calf rearing. Increased sales in the export market for dairy products are difficult to obtain and prices often unattractive. In these circumstances, and bearing in mind that two out of the four new entrants to the EEC have substantial dairy exports, which may be stimulated by Community prices, it seems very likely that the problem of milk surpluses will remain serious unless quotas are introduced or there is a major readjustment of prices.

Much that has been said about the milk market also applies to other products. The sugar surplus could be cured by action on either prices or the quota. The sugar quota, with lower prices for production in excess of the basic quota, provides the sole example in the Community of a system which penalises farmers for excess production. With cereals, as with sugar, there are limited possibilities for use in animal feeds of products suitable for human consumption. Surpluses of beef, as has already been shown, are seasonal. The balance between supply and demand in eggs and pigmeat is likely to become even more delicate following the entry of the new applicants. In most of these markets officially supported prices influence the volume of production. On the evidence to date it seems likely that these will be held at levels tending to encourage surpluses.

We assume therefore a continuing state of surplus of some of the principal agricultural products whether the Community remains with its present membership or is enlarged by the addition of the four applicants. In the last chapter we concluded that the idea of handing over responsibility for dealing with surpluses to producers or 'interprofessional' organisations, while sound in principle, is not likely to be achieved for non-horticultural products in the near future. The limited number of ways in which surpluses can be disposed of by official action (destruction; selling at concessional prices, or even giving away, on the domestic market; transfer with subsidy from one product market to another through denaturing; and export with restitution subsidies) have, of course, all been tried out by the Community. In general the Community has operated a mixed system

[1] Herr H. H. Messerschmidt in a speech to the Conference on 'Profitable Dairying in the '70s', Olympia, October 1970.

consisting partly of intervention buying and subsequent resale and partly of immediate provision of subsidies for export, etc. An important, though perhaps obvious, point arises here. The outlets for surplus disposal remain the same whether intervention buying is used or whether the trade is provided with the required subsidies without an agency intervening to purchase the products and take them off the market. Except that it provides a known minimum floor price intervention buying does nothing which cannot be achieved in other ways.

This point perhaps needs to be stressed. The methods of disposal practised by the intervention agencies working under the Commission have been described in the commodity chapters. The most normal method is for the agency, on instructions from Brussels, to invite tenders from the trade for export restitutions or denaturing premiums. The system is operated in conjunction with permanent restitutions and denaturing premiums. These, if the tender is to be successful, must be set less attractively than the level of tender which the agency, instructed by the Commission, accepts. The permanent restitution and premium can be altered, and thus some flexibility is obtained. The intervention system provides still greater flexibility as no tender need be accepted. But essentially the methods of disposal with or without intervention are the same.

There is therefore some sense in raising the question as to why intervention buying is required at all. It can fairly be pointed out that intervention necessarily involves an additional marketing stage reflected in the costs of administering the agency and, on occasions when the produce has to be moved into a different store, higher transport costs. Doctrinaire non-interventionists might go so far as to argue that any direct intervention on markets by organisations outside the trade is likely to do more harm than good on the grounds that only the trade can fully understand the market, a view which we sympathise with without wholly supporting.

Intervention buying in agricultural markets under EEC circumstances can be justified on four grounds. First, there is a political case both in relation to the farmers who benefit from it, as well as to the taxpayers/consumers who have to bear its net cost. Price levels related to the target prices could of course be maintained without intervention prices. Farmers could be assured that the Commission would set export restitutions, etc., so that these price levels would be achieved. But farmers would undoubtedly feel less secure under such a system. Intervention prices at least provide some sort of floor to the market even if they do not constitute guaranteed prices to farmers. In political terms farmers' organisations are no doubt right to press for retention of intervention prices. The taxpayer/consumer on the other hand has to pay the bill for market support activity whatever form it takes. In trying to draw as much attention as possible to the high cost of this support it has probably suited the Commission to be able to point to stocks of agricultural produce which are owned by the Community and which every day are costing the taxpayer large sums of money for storage.

Second, there may be occasions when the administrative costs of operating an intervention agency are lower than those involved in offering subsidies to the trade. For example in the meat market quite small intervention purchases of livestock or fresh meat have been made in the autumn and the frozen meat subsequently sold at a loss. A subsidy could be provided to allow the trade to do this, but this would be likely to be difficult and expensive to control compared with buying, storing, and selling by the agencies themselves.

Third, for some products at some points of time the world market may be so small that the cost in restitutions of disposal via exports could appear prohibitively expensive. Under these circumstances there is really no alternative but to enter the market and buy for stock in the hope that more favourable opportunities for disposal may eventually occur. The most obvious example here is butter, a product for which outlets are notoriously difficult to find. Even for sugar, for which a more active world market exists, the Community surplus has from time to time become very large in relation to available outlets.

The fourth justification for intervention buying of agricultural products in the EEC—the greater flexibility that it provides to the system of market regulation—has already been briefly mentioned. This important point requires further explanation. The original concept of the Community was that rates for levy and export restitution should normally be in tune with each other. Theoretically the concept may be correct as both are intended to equalise world prices with EEC prices. The practical application of the system has, however, ruled out keeping the two in step. Levies are calculated so as to raise the world price c.i.f. the Community up to a common threshold price which in turn is derived from the target price. This is quite straightforward. The rate of export restitution is intended to subsidise EEC exports by the difference between market prices and world prices. Very frequently EEC market prices have been below target prices, at the intervention level, or even lower. Under these circumstances restitutions set at a similar level to levies might well be excessively generous and lead to larger exports than were really necessary. Furthermore, the export and import markets in, for instance, cereals differ as to qualities and market locations. The Commission has therefore recommended that the two should be kept separate.

Since the threshold price is a fixed price, the calculation of the appropriate levy is far more simple than the establishment of the right rate of restitution, the latter involving knowledge of a wide range of internal market prices as well as of world prices. It is much easier to get the rate of restitution wrong, leading either to insufficient exports and a bottle-neck in the trade, or to a flood of exports, needless disruptions of world trade, and a waste of FEOGA funds. Both levies and restitutions are awarded as a result of application for licences to import or export certain quantities of certain qualities of the products in question, but in neither case does the system allow for quantitative controls on foreign trade, the licences effectively being awarded automatically.

Finally, it must be recognised that levies and restitutions are designed to serve rather different purposes. For some products (e.g. sugar) threshold prices are set so that, in effect, imports are largely prevented. For others (notably cereals) levies are used primarily to adjust world prices to the EEC level rather than to prevent the imports which the Community requires. The threshold prices themselves inhibit imports but the mechanics of the system are not intended to discourage importers from carrying on their trade. By contrast exports with restitutions are not required as a matter of policy for trade reasons, that is to say in order to earn foreign exchange. There would be no reason to encourage trade at a cost in subsidies except for the need to get rid of the market surpluses which arise as a consequence of the Community's price policy for agricultural products. Consequently, and as a result of some bad experiences following setting restitutions too high, the Commission has in recent years adopted a cautious attitude to the level of permanent restitutions and has not attempted to set these subsidies, even if this were possible, on a basis which might be expected precisely to clear markets of the Community's anticipated annual surpluses. It has adopted the same policy over the denaturing premium. Here again it is evidently very difficult to set the subsidy at exactly the right rate. In the case of wheat there is an obvious danger that the denaturing premium could be so attractive as to produce a major switch from one market to another, which in this case would disrupt the feed grains market. The balance is very delicate.

When selling intervention stocks the Commission is able to control by means of subsidies the quantities of surpluses moving into the various market outlets. By using fairly frequent tenders it is better placed to ensure that the subsidies are set at exactly the right point to achieve the objectives. These are the two attractions of the tender system used for the disposal of intervention stocks. The narrower the market outlet (for example the export market for butter) the more inclined the Commission is to use these methods rather than the blunter instrument of permanently available (even though varying) subsidies at levels which might be expected to be attractive to the trade.

We conclude from this examination that intervention buying in the Community is likely to continue. It is possible that in the future the Commission will develop still greater knowledge of the intricate balance of agricultural markets and therefore greater skill in setting subsidies to move surpluses without intervention. But if these surpluses remain as significant as we expect, and if we are right in assuming that official rather than producer-organised action will be required, then there is undoubtedly a good case for continuing to make use of intervention agencies.

CHAPTER 14

Implications for the British Market

Adoption by Britain of the CAP would to a greater or less degree affect every person and organisation concerned with farming, including the agricultural supply industries and the food processing industries, and extending to a wide range of institutions and government departments. For many the calculation of how they would stand as a result of British membership of the Common Market is extremely complex. To illustrate just how complex one might take the case of a biscuit manufacturer. The biscuit industry, as a second-stage processor of farm produce whose purchases include flour, butter, sugar and egg products, might seem only remotely connected with agricultural regulations. Nevertheless it and other processing industries are both subject to them and greatly influenced by them in a variety of ways. Many of the products they use are affected by import controls. For some products there are intervention arrangements, which likewise influence price and availability. For others harmonised quality standards may prove different from those to which national manufacturers have previously been accustomed. One or two (like butter released from cold store) are available at lower prices because of the need to dispose of Community surpluses. But the real complexities begin when exports have to be dealt with. The biscuit industry, like other food processors such as the confectionery industry, is able to claim restitutions on a number of materials that it uses in its exports. There are at least ten ingredients of biscuits on which restitutions may be obtained.[1] A Belgian manufacturer who had recently carried out a careful timing exercise reported to us that it took his office staff four hours and ten minutes to complete the necessary documents for one consignment of biscuits going for export. This was apart from any documentation required by the company internally either for stock control or for invoicing its customer. Admittedly some of this documentation was for national rather than Community purposes, but at least the case illustrates the potential difficulties for companies only indirectly concerned with agriculture, some of whom in Britain may be unaware of what they will have to cope with.

Therefore, in listing the implications of the CAP for agricultural

[1] Maize starch, husked rice, wheat flour, rye flour, white sugar, milk powder (whole or skimmed), concentrated milk, butter, shell eggs, and egg yolks (liquid, frozen or dried).

marketing in Britain the first point to make is that much will be strange and unaccustomed. Farmers will have to get used to new price policies, feed manufacturers to new raw-material costs, and traders to the complexities of Common Market regulations for both international and domestic trade. These difficulties will be aggravated by the transition period which is required for phasing in the foreign-exchange cost to Britain of the CAP, the rise in the cost of living through higher food prices, and the effects on third-country suppliers. From the trade point of view the transition period will present a further complication. At the end of each year of the period Britain will have to change its threshold and other prices as well as levies and restitutions. At the same time EEC prices may change (levies and restitutions of course vary continually) and there will be additional complications over the comparative level of monthly increments, about carry-over stocks, etc. The transition period thus introduces one further element into an already confusing situation.

The Community's policy towards agriculture is of course protectionist. To this extent British producers should welcome the prospect of membership. But the movement from one small (or national) protected market to a much larger (Community) market will have consequences for British producers which may not suit them so well. Existing member countries and two at least of our fellow applicants have surpluses of agricultural products which they will be marketing aggressively, often with the help of public funds, within the protected market. In other words British agriculture (and agricultural merchants, food processors and food distributors) will face much more direct competition from the members of the enlarged Community than exists at present with Britain outside the EEC. Since of all British industries agriculture must be rated to have as great an advantage as any in efficiency over its competitors elsewhere in Western Europe, it must be hoped that access to the larger market of the Community will bring benefits to agriculture, as well as to the food-processing industries. But competition will be severe. In these circumstances all the marketing improvements which have been mentioned so often in previous pages become even more urgent. The wider the market the more important is accurate and comprehensive price information. In competitive conditions adherence to quality standards and fulfilment of delivery obligations become not only desirable but vital if business is to be retained. With a few exceptions, such as cattle breeding, British agriculture has not thought of itself as a competitor in a free multi-national market. It may take some time to get used to the idea. To a lesser extent the same may also apply to food processors. Here too there are some important exceptions, like the confectionery industry, but in general the British food industry has not until very recently been export-minded. Most exporting companies have in any case more experience of Commonwealth and other non-EEC markets.

What part can producer marketing organisations play in these developments? All the existing trends in marketing should be working in their favour. British membership of the Common Market would give them a further boost with Community policy strongly favourable to a major extension of the powers and influence of producer marketing organisations. Many observers of agricultural co-operation in Britain have felt some dismay at the way the movement has developed, or rather failed to develop. It remains divided between groups and societies, and between societies themselves lacking commercial ties and often competing against each other. A few federal organisations have been established, but so far only Farmers' Overseas Trading Ltd, dealing in cereals and linked with Eurograin, the European co-operative brokerage organisation, has made much progress. Some of the groups are soundly established and well managed, but others suffer from a shifting membership, poor discipline, or inadequate capital. Open conflict no longer exists between the groups, centred on the NFU, and the traditional co-operatives, members of the Agricultural Co-operative Association. But there are very few examples of effective collaboration between the two. Compared with the Raiffeisen organisation in Germany, or CEBECO and CIV in the Netherlands (backed by the resources of the two recently merged agricultural co-operative banks which attract over 40 per cent of all deposits) co-operatives in Britain are pitifully weak financially. They have made some links with those on the Continent but these are nothing like as strong as the commercial relations that now exist, for instance, between German and French co-operatives. Finally, the agricultural co-operatives have so far failed to grasp a possible opportunity available to them, the establishment of close links with the consumer co-operative movement.

Admittedly the links are also fairly tenuous in most EEC member countries, but the consumer co-operatives there are weak in national terms compared with British co-operative retail societies, and in some countries, France for instance, are only of any importance in certain regions. The links therefore tend to be informal, the difference in commercial importance between the two parties providing a handicap to the development of a commercial relationship. The British retail societies, particularly if their buying power is grouped under the CWS, represent much more attractive customers for farmers. However understandable the reasons, it remains a major disadvantage for British agricultural co-operatives that few have so far been able to persuade the retail societies that they could do an important job for them. The difference of interest between the two sides, as in any buyer/seller relationship, need not rule out the possibility of closer trading arrangements. At this stage the onus seems to be on the agricultural co-operatives to show what they could offer to their colleagues on the other side of the co-operative movement.

The structure of agricultural co-operation in the six member countries is still evolving. The relationship between producer groups and traditional co-operatives has, as in Britain, yet to be resolved. But at least one can say with confidence that the principal organisations (the Federconsorzi, the Raiffeisenverband, CEBECO, the Boerenbond and so on) are there to stay. In Britain there is no established central commercial organisation of comparable influence.[1] We concluded in Chapter 12 that the EEC producer organisations were in general far from being strong enough to take on the enlarged 'market responsibilities' envisaged in the Mansholt Plan. But in ten or twenty years' time the situation may be very different. In Britain, however, the seeds have yet to be sown. For all the main products except milk, and failing the existence of a Board for most others as well, producer marketing is weak and disorganised. British agricultural co-operation has yet to solve its structural problems, and to arrive at a form of commercial organisation that is effective even in national terms. If it fails to do so in the wider context of the EEC, and of the closer contacts that this will bring with other and stronger co-operatives, it may have lost its last opportunity.

Examination of the official institutions involved in agricultural marketing in the EEC has been the other principal object of this study. Member countries are allowed a fairly wide discretion as to the form of these institutions, and therefore as to the way in which the CAP is implemented. Chapter 3 and the commodity chapters in Part 2 have indicated the considerable variations in practice. Within each country the ultimate authority for all intervention activity and its financial control remains of course with the government. The variations arise through differences in the methods of delegating responsibilities for intervention to other bodies.

If Britain joins the EEC the Ministry of Agriculture, Fisheries and Food would be the government department with the principal responsibility for implementing the CAP. Levies on imports would be collected by HM Customs and Excise and paid to the Treasury, which would then remit to FEOGA. Applications for licences to import would be made to the intervention agency concerned (see below), which would then issue the licences. Exporters too would apply in the first place for licences to the intervention agency. This would vet the applications and approve them, stamping on the licence the appropriate rate of restitution. Payments in respect of restitutions could be made either by the intervention agency or by the Ministry of Agriculture direct, reimbursement being made by the Treasury. If the Ministry made the payments the work could be done by the Ministry's appropriation, accounts and data-processing division at Guildford. This is currently responsible for issuing deficiency payments for cereals against documents prepared by the Ministry's divisional offices on the basis of certificates issued by authorised merchants; and for fatstock against documents processed by the Meat and Livestock Commission on the basis of certificates of licensed auctioneers and slaughterhouses, supported by the Commission's staff of inspectors. The Guildford office's computer, which also deals with the payment of other grants and subsidies such as the fertiliser subsidy, at present issues 4 to 5 mn cheques a year direct to farmers. However, the decision to implement government support for agriculture largely through frontier controls rather than deficiency

---

[1] The Central Council for Agricultural and Horticultural Co-operation, which has important responsibilities for promoting co-operative activity, is not a trading organisation.

payments could already have considerably reduced the work of this division by the time transitional arrangements started to come into force.

Membership of the EEC will necessarily involve the establishment in Britain of one or more organisations to deal with intervention for those products for which provision for intervention has been made in the regulations. For reasons set out in the previous two chapters we consider that official intervention is likely to remain a feature of the CAP for the foreseeable future. Bearing in mind the member countries' discretion in this matter, how should Britain set up an intervention system? Although the answer to this question will depend mainly on an assessment of what is the cheapest and most efficient system, one must first form some view as to the likely extent and frequency of market intervention in Britain. This is by no means easy, as the Community has already discovered, since so much depends on seasonal factors affecting production, the course of world prices and other factors which can be no more than guessed at. Earlier chapters have already given examples of the variations that have occurred in intervention from year to year. The point is well illustrated by the extent of softwheat intervention in the years 1968/69 and 1969/70. Intervention purchases in the Community totalled 3·8 mn tons in one year and 1 mn tons in the other. In 1968/69 ONIC bought wheat in each of the nine months between September and May to a total of 650,000 tons. In the following year intervention was limited to only one month (September) and amounted to only 12,850 tons for the whole season. This was mainly due to speculative movements of grain into Germany which anticipated changes in exchange-rate parities. The fact that, for reasons of this kind, accurate prediction is impossible of how much and how often intervention is likely to occur must strongly influence any view of the form the intervention agencies should take.

Member countries differ in the extent to which they allow or encourage interested parties (farmers, merchants, international traders and processors) to take some part in intervention activities. These differences will already be evident from descriptions given of the Boards of the various agencies. Our own view is that some degree of 'interprofessionalism' is of value, that it keeps the agencies better informed on technical questions, and that it helps to secure collaboration in the intervention system on the part of the trade. In suggesting this we are, of course, well aware that this participation is largely a charade, since under the EEC system the government department responsible for intervention has very limited discretion, and the agency itself, to which the job is delegated, virtually no discretion at all. Its main use to the 'professions' is the opportunity which it can sometimes afford of expressing their point of view at Management Committee level in Brussels.

A major difference between intervention agencies in the member countries consists of the use of an umbrella organisation, as in Italy, the Netherlands, Belgium and Luxemburg, or of separate agencies for individual products as in France or Germany. If no organisation were already at hand to do the work, or if existing organisations lacked some feature considered to be essential, such as interprofessionalism (or, of course, if they were liable to be abolished), then there would seem to be a good case for establishing a new body in Britain charged with all EEC intervention responsibilities. Although there are different technical problems involved in the various products subject to intervention, there would be likely to be some economies of scale to be obtained in an umbrella organisation, since staff could be shifted between products, depending on the volume of work.

As it is, however, we prefer the solution of giving these responsibilities, where possible, to the organisations that already exist and which could gradually build up the required expertise without adding greatly to their staff. In earlier chapters we have therefore recommended that in due course the Sugar Board, the Meat and Livestock Commission and the Home-Grown Cereals Authority should be given this work for their respective products. For the other products the Ministry of Agriculture could retain sole responsibility, at any rate until a need for intervention became established. This seems unlikely for oilseeds, deficiency payments for which, however, would be paid by the Ministry in the way already established for cereals. In the case of horticulture a British government may be more inclined than are those of the present member governments to undertake second-stage intervention buying in the appropriate circumstances of very low prices, given the difficulties likely to face fruit and vegetable growers generally in Britain, in the early years of membership at any rate. If Community regulations were established for potatoes, the Potato Marketing Board would obviously be a suitable agency. This leaves dairy products as the sole candidate for the eventual establishment of a new intervention agency. Here we have argued that the Milk Marketing Boards, being essentially producer organisations, as well as being already engaged in processing on their own account, would be inappropriate to undertake an intervention role. In any case one intervention agency only is required for the whole UK. It would therefore seem desirable to set up a Dairy Commission whose Board would be representative of producers, processors and distributors, and whose permanent staff would probably be provided mainly by the Ministry of Agriculture and the MMBs.

All the agencies would of course be functioning for the UK as a whole, being the member country. In Northern Ireland, therefore, there are two possible courses of action. Either each agency could set up a local sub-office in Belfast, or else all intervention and other functions could be carried out locally by the Northern Ireland Ministry of Agriculture on behalf of the national agencies. The latter course seems the more likely to be adopted.

If arrangements were made along the lines suggested above it should be possible to administer the EEC agricultural regulations, complicated though they are, without superimposing any massive new bureaucratic structure on existing organisations in Britain. Assuming the redeployment of staff of some of these organisations and the use, where possible, of an existing office accommodation it should also be possible to avoid incurring very large extra administrative costs. At a very rough guess, based on the experience of the present members of the Community, these extra costs should not exceed £1 mn a year at current prices. Clearly, year-to-year differences in the level of intervention activity will lead to variations in administrative costs. These are especially likely to occur during the transition period, which will provide an opportunity for the agencies to establish themselves and to acquire experience of the market regulations for the various agricultural products.

PART FOUR

Appendices

APPENDIX A

Agricultural Marketing in Other Countries Applying for EEC Membership

Since the 1961-3 negotiations it has been the intention of three countries, Ireland, Denmark and Norway, to join the EEC at the same time as Britain, provided each could obtain satisfactory terms for entry. This study would not be complete without some account of the agricultural marketing systems and institutions in each of these three countries. Such a description might be of interest as a comparison with the situation in Britain and that of the existing member countries. It becomes more relevant if the applications for membership of all four are successful, because in that event all of their organisations will be incorporated into the EEC marketing system and their peculiarities will be a direct concern for their fellow members.

Britain's three fellow applicants share a number of common features. All are small countries (the total population of all three together scarcely exceeds a quarter of the United Kingdom), in which agriculture still occupies a rather large proportion (about 10 to 12 per cent) of the working population. They are all countries in which small farms predominate, co-operation is strong (much less so in Ireland than in the Scandinavian countries) and government policy has been firmly directed towards improving the marketing of farm produce. In all three the growth of farm incomes has tended to lag behind that of other sectors, giving cause for political concern, since in these countries agriculture possesses a social and political importance out of proportion to its share of the total population.

In each country structural policy calls for a reduction in the farm population and amalgamation of the more uneconomic holdings. As this policy proceeds, the political importance of farmers and their organisations will decline. But agriculture will remain an influential sector in these countries, in Ireland and Denmark partly because of the high proportion of export earnings derived from agriculture, and in Norway because the government is anxious for defence reasons to avoid depopulation of the more remote rural areas.

Ireland

Entry into the EEC would be likely to present problems for Irish industry, which has been sheltered from foreign competition and has received subsidies and tax concessions that might not be acceptable to the Community. Increases in food prices following adoption of the CAP would also cause difficulties, especially as the general level of prices has been rising sharply in the recent past. But for agriculture the outlook seems very promising. Ireland exports over half of its gross agricultural output. The possibility of selling a much larger proportion of these exports in the protected markets of an enlarged Community and at EEC prices is most appealing. The EEC guide price for cattle is about 60 per cent higher than the average level of prices for fat cattle in Ireland, and there is approximately the same difference between the Community's target price for milk and the average price obtained by the Irish producer for manufacturing milk.

Appendices

For most of the principal agricultural products Boards or Commissions have been established which play an important role in marketing, notably for exports. The activities of these organisations deserve to be described not only because Ireland is a major supplier of meat, livestock and dairy products to the UK, but also because their possible adaptation to suit EEC requirements throws further light on the situation of comparable bodies in the UK. Some of these Boards or Commissions might take on the responsibility for market intervention in Ireland.

There are two organisations in the meat and livestock section. The Pigs and Bacon Commission, originally set up in 1939 but reconstituted in 1961, has as its primary function the responsibility to produce and market all bacon destined for export. Bacon factories are obliged to sell all export bacon to the Commission. By voluntary agreement with the factories export marketing of pork has also been taken over by the Commission since 1965. The Commission consists of three representatives of the processors, nominated by the Irish Bacon Curers' Society, two of the producers, nominated by producer organisations, and one nominee of the Ministry of Agriculture. An outside Chairman is elected by the members. The Commission's costs are financed out of a levy paid by the processors. For 1969/70 the levy was fixed at 17s 0d per pig, an increase of 3s 0d over the previous year.

The Irish market for pigmeat is closely controlled. There are guaranteed minimum prices to producers for four grades of bacon pig and to the bacon factories for all bacon sold to the Commission for export. Imports of bacon and pigs are prohibited on veterinary grounds and, as a consequence, domestic prices are often higher than export prices. The domestic retail price of pigmeat is also controlled. The UK is the main export market. There is a quota of about 28,000 tons of bacon under the Bacon Sharing Understanding (28,215 tons were exported to the UK in 1968/69). The UK also imported some 12,000 tons of Irish pork. About 6,000-7,000 tons of pork are exported annually to the Continent, mainly Italy. A little goes to Japan and Canada. Exporting was never in the hands of the wholesale meat trade, and it is doubtful whether factories would want to go back to the previous situation in which each factory sold on commission on Smithfield. The Commission has largely cut out commission agents in its UK pork sales, which are direct at a fixed price. Bacon is sold by an archaic system on the London Provision Exchange through commission agents (some of whom may also be wholesalers). Prices are fixed each Thursday for the whole of the current week by Pricing Committees appointed by the shippers of each importing country.

The disappearance of the Understanding should offer a good opportunity to obtain a larger share of the UK market. From the production point of view the industry is competitive. The marginal producer is tending to disappear, units are becoming larger, and management standards improving. The proportion of 'A Special' carcases delivered to factories has greatly increased in recent years, largely thanks to the Commission's technical services. The UK market for pork, where Irish quality is said to be equal to Danish and Irish pork commands a premium over British, will obviously remain the most easily accessible in an enlarged EEC, though shipping costs to the UK tend (for conference reasons) to be at least as high as those to the Continent. Dutch interest in bacon is relatively small, and very little fresh pork is at present exported by the Netherlands to the UK; it is mainly canned.

The Pigs and Bacon Commission has all the makings of a recognisable interprofessional organisation. The Minister's nominee would presumably have to be eliminated, and replaced perhaps by a third producer representative. If it is to continue its trading role it could hardly qualify as the intervention agency, though well equipped to be so. It seems unlikely that its monopoly (or rather monopsony) in the field of export products would arouse any objection among producers or processors.

The Irish Livestock and Meat Commission was only established in 1969 and it is therefore somewhat early to arrive at any judgement about its performance. It was set up to develop and expand export markets for livestock meat, and meat products. It has

Appendix A

taken over from the Department of Agriculture the responsibility for organising foreign trade shows and the promotion of Irish products in export markets. So far its main activities have been in market research, market intelligence for Irish producers and processors and the organisation of a carcase classification and grading system. The Commission is financed by a direct grant from the Exchequer plus a levy paid by producers. There are 10 members of the Commission.

The terms of reference of the Commission specifically excludes trading. Nevertheless, it is possible to envisage that the Commission could ultimately take on this function and thus fulfil a comparable role to that of the Pigs and Bacon Commission. Such a move would of course be opposed by the trade. The case for a monopolistic export organisation for meat and livestock is much reduced by the concentration that is occurring in these trades. Policy is now directed towards encouraging exports of meat in preference to live cattle. Meat exporting is becoming increasingly concentrated. The largest export firm, which has recently been bought out by a co-operative, Cork Marts, is responsible for nearly half of Irish boned-meat exports and close to one third of prime meat exports. A company of this kind is capable of controlling closely the quality of its products and also of engaging in large-scale contracts direct with the more important overseas buyers. It is also capable of carrying out its own market research and as a result is unlikely to benefit greatly from the Commission's activities except from the expenditure on promotion.

An enlarged Community offers a considerable opportunity for Irish exports of meat and livestock which, at around £100 mn a year, already make up about a third of total exports. Over recent years Irish exports to the existing member countries have fallen very significantly. (From 81,000 live cattle and 18,800 tons of meat in 1965 to 1,800 live cattle and 1,600 tons of meat in 1969.) Following membership this trend should be decisively reversed. Supplies available for export should increase as producers respond to the higher EEC prices and home consumption declines as a result of the rise in retail prices. Depending on how British production reacts to EEC price levels, the UK market would be likely, for geographical reasons, to remain by far the most important export market for Irish meat and livestock.

As the chief function of the Commission is promotion, it would be unlikely to develop into an intervention agency, though it would be possible for a separate division to be established for this purpose within the Commission. Alternatively, and failing the creation in Ireland of an umbrella-type agency for all products subject to intervention activity under EEC regulations, it would be necessary to set up a new body to take on these responsibilities.

The Irish Dairy Board took over in 1961 from the Ministry of Agriculture's Butter Marketing Committee, which used to export part of the national butter surplus and store the rest. In 1964 it took on overseas marketing of other products, with the exception of fresh cream, for which the Board collaborates with the Irish Cream Exporters' Association, control having been vested in the Board only since 1969. Products are either marketed directly by the Board or under its licence. Animal feeds containing milk powder are not under its control. Nor is liquid milk, for which there are special Supervisory Boards in the two main consumption centres, Dublin and Cork. The Board is therefore responsible only for what in Ireland is known as 'creamery' milk, i.e. that destined for manufacturing.

There are 9 members of the Board, 4 elected by producers (currently 2 from the National Farmers' Association and 2 from the Irish Creamery Milk Suppliers' Association), 3 by cheese, chocolate crumb, and milk-powder manufacturers, 1 civil servant nominated by the Minister of Agriculture, and 1 nominee of the Dairy Disposal Company, of which the government through the Ministry holds 100 per cent of the equity. The Board's staff numbers 160.

The activities of the Board and the organisation of the Irish Dairy Industry must be viewed against the small-scale structure of milk production in Ireland. There are about 105,000 producers in the Republic, the average size of herd being only 9 cows. Average yields are low, only about 530 gallons (2,420 litres) per cow annually. All milk except that sold under contract for the liquid market is obligatorily sold to co-operative creameries, of which there are between 160 and 170 (including those of the Dairy Disposal Company, which is not strictly speaking a co-operative). An attempt is being made to group processing into 19 regional units, by agreement between the Ministry and the ICMSA, a number of smaller creameries being closed down or surviving merely as collecting points. Second-stage distribution is to a great extent diversified. All processing plants have some private participation, ranging from 20 to 80 per cent, including Unigate, Fry-Cadbury, Express Dairy, Glaxo, L. E. Pritchett, and Borden. The private sector has taken the co-operatives into partnership as a matter of convenience to help ensure supplies of raw milk.

The Board's main function is as an intervention agency for butter. There is no intervention price for skim. On the basis of the butter intervention price, a creamery derives a minimum price per gallon paid to producers. There are in fact quite wide variations in these payments as between co-operatives, though competition is largely theoretical owing to agreements not to poach each other's members. The Board has three sources of income: the return from the market, a producer levy (3d a gallon since June 1968), and direct subsidy. Levy income is expected to cover about one third of the Board's trading loss, all administrative costs, and all marketing expenses less a direct government grant of £50,000. In 1969 it spent £31 mn, of which roughly £20 mn went on the price allowance and the balance on its export deficit.

Eighty per cent by value of exported produce goes to the UK, including 30,000 tons of annual butter quota and 35,000 tons of the unofficial two-year cheese quota. The UK also allows imports of fresh cream. The balance of the butter (12,000 to 14,000 tons) is sold in other countries, especially the Mediterranean and Muslim area, at residual world prices, of £60 to £70 a ton—which, considering storage charges are 30s 0d a week, is better than nothing. The stored stock is currently down to 10,000 tons from a peak of 30,000 tons.

The milk set-up in Ireland, being more analagous to that in member countries of the Six than to that in the UK, seems to present fewer problems of adaptation—at least fewer philosophical ones. The Minister's nominee would be ineligible to remain on the Board if it were to seek recognition, which would be likely to be granted, as an interprofessional organisation. Its trading activities would, however, seem to preclude any role as intervention agency. The staff trained in this aspect of the Board's present work could be transferred to a separate agency, or to the national agency if the government decided to have intervention for all products under the same roof on the Belgian model. Government price support would disappear, but would be replaced by that of FEOGA, acting through the intervention agency, for butter and skim (intervention and export restitutions to third countries) and certain other products (restitutions). Since the EEC target price is in the region of double the present Irish producer price, a boost to production seems inevitable. The Irish system presents no problem of the national pooling arrangements frowned on by the Commission.

The Irish Sugar Company Ltd has a monopoly *de facto* of refining in the Republic, though not *de jure* since the Sugar Manufacture Act 1933 merely enabled the setting up of a company to acquire, erect and operate sugar factories whose entire equity capital shall be held by the state, some preference shares being held by members of the public. A maximum dividend of 5 per cent is payable on the ordinary shares, but normally the divident is 2½ per cent. Initially, a factory at Carlow was acquired in 1933 from Belgian interests. There are now 4 factories. Contracts are entered into annually with growers by the Company on an acreage basis, and the price (linked to a 15·5 per cent sugar content) negotiated annually with the Beet and Vegetable Growers' Association. A representative of the Association is present at weighing and taring.

The total of quotas has recently been increased by 4,000 to 65,000 acres, the largest factory quota being that at Carlow, Co. Carlow (25,000 acres), and the smallest at Tuam, Co. Galway (9,000 acres), with Mallow, Co. Cork, and Thurles, Co. Tipperary, in between. The quotas are geared to factory capacity and to domestic sugar consumption. Imported raws are refined and sold to processing firms for re-export, mainly as chocolate crumb. Imports are in general from the same sources as the UK, but 7,000 tons were imported from the EEC in 1968.[1] In addition, the Company supplies Northern Ireland with its total requirements of refined sugar (about 10,000 tons) and has a small quota on the US market. Control of imports is similar to the UK system, the surcharge being used by the Sugar Company to subsidise domestic beet growers. The retail price of sugar is controlled (currently 4p per lb). The present producer price is the equivalent of about £8 per ton at 16 per cent sugar content. Pulp is sold to the growers, who are entitled to 1·5 cwt of dried molass pulp at 77½p for every ton of beets delivered. Delivery to factory of clean beets is free; i.e. producers pay full freight, but receive a rebate according to the degree of cleanliness.

The Company's hope is that Ireland would be allotted a quota at least equivalent to current output of sugar, say 180,000 tons, sufficient to satisfy domestic demand, including that of the North. (It would expect to pass on in cash form to the producer some of the benefit from the guaranteed sugar price but services provided in the form of credit, etc., would, of course, have to be taken into consideration.) On the other hand, it would not be averse to obtaining access to the British market, through being given a somewhat larger national quota, taking the place of part of the CSA quota at present supplied by Australia. Since the Irish Sugar Company is not a *de jure* monopoly it would appear to be in theory less vulnerable than the British Sugar Corporation to EEC regulations, even if in practice there is not much to choose between the two. In any case, it could hardly qualify as the intervention agency.

The Irish cereals market is subject to a high degree of government intervention. In addition to import controls, the government decides the price to be paid by millers for millable wheat provided production does not exceed the quantity prescribed for use by the milling industry (240,000 tons in 1969). The price varies according to moisture content, bushel-weight screenings content and time of delivery. The millers are obliged to take a certain proportion of their requirements from domestic production. Any production in excess of the prescribed quantity is bought by the Grains Board and disposed of in denatured form, the loss on the operation being financed partly by a levy on all millable wheat and partly by a government subsidy. The price of feed barley is not controlled, but an assurance is given that a minimum price will be provided for all barley offered for sale by growers, the purchase being made by the Grains Board. There is no state intervention for malting barley, which is marketed on contract between farmers and maltsters. Since 1968 there has been a floor-price scheme for oats grown in certain areas of the country. This scheme also is operated by the Grains Board.

The Board receives from the trade offers by tenders for imports. Quantities purchased are then sold on to domestic merchants at cost. In addition, the Board fulfils the functions mentioned above of taking up and disposing of surplus quantities of millable wheat and carrying out intervention in the barley and oats markets if this is necessary to implement minimum and floor prices. Its total trading in cereals has recently been running at about 350,000 tons a year. The Board consists of 8 members, all nominated by the Minister, and

---

[1] Under the terms of the Anglo-Irish Sugar Agreement the British Sugar Board is obliged to buy 10,000 tons of refined beet sugar a year from the Irish Sugar Company and then re-sell it on the spot to the Sugar Company at a price which yields on average a profit of £150,000 a year to the Sugar Company. This is a compensating arrangement to atone for the worsening to the extent of ½d a lb. or approximately £150,000 a year of the competitive position of Irish sugar entering the British market, as sugar or in goods, as a result of changes made in the British sugar levy in December 1961. While the Agreement does not limit the quantity of sugar goods exported to the United Kingdom it provides that the Sugar Company should confine its exports to that market of refined sugar to 10,500 tons a year for delivery to the Six Counties. In addition, any sugar imports required by the Sugar Company, other than for exports to non-United Kingdom destinations, must be purchased from the British Sugar Board, i.e. in effect to be of Commonwealth origin. These purchases represent the bulk of the Sugar Company's imports and are made at current world prices.

drawn half from producers and half from the trade, plus a Chairman. There is a staff of about 20. Administrative costs in 1969 were about £40,000.

Under the CAP the wheat price would be similar to the current guaranteed price, the difference depending on the manner in which the target and intervention prices are derived. The barley price, however, would be considerably higher, about £5 a ton above the minimum set for 1969. The price of oats would be likely to move in sympathy with the change in the barley price. Feed-grain production could therefore be expected to rise. This might have an adverse affect on imports, which amounted to a little over 200,000 tons in the cereal year 1969, of which about half was maize, but total demand for feed should rise as the livestock sector expands. Application of the CAP would involve some changes in the marketing system for cereals, but none of these would be very drastic. For instance, the price-equalisation scheme for maize financed through a levy on imports would be abolished. The flour mills' production quotas would come to an end, and there might have to be changes in the system of licensing of authorised purchasing agents. The quantitive control of imports exercised by the Grains Board would be abolished.

The Grains Board is already fulfilling the general function of an intervention agency. It has experience of buying cereals, controlling quality, storing its purchases and then reselling. For the other commodities for which market intervention organisations are required under the CAP there appears to be a good case for starting afresh and creating new intervention bodies or possibly one umbrella organisation. It is difficult to envisage that the intervention function could be satisfactorily added to a promotional organisation like the Livestock and Meat Commission or to a producing and trading organisation like the Sugar Company. But the Grains Board, shorn of its import-control function, is tailor-made to act as an EEC intervention agency.

Entry into the EEC provides an opportunity to re-examine the structure of agricultural marketing in Ireland, to assess its weaknesses and to clarify the functions of the various Boards, Commissions and other bodies engaged in it. The most pressing need seems to be the development of stronger producer organisations capable of taking part in market research and development. These are particularly required for horticultural marketing. The role of the state might, with advantage, be reduced whether Ireland enters the EEC or remains outside. Intervention agencies are required under the CAP but, apart from these, direct government involvement in agricultural markets might be limited to exercising quality controls and statutory regulations concerning health and hygiene on behalf of consumers of food and users of feedingstuffs.

Denmark

Like Ireland, Denmark exports a large proportion (about two thirds) of its agricultural output. Considerable benefits to Danish farmers should therefore follow from full and unrestricted access to the protected EEC market. Dairy farmers and producers of beef cattle should gain to about the same extent. The rise in prices, which will be in excess of 60 per cent, should stimulate production, which has recently been static or declining. Cereal producers, who already have the benefit of guaranteed prices, will gain from adoption of the EEC prices. Allowing for increased input costs, the effects on the pig-meat industry will be approximately neutral. The whole of the poultry industry will be disadvantaged as a result of the steep rise in feed costs. Any changes in sugar-beet production, which is controlled by quotas and marketed on contracts with the Danish Sugar Company, would depend on the sugar quota allocated to Denmark under the EEC regulations.

Agricultural marketing in Denmark is theoretically free from state interference, the role of the government being largely confined to import controls, a few measures of price support, and the usual legislation regarding fair trading practices, cartels and so on. The most noticeable feature of marketing is the great strength of producer organisations which have got together with processors and exporters to form a number of boards or committees. This system of co-operative marketing developed, as in the Netherlands, in the thirties when Denmark was faced with the problem of how to respond to depressed world markets. So-called export committees were set up under the Ministry of Agriculture, but in fact from the outset these committees were dominated by and effectively run by the farmers' organisations and the trade. They were given a surprising degree of financial autonomy, including the responsibility for receiving and using the levies on exports which were introduced shortly before the war. Soon after the war, as a result of pressure from the private trade, the ministerial committees were dissolved. The granting of licences, which is normally only a formality, was retained by the Ministry, but the important powers to make marketing regulations were left with the co-operatives and private export organisations functioning in committees without formal links with the government. These committees still receive the revenue from export levies which are imposed by the Ministry. The rather centralised character of agricultural marketing in Denmark is strengthened in two other ways. For some farm products there is legislation limiting exporting to certain licensed exporters or processors. The Ministry of Agriculture is often reluctant to issue licences to new applicants. Second, the administration of the government grant for promotion of sales of agricultural products is the responsibility of a committee which is dominated by representatives of the co-operatives.

The marketing of Danish pigs to the bacon factories and of bacon and other pigmeat products (about 80 per cent for export) is a model of how a closely controlled producer organisation should operate. Supplies of weaners are organised through auctions run by farmers' unions. Farmers specialising in fattening are almost invariably members of the co-operatives to which they are obliged to deliver all pigs of appropriate size and quality. All except one of the co-operative bacon factories and all the handful of private factories are members of the Export Association of Danish Bacon Factories which operates something close to a monopoly of export sales. The Association is the sole supplier to the British market and is responsible for maintaining the required quality and for assuring the supplies to meet the Danish quota under the Bacon Understanding. On the domestic market the Association supplies pigmeat to the meat processors and is responsible for operating the minimum-price system, for collecting levies on all slaughtered pigs, and for making refunds if the pigmeat is exported.

The Danish dairy industry is similarly concentrated. At the head is the Federation of Danish Dairy Associations which is dominated by the co-operatives since they receive about 85 per cent of total milk output. Members of the Federation have to comply with its regulations provided that they receive the support of three-quarters of delegates at a meeting. The Federation operates the levies on dairy products in the domestic market, which are passed on to producers as supplementary payments. These are calculated in order to equalise export and domestic prices so that dairies are indifferent as to which market they sell to.

Of total deliveries of milk to dairies in 1969, about 64 per cent was used for butter and 14 per cent for cheese. About two-thirds of butter and cheese production is exported. The Export Committees for these two products are therefore of considerable importance. The Committees were established in 1950 as successors to the ministerial committees mentioned earlier. The Butter Export Committee controls the number of firms permitted to export and supervises quality. Permission to export to Britain, which accounts for over 95 per cent of export sales, is limited to five exporters, and of these one co-operative organisation alone does about 80 per cent of the trade. The Butter Export Committee operates a large cold store in Esbjörg in conjunction with OXEXPORT (see below). This is used for intervention stocks bought by the Committee with finance from the Promotion Fund. The Cheese Export Committee supervises a much less centralised trade. There are about 50 exporters who have to obtain an authorisation to engage in the export trade but do not require licences for each transaction. Cheese imports (unlike butter) are uncontrolled. The Committee, however, exerts tight control on the quality of cheese offered for export, and awards subsidies for certain types in certain markets, part of the resources for these activities coming from the Export Promotion Fund. At present the Committee takes a responsibility for ensuring that the minimum import prices on cheeses sold to the EEC are complied with. There is a separate organisation for exporters of milk powder and condensed milk called FAMEX, which also benefits from the Export Promotion Fund.

The remaining agricultural export of importance, cattle beef and veal, lacks the strong market organisation of pigmeat and dairy products. The reason for this is not to be found in lack of exports of these products. A survey quoted in a recent paper on the subject of agricultural marketing in Scandinavia[1] showed that of total meat output in 1968, 60 per cent was exported either as live animals or as carcases and cuts. The principal cause of the diversity of marketing organisation for cattle and meat derives from the complexity of this trade and the absence of the classification standards which have been successfully applied to pigmeat and dairy products.

Danish producers usually sell their cattle through markets either using commission agents or working through a marketing group. Alternatively, sales can be made direct to slaughterhouses, including those owned by co-operatives, and this type of marketing is increasing in importance. The export trade is divided roughly 60/40 between the co-operatives and the private trade. The former are grouped together in OXEXPORT, the successor organisation to the ministerial cattle and meat export committee. The private trade, which consists of about 80 firms, also possesses a trade association. The two collaborate on policy matters and have been jointly concerned in the organisation of intervention buying of cattle and the sale of surpluses as frozen meat in export markets. This intervention activity has been financed out of the sales promotion fund as in the case of butter.

The organisation of poultry and egg marketing in Denmark is similar to that for the products described already. There are export committees for both poultry and eggs. Four large co-operative slaughterhouses with a turnover of about 120 mn kr a year take slightly under half total broiler production, the remainder going to a number of smaller private slaughterhouses. Both co-operatives and the private trade are associated in the export committee which regulates the increasing volume of exports, imposes levies to form a price-equalisation fund and possesses powers to make intervention purchases if this is necessary to maintain prices. Egg producers, who still number about 12,000, have to sell their production to authorised packing stations, with the exception of farm-gate sales which may not be advertised. The packing stations are divided roughly equally between the co-operatives and the private trade. Exports are controlled through the requirement of a general authorisation to export and licences for specific shipments. As in the case of other products, a levy is imposed on eggs sold on the domestic market, the proceeds being used to provide supplementary payments for exports.

The marketing systems for other agricultural products in Denmark need to be only briefly noted. There is an export committee for potatoes, organised similarly to those described above, but not for sugar, since exports, which are very small (mostly to Sweden), are handled by the Danish Sugar Company with its monopoly of refining. The cereals market is unrestricted, except for controls on imports through a levy system similar to that of the EEC. Farmers receive guaranteed prices administered through authorised merchants and millers. Production of cereals has increased in recent years and surpluses have arisen despite the obligation of flour millers to use a certain proportion of domestic wheat. Subsidies are paid by the Export Promotion Fund for exports and for denatured cereals sold back to livestock producers by the authorised merchants. Private firms are much stronger in the marketing of cereals than in the case of the other main agricultural products.

Adoption of the EEC marketing system would necessitate the establishment in Denmark of an official intervention agency for cereals. This agency would appropriately be associated directly with the Ministry of Agriculture, but the long tradition of participation by producers' organisation in all market regulations would mean that its character

[1] E. Mortensen, *Agricultural Marketing in Scandinavia*, a paper presented at the International Legal Conference on the Expansion of the European Communities, Dublin, October 1970.

would be likely to be interprofessional. For other products, Boards or Committees exist, but their mixed functions—market regulations, promotion and trading—might create difficulties for grafting on a further responsibility. In Denmark's case the most convenient course of action might be to make use of the need to create an organisation for cereals as an opportunity to create a small umbrella agency for all intervention products, which would collaborate closely with the producers and trade organisations, while retaining the ultimate financial responsibility for intervention and acting as the link with Brussels.

Norway

Farming in Norway differs from Ireland and Denmark in three important respects. The average size of holding is smaller, about 5 ha, with some 85 per cent of the farms under 10 ha. Second, and no doubt partly as a consequence of this, the Norwegian policy has been far more protective to agriculture. Prices are kept high by import controls and other methods, cereal and milk prices being substantially above even the EEC level. Third, Norway only exports very limited quantities of agricultural products. Consequently marketing policies are primarily directed at the home market.

Agricultural policy in Norway is based on agreements reached biannually between the government and the farmers' organisations and ratified by the Storting. The key organisation for marketing is the State Grain Corporation which exercises a monopoly on all purchases of grain, both imported and home-grown. Levies imposed on imported grains, to bring prices up to the levels agreed for the domestic market at the biannual reviews, are paid into the Feed Fund. Additional finance is provided by levies on feedingstuffs. This Fund is used to pay for a variety of price-equalisation schemes, transport rebates, etc., for producers of livestock and livestock products.

Under the Agricultural Marketing Act of 1936 a number of co-operative marketing associations have been established. All milk is delivered to co-operatives, whose association, the Norwegian Dairy Sales Central, administers the guaranteed price system and has a monopoly on exports of butter and cheese. The co-operatives control about 80 per cent of livestock slaughterhouses and about 60 per cent of meat wholesaling. Their association, the Norwegian Meat Sales Central, has powers to intervene in markets to support wholesale prices at the agreed levels. Subsidies for intervention are provided by the Feed Fund. A similar system exists in egg marketing. These associations are empowered to raise levies on producers, the proceeds of which are paid into a Product Fund used for a wide range of market development purposes.

The problems raised for Norway by EEC membership are mainly related to agricultural prices, a transition period and special aid for problem areas, rather than to the organisation of marketing of farm products. The monopoly position of the Grain Corporation would presumably have to be abandoned, but this organisation could conveniently become the intervention agency for cereals. The marketing associations could very easily be adapted to continue with intervention responsibilities under the EEC marketing system. Indeed, these specialised co-operatives operating close controls on highly regulated markets appear to correspond in many respects with what is envisaged by the Mansholt proposals discussed in Chapter 12.

APPENDIX B

Intervention Purchases EEC 1967/68—1969/70

(tons)

		1967/68	1968/69	1969/70
CEREALS				
Soft Wheat	Belgium	17,000	220,000	20,000
	France	92,000	650,000	13,000[a]
	Germany	736,000	1,983,000	979,500
	Italy	252,000	889,000	362,000
	Netherlands	—	105,000	9,000
	Total EEC	1,097,000	3,847,000	1,383,500
Hard Wheat	Italy	11,000	13,000	14,000
Barley	Belgium	—	11,000	—
	France	360,000	176,000	3,500
	Germany	168,000	484,000	219,000
	Netherlands	—	15,500	11,500
	Total EEC	528,000	686,500	234,000
Rye	France	2,000	3,500	1,000
	Germany	151,000	357,000	360,500
	Netherlands	—	500	7,500
	Total EEC	153,000	361,000	369,000
DAIRY PRODUCTS				
Butter	Belgium	23,000	27,000	28,000
	France	177,000	162,000	139,000
	Germany	146,000	142,000	174,000
	Italy	1,000		—
	Netherlands	44,000	74,000	75,000
	Total EEC	391,000	405,000	416,000
Dried skim	Belgium	—	34,500	10,000
	France	—	150,000	39,000
	Germany	—	54,000	66,000
	Italy	—	—	—
	Netherlands	—	40,000	25,000
	Total EEC	—	278,000	140,000

Appendix B

		1967/68	1968/69	1969/70
LIVESTOCK AND MEAT				
Beef	Belgium	—	..	—
	France	63,000	17,000	—
	Germany	9,000	9,000	7,500
	Italy	—	—	—
	Netherlands	—	—	—
	Total EEC	72,000	26,000	7,500
Pigmeat	Belgium	—	—	—
	France	—	90	—
	Germany	—	1,560	—
	Italy	—	480	—
	Netherlands	—	20	—
	Total EEC	—	2,150	—
SUGAR	Belgium	—	—	..
	France	—	—	127,000
	Germany	—	85,000	25,500
	Italy	—	—	—
	Netherlands	—	—	—
	Total EEC	—	85,000	154,500
OILSEEDS				
Rapeseed	Belgium	—	—	—
	France	—	—	—
	Germany	360	170	120
	Italy	—	—	—
	Netherlands	—	—	—
	Total EEC	360	170	120
Sunflowerseed	France	870	450	500
	Italy	—	—	—
	Total EEC	870	450	500
OLIVE OIL	Italy	13,000	—	—
FRUIT AND VEGETABLES				
Cauliflowers	Belgium	1,100	—	—
	France	23,700[b]	5,600[b]	4,300[b]
	Italy	11,800	—	—
	Netherlands	900	—	—
	Total EEC	37,500	5,600	4,300

Appendix B

		1967/68	1968/69	1969/70
Tomatoes	France	2,010	1,800	1,670
Peaches	France	—	82,600	—
	Italy	—	17,600	—
	Total EEC	—	100,300	—
Pears	Belgium	—	20,500	—
	France	490[b]	55,000[b]	—
	Italy	—	74,000	120,000[b]
	Netherlands	—	61,000	200
	Total EEC	490	210,500	120,200
Apples	Belgium	4,300	600	17,400
	France	119,000[b]	20,100[b]	70,000[b]
	Italy	167,000[b]	—	n.a.
	Luxemburg	—	—	..
	Netherlands	9,300	—	23,000
	Total EEC	299,000	20,700	n.a.
Oranges	Italy	31,600	34,600	85,000[b]

[a] excluding 'B' type intervention
[b] provisional
.. negligible
n.a. not available

Source: EEC Commission (FEOGA)

Note: All figures are rounded. In certain cases quantities have been derived from total FEOGA disbursements divided by average prices per ton.

APPENDIX C

Expenditure from Guidance Section of FEOGA 1964/68

	Number of Schemes	Cost UA '000	Percent of Total Cost		Number of Schemes	Cost UA '000	Percent of Total Cost
Improving Structure of Production				**Improving Structure of Production and Marketing (Mixed Schemes)**			
Belgium	27	2,721	2·8	Belgium	3	274	3·6
France	101	27,828	29·0	France	10	1,334	17·6
Germany	88	25,922	27·1	Germany	3	219	2·9
Italy	172	31,269	32·6	Italy	23	5,156	68·1
Luxemburg	1	125	0·1	Luxemburg	4	464	6·1
Netherlands	36	8,063	8·4	Netherlands	1	120	1·7
Total EEC	425	95,928	100·0	**Total EEC**	44	7,567	100·0

Improving Structure of Marketing

	Number of Schemes	Cost UA '000	Percent of Total Cost		Number of Schemes	Cost UA '000	Percent of Total Cost
Cereals				*Fruit and Vegetables*			
Belgium	2	599	17·1	Belgium	20	2,319	9·7
France	6	1,353	38·6	France	10	3,246	13·6
Germany	5	199	5·7	Germany	25	2,686	11·3
Italy	3	895	25·6	Italy	115	12,544	52·6
Luxemburg	1	250	7·1	Luxemburg	—	—	—
Netherlands	5	206	5·9	Netherlands	22	3,054	12·8
Total EEC	22	3,502	100·0	**Total EEC**	192	23,849	100·0
Dairy Products				*Wine*			
Belgium	28	6,747	23·4	Belgium	—	—	—
France	10	1,522	5·3	France	4	256	2·9
Germany	58	16,220	56·3	Germany	10	1,994	22·9
Italy	20	2,298	8·0	Italy	57	6,470	74·2
Luxemburg	1	800	2·8	Luxemburg	—	—	—
Netherlands	10	1,184	4·2	Netherlands	—	—	—
Total EEC	127	28,771	100·0	**Total EEC**	71	8,720	100·0
Meat				*Miscellaneous*			
Belgium	5	922	7·8	Belgium	2	350	4·1
France	21	5,403	45·8	France	1	218	2·6
Germany	20	4,263	36·1	Germany	6	1,435	16·8
Italy	7	636	5·4	Italy	36	4,263	49·9
Luxemburg	—	—	—	Luxemburg	1	500	5·9
Netherlands	4	579	4·9	Netherlands	14	1,779	20·7
Total EEC	57	11,803	100·0	**Total EEC**	60	8,545	100·0

Appendix C

	Number of Schemes	Cost UA '000	Percent of Total Cost		Number of Schemes	Cost UA '000	Percent of Total Cost
Total Marketing Schemes							
(a) by countries:				(b) by products:			
Belgium	57	10,938	12·8	Cereals	22	3,502	4·1
France	52	12,028	14·1	Dairy			
Germany	124	26,796	31·4	Products	127	28,801	33·8
Italy	238	27,106	31·8	Meat	57	11,803	13·9
Luxemburg	3	1,550	1·8	Fruit and			
Netherlands	55	6,802	8·1	vegetables	192	23,849	28·0
				Wine	71	8,720	10·2
				Miscellaneous	60	8,545	10·0
Total EEC	529	85,220	100·0	**Total EEC**	529	85,220	100·0

		UA '000	Percent of total annual expenditure
(c) by years:			
1964		4,844	53·5
1965		8,471	49·4
1966		25,402	61·1
1967		11,078	42·5
1968		35,425	37·3

Total Expenditure from Guidance Section

(a) by countries:				(b) by years:			
Belgium	87	13,933	7·4	1964	57	9,057	4·8
France	163	41,190	21·8	1965	97	17,134	9·1
Germany	215	52,937	28·1	1966	254	41,587	22·0
Italy	433	63,531	33·7	1967	152	26,040	13·8
Luxemburg	8	2,139	1·1	1968	438	94,897	50·3
Netherlands	92	14,985	7·9	(1969)[a]	(663)	(159,998)	—
Total EEC	998	188,715	100·0	**Total EEC**	998	188,715	100·0

(c) by type of expenditure:			
Improving structure of production	425	95,928	50·8
Mixed schemes	44	7,567	4·0
Improving structure of marketing	529	85,220	45·2
Total EEC	998	188,715	100·0

[a] no breakdown yet available
Source: EEC Commission (FEOGA)
see p. 270

APPENDIX D

UK/EEC Conversion Factors

To convert			Multiply by
Areas			
Hectares	to	Acres	2·4711
Acres	to	Hectares	0·40468
Yields			
Quintals (100 kg.)/Hectare	to	Hundredweights (112 lb.)/Acre	0·79657
Cwt./Acre	to	Qls/Ha	1·25538
All commodities by weight			
Units of Account ($)/metric ton (1,000 kg.)	to	£/long ton (2,240 lb.)	0·42336
£/long ton	to	UA/m. ton	2·36207
UA/100 kg.	to	shillings/hundredweight (112 lb.)	4·2336
sh./cwt.	to	UA/100 kg.	0·236207
p./cwt.	to	UA/100 kg.	1·181035
Milk			
sh./gallon	to	UA/100 kg.	2·56283
UA/100 kg.	to	sh./gall.	0·390194
UA/100 kg.	to	p./gall.	0·78039

£1 = UA 2·40
UA 1·00 = £0·4166
1 kilogramme = 2·2046 pounds
100 kg. = 220·462 lb.
1 long ton = 1·016 metric tons
1 metric ton = 0·9842 long tons
1 gallon = 4·54596 litres
1 litre = 0·21997 gallons
1 gallon milk weighs 10·3 lb.
1 litre milk weighs 1·028 kg.

Index

Index

Index

ACA (Agricultural Co-operative Association), 20, 251
Agricultural Acts
  1937, 61
  1947, 3, 16, 19 n, 21–2
  1958, 115
  1970, 164
Agricultural Holdings Acts (1875 to 1923), 18 n, 19 n
Agricultural Marketing Acts
  1931, 12, 14
  1933, 12, 14
  1933 (N. Ireland), 130
  1949, 15, 16
  1958, 107, 114
agricultural population reduction, 7, 8
Agriculture and Horticulture Acts, 1964 and 1967, 204
AIMA (Azienda di Stato per gli Interventi nel Mercato Agricolo)
  cereals, 73
  cheese, 93
  deficiency payments, 43, 212
  financing difficulties, 43
  fruit and vegetables, 198
  oilseeds, 215
  olive oil, 212
  not 'interprofessional', 50
  staffing, 43
Anglo-Irish Sugar Agreement, 183, 263 n
animal feedingstuffs, 57–8, 76
  industry, 60, 73, 141, 250
  port mills, 59–60
  utilisation of denatured butter, 84
    milk powder, 97, 245
    sugar, 184
    wheat, 67–8
AOS (Agricultural Organisation Society), 19–20
apples, 187, 189, 191 n, 196, 200, 203
artichokes, 190, 200

Ashton Report (1970), 121, 131, 147–8
auctions
  cattle, 124, 132, 135, 141, 143
  fruit and vegetable, 197
  see also clock auctions
Australia, meat exports, 146, 149
AWS (Agricultural Wholesale Society), 19, 20

bacon, *see* pigmeat
bacon industry,
  Denmark, 265
  GB, 14, 129
  Ireland, 260
  Northern Ireland, 129, 147–8
Bacon Understanding (UK market) (1969), 129, 131, 146, 260, 265
barley
  guaranteed prices, UK, 12
  EEC prices, 71
break-crops, 171, 215
Brewers' Society, 219–20
British entry into EEC, *see* enlargement of the EEC
British Sugar Act, 1925, 183
British Sugar Board, 182–5, 254, 263 n
British Sugar Corporation, 172, 182, 184–5, 263
Britton Report (1969), 57, 58, 59, 60, 63 n, 64
Butter Export Committee (Denmark), 265

CACEPA (Centre d'Action Concertée des Entreprises de Produits Alimentaires), 29 n
car ownership, 11, 25
cash-and-carry, 27, 28, 36
cauliflowers, 187, 200–4
CENECA (Centre National des Expositions et Concours), 47, 140
Census of Distribution (1966), 127

278　　　　　　　　　　　　　　　*Index*

Central Council for Agricultural and
　　Horticultural Co-operation, 128,
　　231, 252 n
cereals, 57–78
　co-operative marketing, 17
　EEC regulations, 65–74
　intervention, 68–72, 75 n
　levies, 65–7
　marketing systems
　　Denmark, 266
　　Ireland, 263
　　Norway, 267
　monthly price increments, 75
　storage, 60–1, 63–4, 69, 71–3, 78
chain stores, 24, 26, 27, 141, 195–6, 202
Channel Tunnel, 103
citrus, 191 n, 199
clock auctions (*veilingen*), 234
　fruit and vegetables, 18, 194–6, 201–2,
　　206
　pigs, 143
CNCA (Caisse Nationale du Crédit
　　Agricole), 44, 98, 138, 225
COFREDA (Compagnie pour Favoriser
　　la Recherche et le Développement
　　des Débouchés Agricoles), 47,
　　140, 236–7
COGECA (Comité Général de la
　　Coopération Agricole des Pays
　　de la Communauté), 239–40
colza, *see* rapeseed
Comité Européen du Commerce
　　Inteuropéen des Pommes de
　　Terre, 224
Commonwealth Sugar Agreement
　　(CSA), 181
compound feeds, *see* animal feedingstuffs
concentration of food industries, 30–1
　dairy industry, 86, 87, 88, 89, 94–6,
　　100, 108, 118, 265
　meat processing, 144
　sugar refining, 173, 178, 180, 184
consorzi agrari, *see* Federconsorzi
contracts, production, 31–2
　broilers, 153, 159
　eggs, 160, 164, 167
　meat, 126, 132, 135–9, 143, 145
　processing peas, 31
　sugar-beet, 15, 31, 172, 176, 181
co-operative chains, 127
co-operatives, agricultural
　CEBECO, 65, 251
　cereals, 17, 33–4, 60, 62–5, 73–4
　cheese *fruitières*, 17, 94
　CMC (Coöperative Mellicentrale), 89

dairy products
　Belgium 86
　Denmark, 265
　France, 33, 35, 94–7
　Germany, 33–5, 100–1
　Ireland, 19, 262
　Italy, 92–3
　Luxemburg, 89
　Netherlands, 35, 88–9
　Northern Ireland, 119–21
　Norway, 267
　Scotland, 19
eggs and poultry-meat, 158, 161,
　　163–4, 166
exercise of countervailing power, 122
exercise of monopoly, 241–2
fiscal aids, 233
fruit canning, 200
fruit and vegetables, 195–9
Groupe Lafayette, 202
Groupe MacMahon, 32, 202
involvement in retailing, 32
links with private firms, 96 n
livestock and meat, 17, 135, 139, 142
organisational problems, 232–3
origins and development
　Britain, 18–21
　Continental Europe, 17–18
　Denmark, 264
　Ireland, 19
　Norway, 267
political and religious affiliations,
　　231–2
potatoes, 221
Raiffeisen verband, 241, 251
requirement societies, 19
sugar refining, 180
transnational links, 65, 96, 239–40
see also producer groups
co-operatives, consumer, 28, 202
co-operatives, retailing, 26, 27, 28
COPA (Comité des Organisations
　　Professionelles Agricoles), 239
corn merchants, 19, 58, 61
Corn Production Act, repeal of, 12
corned beef, *see* meat
Council of Ministers of the EEC and
　　the Manshott Plan, 6, 9, 79, 239,
　　241
countervailing charges, fruit and
　　vegetables, 189
Creamery Proprietors' Association, 117
credit
　merchant credit, 32, 58, 62, 128
　subsidies, 5, 205
Crédit Agricole, *see* CNCA

crofting, 19
Cutforth Commission (1936), 110-11, 114
CWS (Co-operative Wholesale Society), 122, 126, 166, 251

Dairy Commission proposed as intervention agency, 116-17, 254
dairy-herd size, 80, 87, 91, 94, 99, 261
dairy products, *see* milk
Davis Committee (1963), 110-11
demand for food, *see* food consumption
denaturing with premium
  butter, 84
  sugar, 40, 177, 179, 185
  wheat, 40, 67-8, 248
Denmark, *see* enlargement of the EEC
deficiency payments, 5
  British system, 3, 12, 21, 23, 61
    cereals, 62, 77
    livestock, 145
    wool, 224
  use in EEC, 4, 43, 49
    durum wheat, 74
    olive oil, 210-12
    rapeseed, 209, 213-14
departmental stores (food sections), 24, 27
directives on structural reform, 9
discount stores, 25
DOM (Départements d'Outre-Mer), 48, 174-5
Duhamel, Jacques, 8
durum wheat deficiency payments, 4, 74
DWV (Deutsche Wollverwertung), 226

Egg Authority (British), 152, 164-6
eggs and egg products, 152-70
  breaking-out, 156, 168
  grading and packing regulations, 169
  intra-Community trade, 153
  market structure, Belgium, 157
    Britain, 166-7
    Denmark, 266
    France, 160-1
    Germany, 162-3
    Netherlands, 158
    Northern Ireland, 169-70
  minimum import prices, 152, 154, 156-7 n
  producer organisation of market, 161-2, 166-7
enlargement of the EEC, implications for applicant countries
  Britain
    cereal marketing and storage, 75-8

eggs and poultry-meat, 164-9: concentration of packing stations, 166, 168; demand for egg products, 168; EEC grading regulations, 169; role of Egg Authority, 165
food exports, 250
food processing industries, 250
future of co-operation, 251
hops, future of Marketing Board, 220
horticulture: disposal of surpluses, 205; flowers and flower bulbs, 207; intervention role of co-operatives and groups, 203-4
intervention agencies, 116, 150-1, 253-5
livestock marketing: bacon industry, 129; frozen meat imports, 149-50; sheepmeat, 146-8
milk marketing, England and Wales, 107-18: allocation of balancing supplies, 116-17; maintenance of countervailing power, 108; regional price differentials, 109-10, 114, 117; regional price pooling, 110-11, 116; regionalisation of Board activities, 116-17; retail price regionalisation, 112; role of Board as intervention agency, 116; satisfaction of winter milk demand, 106, 116
milk marketing, Northern Ireland and Scotland, 118-22: butter production, 119; concentration of dairy industry, 118; imports from Irish Republic, 120-1; liquid milk demand, 118-19; MMBs, 118, 120-1; non-processed milk, 119; transport costs, 118
milk marketing, UK, 101, 122: manufacturing rebates, 103, 117; milk imports, 103; Milk Marketing Scheme, 107; milk retail prices, 104; MMBs, 102-3, 105; pooling produce returns, 104-5; seasonality of supplies 105-6; zoning of collection, 106-7
Northern Ireland: bacon industry, 148; eggs and poultry-meat, 169-70; intervention arrangements, 254; meat processing, 148; seed potatoes, 224
oilseed rape: production, 216, 220
  deficiency payments, 217

Index

Enlargement of the EEC—*contd.*
  potatoes, future of Marketing
    Board, 224
  producer marketing organisations,
    250–1
  sugar marketing: CSA, 181–2;
    role of British Sugar Board, 182
  wool marketing, future of Marketing
    Board, 227
  Denmark, 264–7
    effect of EEC prices, 264
    intervention arrangements, 266–7
  Ireland, 259–64
    cereal marketing, 264
    effects of EEC prices, 259–60
    exports: beef, 261; butter, 262;
      pigmeat, 260
    intervention arrangements, 260–1,
      264
    sugar quota, 265
  Norway
    future of Grain Corporation, 267
    intervention arrangements, 267
Eurograin, 65, 251
European Social Fund, 112
EVSt (Einfuhr- und Vorratstellen)
  for cereals and feedingstuffs, 65, 70–1
  for livestock, 142–3
  for oils and fats, 101, 214–15
  for sugar, 180
  intervention and other activities, 42
  origins, 41; staffing, 42, 70
export restitutions, *see* restitutions
export subsidies, *see* restitutions

farm incomes
  Mansholt Plan, 6
  parity with non-farm, 4, 5, 6
farmers' organisations
  Belgische Boerenbond, 86, 143, 195,
    231, 241, 251
  CNJA (Centre National des Jeunes
    Agriculteurs), 46 n
  Confederazione dell'Agricoltura
    Italiana, 198
  Confederazione Italiana degli
    Coltivatori Diretti, 198
  CPL (Centrale Paysanne Luxem-
    bourgeoise), 89, 144
  Deutscher Bauernverband, 197
  FNSEA (Fédération Nationale des
    Syndicats d'Exploitants Agricoles),
    46 n
  NFU (National Farmers' Union), 15,
    52, 251
Fatstock Guarantee Scheme, 124, 125

Federal Trust Report, 243
Federconsorzi, 42, 231, 234, 241, 251
  cereal marketing, 73–4
  dairy product processing, 93
  fruit and vegetable marketing, 198
  wool marketing, 226
feedgrains
  imports, 60
  North America, 5
FEOGA (Fonds Européen de Garantie
  et d'Orientation Agricole)
  cost of intervention, 244
  Guarantee Section, 5, 81, 84, 269–70
  Guidance Section, 9, 112, 156, 165,
    239, 240 n
  payments to intervention agencies,
    39, 43, 215
  payments to producer groups, 155,
    165, 192, 200, 238
fertilisers
  sale by corn merchants, 58, 61
  subsidies, 5
  transport, 58
FIRS (Fonds d'Intervention et de
  Régularisation du marché du
  Sucre)
  constitution and staffing, 48
  intervention and other activities, 49, 180
flowers and bulbs, 205–7
Fonds de Développement Economique
  et Social, 225
food consumption, 11, 17, 23, 245
  beef, 9
  convenience foods, 25, 29–30
  eggs, 153
  dairy products, 86, 88, 99
  fruit and vegetables, 186, 188, 205
  health foods, 35
  liquid milk, 12, 80, 86, 88, 90, 94, 118
  meat, 123, 134, 139, 144
  pigmeat, 9
  potatoes, 222
  poultry-meat, 9, 153, 158–9
  sugar, 172
food distribution, 14, 23–8
  advertising, 29, 127
  assortment, 24–5, 29, 34
  dairy products, 12, 87, 89, 93, 96,
    101, 262, 265
  eggs, 31, 155, 160–3, 266
  fruit and vegetables, 195, 197, 199–202
  investments, 24, 26
  meat, 126, 128, 135–42, 144–5
  milk, liquid, 12, 85, 88–9, 97, 104,
    112–13
  potatoes, 222

poultry-meat, 158–63, 266
product innovation, 29–30
research development, 29
turnover, 24, 27–30
see also chains, co-operative chains, supermarkets, voluntary chains
food industries, 30–1
  bacon and pigmeat, 126, 129–30, 148, 260, 265
  biscuit, 84, 250
  cereals, 63, 73, 76
  confectionery, 84, 250
  dairy, 30, 86, 88–9, 94–6, 100, 108, 118, 120, 262, 265
  fruit and vegetable canning, 30, 197, 199, 201
  meat, 132, 148
  oilseed crushing, 209, 216
  pasta, 73, 153, 159
  potato processing, 222–3
  sugar, 173, 178, 180, 184, 262
  see also concentration of industry
food retailing, *see* food distribution
food wholesaling, 27–8
FORMA (Fonds d'Orientation et de Régularisation des Marchés Agricoles)
  aid to producer groups, 137, 200, 202, 225
  connection with SOPEXA, CENECA, and COFREDA, 47, 140
  dairy products, 97–8
  financing, 46
  intervention activities, 47 (*see also* Interlait and SIBEV)
  payment of grants, 47
  staffing, 46–7
Forward Contract Bonus Scheme (UK), 77
fuel subsidies, 5

GAEC (*groupement agricole pour exploitation en commun*), 138, 235–6
GATT (General Agreement on Tariffs and Trade), 149, 191, 210
Geneva Protocol (fruit and vegetable standards), 190, 203
glasshouses, 188, 205, 232
grain importers, 63, 73
grain shippers, 63
grains, *see* cereals and under individual crops
group trading, *see* producer groups
guaranteed prices, 3, 12, 21
  bacon, 260

cereals, 61
meat, 124
guide prices
  meat, 132
  sugar, 175

Hague, The, Conference (1969), 9
hard wheat
  imports, 76
  see also durum
health regulations, milk, 84–5, 89, 102 n, 120
HGCA (Home-Grown Cereals Authority), 59, 76–7, 254
HM Customs and Excise, 183, 252
hops, 218–20
  EEC production, 218
  marketing in England, 219
horticulture, 186–207
  disposal of surpluses, 192, 205
  market support arrangements, 191–2
  non-edible products, 205–7
  top-fruit production, 187
  vegetable production, 187
Horticulture Act, 1960, 204
hygiene regulations, *see* health regulations
hypermarché, 25–6

import levies, *see* levies on imports
imports of food
  France
    sheepmeat, 149
  Italy
    meat, 144–5
    milk, 92
    sugar, 180
  UK
    bacon, 129, 146, 260, 265
    butter, 262, 265
    maize, 60, 76
    meat, 123, 146, 149, 261
    milk, 103, 120
    pork, 260
    rapeseed, 216
    wheat, 67–8, 76
Interlait (Société Interprofessionnelle du Lait et de ses Dérivés)
  constitution, 45
  intervention buying and storage, 98–9
International Sugar Agreement, 183
'interprofessionalism'
  at Community level, 165, 240, 245
  in intervention agencies, 49, 51, 62, 70, 253
  in sugar production, 175

'interprofessionalism'—contd.
  Belgium, 87
  Britain, 113–16
  France, 44–6, 48–9
  Germany, 42
  Italy, 43
  Netherlands, 40 n
intervention agencies, 37–52
  activities, 50
  applicant countries
    Britain, 76–8, 116, 253–5
    Denmark, 266–7
    Ireland, 264
    Norway, 267
  cost, 50–1
  extent of 'interprofessionalism', 49, 51–2
  financing, 77
  staffing, 50
  'umbrella' type, 50
  see also AIMA (Italy), EVSt (Germany), FIRS (France), FORMA (France), Interlait (France), OBEA (Belgium), ONIC (France), SER (Luxemburg), SIDO (France), SNIPOT (France), VIB (Netherlands)
intervention buying and storage, 5, 22, 62, 246–7
  cereals, 68–9, 72, 75–8
  dairy products, 23, 83, 87, 98, 119, 262
  meat, 140, 150
  olive oil, 210
  rapeseed, 209, 212, 214–15
  sugar, 179–80
intervention points, designation of
  cereals, 69–70, 71, 72, 75 n
  in UK, 75–6, 78
intervention policy, 4, 6, 22–3, 244–7
  beef and veal, 133
  cereals, 263
  dairy produce, 262
  pigmeat, 134, 134 n
  sugar, 175
intervention stocks, disposal of, 74–5, 248
  Belgium, 39
  France, 48, 70
  Ireland, 262
  Luxemburg, 40
  Netherlands, 41, 72
  butter, 83–4
  skim milk powder, 84
intra-Community trade
  cereals, 65

dairy produce, 81, 87
eggs, 153–4, 155
fruit and vegetables, 186, 196–7
livestock, 135
meat, 135
poultry-meat, 153–4
Irish Dairy Board, 121, 261–2
Irish Grains Board, 263–4
Irish Sugar Company, 262–3

Joint Committees (Milk Marketing Scheme), 113, 117

Karmel Committee of Investigation (1969), 109 n, 110–12, 114
Knapp Report (1965), 19 n, 21

lamb, see sheep, meat
land reclamation, 9
Land Settlement Acts (Ireland), 1881 &c, 19
land tenure, Britain, 18
land use
  forestry, 9
  recreation, 9
lettuces, 187, 194
levies on imports
  fixing by Commission, 52
  influence of Management Committees, 52–3
  method of fixing
    beef and veal, 132–3
    cereals, 65–7
    dairy products, 82–3
    eggs and egg products, 154
    olive oil, 211
    pigmeat, 134–5
    poultry-meat, 154, 156–7 n
  procedure in Belgium, 38
    France, 48
    Germany, 71
    Italy, 42–3
    Luxemburg, 39
    Netherlands, 40
  system, 45, 22, 61, 247–8
Linlithgow Committee (1924), 14, 19
livestock, 123–151
  markets, 124, 135, 141, 143
  see also meat
Livestock and Meat Commission (Ireland), 260–1
Lucas Committee (1947), 14–15, 114 n
lucerne, 138
Luxemburg Protocol, 39–40, 144

maize
  imports, 60, 76

prices, 71, 73
Management Committee, 41, 52–3, 253
  beef, 149
  fruit and vegetables, 189–90, 192
  olive oil, 211–12
  sugar, 48, 184
Mansholt Plan, 8, 17, 244
  farm incomes, 6
  intervention policy, 67
  market policy, 7
  price policy, 6
  producer groups, 238
  product councils, 51–2
  structure, 7
  surpluses, 7
margarine, 210
marginal farms, 7
market intelligence, 71, 243, 261
  cereals, 59
  eggs, 165
  meat, 145, 150
Marketing Boards, 13–16
  Egg, 13, 16, 152, 164
  Hops, 13, 15, 219
  Milk, 12–13, 15, 20, 102–22
    Aberdeen and District, 118 n
    England and Wales, 107–18, 254
    North of Scotland, 118 n
    Northern Ireland, 119–22
    Scottish, 118
  Pigs and Bacon, 13–15
  Pigs (Northern Ireland), 13, 129–31, 147–8
  Potato, 13, 15, 221, 224, 254
  Seed Potato (Northern Ireland), 224
  Tomato and Cucumber, 13, 16
  Wool, 16, 224–5, 227
meat, 123–51
  carcase classification, 125, 140, 145, 150, 261
  corned beef, 133, 149
  deadweight sales, 124–6, 131, 139, 143
  frozen, 133, 149–50
  import quotas, 133
  liveweight sales, 124–5, 139–41
  seasonality of supplies, 146
  see also livestock and poultry-meat
Meat and Livestock Commission, 123, 124, 150–1, 252, 254
milk and dairy products, 79–122
  butter,
    Belgium, 87
    France, 95
    Luxemburg, 90
    Netherlands, 89
    Northern Ireland, 120

cheese,
  Cheddar, 87, 119
  Cheshire, 119
  Emmenthal, 93
  Gorgonzola, 93
  Gouda, 87, 89
  Grana-Padano, 83, 92–3
  Gruyère, 94
  Provolone, 92
  soft, 83, 87
  storage costs, 93
milk, condensed, 88, 104, 119–20
milk, liquid (raw or processed)
  accommodation supplies, 88, 97–8, 100, 117
  Channel Island, 84 n
  collection costs, 97
  compositional quality, 85
  consumption, 12, 85–6, 90–1, 99
  delivery to dairies, 79, 81, 85, 86, 88–9, 94, 99
  distribution, 12, 81, 85, 104, 112–13
  draft Regulation, 82, 84–5, 102, 112
  free circulation, 85, 90, 92, 103, 120
  house-to-house delivery, 86, 88–9, 113
  Irish Republic, 261
  prices, 12, 85, 92, 97–8, 104, 109–12, 114, 117
  production forecasts (1975), 86, 88, 91, 94, 97, 99
  regional production, 90, 94, 99
  seasonality of supplies, 80–1, 88, 105–6, 111, 116
  standardisation, 84 n
  urban supplies, 85–6, 88, 97, 113
  utilisation for manufacture, 82, 87–90, 93
  yields, 79–80, 88–90, 94, 99, 261
  zoning systems, 91–2, 100–1, 106–7, 111
milk, sterilised, 85, 87
skim milk powder, 83, 84, 89, 95, 120
structure of production and manufacture
  Belgium, 86–7
  Denmark, 265
  England and Wales, 107–18
  France, 94–8
  Germany, 99–101
  Ireland, 261–2
  Italy, 90–3
  Luxemburg, 89–90
  Netherlands, 88–9
  Northern Ireland, 119–21
  Scotland, 118
whey and whey powder, 83, 89

Milk and dairy products—*contd.*
  yoghurt and fresh products, 87–9, 96, 120, 121
  see also enlargement of the EEC
Milk Distributive Council, 114
Ministry (Minister) of Agriculture, Fisheries and Food, 77, 114–16, 217, 252, 254
Ministry (Minister) of Agriculture, Northern Ireland, 130, 147, 151, 254
monthly price increments
  cereals, 75 n
  oilseeds, 213
  olive oil, 211
multiple stores, *see* chain stores
mutton, *see* sheep, meat

National Farmers' Union, 52, 251
  attitude to co-operation, 20
  attitude to marketing, 15, 20
  Livestock Producers' Marketing Association, 127
National Mark Scheme, 1928, 14, 19
New Zealand
  dairy products, 5
  lamb, 125, 146, 149
Northern Ireland
  bacon industry, 129–31
  future of dairy production, 119–21
  meat industry, 132
  see also enlargement of the EEC
Norway, *see* enlargement of the EEC

oats, imports of, 73
OBEA (Office Belge de l'Economie et de l'Agriculture)
  dairy products, 87
  history, 37–8
  intervention activities, 39
  meat, 143
  oilseeds, 214
  staffing, 389
  sugar, 179
oilseeds
  deficiency payments, 49, 209, 213–14
  intervention, 49, 212, 214–15
olive oil, 4, 208, 210–12
ONIC (Office National Interprofessionnel des Céréales)
  administering of levies, 65
  intervention, 68–9, 253
  sale of stocks, 70
  storage, 69
  budget, 45
  constitution, 44–5

origins, 44, 61
onions, 187
ONL (Office Nationale du Lait—Belgium), 87–8
orchards, grubbing premium, 5, 193
'own-brand' products, 31, 127
OXEXPORT (Denmark), 265–6

Padfield case, 109–10, 114
peaches, 187, 191 n, 196, 199, 200
pears, 187, 191 n, 199–200, 203
peas, 188
pensions for farmers, 4, 5
pig-herd size, 130
pigmeat, 14
  cyclical production, 92
  EEC system, 134
  market structure
    Belgium, 143
    Britain, 126
    France, 137–9
    Germany, 140
    Italy, 92, 144–5
    Netherlands, 143–4
    Northern Ireland, 129–30, 148
  see also bacon
Pigs and Bacon Commission (Ireland), 260
Plunkett, Horace, 19
pool price (milk), 97, 105, 110–11, 116
potatoes, 220–4
  Denmark, 266
  French buffer stock, 223–4
poultry-meat, 152–170
  broiler production, 158–60, 163–4, 266
price fixing, 16, 85
price-reporting, 234
  cereals, 65, 71, 77
  dairy products, 82
  sugar, 49, 185
Prices and Incomes Board, 104, 108, 109, 112–13
producer groups, 5, 9, 34
  cereals, 59, 60, 234
  Commission's policy, 237
  eggs and poultry-meat, 161–2, 237
  France, 102–3, 161–2, 235–6
  fruit and vegetables
    Belgium, 194–5
    France, 199–202, 237
    Germany, 196–8
    Italy, 198–9
    Luxemburg, 196
    Netherlands, 196
  Germany, 234
  hops, 218–19

meat, 127–8, 135, 142
pigmeat and weaners, 130, 135, 139, 143
potatoes, 221–3, 237
wool, 225
producer levies, 165, 194
  France, 45, 77, 103, 161
  Germany, 234
  Irish Republic, 262
  Northern Ireland, 130
  UK, 77, 114, 164
producer prices
  cereals, 8
  milk, 81–2, 109–10
  policy, 3, 4, 6, 9, 10, 21, 243–4
  rapeseed, 216
  sugar, 8, 176
producer responsibility for market organisation, 51–2, 240–2, 252
producer-retailers, milk, 81, 86, 97
production grants, 5
Produktschappen (Netherlands Commodity Boards), 40
  for dairy products, 35
  for grains, 65
  for margarine, fats and oils, 214
  for potatoes, 223
protection of agriculture
  EEC countries, 4
  history, 4, 12

quality standards for farm produce
  carcase meat, 125, 140, 144
  eggs, 156
  flowers and bulbs, 205–7
  fruit and vegetables, 31, 34, 189, 191
  hops, 219
  live cattle, 142
  potatoes, 13, 34, 224
  poultry-meat, 31
quotas
  on imports, 5, 14, 119
  on production, 8
    hops, 13, 218
    sugar, 8, 22, 174–6
    sugar-beet, 176, 178, 262

Raiffeisen, F. W., 17
raisin seed, 208
rapeseed
  deficiency payments, 209, 213–14
  intervention, 209, 212, 214–15
  location of production, 208, 216
regional policy, 8, 112, 147
Regulations of the EEC
  19/2 (cereals), 22, 65

23/2 (fruit and vegetable grading), 190
26/2 (exemption from Article 85 for producer groups), 239
136/66 (vegetable oils and oilseeds), 208
158/66 (fruit and vegetable grading), 190
159/66 (fruit and vegetable producer groups), 204
121/67 (pigmeat), 134
122/67 (shell eggs and egg products), 154
123/67 and 199/67 (poultry-meat and derived products), 154
1009/67 (sugar), 174
234/68 (flower and plant standards), 206
315/68 (flower bulbs), 206
316/68 (flower grading), 206
1414/69 (cereals), 68
2511/69 (citrus), 193
2513/69 and 2514/69 (fruit and vegetable imports), 190
2515/69 (fruit and vegetable marketing), 190
2516/69 (fruit and vegetable grading), 190
2517/69 (grubbing grants), 193
draft regulation for liquid milk, 82, 84–5, 102, 112
Reichsnährstand, 41 n
remote areas, 111–12
restitutions on exports, 5, 247–8
  award procedure
    Belgium, 38
    France, 48
    Germany, 71
    Italy, 42–3
    Luxemburg, 39
    Netherlands, 41
  beef, 133, 143
  cereals,
    normal, 67
    special (tendering), 67
  dairy products
    open tendering, 84, 87
    special, 83–4
  fixing by Commission, 52
  influence of Management Committees, 52–3
  olive oil, 210
  rapeseed, 212
  sugar, open tendering, 177
retraining grants for farmers, 45
Rippon, Geoffrey, 106

sales promotion, 47, 140, 234, 243
self-service retailing
   development in Britain, 23–7, 125
   on the Continent, 23–7
SER (Service d'Economie Rurale), Luxemburg, 39–40, 74, 144
sheep
   meat, 125, 149
   milk, 90
   wool, 224–7
SIBEV (Société Interprofessionnelle du Bétail et de la Viande), 46, 134 n, 140
SICA (Société d'Intérêt Collectif Agricole), 97 n, 136–9, 200–2, 235–6
SIDO (Société Interprofessionnelle des Oléagineux)
   administration of deficiency payments, 49, 215
   constitution, 49
SILIN (Société Interprofessionnelle des graines et huiles de Lin), 49
single-suckled beef herds, 79, 132, 139
slaughtering premium for cows, 5, 244–5
sluice-gate prices
   eggs and egg products, 154–5
   pigmeat, 134
   poultry-meat, 155–7
SNIPOT (Société Nationale Interprofessionnelle pour les Pommes de Terre), 47, 223
SOPEXA (Société pour l'Expansion des Ventes de Produits Agricoles et Alimentaires), 47, 140
standard quantities
   cereals, 21
   milk, 21, 81, 105
store cattle, 138–9
Strutt Committee (1970), 5
subsidies
   eggs, 16
   fertilisers, 5
   fuel, 5
sugar, 171–85
   BSC's monopoly, 184
   development of production in Europe, 171–2
   factory quota system, 176, 178
   future role of Sugar Board, 184–5
   intervention, 185
   location of production, 172–3
   producer control of factories, 173
sunflower seed, 208

supermarkets
   development in Britain, 23–7, 126–7
   on the Continent, 23–7
   direct sales by producer organisations, 32, 34 n, 138–9, 153, 159, 160–1, 195–6, 199
surpluses, 4, 6, 7, 8, 239, 243–5
   apples and pears, 189, 191, 194–5
   beef, 245
   cereals, 71
   milk, 245
   sugar, 245
Sweden, food distribution, 23
Switzerland, food distribution, 23

table-grapes, 187, 190, 191 n, 195, 199
television, 11
threshold prices, 5
   cereals, 76, 248
   dairy products, 82
   sugar, 176, 248
tomatoes, 187, 190, 191 n, 203, 232
transport
   cereals, 58, 69–70
   milk, 97, 103, 108–10, 118
Treaty of Rome
   Article 39, 3
   Article 85, 103, 238
   Article 86, 103
   Luxemburg Protocol, 39–40, 144

UK Milk Fund, 105 n, 119
   see also standard quantities
Ulster Bacon Agency, 131

variety stores (food sections), 24, 27
Vedel Report (1969), 8–9, 17, 243
vegetable oils and oilseeds, 208–17
   imports into EEC, 209
veilingen, see clock auctions
Verdon-Smith Committee (1964), 114 n, 123
vertical integration, 31–2, 128, 130, 135, 138, 141, 143–4, 158–9, 163, 241
VIB (Voedselvoorzienings In- en Verkoopbureau)
   activities, 41
   cereals, 71
   dairy products, 89
   delays in settlement, 50 n
   history, 40
   meat, 144
   relation to *Produktschappen*, 41
   staffing, 40
   sugar, 179
voluntary chains, 26–8, 36, 127

wheat
  guaranteed prices, UK, 12
  North America, 5, 12
  see also cereals
Wheat Act, 1932, 61
wool, 224–7
  EEC marketing, 225–6
  EEC production, 225
world economic crisis, 14
Wright Commission (1968), 16, 114 n, 164

yields, 7
  eggs, 155
  milk, 79–80, 88–90, 94, 99, 261
Yugoslavia, meat exports (special levy), 145

ZMP (Zentrale Markt- und Preisberichtung), 71
zoning, milk supplies, 85
  Germany, 100
  Italy, 91–2
  UK, 106